INSTRUCTOR'S MANUAL

to accompany

Barnet • Berman • Burto • Cain

Introduction to Literature

Eleventh Edition

An Imprint of Addison Wesley Longman, Inc.

New York • Reading, Massachusetts • Menlo Park, California • Harlow, England
Don Mills, Ontario • Sydney • Mexico City • Madrid • Amsterdam

Executive Editor: Lisa Moore
Supplements Editor: Lily P. Eng
Electronic Page Makeup: David Munger/ DTC

Instructor's Manual to accompany **Barnet/Berman/Burto/Cain,** *Introduction to Literature,* **Eleventh Edition**

ISBN: 0-673-54282-3

97 98 99 00 01 9 8 7 6 5 4 3 2 1

Contents

CHAPTER 10
The Novel

PART THREE
Poetry

CHAPTER 11
Approaching Poetry: Responding in Writing

CHAPTER 12
Lyric Poetry

CHAPTER 21
Three Poets in Depth   **297**

Preface

What follows is something close to a slightly organized card file. In the course of teaching many of the materials in this book, we have amassed jottings of various sorts, and these may be of some use to others as well as to ourselves. Perhaps most useful will be the references to critical articles and books from which we have profited. We have plowed through a fair amount of material and tried to call attention to some of the best. We have also offered suggestions for theme assignments, but many of the questions printed at the ends of selections in *Literature* are suitable topics for writing. The point of these questions is to stimulate critical thinking.

We have offered, too, relatively detailed comment on some of the stories, poems, and plays. These may serve to give an instructor a jumping-off place for these selections and others to which they are connected.

A Note on Reference Books

There are many good reference books, but we'll mention here the core group that we could not survive without. Most are updated every few years. When new, they are expensive, but often you can fill out your reference shelf by checking what's available in used bookstores.

At the bare minimum, we urge students to read with an excellent dictionary, such as *The American Heritage Dictionary*, 3rd edition, nearby. We also recommend that they do some of their reading, especially when preparing for paper assignments, in the reference room of the library.

Annals of American Literature, ed. Richard M. Ludwig and Clifford A. Nault, Jr.

Benét's Reader's Encyclopedia. ed. Katharine Baker Siepmann

Benét's Reader's Encyclopedia of American Literature, ed. George Perkins, Barbara Perkins, and Philip Leininger

The Bible, King James Version, and a concordance, such as Strong's

Brewer's Dictionary of Phrase and Fable

The Cambridge Biographical Encyclopedia, ed. David Crystal

The Cambridge Dictionary of American Biography, ed. John S. Bowman

The Cambridge Encyclopedia of the English Language, ed. David Crystal

The Cambridge Guide to Literature in English, ed. Ian Ousby

The Columbia Encyclopedia

The Concise Dictionary of American Biography

The Encyclopedia of World Facts and Dates, ed. Gordon Carruth

The Feminist Companion to Literature in English: Women Writers From the Middle Ages to the Present, ed. Virginia Blain, Isobel Grundy, and Patricia Clements

Merriam-Webster's Encyclopedia of Literature

The New Princeton Encyclopedia of Poetry and Poetics, ed. Alex Preminger and T. V. F. Brogan

The Oxford Classical Dictionary, ed. N. G. L. Hammond and H. H. Scullard

The Oxford Companion to American Literature, ed. James D. Hart

The Oxford Companion to Classical Literature, ed. M. C. Howatson

The Oxford Companion to English Literature, ed. Margaret Drabble

The Oxford Companion to the English Language, ed. Tom Macarthur

The Oxford Companion to Women's Writing in the United States, ed. Cathy N. Davidson and Linda Wagner-Martin

The Oxford English Dictionary

You'll want to supplement this list with favorites of your own, along with anthologies of American, English, and World literatures, which are handy both for their selections and headnotes.

The First Meeting

The night before the first class, every teacher knows the truth of Byron's observation: "Nothing so difficult as a beginning." What to do in the first meeting is always worrisome. Students will not, of course, have prepared anything, and you can't say, "Let's open the book to page such-and-such," because half of them won't have the book. How, then, can one use the time profitably? A friend of ours (Marcia Stubbs of Wellesley College) offers a suggestion. We have tried it and we know it works, so we suggest that you consider it, too, if you are looking for an interesting beginning.

Begin reading the Japanese anecdote (text, p. 53) aloud, stopping after "A heavy rain was still falling." Then ask, "What do you think will happen now?" Someone is bound to volunteer "They'll meet someone." Whom will they meet? (It may be necessary to say at this point that Tanzan and Ekido are both men.) You will certainly be informed that if two men meet someone, it will be a woman. Continue reading, "Coming around the bend they met a lovely girl." After "unable to cross the intersection," ask again what will happen, and entertain answers until you get an appropriate response. Read again, and pause after "temple." Who are Tanzan and Ekido? The temple may suggest to someone that they are monks; if not, provide the information. Continue reading, up through "Why did you do that?" Now inform the class that the story ends with one more line of print, and ask them to supply the brief ending. The students will then see the perfect rightness of it.

The point of the exercise: First a story sets up expectations, partly by excluding possibilities. (A relevant remark by Robert Frost can be effectively introduced at the first meeting. A work of literature—Frost is talking about a poem, but we can generalize—"assumes direction with the first line laid down.") After the first line or so, the possibilities are finite. The story must go on to fulfill the expectations set up. At the same time, a story, to be entertaining, must

3

surprise us by taking us beyond what we have imagined and expect. But the fulfillment and the surprise must be coherent or the storyteller will appear arbitrary and the story, no matter how entertaining, trivial. (Notice E. M. Forster's pertinent comment, "Shock, followed by the feeling, 'Oh, that's all right,' is a sign that all is well with the plot.")

By satisfying expectations, literature confirms the truth of our own experience, teaching us that we are not alone, not singular; our perceptions, including moral perceptions (e.g., cause leads to effect, guilt leads to punishment or retribution) are shared by other human beings, people who may not even be of our own century or culture. Something along these lines can be suggested at the first meeting; subsequent meetings can be devoted to showing that literature, by exceeding and yet not violating our expectations, can also expand our powers of observation, imagination, and judgment.

The first chapter ("Reading and Responding to Literature") is fairly short; it can be given as the first reading assignment, and since it includes two very short poems (both called "Immigrants") and two very short prose narratives ("The Prodigal Son," and Grace Paley's "Samuel"), the discussion in class can hardly flag.

If, however, you prefer to skip the first chapter and you plan to spend the first few weeks on fiction, you may want to begin with Chapter 2, or Chapter 3, which include Chopin's "Story of an Hour" and Hemingway's "Cat in the Rain," along with comments about annotating and keeping a journal. If none of this pedagogical material appeals to you, you may want to give as the first assignment—that is, the reading for the next meeting—Poe's "The Cask of Amontillado.". The story is short and arresting, and it is familiar to many students. There will almost certainly be ample discussion in class, yet even students who come to class thinking they know the story well will probably leave class having learned new things about it. And in any case, an instructor who wishes to follow up on the lessons of "Muddy Road"—not the theme of the story but the lessons about plot and characterization—can examine Poe's story with an eye toward the way one episode follows another, arousing curiosity and then satisfying it. Shirley Jackson's "The Lottery" can be used in a similar fashion.

In closing, we'd like to mention one other tip for the first meeting that we have been using often in recent years, as we have tried to emphasize writing as a part of the Introduction to Literature course. Make a copy of a short poem—by Blake, Dickinson, or Frost, for example—that the students can examine. Read it aloud. And then ask two or three questions, to which students respond by writing in their notebooks. The questions can be fairly general, such as "what do you find especially interesting in this poem?" Or they can be specific, keyed to the meaning of a stanza or an image.

The value of this approach is that it connects the course, right away, to *writing*. In addition, after the students are done writing, the questions and responses can be made the basis for some discussion. Yes, it is only the first meeting, but it is good to get the students talking from the beginning, and frequently students will be more ready to speak if they have written something: they feel more committed to the response, because they have set it down on paper. There is always the risk, too, that if the instructor does all of the talking on the first day, he or she might create the impression that it's the instructor's voice that really counts, and that the students in the course will play secondary, rather than primary and active, roles in it.

PART ONE:

Reading, Thinking, and Writing Critically about Literature

CHAPTER 1

Reading and Responding to Literature

This chapter begins with two very short poems. If you want to begin by teaching fiction, you may want to skip this chapter and start with Chapter 2 or 3 (Chopin's "Story of an Hour" and Hemingway's "Cat in the Rain"). On the other hand, we think these two poems make a good introduction to literature, and in any case, since they are closely followed by two short works of prose, The Parable of the Prodigal Son and Grace Paley's "Samuel," you can use the chapter even if you devote the first third of the course to fiction.

ROBERT FROST

Immigrants (p. 4)

PAT MORA

Immigrants (p. 7)

These two poems are discussed at some length in the text. Those words may sound ominous, even deadly, but we are sure you will find that much remains to be done in class. Enough questions are raised in the text to stimulate lots of discussion.

    The text makes the point that Frost's poem was written for an anniversary celebration of the arrival of the *Mayflower,* and that is really all that students need to know about the background, but instructors may be interested in a bit more. The lines originally were the fourth stanza of a long poem that Frost wrote in 1920, "The Return of the Pilgrims," for *The Pilgrim Spirit—A Pageant in Celebration of the Landing of the Pilgrims at Plymouth, Massachusetts, December 21, 1620,* organized by George Pierce Baker. The literary aspects of the pageant were published (under the title just given) in 1921, but Frost never again reprinted the entire poem. Instead, he extracted only this one stanza from his poem, called it "Immigrants," and printed it in *West-Running Brook* (1928) and in many of his later volumes.

In the text, in our discussion of Frost, we ignore one large matter—the speaking voice. We omitted this issue because we felt we had talked enough (maybe more than enough) about the poem, and because the matter of voice is fairly subtle, but instructors may want to ask several students to read the poem aloud, and then to discuss the voice. Briefly, it seems to us that in this poem we get an authoritative voice—a voice which is by no means offensive but which is highly confident and which by its confidence (and its mastery of form) inspires confidence or faith in its assertion.

Pat Mora's voice in her "Immigrants" is marvelously different—for one thing, we get (as our comment in the text tries to suggest) *several* voices in her poem. Where Frost gives us the voice of the poet as an assured elder statesman (though he was only 46 at the time), Mora gives us the voices of the uneasy immigrants as well as the voice of the ironic commentator.

At least three voices are heard in Mora's poem: the voice of the immigrant who hopes that his or her child will resemble Americans (WASPS, that is); the voice of the immigrant who fears that the child will not be liked because the child will not seem sufficiently American; and the ironic voice of the poet, expressing skepticism about the hopes for assimilation to an Anglo-American model.

The almost comic glimpse of imperfect pronunciation given in line 8 ("hallo, babee, hallo")—the speaker of the poem here seems to have a somewhat superior attitude—disappears in the last three lines which, though written in English, sympathetically represent the fear that is thought "in Spanish or Polish." If you discuss these lines, you may want to invite students to express their opinions about why "american" is not capitalized in the last two lines, even though it is capitalized in the first ("the American flag"), and "Spanish" and "Polish" are capitalized. It's our guess that by not capitalizing "american" in the last two lines the poet implies that it's not all that wonderful to become an "american," indeed there may be a loss in changing from "Spanish" or "Polish" to "american."

Put it this way: the poem shifts from the eager activity of immigrant parents (presented almost comically in lines 1-7) to a more sympathetic presentation of deep fears in lines 8-14, but the whole is complicated by the author's implied criticism (chiefly through "american") of the immigrants' understandable but mistaken activity.

In short, we think that if you ask several students to read both of the poems aloud, students will enjoy what Frost in a letter called "the sound of sense," and they will also see that works of literature have an almost palpable sensuous appeal. They will see, too, that Mora's poem is able to hold its own in the company of Frost's. We confess that we are unable to think of a more effective way than this if one wants to introduce students to the idea of "multiculturalism."

One last word about this part of the chapter, specifically about Frost's poem. A reader of our manuscript objected that Frost offered an offensive mythic view of America (the land of freedom and opportunity) and that in our commentary we had bought this myth. He suggested that many immigrants—especially the Asian laborers in the nineteenth century—had been imported as cheap labor, and existed virtually as chattel. And before the Asians came, thousands of English, for instance, had come as indentured servants, obliged to work for years before they could be free. Still, it seems evident that even for these people life in America promised opportunities that were unavailable in the Old Country. Similarly, for those Asians who came here, life in this country (or Hawaii)—however grinding—must have seemed preferable to life in China or Japan or the Philippines. For instance, the Japanese who worked in the sugar plantations of Hawaii (beginning in 1868) endured terrible conditions, but the prospects were better for them than was life in Japan, and at the end of their contractual period most of them elected *not* to return to Japan. In time, of course, many of these people migrated to the mainland. Our own instinct is *not* to go into this issue in discussing Frost's poem, partly because we do not find his view offensive, but chiefly because we want to talk about literature, not about history.

Note: Our text includes a fair number of other poems by Robert Frost, and one other poem ("Sonrisas," also on conflicting identities) by Pat Mora.

The best book on Robert Frost is Richard Poirier, *Robert Frost: The Work of Knowing* (1977), Also helpful are: Reuben A. Brower, *The Poetry of Robert Frost: Constellations of Intention* (1963); and William H. Pritchard, *Frost, A Literary Life Reconsidered* (1984). For a good collection of Frost's prose pieces and letters on literary criticism and poetry, see *Robert Frost on Writing,* ed. Elaine Barry (1973). Serious students will consult *Robert Frost: Collected Poems, Prose, and Plays,* published in the Library of America series (1995).

We tend ourselves not to refer much, if at all, to secondary sources during the early weeks of the course: The main goal then, for us, is to focus the attention of students on the text at hand and equip them to state their responses to it. But from experience we know that a student is likely to ask early on, usually at the time of the first paper assignment, "Do you want us to use criticism?" Here, each instructor will fall back on his or her own preferences. Some will agree with us and judge that students, in getting underway, benefit most from their own engagement with the works; these instructors see criticism as coming into play later, once students are more confident about their own interpretations. Other instructors, however, find it valuable to use criticism right from the start, as a means of encouraging students to connect their experiences in the classroom and in papers to the larger "conversation" about this or that particular author.

Perhaps the main point is that instructors should give some thought to the question that, no doubt, a number of students will be wondering about: "Am I allowed to use criticism?" Take the question seriously, and have your answer ready for it. If no student asks the question, raise it yourself: rest assured that members of the class will be glad that you did.

Whether you are willing to let your students use criticism or not, we suggest that you stress to them that *they* have the capacity themselves to analyze literary texts well. In our view, one of the important aims of the first weeks is to boost the students' confidence, making them see and believe that they *can* respond cogently and coherently to literature, and, furthermore, that their pleasure in literary works will grow as they become more articulate about describing the nature and shape of their responses.

LUKE

The Parable of the Prodigal Son (p. 8)

A bibliographic note about parables may be useful. In the *Encyclopedia Britannica,* in a relatively long article entitled "Fable, Parable, Allegory," fable and parable are defined as "short, simple forms of naive allegory," and yet a few paragraphs later the article says that "The rhetorical appeal of a parable is directed primarily toward an elite, in that a final core of its truth is known only to an inner circle, however simple its narrative may appear on the surface...." Perhaps, then, a parable is not a "naive allegory." Two other passages from the article are especially interesting: "The Aesopian fables emphasize the social interaction of human beings," whereas "parables do not analyze social systems so much as they remind the listener of his beliefs." That may not always be true, but it is worth thinking about.

The traditional title of this story is unfortunate, since it makes the second half of the story (the father's dealings with the older brother) superfluous. Joachim Jeremias, in *The Parables of Jesus,* suggests that the work should be called "The Parable of the Father's Love."

Here is a way to provoke thoughtful discussion of the parable. Roger Seamon, in "The Story of the Moral: The Function of Thematizing in Literary Criticism," *Journal of Aesthetics and Art Criticism* 47 (1989): 229-36, offers an unusual way of thinking about this parable. He summarizes his approach as follows:

> I want to reverse the traditional and common sense view that stories convey, illustrate, prove or emotionally support themes. Morals and themes, I argue, convey to audiences what story is to be made out of sentences. The story flows, so to speak, from theme, rather than the theme following from the story. (230)

He goes on to suggest an experiment. "Imagine," he says, that instead of reading a story that traditionally is called "The Prodigal Son,"

> we were to find the same set of sentences in another book under the title "The Prodigal Father," and at the end we found the following moral: "waste not your heart on the unworthy, lest you lose the love of the righteous." We now go back and re-read the sentences, and we find that *we are now reading a different story.* In the new story the father's giving the son money is wrong.

Seamon goes on to say that in *this* story the son's confession is "a way of evading responsibility for his error," and that the father is as prodigal with his love as he was with his property. In this version (remember: the sentences are identical, but the title is different), Seamon claims "The story concludes with the father happily returning to his error. The absence of poetic justice at the end is meant to arouse our indignation" (232).

It's interesting to hear students respond to this view. Of course Seamon's title, "The Prodigal Father," is merely his own invention, but the conventional title ("The Prodigal Son") has no compelling authority. The question is this: Once we apply Seamon's title, do we read the story the way he suggests—that is, do we see the father as blameworthy and the stay-at-home son as justified? If not, why not? Again, Seamon's point is that although the common-sense view holds that the story yields a moral, in fact the reverse is true: the moral (i.e. the theme we have in mind) yields the story. For Seamon, "A thematic statement conveys information about how the critic constructs the *nature and motivations of the characters,* [and] *the value of their actions. . ."* (233). True, but can't we add that the skilled critic, i.e., reader, is in large measure guided by the author who knows (again, at least in large measure) how to control the reader's response? Seamon apparently takes a different view, for he holds that "the sentences used to project the events are not, in themselves, sufficient to tell us how we are to characterize or evaluate what is going on." Our response to Seamon is of no importance; what is important is to get students to think about why they do or do not accept the view that the story might be entitled "The Prodigal Father."

We spend some time in class teaching this parable because we find the artistry admirable—and also because the story is profound. One small but telling artistic detail may be noted here, a detail mentioned by Joachim Jeremias, who points out that the elder son, speaking to his father, "omits the address"; we had never noticed this, but now it seems obvious, and surely it is revealing that when the younger son addresses his father he says, "Father," and that when the father addresses the older son he says, "Son." The older son's lack of address, then, speaks volumes: he refuses to see himself as bound by family ties of love—a position evident also when, talking to his father, he identifies the prodigal not as "my brother" but as "this thy son." The story is (among many other things) an admirable example of work in which a storyteller guides an audience into having certain responses.

It's also worthwhile in class to spend some time cautioning against a too-vigorous attempt to find meaning in every detail. (Professionals as well as students sometimes don't know when to leave well enough alone. For instance, a writer in *Studies in Short Fiction* 23 (1986), talking about Updike's "A & P," says that Queenie's *pink* bathing suit "suggests the emerging desires competing with chastity." But come to think of it, this statement isn't surprising, considering what has been said about the pink ribbon in "Young Goodman Brown." One writer, for instance, says it symbolizes feminine passion, and another says it symbolizes a state between the scarlet of total depravity and the white of innocence.)

To illustrate the danger of pressing too hard, you might mention medieval allegorizations of the story. The gist of these is this: the older brother represents the Pharisees and teachers who resented the conversion of the Gentiles. Thus the fact that the older brother was in the fields when the prodigal returned was taken as standing for the remoteness of the Pharisees and the teachers from the grace of God. The younger brother, according to medieval interpretations, represents the Gentiles, who wandered in illusions and who served the devil (the owner of the swine) by tending the devil's demons (the swine). The pods that the prodigal ate represent either the vices (which cannot satisfy) or pagan literature (again, unsatisfying). The father represents God the Father; his going forth to meet the prodigal stands for the Incarnation; his falling on the neck of the prodigal stands for the mild yoke that Christ places on the neck of his followers (Matthew 11:29-30). The music which the older brother hears represents the praise of God, and the feast of the fatted calf represents the Eucharist. A great deal more of this sort of thing can be found in Stephen L. Wailes, *Medieval Allegories of Jesus' Parables* (236-45). The point should already be clear. On the other hand, it's also worth mentioning that the medieval interpreters of the parable at least paid it the compliment of taking it seriously. Odd as the interpretations now seem, they were the result of an admirable love of the word, and surely such an excess is preferable to indifference.

Is the parable an allegory? No, and yes. Certainly it does not have the detailed system of correspondences that one associates with allegory. Moreover, since the prodigal says, "Father, I have sinned against heaven and. . . thee," the father cannot be said to represent heaven, i.e., God. And yet, as Jeremias says (131):

> The parable describes with touching simplicity what God is like, his goodness, his grace, his boundless mercy, his abounding love.

Need a reader believe in God or in the divinity of Jesus in order to value this story? The point is surely worth discussing in class. Many students will say that religious belief is not necessary to appreciate the artistry of the parable and to benefit from the moral lesson that it teaches. But for other students, this parable will be understood within the context of their own religious views and values. The discussion in class of the parable, we have found, can often take on a curious shape, with some students sounding like literary critics and others a bit like priests and ministers.

Usually all that's needed is some acknowledgment from the instructor that the story of the prodigal son is profound on at least two levels, meaningful (and moving) for believers and nonbelievers alike. But we have sometimes used the occasion to describe briefly for students the connections between reading the sacred books of religious traditions and interpreting literature, as the students are learning to do in their course. "Close reading" can come to strike some students as more accessible, as more *possible* for them, when they realize that versions of it can be found outside the college and university classroom. It's curious that students frequently begin their literary work by saying that they find "close reading" to be strange, foreign, forced, even though they are in fact accustomed to careful analysis of texts in their religious practices and observances. You might help them move more readily into their literary work by pointing out the connections between what they have done, if they are religiously observant and are students of sacred scriptures, and what they are now learning to do.

GRACE PALEY

Samuel (p. 12)

"All those ballsy American stories," Grace Paley has said of much of the American canon, "had nothing to say to me." Is she, then, a feminist writer? She denies it, insisting that she is something rather different, "a feminist and a writer." Some instructors may wish to have a class consider in what ways, if any, "Samuel" is the work of a feminist.

There is a particularly female insight in the last two paragraphs of "Samuel" which (though the second of these mentions Samuel's father) focus on Samuel's mother. The first of these paragraphs emphasizes the mother's agony when she learns of her son's death; the final paragraph, describing a later time, emphasizes a grief that is less visible or audible but that is perhaps even more painful, for this grief is stimulated by the sight of her newborn baby: "Never again will a boy exactly like Samuel be known."

Interestingly, the narrator (can we say the female author?) conveys a good deal of enthusiasm for what some people might regard as offensive macho displays of jiggling on the subway, riding the tail of a speeding truck, and hopping on the tops of trucks. Paley makes these actions sympathetic partly by implying that they take real skill, partly by implying that the show-off performing kids usually turn out to be very decent guys (one daredevil has graduated from high school, is married, holds a responsible job, and is going to night school), and partly by mildly discrediting those who oppose them. Thus one lady who disapproves of the jigglers thinks, "Their mothers never know where they are," but the narrator immediately assures us that the mothers of these boys did know where they were, and, moreover, the boys had been engaged in the thoroughly respectable activity of visiting a "missile exhibit on Fourteenth street."

Like this woman, the man who pulls the alarm cord is somewhat discredited: he is "one of the men whose boyhood had been more watchful than brave." Although it's no disgrace for a boy to be "watchful," the sentence probably guides most readers to feel some scorn for the man who (so to speak) was never a boy. Many readers will feel that although the man "walked in a citizenly way" to pull the cord, he is motivated less by an impulse of good citizenship than (though probably he doesn't know it) by resentment, by irritation that these children are experiencing a joy that he never experienced in his childhood. On the other hand, Paley does not present him as a villain, and the story is not chiefly concerned with his guilt. By the end of the story, readers are probably so taken up with the mother's grief that they scarcely remember the man.

Although "Samuel" resembles a fable in that it is fairly brief, is narrated in an apparently simple manner, and concludes with a message, it differs significantly from a fable. Most obviously, it does not use the beasts, gods, and inanimate objects that fables commonly use. In fact, these are not essential in fables. More significantly, the characters in "Samuel" are more complicated, since the noisy boys are treated sympathetically and the apparently respectable adults are treated ironically. Finally, where the fable traditionally utters or implies a hard-headed, worldly-wise (and often faintly cynical) message, the message uttered at the end of "Samuel" arouses the reader's deepest sympathy.

On Paley, see N. Isaacs, *Grace Paley, A Study of the Short Fiction* (1990); J. Taylor, *Grace Paley, Illuminating the Dark Lives* (1990); and Judith Arcana, *Grace Paley's Life Stories: A Literary Biography* (1993).

TOPICS FOR CRITICAL THINKING AND WRITING

1. If you had been on the train, would you have pulled the emergency cord? Why, or why not?
2. Write a journalist's account (250-300 words) of the accidental death of a boy named Samuel. Use whatever details Paley provides, but feel free to invent what you need for an authentic news story.

COUNTEE CULLEN

Incident (p. 15)

The poem seems to be of the utmost simplicity: twelve lines without any figures of speech and without any obscure words. But it has its complexities, beginning with the title.

Our first question in the text asks students to think about the word "incident." It's our impression that an "incident" is usually a minor affair—something detached from what comes before and after, and of little consequence. For instance: "During the banquet a waiter dropped a tray full of dishes, but apart from this incident the affair was a great success." There are of course plenty of exceptions, such as the famous "Incident at Harpers Ferry," but we think that on the whole an incident is (1) minor and (2) a distinct occurrence.

Cullen's title therefore is ironic; the episode might seem to be minor, but in fact it has left an indelible mark on the speaker's mind (and on the minds of countless readers). And since it continues to have its effect, it is not something separate and done with. The apparent simplicity, then, of the title and of the entire poem, is deceptive, since this seemingly trivial and unconnected episode stands for, or embodies, an enormous force in American life.

It's a good idea to ask a student to read the poem aloud in class (true for all poems, of course), so that students can hear the rhythms. On the whole, "Incident" sounds like a happy jingle, but of course that is part of the irony. Two details that strike us as especially effective are the enjambments in lines 7 and 11.

Of the other ten lines, nine end with some mark of punctuation, and the other one ("I saw the whole of Baltimorean") could be complete in itself. But in the seventh line we are propelled into the horrible event of the eighth line ("And so I smiled, but he poked out / His tongue, and called me 'Nigger'"); and in the eleventh line we are propelled into the final line, the line that tells us that this whole "incident" was by no means trivial ("Of all the things that happened there / That's all that I remember").

Studies of Countee Cullen include: Helen J. Dinger, *A Study of Countee*

Cullen (1953); Stephen H. Brontz, *Roots of Negro Racial Consciousness—The 1920s: Three Harlem Renaissance Authors* (1954); Blanche E. Ferguson, *Countee Cullen and the Negro Renaissance* (1966); and Margaret Perry, *A Bio-Bibliography of Countee P. Cullen* (1969).

Instructors will find these secondary sources to be helpful, but none of them offers help on one issue that will be in the air when Cullen's poem is discussed. "Nigger," in line eight, is an ugly, offensive word—which is central to Cullen's point in the poem, but which is nonetheless a hard word for the teacher and for students to say aloud and to analyze.

We know some instructors who press hard on the word "Nigger" in class: they want the students to feel very vividly the crude bigotry and shock of the term. This approach, we confess, does not work for us, and so we follow a different path. Often, after we have read the poem and begun to examine it with students, we have paused to say outright that it's hard to use and talk about offensive racial and ethnic slurs and epithets. Yes, one of them is in Cullen's poem, and thus it has to be considered as essential to its meaning. But, still, we tell and teach ourselves that such words are wrong— that they should not be used, ever, because they are offensive—and thus it cuts against our principles and (we hope) our practice to hear ourselves voicing them.

This may or may not be the best approach, but at the least it acknowledges for students that *something* is awry and uncomfortable in the room when the instructor and students start using the word "nigger" or other words like it. Keep in mind what the students are or might be thinking and feeling. Be aware of, and talk about it. The tone of the class will be better, we believe, if you are sensitive to this issue and seek as best you can to address it carefully. The mistake would be to assume that, in a classroom context, ugly, offensive words will be heard by students neutrally, dispassionately.

CHAPTER 2

Writing about Literature: From Idea to Essay

KATE CHOPIN

The Story of an Hour (p. 19)

The first sentence of the story proves to be essential to the end, though during the middle of the story the initial care to protect Mrs. Mallard from the "sad message" seems almost comic. Students may assume, too easily, that Mrs. Mallard's "storm of grief" is hypocritical. They may not notice that the renewal after the first shock is stimulated by the renewal of life around her ("the tops of trees. . . were all aquiver with the new spring of life") and that before she achieves a new life, Mrs. Mallard first goes through a sort of death and then tries to resist renewal: Her expression "indicated a suspension of intelligent thought," she felt something "creeping out of the sky," and she tried to "beat it back with her will," but she soon finds herself "drinking the elixir of life through that open window," and her thoughts turn to "spring days, and summer days." Implicit in the story is the idea that her life as a wife—which she had thought was happy—was in fact a life of repression or subjugation, and the awareness comes to her only at this late stage. The story has two surprises: the change from grief to joy proves not to be the whole story, for we get the second surprise, the husband's return and Mrs. Mallard's death. The last line ("the doctors. . . said she had died. . . of joy that kills") is doubly ironic: The doctors wrongly assume that she was overjoyed to find that her husband was alive, but they were not wholly wrong in guessing that her last day of life brought her great joy.

In a sense, moreover, the doctors are right (though not in the sense they mean) in saying that she "died of heart disease." That is, if we take the "heart" in a metaphorical sense to refer to love and marriage, we can say that the loss of her new freedom from her marriage is unbearable. This is not to say (though many students do say it) that her marriage was miserable. The text explicitly says "she had loved him—sometimes." The previous paragraph in the story nicely calls attention to a certain aspect of love—a satisfying giving of the self—and yet also to a most unpleasant yielding to force: "There would be no one to live for her during those coming years; she would live for herself. There would be no powerful will bending her in that blind persistence with which men and women believe they have a right to impose a private will upon a fellow-creature."

A biographical observation: Chopin's husband died in 1882, and her mother died in 1885. In 1894 in an entry in her diary she connected the two losses with her growth: "If it were possible for my husband and my mother to come back to earth, I feel that I would unhesitatingly give up every thing that has come into my life since they left it and join my existence again with theirs. To do that, I would have to forget the past ten years of my growth—my real growth."

Note: the chapter includes another work by Chopin, "Ripe Figs," and Chapter 4 includes "The Storm."

Good secondary sources include: Per Seyersted, *Kate Chopin* (1969); and a more recent biography, Emily Toth, *Kate Chopin* (1990).

TOPIC FOR CRITICAL THINKING AND WRITING
Chopin does not tell us if Mrs. Mallard's death is due to joy at seeing her husband alive, guilt for feeling "free," shock at the awareness that her freedom is lost, or something else. Should the author have made the matter clear? Why, or why not?

KATE CHOPIN

Ripe Figs (p. 42)

This story teaches marvelously. Some stories supposedly teach well because the instructor can have the pleasure of showing students all sorts of things that they missed, but unfortunately stories of that kind may, by convincing students that literature has deep meanings that they don't see, turn students away from literature. "Ripe Figs" teaches well because it is a first-rate piece that is easily accessible.

Elaine Gardiner discusses it fully in an essay in *Modern Fiction Studies* 28:3 (1982), reprinted in Harold Bloom's collection of essays *Kate Chopin* (1987), pp. 83-87. Gardiner's essay is admirable, but instructors will be interested to find that their students will make pretty much the same points that Gardiner makes. Gardiner emphasizes three of Chopin's techniques: her use of *contrasts, natural imagery,* and *cyclical plotting.*

The chief contrast is between Maman-Nainaine and Babette, that is, age versus youth, patience versus impatience, experience versus innocence, staidness versus exuberance. Thus, Chopin tells us that "Maman-Nainaine sat down in her stately way," whereas Babette is "restless as a hummingbird," and dances. Other contrasts are spring and summer, summer and fall, figs and chrysanthemums.

Speaking of natural imagery, Gardiner says, "Not only are journeys planned according to when figs ripen and chrysanthemums bloom, but places are defined by what they produce; thus, Bayou-Lafourche, for Maman-Nainaine, is the place 'where the sugar cane grows.'" Gardiner calls attention to the references to the leaves, the rain, and the branches of the fig tree, but of course she emphasizes the ripening of the figs (from "little hard, green marbles" to "purple figs, fringed around with their rich green leaves") and the flowering of the chrysanthemums. The contrasts in natural imagery, Gardiner says, "ultimately convey and emphasize continuity and stability."

Turning to cyclical plotting—common in Chopin—Gardiner says, "With the ripening of the figs in the summertime begins the next period of waiting, the continuance of the cycle, both of nature and of the characters' lives.... The reader finishes the sketch anticipating the movements to follow—movements directed by the seasons, by natural happenings, by the cyclical patterns of these people's lives."

WILLIAM BLAKE

Infant Joy (p. 43)

In addition to the infant there is a second speaker, an adult—presumably the mother, but nothing in the text rules out the possibility that the adult speaker is the father.

The infant speaks the first two lines, the adult (asking what to call the infant) speaks the third. The infant replies, "I happy am, / Joy is my name," and the adult is then moved to say, "Sweet joy befall thee." Is it too subtle to detect a difference between the infant, who knows only that it is happy, and the adult, who, in saying "Sweet joy befall thee" is introducing (to the edges of our mind, or, rather, to the depths of our mind) the possibility that—life being what it is—joy may *not* befall the infant? That is, even here, in the *Songs of Innocence*, we may detect an awareness of a fallen world, a world where in fact people do not always encounter "Sweet joy."

The second stanza apparently is spoken entirely by the adult, but the language of the first two lines ("Pretty joy! / Sweet joy but two days old") is close to the language of the infant—not to the language of a real infant, of course, but to the language of Blake's infant, who began the poem by saying "I have no name, I am but two days old." Still, there is a difference between the speakers. The mother sings (a lullaby?), partly out of her own joy, and partly, perhaps, to reassure the infant (at least that is more or less the function of lullabies in real life).

For introductory students, secondary sources on Blake can offer more harm than good. We favor turning students toward Blake's *Poetical Sketches* and *Songs of Innocence and of Experience.* For the ambitious, the next steps might include: *The Poetry and Prose of William Blake,* David Erdman and Harold Bloom (rev. ed., 1982); and *Blake's Poetry and Designs,* ed. Mary Lynn

Johnson and John E. Grant (1979).

What of Blake's illustration for the poem? The best discussion of the picture is Andrew Lincoln's, in his edition of Blake's *Songs of Innocence and Experience* (1991), which is volume 2 in the series called *Blake's Illuminated Books*, gen. ed. David Bindman. We quote Lincoln's chief points:

> The figures within the opened petals enact an Adoration scene. A mother in a blue dress nurses a baby in her lap, while a winged girl-angel stands with arms reaching out towards the infant.

> The petals of the flower seem protective, although those that curl over from the left may suggest containment, hinting perhaps at the potential constraints that face the newborn child.

> There are other images of constraint here. In the design, the drooping bud at the right may recall the temporal process in which flowers unfold and decay, while in the song joy is at once a present state of being and a hope for an uncertain future.

WILLIAM BLAKE

Infant Sorrow (p. 44)

In "Infant Joy" we saw not only the child's view but also the parent's. Here we see only the child's view, which regards the adult embrace not as an act of love but as a threatening constraint. It's not a question of which view—"Infant Joy" or "Infant Sorrow"—is truer. Both are true. In "Infant Sorrow" Blake lets us see life from the point of view of the infant, a creature who is helpless, distrustful of the parents, presciently aware that it has entered a "dangerous world" and aware that its cries sound like those of a "fiend" to all who cannot understand its distress.

The first stanza emphasizes physical actions—of the mother in labor, of the sympathetic father, and of the babe itself ("piping loud"). There is action in the second stanza too, but there is also something more; there is thought, really strategy. Confined by the father at the beginning of the second stanza, the infant decides it is best to turn to the mother ("I thought best / To sulk upon my mother's breast"), but in any case the infant is still trapped.

PART TWO:

Fiction

CHAPTER 3

Approaching Fiction: Responding in Writing

ERNEST HEMINGWAY

Cat in the Rain (p. 48)

To the best of our knowledge "Cat in the Rain" has not been anthologized in college textbooks of this sort, but we think that it ought to be better known, and we find that it provokes lively discussion when used as an introduction to fiction.

The best published discussion is David Lodge's "Analysis and Interpretation of the Realist Text," *Poetics Today* 1 (1980): 5-19; conveniently reprinted in Lodge's *Working with Structuralism* (1981). Lodge begins by summarizing Carlos Baker's discussion, in which Baker (in *Ernest Hemingway: The Writer as Artist* [1952]) assumed that the cat at the end is the cat at the beginning. As Lodge puts it, in this reading

> [T]he appearance of the maid with a cat is the main reversal in Aristotelian terms in the narrative. If it is indeed the cat she went to look for, then the reversal is a happy one for her, and confirms her sense that the hotel keeper appreciated her as a woman more than her husband.

On the other hand, Lodge points out, if the cat is not the same cat,

> We might infer that the padrone, trying to humour a client, sends up the first cat he can lay hands on, which is in fact quite inappropriate to the wife's needs. This would make the reversal an ironic one at the wife's expense, emphasizing the social and cultural abyss that separates her from the padrone, and revealing her quasi-erotic response to his professional attentiveness as a delusion.

Lodge goes on to discuss a very different interpretation by John Hagopian, published in *College English* 24 (Dec 1962): 220-22, in which Hagopian argued that the story is about "a crisis in the marriage... involving the lack of fertility, which is symbolically foreshadowed by the public garden (fertility) dominated by the war monument (death)." For Hagopian, the rubber cape worn by the man in the rain "is a protection from rain, and rain is a fundamental necessity for fertility and fertility is precisely what is lacking in the American wife's marriage." Put bluntly, Hagopian sees the rubber cape as a condom. Lodge correctly points out that although rain often stands for fertility, in this story the rainy weather is contrasted with "good weather." What the rubber cape does is emphasize the bad weather, and thus emphasizes the padrone's thoughtfulness (and the husband's indifference).

Lodge's careful and profound article can't be adequately summarized, but we'll give a few more of his points. Near the end of the story, when we read that "George shifted his position in the bed," a reader may feel that George will put down the book and make love to his wife, but this possibility disappears when George says, "Oh, shut up and get something to read."

Taking Seymour Chatman's distinction between stories of *resolution* (we get the answer to "What happened next?") and stories of *revelation* (events are not resolved, but a state of affairs is revealed), Lodge suggests that this story seems to share characteristics of both: it is, one might say, a plot of revelation (the relationship between husband and wife) disguised as a plot of resolution (the quest for the cat). The ambiguity of the ending is therefore crucial. By refusing to resolve the issue of whether the wife gets the cat she wants, the implied author indicates that this is not the point of the story.

On point of view, Lodge demonstrates that Hemingway's story is written from the point of view of the American couple, and from the wife's point of view rather than the husband's. (Of course he doesn't mean that the entire story is seen from her point of view. He means only that we get into her mind to a greater degree—e.g., "The cat would be round to the right. Perhaps she could go along under the eaves"—than into the minds of any of the other characters.) Lodge's argument is this: at the end, when the maid appears "the narration adopts the husband's perspective at this crucial point," and so that's why we are told that the maid held *a* cat rather than *the* cat. After all, the man had not seen the cat in the rain, so he can't know if the maid's cat is the same cat.

Finally, another discussion of interest is Warren Bennett, "The Poor Kitty... in 'Cat in the Rain,'" *Hemingway Review* 8 (Fall 1988) 26-36 Bennett reviews Lodge's discussion of Baker and Hagopian and insists that the wife is not pregnant (Lodge had suggested, in arguing against Hagopian, that the wife *may* be pregnant). Bennett says that

> [T]he girl's feelings as she thinks of the padrone pass through three stages, tight inside, important, and of momentary supreme importance, and these stages reflect a correspondence to the sensations of desire, intercourse, and orgasm.

Not all readers will agree, though probably we can all agree with Bennett when he says that "The wife's recognition of the padrone's extraordinary character suggests that her husband, George, lacks the qualities which the wife finds so attractive in the padrone. George has neither dignity, nor will, nor commitment."

In any case, Bennett suggests that when the wife returns to the room "her sexual feelings are transferred to George. She goes over to George and tries to express her desire for closeness by sitting down 'on the bed.'"

Bennett's article makes too many points to be summarized here, but one other point should be mentioned. He says that female tortoise-shell cats do not reproduce tortoise-shells, and that males are sterile. Since he identifies the woman with the cat, he says that the woman's "destiny is that of a barren wandering soul with no place and no purpose in the futility of the wasteland *In Our Time.*"

Bennett's article is reprinted in the excellent collection, *New Critical Approaches to the Short Stories of Ernest Hemingway,* ed. Jackson J. Benson (1990). There have been a number of noteworthy biographies of Hemingway published recently, including Kenneth S. Lynn, *Hemingway* (1987), and James R. Mellow, *Hemingway: A Life Without Consequences* (1992).

An audiocassette of Ernest Hemingway reading is available from Longman.

CHAPTER 4

Stories and Meanings: Plot, Character, Theme

ANTON CHEKHOV

Misery (p. 58)

Like all good stories, this one can be taught in many ways. Since we teach it at the beginning of the course, we tend to emphasize two things: the artistry of the story and the reader's response, especially the reader's response to the ending. But first we want to mention that plot is given little emphasis. The cabman encounters several passengers, but these encounters do not generate happenings—actions—in the obvious or usual sense, though of course they are in fact carefully arranged and lead to the final action when Iona speaks to the mare. Second, we want to mention that we believe that writers usually express their values in the whole of the story, not in a detachable quotation or in a statement that a reader may formulate as a theme. Chekhov himself made a relevant comment to an editor: "You rebuke me for objectivity, calling it indifference to good and evil, absence of ideals and ideas, etc. You would have me say, in depicting horse thieves, that stealing horses is evil. But then, that has been known for a long while, even without me. Let jurors judge them, for my business is only to show them as they are."

By "the artistry," we mean chiefly the restrained presentation of what could be a highly sentimental action. Chekhov does not turn Iona into a saint, and he does not turn the other characters into villains. The passengers are unsympathetic, true, but chiefly they are busy with their own affairs, or they are drunk (One of the drunks is a hunchback, and although we feel that he behaves badly toward Iona, we feel also that nature has behaved badly toward him.) Second, Chekhov does not simply tell us that the world is indifferent to Iona; rather, he takes care to *show* the indifference before we get the explicit statement thatIona searched in vain for a sympathetic hearer. Third, it seems to us that the episodes are carefully arranged. First we get the officer, who, despite his initial brusqueness, makes a little joke, and it is this joke that apparently encourages Iona to speak. The officer displays polite interest—he asks of what the boy died—and Iona turns to respond, but the passenger immediately (and not totally unreasonably) prefers the driver to keep his eyes on the road. Next we get the drunks, who can hardly be expected to comprehend Iona's suffering. All of this precedes the first explicit statement that Iona searches the crowd for a single listener. Next, in an extremely brief episode (we don't need much of a scene, since we are already convinced that Iona cannot find an audience) the house-porter dismisses him, and finally, again in a very brief scene, even a fellow cabman—presumably exhausted from work—falls asleep whileIona is talking. But again Chekhov refrains from comment and simply shows us Iona going to tend his horse. At this point Iona does not intend to speak to the animal, but the sight of the horse provokes a bit of friendly talk ("Are you munching"?), and this naturally leads to a further bit of talk, now about the son, couched in terms suited to that horse—and this, in turn, opens the floodgates.

So far as responses go, all readers will have their own, but for what it's worth, we want to report that we find the ending not so much painful as comforting. The tension is relieved; Iona finds an audience after all, and if the thought of a man telling his grief to his horse has pathos, it also has its warmth. It seems to us to be especially satisfying, but we will have to explain our position somewhat indirectly. First, we will talk about attempts to state the theme of the story.

In the text we give the attempts of three students to state the theme. Of the three, we find the third ("Suffering is incommunicable, but the sufferer must find an outlet") the closest to our response. That is, we are inclined to think that the reason Iona cannot tell his story to the officer or to any other person is that grief of this sort cannot be communicated. It isolates the grief-stricken person. One notices in the story how much physical effort goes into Iona's early efforts to communicate with people. As a cabman, of course, he is in front of his passengers, and he has to turn to address his audience. At first his lips move but words do not come out, and when he does speak, it is "with an effort." Near the end of "Misery," just before he goes to the stable, Iona thinks about how the story of his son's death must he told:

> He wants to talk of it properly, with deliberation. He wants to tell how his son was taken ill, how he suffered, what he said before he died, how he died. He wants to describe the funeral. and how he went to the hospital to get his son's clothes. He still has his daughter Anisya in the country. And he wants to talk about her too. Yes, he has plenty to talk about.

Now, we are all decent people—not at all like the brusque officer or the drunken passengers or the indifferent house-porter or the sleepy young cabman—but which of us could endure to hear Iona's story? Which of us really could provide the audience that he needs? Which of us could refrain from interrupting him with well-intended but inadequate mutterings of sympathy, reassurances, and facile pity? Iona's grief is so deeply felt that it isolates him from other human beings, just as the indifference of other beings isolates them from him. Overpowering grief of this sort sets one apart from others. We hope we are not showing our insensitivity when we say that the mare is the only audience that can let Iona tell his story, in all its detail, exactly as he needs to tell it. And that is why we think that, in a way, this deeply moving story has a happy ending.

Chekhov once said that the aim of serious literature is "truth, unconditional and honest." He stated, too, that, in his estimation, "the artist should be, not the judge of his characters and their conversations, but only an unbiased witness." Both of these observations can prove useful in opening up the story for discussion. Ask students to point to moments in the text where Chekhov's intentions for his art are realized.

Much of the best scholarship focuses on Chekhov's plays, but for the stories (and for sensitive treatments of his central themes) we can recommend the discussions in D. Rayfield, *Chekhov: The Evolution of His Art* (1975); Beverly Hahn, *Chekhov: A Study of the Major Stories and Plays* (1977); *Chekhov: New Perspectives*, ed. René Wellek and N. D. Wellek (1984).

For biography: Ernest J. Simmons, *Chekhov: A Biography* (1962).

Students can be encouraged to seek out an excellent selection of stories, supplemented by critical essays: *Anton Chekhov's Short Stories: Texts of the Stories, Backgrounds, Criticism*, ed. Ralph E. Matlaw (1975).

KATE CHOPIN

The Storm (p. 65)

Chopin wrote this story in 1898 but never tried to publish it, presumably because she knew it would be unacceptable to the taste of the age. "The Storm" uses the same characters as an earlier story, "The 'Cadian Ball," in which Alcée is about to run away with Calixta when Clarisse captures him as a husband.

Here are our tentative responses to the topics for discussion and writing in the text.

1,2. (On the characters of Calixta and Bobinôt). In Part I, Bobinôt buys a can of shrimp because Calixta is fond of shrimp. Our own impression is that this detail is provided chiefly to show Bobinôt's interest in pleasing his wife, but Per Seyersted, in *Kate Chopin*, finds a darker meaning. Seyersted suggests (223) that shrimp "may represent a conscious allusion to the potency often denoted by sea foods." (To the best of our knowledge, this potency is attributed only to oysters, but perhaps we lead sheltered lives.) At the beginning of Part II Calixta is "sewing furiously on a sewing machine," and so readers gather that she is a highly industrious woman, presumably a more-than-usually diligent housekeeper. The excuses Bobinôt frames on the way home (Part III) suggest that he is somewhat intimidated by his "overscrupulous housewife." Calixta is genuinely concerned about the welfare of her somewhat simple husband and of her child. The affair with

Alcée by no means indicates that she is promiscuous or, for that matter, unhappy with her family. We don't think her expressions of solicitude for the somewhat childlike Bobinôt are insincere. We are even inclined to think that perhaps her encounter with Alcée has heightened her concern for her husband. (At least, to use the language of reader-response criticism, this is the way we "naturalize"—make sense out of—the gap or blank in the narrative.)

3. Alcée's letter to his wife suggests that he thinks his affair with Calixta may go on for a while, but we take it that the affair is, like the storm (which gives its title to the story), a passing affair. It comes about unexpectedly and "naturally": Alcée at first takes refuge on the gallery, with no thought of entering the house, but because the gallery does not afford shelter, Calixta invites him in, and then a lightning bolt drives her (backward) into his arms. The experience is thoroughly satisfying, and it engenders no regrets, but presumably it will be treasured rather than repeated, despite Alcée's thoughts when he writes his letter.

4. Clarisse's response. By telling us, in Part V, that Clarisse is delighted at the thought of staying a month longer in Biloxi, Chopin diminishes any blame that a reader might attach to Alcée. That is, although Alcée is unfaithful to his wife, we see that his wife doesn't regret his absence: "Their intimate conjugal life was something which she was more than willing to forego for a while."

5. Is the story cynical? We don't think so, since cynicism involves a mocking or sneering attitude, whereas in this story Chopin regards her characters affectionately. Blame is diminished not only by Clarisse's letter but by other means. We learn that at an earlier time, when Calixta was a virgin, Alcée's "honor forbade him to prevail." And, again, by associating the affair with the storm, Chopin implies that this moment of passion is in accord with nature. Notice also that the language becomes metaphoric during the scene of passion. For instance, Calixta's "lips were as red and as moist as pomegranate seed," and her "passion... was like a white flame," suggesting that the characters are transported to a strange (though natural) world. There is, of course, the implication that people are less virtuous than they seem to be, but again, Chopin scarcely seems to gloat over this fact. Rather, she suggests that the world is a fairly pleasant place in which there is enough happiness to go all around. "So the storm passed and everyone was happy." There is no need to imagine further episodes in which, for instance, Calixta and Alcée deceive Bobinôt; nor is there any need to imagine further episodes in which Calixta and Alcée regret their moment of passion.

Two additional points can be made. First, there seems to be a suggestion of class distinction between Calixta and Alcée, though both are Creoles. Calixta uses some French terms, and her speech includes such expressions as "An' Bibi? he ain't wet? Ain't hurt?" Similarly Bobinôt's language, though it does not include any French terms, departs from Standard English. On the other hand, Alcée speaks only Standard English. Possibly, however, the distinctions in language are also based, at least partly based, on gender as well as class; Calixta speaks the language of an uneducated woman largely confined to her home, whereas Alcée—a man who presumably deals with men in a larger society— speaks the language of the Anglo world. But if gender is relevant, how can one account for the fact that Bobinôt's language resembles Calixta's, and Clarisse's resembles Alcée's? A tentative answer: Bobinôt, like Calixta, lives in a very limited world, whereas Clarisse is a woman of the world. We see Clarisse only at the end of the story, and there we hear her only through the voice of the narrator, but an expression such as "The society was agreeable" suggests that her language (as might be expected from a woman rich enough to take a long vacation) resembles her husband's, not Calixta's.

KATE CHOPIN

Désirée's Baby (p. 69)

Students tend to differ in their responses to this story, and in particular to the ending. In the final lines, Armand learns that his own mother "belongs to the race that is cursed with the brand of slavery." The point is that he carries within himself the traces of the "black" race that he found intolerable in his wife, whom he has exiled from his presence and who, apparently, commits suicide along with their child.

But what exactly is it that Armand learns? Is he learning with a shock something he never suspected, or, instead, something he sensed was true (or might have been true) all along? Some students contend that the letter from his mother that Armand reads stuns him with its sudden, shocking disclosure, whereas others maintain that he really knew the truth all along, or, that he may not have known the truth for sure but likely suspected it.

We tend to start the class, then, by asking the students for their responses to the ending of the story. And we have always found some version of this sharp difference in interpretation to emerge from the opening discussion. There is of course a risk in keying the structure of the class to a debate; sometimes the positions can become too polarized, too rigidly upheld. The way to avoid this is to keep pressing the students to connect their positions to details in the language, moments in the story's unfolding narrative. As the students talk about the ending, ask them to explain where, earlier in the story, they find evidence that supports their interpretation.

On the one hand, this reminder spurs the students to seek evidence for their statements about the text: they must return to the text and its organizations of language. On the other hand, this close attention to passages usually complicates the polarized terms of the debate, making the story more complex and harder to simplify.

Notice, for example, the detail about Armand that Chopin gives half-way through: "And the very spirit of Satan seemed suddenly to take hold of him in his dealings with the slaves." This is the kind of detail that is worth lingering over. Does Armand begin to act cruelly because of his rising anger at his wife and child? Or, somewhat differently, because he knows on some level that he cannot deny the truth about who he is—the truth that his mother's letter will later confirm?

In her biography of Chopin (1990), Emily Toth states that "Désirée's husband, Armand, has a relationship with the slave La Blanche." We are not sure that the text sustains this intriguing idea, but it's a useful comment to mention in class, for it returns the students once more to the text, leading them to focus on a key passage in order to test whether they agree with Toth or not. Students are frequently unsure about how to make use of secondary sources in their own analytical essays, and an example like this one, which a student could cite for agreement or disagreement and *work with*, can be instructive to them.

We might mention a couple of assignments that have gone over well for Chopin's story. On occasion we have asked students to "complete the story": Write a new final paragraph that presents Armand's reaction to his mother's letter. Sometimes we have also assigned a student to present an oral report on the term "miscegenation," which derives from the title of a faked anonymous pamphlet written during the Civil War. The authors, David Goodman Croly and George Wakeman, were Democratic newspapermen, and their pamphlet (which they pretended had been written by a member of the Republican Party) was designed to discredit Abraham Lincoln and his fellow Republicans by revealing that they favored interracial marriages—which was untrue. The student might be directed to dictionaries and encyclopedias and, for more detail, to George M. Fredrickson, *The Black Image in the White Mind: The Debate on the Afro-American Character and Destiny, 1817-1914* (1971), which includes an insightful account of how the term "miscegenation" arose and gained prominence.

CHAPTER 5

Narrative Point of View

A good deal of critical discussion about point of view is in Wayne Booth, *The Rhetoric of Fiction*; for a thorough history and analysis of the concept, consult Norman Friedman, "Point of View in Fiction," *PMLA* 70 (December 1955): 1160-84. Also of interest is Patrick Cruttwell, "Makers and Persons," *Hudson Review* 12 (Winter 1959-1960): 487-507.

Among relatively easy stories in other chapters that go well with discussions of point of view are Poe's "The Cask of Amontillado," Frank O'Connor's "Guests of the Nation," Alice Walker's "Everyday Use," Toni Cade Bambara's "The Lesson," and Amy Tan's "Two Kinds"—all first-person stories. V. S. Naipaul's "The Night Watchman's Occurrence Book" is a delightful story told through entries in a hotel logbook. (More difficult first-person stories are Gilman's "The Yellow Wallpaper" and Joyce's "Araby.")

JOHN UPDIKE

A & P (p. 79)

It may be useful for students to characterize the narrator and see if occasionally Updike slips. Is "crescent," in the third sentence too apt a word for a speaker who a moment later says, "She gives me a little snort," and "If she'd been born at the right time they would have burned her over in Salem"? If this is a slip, it is more than compensated for by the numerous expressions that are just right.

Like Frank O'Connor's "Guests of the Nation," "A & P" is a first-person story, and in its way is also about growing up. Invite students to characterize the narrator as precisely as possible. Many will notice his hope that the girls will observe his heroic pose, and some will notice, too, his admission that he doesn't want to hurt his parents. His belief (echoing Lengel's) that he will "feel this for the rest of his life" is also adolescent. But his assertion of the girls' innocence is attractive and brave.

Some readers have wondered why Sammy quits. Nothing in the story suggests that he is a political rebel, or that he is a troubled adolescent who uses the episode in the A & P as a cover for some sort of adolescent emotional problem .An extremely odd article in *Studies in Short Fiction*, 23 (1986): 321-23, which seeks to connect Updike's story with Hawthorne's "Young Goodman Brown," says that "Sammy's sudden quitting is not only a way of attracting the girls' attention but also a way of punishing himself for lustful thoughts." Surely this is nonsense, even further off the mark than the same author's assertion that Queenie's pink bathing suit "suggests the emerging desires competing with chastity" (322). Sammy quits because he wants to make a gesture on behalf of these pretty girls, who in appearance and in spirit (when challenged, they assert themselves) are superior to the "sheep" and to the tedious Lengel. Of course Sammy hopes his gesture will be noticed, but in any case the gesture is sincere.

What sort of fellow is Sammy? Is he a male chauvinist pig? An idealist? A self-satisfied deluded adolescent? Someone who thinks he is knowledgeable but who is too quick to judge some people as sheep? Maybe all of the above, in varying degrees. Certainly his remark that the mind of a girl is "a little buzz, like a bee in a glass jar," is outrageous—but later he empathizes with the girls, seeing them not as mindless and not as mere sex objects but as human beings who are being bullied. If we smile a bit at his self-dramatization ("I felt how hard this world was going to be to me hereafter"), we nevertheless find him endowed with a sensitivity that is noticeably absent in Lengel.

Helpful studies of Updike include: George W. Hunt, *John Updike and the Three Great Secret Things: Sex, Religion, and Art* (1980); *Critical Essays on John Updike*, ed. William R. McNaughton (1982); Donald J. Greiner, *John Updike's Novels* (1984); and Julie Newman, *John Updike* (1988).

Students will likely be familiar with Updike's name; some will have seen the film version of his novel, *The Witches of Eastwick* (1984). But because he has written so much, students may be unsure what by Updike they should read. For starters, we recommend the early novel, *Rabbit, Run* (1960), and the short story collections, *Pigeon Feathers* (1962) and *Problems* (1979).

TOPICS FOR CRITICAL THINKING AND WRITING
1. Sammy: comic yet heroic?
2. What kind of person do you think he is?
3. Updike has said what he thinks stories should do:

> I want stories to startle and engage me within the first few sentences, and in their middle to widen or deepen or sharpen my knowledge of human activity, and to end by giving me a sense of completed statement.

In your opinion does " A & P" meet his criteria? Explain.

JOHN UPDIKE

The Rumor (p 83)

One might almost have thought that the emergence of the gay liberation movement had put an end to all talk about "latent" homosexuality, but it hasn't;

indeed, although sexual identity is much talked about, it remains at least as mysterious as ever.

One of the interesting things about "The Rumor" is that it is about sex and yet it has very little sexual action in it. We hear that Sharon had sex with Frank when she was sixteen, that they "made love just two nights ago," that Frank had had a "flurry of adulterous womanizing," and (about a third of the way through the story) that Frank, after the rumor has changed everything, engages in "pushing more brusquely than was his style at her increasing sexual unwillingness," but that's pretty much it, as far as sexual activity goes. Yet the story glances at a wide spectrum of sexual activity. We can begin with heterosexuality:

1. Frank and Sharon married partly as a way of getting out of Cincinnati. ("Their early sex had been difficult for her; she had submitted to his advances out of a larger, more social, rather idealistic attraction. She knew that together they would have the strength to get out of Cincinnati and, singly or married to others, they would stay.")
2. Frank has had adulterous heterosexual affairs—but after the rumor has reached his ears, he wonders if these were not really a manifestation of his homosexuality.

As for homosexuality:

1. The unambiguous homosexuality of Walton Fuller and Jojo, and of others who make up "the queer side" of the art world;
2. the part of Frank's nature that, as he now sees it, is homosexual. Here too we find a spectrum. Probably some of Frank's speculations strikes a reader as tenuous (e.g., his belief that his attraction to "stoical men" had a homosexual component). The passage about the golfing trip in Bermuda, however, is more convincing; Frank "had felt his heart make many curious motions, among them the heaving, all-but-impossible effort women's hearts make in overcoming men's heavy grayness and achieving—a rainbow born of drizzle—love." Finally, at the end of the story, it seems clear that Frank's interest in Jojo, which he characterizes as "Hellenic friendship," is a mixture of the physical ("that silvery line of a scar,... lean long muscles,... white skin") and the intellectual and paternal (Jojo now seems unexpectedly "intelligent," and someone who "needed direction").

Is Frank a homosexual? Any answer would of course have to say what homosexuality is, or, more precisely, would have to say what it means to be a homosexual. It's our sense of the story that as the rumor persists, Frank finds in himself things that seem to confirm it, that is, he begins to take his identity from the identity ascribed to him. He now looks back on various episodes and sees in them a homosexual slant which cannot quite be disproved, though it cannot be proved either, for example, the idea that his adulterous affairs were an attempt to deny his essential homosexuality.

The first half of the story pretty clearly establishes Frank—or seems to establish him—as heterosexual, though even here there are some ambiguous notes. For instance, when he first denies that he has a lover, he does so "too calmly." We take the comment to reflect Sharon's perception, but it comes from the omniscient narrator and therefore can at least be conceived as an authoritative comment. Similarly, Frank's hostile comment about gays—"You know how gays are. Malicious. Mischievous"—sounds like the unambiguous comment of a straight male; yet of course it can be taken as a reflection of Frank's insecurity, a disparaging comment made by someone unsure of his own masculinity. (By the way, the comment is *Frank's*, not—as some students may think—Updike's.)

The idea that gays are "malicious" probably is fairly common among straight men; what is especially interesting in this story is that Updike goes on to use the words "malice" and "maliciousness" in connection with Frank's behavior: "Frank sensed her discomfort and took a certain malicious pleasure in it," and Sharon's belief in the rumor "justified a certain maliciousness" on Frank's part. So, again, we get Frank taking his identity from society's view; if (at least in Frank's view) gays are malicious, Frank—now rumored to be gay—will be malicious. In any case, the first half of the story is largely devoted to setting forth the rumor and to giving evidence of Frank's heterosexuality, and the second half of the story is largely devoted to Frank's perception (creation?) of himself as a homosexual. Whereas in the first half of the story, his denial increased his wife's belief in the truth of the rumor and indeed the very "outrageousness" of the rumor paradoxically served to confirm her suspicions, now, in the second half we find a new belief (Frank's) based, it may seem to most readers, on evidence almost equally insubstantial. In the first half she spied on him, looking for tiny clues (e.g., his response to a waiter) and interpreting them in one way, and in the second half he spies on himself, equally attentive to tiny clues, and equally seeing the evidence only one way.

Does Updike take a stand on the nature/nurture argument about gender identity? We don't think so (and we certainly don't think a writer of fiction need do so), but he does force the issue into a reader's mind. Frank himself sometimes seems to incline to the "nature" view, for instance when he thinks of himself as someone likely to be a homosexual because he is a man with "a slight build, with artistic interests," but at other times he senses that what he is depends on what is around him: "Depending on which man he was standing with, Frank felt large and straight and sonorous, or, as with Wes, gracile and flighty."

A word about some of the questions we ask in the text. Question 1: The point of view in the first paragraph is omniscient (we are told about the feelings of both characters). Question 2: As we have already said, in "Frank said, too calmly," the reader enters into Sharon's mind, that is, here (and in some other passages early in the story) the "central intelligence" is Sharon. Question 3: Here (and in much of the second half of the story) we get into Frank's mind, "annoyingly, infuriatingly" (his response to her action).

CHAPTER 6

Allegory and Symbolism

"Allegory" and "symbolism" have accumulated a good many meanings. Among the references to consult are Edwin Honig, *The Dark Conceit*; C. S. Lewis, *The Allegory of Love*; and Dorothy Sayers, *The Poetry of Search*.

Among highly symbolic stories in the book are Kafka's "The Metamorphosis" and Viramontes's "The Moths," but of course less evident symbols appear in almost all stories. "Araby" is a good story to focus on if one wants to get into a discussion of how far to press details for symbolic meanings.

In our discussion of the Parable of the Prodigal Son (in this manual, Chapter 1), we have already talked about pressing a work very hard in an effort to make it an allegory, and we have also mentioned that some readers put an awful lot of weight on details. How much emphasis should one put on the fact that a girl's bathing suit is pink (in Updike's "A & P"), or on the rusty bicycle pump in "Araby"? Different readers will have different answers. (Our own answer is that much depends on the amount of weight that the author gives to the details.)

NATHANIEL HAWTHORNE

Young Goodman Brown (p. 96)

Lea B.V. Newman's *A Reader's Guide to the Short Stories of Nathaniel Hawthorne* (1979) provides a valuable survey of the immense body of criticism that "Young Goodman Brown" has engendered. (By 1979 it had been discussed in print at least five hundred times.) We can begin by quoting Newman's remark that the three chief questions are these: "Why does Brown go into the forest? What happens to him there? Why does he emerge a permanently embittered man?"

Newman grants that there is a good deal of "ambivalence" in the story, but she finds most convincing the view that Brown is a victim, a man who "is deluded into accepting spectral evidence as conclusive proof of his neighbors' depravity." Newman also finds convincing another version of the "victim" theory, this one offered by psychologists who hold that "Brown is a sick man with a diseased mind who cannot help what he sees in the forest or his reaction to it." But her survey also includes references to critics who see Brown "as an evil man who is solely responsible for all that happens to him" (342-44).

Various critics—it almost goes without saying—press various details very hard. For instance, one critic says that Faith's pink ribbons symbolize Brown's "insubstantial, pastel-like faith." (Instructors expect to encounter this sort of reductive reading in essays by first-year students, but it is disappointing to find it in print.) How detailed, one might ask, is the allegory? Probably most readers will agree on some aspects: the village—a world of daylight and community—stands (or seems to stand) for good, whereas the forest—a dark, threatening place—stands (or seems to stand) for evil. The old man—"he of the serpent"—is the devil. But, again, as Newman's survey of criticism shows, even these interpretations have been debated.

The journey into the forest at night (away from the town and away from the daylight) suggests, of course, a journey into the dark regions of the self. The many ambiguities have engendered much comment in learned journals, some of which has been reprinted in a casebook of the story, *Nathaniel Hawthorne: Young Goodman Brown*, ed. Thomas E. Connolly. Is the story—as David Levin argues in *American Literature* 34 (1962): 344-52—one about a man who is tricked by the devil, who conjures up specters who look like Brown's neighbors in order to win him a damnable melancholy? Does Faith resist the tempter? Does Goodman (i.e., Mister) Brown make a journey or does he only dream that he makes a journey? Is the story about awareness of evil, or is it about the crushing weight of needlessly assumed guilt? That is, is the story about a loss of faith (Austin Warren, in *Nathaniel Hawthorne*, says it is about "the devastating effect of moral skepticism"), or is it about a religious faith that kills one's joy in life? And, of course, the story may be about loss of faith not in Christ but in human beings; young Goodman Brown perceives his own corruption and loses faith in mankind.

With a little warning the student can be helped to see that the characters and experiences cannot be neatly pigeonholed. For example, it is not certain whether or not Faith yields to "the wicked one"; indeed, it is not certain that Brown actually journeyed into the woods. Richard H. Fogle points out in *Hawthorne's Fiction* that "ambiguity is the very essence of Hawthorne's tale." Among other interesting critical pieces on the story are Marius Bewley, *The Complex Fate*; Thomas Connolly, "Hawthorne's 'Young Goodman Brown': An Attack on Puritanic Calvinism," *American Literature* 28 (November 1956): 370-75; and Frederick C. Crews, *The Sins of the Fathers: Hawthorne's Psychological Themes*. Connolly argues that Brown does not lose his faith, but rather that his faith is purified by his loss of belief that he is of the elect. Before the journey into the woods, he believes that man is depraved, but that he himself is of the elect and will be saved. In the forest he sees "a black mass of cloud" hide "the brightening stars," and (according to Connolly) his faith is purified, for he comes to see that he is not different from the rest of the congregation.

On the other hand, one can point out (as J. L. Capps does, in *Explicator*, Spring 1982), that only once in the story does Hawthorne use the word "hope" ("'But where is Faith' thought Goodman Brown; and as hope came into his heart, he trembled"), and the word "charity" never appears, indicating that Brown lacks the quality that would have enabled him to survive despair.

Speaking a bit broadly, we can say that critics fall into two camps: those who believe that Goodman Brown falls into delusion (i.e., misled by the devil, he destroys himself morally by falling into misanthropy), and those who believe that he is initiated into reality. Thus, for readers who hold the first view, Brown's guide into the forest is the devil, who calls up "figures" or "forms" of Brown's acquaintances, and it is Brown (not the narrator) who mistakenly takes the figures for real people. Even what Brown takes to be Faith's pink ribbon is for the narrator merely "*something* [that] fluttered lightly down through the air, and caught on the branch of a tree." In this view, (1) the fact that Faith later wears the ribbon is proof that Brown has yielded to a delusion, and (2) we are to judge Brown by recalling the narrator's objective perceptions. For instance, Brown's guide says that "evil is the nature of mankind," and Brown believes him, but the narrator (who is to be trusted) speaks of "the good old minister" and of "that excellent Christian," Goody Cloyse. There is much to be said for this view (indeed much has been said in journals), but against it one can recall some words by Frederick Crews: "The richness of Hawthorne's irony is such that, when Brown turns to a Gulliver-like misanthropy and spends the rest of his days shrinking from wife and neighbors, we cannot quite dismiss his attitude as unfounded" (*The Sins of the Fathers*, 106).

We'd urge instructors to pay special attention to the words spoken by the "sable form" among the fiend worshipers, about three-quarters into the story: "There are all whom ye have reverenced from youth." This is one of Hawthorne's most powerful visions of evil, and it is notable how he involves and implicates the mind of the reader in his dark imaginings. Hawthorne does not state explicitly, for example, that the widow referred to in this paragraph has *poisoned* her husband. Nor does he say outright that the fair damsels are burying children conceived out of wedlock, children whom, apparently, the fearful, ashamed mothers have murdered. The point of the words used in the speech—we find them terrifying—is that they evoke sins and crimes that Hawthorne makes the reader imagine and identify in himself or herself. You might ask the class why Hawthorne does this, and what it is about the nature of the heart and mind he is seeking to explore through this technique.

Good recent biographies include: James R. Mellow, *Nathaniel Hawthorne In His Times* (1980); and Edwin Haviland Miller, *Salem Is My Dwelling Place: A Life of Nathaniel Hawthorne* (1991). Instructors might also refer to *The Scarlet Letter*, ed. Ross C. Murfin (1991), a volume in the Bedford Case Studies in Contemporary Criticism series. This edition presents the text of the novel and essays that exemplify five critical approaches to it.

TOPICS FOR CRITICAL THINKING AND WRITING

1. Ambiguity in "Young Goodman Brown."
2. What are the strengths and weaknesses of the view that Brown is tricked by the devil, who stages a show of specters impersonating Brown's neighbors, in order to destroy Brown's religious faith?
3. Brown's guide says, "Evil is the nature of mankind," but does the story say it?
4. Is the story sexist, showing Brown more horrified by his wife's sexuality, than his own?
5. Retell the story using a modern setting. Make whatever changes you wish, but retain the motif of the temptation of a man and a woman by evil.
6. What do you think Hawthorne gains (or loses) by the last sentence?

EUDORA WELTY

A Worn Path (p. 105)

In an essay in the *Georgia Review* (Winter 1979), Eudora Welty (speaking mainly of her first story, "The Death of a Traveling Salesman") says that her characters "rise most often from the present," but her plots are indebted to "the myths and fairy tales I steeped myself in as a young reader.... By the time I was writing stories I drew on them as casually as I drew on the daily newspaper or the remarks of my neighbors."

Clearly "A Worn Path" draws on the myth of the phoenix, the golden bird that periodically consumes itself in flames so that it, rising from ashes, may be renewed. Phoenix Jackson renews her ancient body on each visit to the doctor's remote office. The chief clues: the woman's name ("Phoenix"), the story's early description of her (her stick makes a sound "like the chirping of a solitary little bird"; "a golden color ran underneath, and the two knobs of her cheeks were illuminated by a yellow burning under the dark"), a reference to cyclic time ("I bound to go to town, mister. The time come around"—and the time is Christmas, i.e., a time of renewal), her "ceremonial stiffness" in the doctor's office, and finally, the words "Phoenix rose carefully."

The myth is wonderfully supported by details, details that are strictly irrelevant (e.g., Phoenix's deception of the hunter, which nets her a nickel, and her cadging of a nickel's worth of pennies from the nurse), but that make the character unsentimental and thoroughly convincing.

A writer in *Studies in Short Fiction* 14 (1977): 288-290 argues: "The journey to Natchez... becomes a psychological necessity for Phoenix, her only way of coping with her loss and her isolation.... Having at first made the journey to save the life of her grandson, she now follows the worn path each Christmas season to save herself" (289). On the other hand, not all of the criticism of the story is on this level. For a good discussion, see Alfred Appel, *A Season of Dreams: The Fiction of Eudora Welty* (1965).

Students will enjoy browsing in Welty's *Collected Stories* (1980). Also worthy of mention are her novels *Delta Wedding* (1946) and *The Optimist's Daughter* (1972); her prose collection, *The Eye of the Story: Selected Essays and*

Reviews (1978); and her eloquent account of her youth and writing career, *One Writer's Beginnings* (1984).

For secondary sources: Michael Kreyling, *Eudora Welty's Achievement of Order* (1980); Ruth M. Vande Kieft, *Eudora Welty* (rev. ed., 1987); and Peter Schmidt, *The Heart of the Story: Eudora Welty's Short Fiction* (1991).

TOPICS FOR CRITICAL THINKING AND WRITING

1. Is the story sentimental? (We'd say no, for several reasons: Phoenix, though old and—at moments—mentally failing, is dignified and never self-pitying; the writer, letting Phoenix tell her own story, never asks us to pity Phoenix; Phoenix exhibits both a sense of humor and a sense of self-reliance, and on those occasions when she needs help she exhibits no embarrassment. Her theft of the nickel and her shrewdness in getting the nurse to give her another nickel instead of "a few pennies" also, as mentioned a moment ago, help to keep her from being the sentimental old lady of Norman Rockwell pictures.)

2. Write a character sketch (250-300 words) of some old person whom you know. If possible, reveal the personality by showing him or her engaged in some characteristic activity.

CHAPTER 7

In Brief: Writing about Fiction

EDGAR ALLAN POE

The Cask of Amontillado (p. 116)

Because many students will have read this story in high school, it can be used effectively as the first assignment: they will start with some ideas about it, and at the end of the class discussion they will probably see that they didn't know everything about the story. It may be well to begin a class discussion by asking the students to characterize the narrator. The opening paragraph itself, if read aloud in class, ought to provide enough for them to see that the speaker is probably paranoid and given to a monstrous sort of reasoning, though, of course, at the start of the story we cannot be absolutely certain that Fortunato has not indeed heaped a "thousand injuries" on him. (In this paragraph, notice too the word "impunity," which we later learn is part of the family motto.) When we meet Fortunato, we are convinced that though the narrator's enemy is something of a fool, he is not the monster that the narrator thinks he is. And so the words at the end of the story, fifty years later, must have an ironic tone, for though *in pace requiescat* can apply to Fortunato, they cannot apply to the speaker, who is still talking (on his deathbed, to a priest?) of his vengeance on the unfortunate Fortunato.

The story is full of other little ironies, conscious on the part of Montresor, unconscious on the part of Fortunato:

- The narrator is courteous but murderous;
- The time is one of festivity but a murder is being planned;
- The festival of disguise corresponds to the narrator's disguise of his feelings;

- Fortunato thinks he is festively *disguised* as a fool, but he *is* a fool;
- He says he will not die of a cough, and the narrator assures him that he is right;
- Fortunato is a Freemason, and when he asks the narrator for the secret sign of a brother, the narrator boldly, playfully, outrageously shows him the mason's trowel that he will soon use to wall Fortunato up.

But what to make of all this? It has been the fashion, for at least a few decades, to say that Poe's situations and themes speak to our anxieties, our fear of being buried alive, our fear of disintegration of the self, and so on. Maybe. Maybe, too, there is something to Marie Bonaparte's interpretation: she sees the journey through the tunnel to the crypt as an entry into the womb; the narrator is killing his father (Fortunato) and possessing his mother. And maybe, too, there is something to Daniel Hoffman's assertion in *Poe Poe Poe Poe Poe Poe Poe* (223) that Montresor and Fortunato are doubles: "When Montresor leads Fortunato down into the farthest vault of his family's wine-cellar, into a catacomb of human bones, is he not... conducting his double thither? My treasure, my fortune, down into the bowels of the earth, a charnel-house of bones." Maybe.

In addition to Hoffman's book (1972), we can recommend Kenneth Silverman's fine biography, *Edgar Allan Poe: Mournful and Never-Ending Remembrance* (1991).

A videocassette of Edgar Allan Poe's "The Cask of Amontillado" is available from Longman. An audiocassette of Basil Rathbone reading Edgar Allan Poe's "The Cask of Amontillado" and "The Pit and the Pendulum" is also available from Longman.

ANN GERAGHTY

Revenge, Noble and Ignoble (Student Essay) (p. 123)

We think this is an excellent essay—clearly written and effectively argued—but we think that if it had been revised yet once more it would have been even better. As we see it, the writer offers not one thesis but two: (1) Montresor is insane, and (2) the story is appealing because Montresor's insanity is of a special sort, rooted in his concept of honor, a concept that leads him to think of the killing as a solemn sacrifice (an "immolation").

We would have been happier if the student had somehow combined these two points more clearly, and had perhaps indicated the thesis (the combined points) earlier in the essay, perhaps even in the title. For instance, the essay might have been called "Insane but Noble Revenge." Having said what we have just said, we want to reiterate our view that we think the essay is strong. We should add that, in a conference after the essay was returned, the student said, quite reasonably, that her thesis was that Montresor is mad, and that the material about the family honor was offered not as second point but as an explanation of exactly what sort of madness was displayed.

The basic thesis, stated at the end of the second paragraph, is that Montresor is insane. Again, we would have liked a title that glanced at the point made in the second half of the essay, but we find Geraghty's title sufficiently interesting and sufficiently relevant, and we find the first two paragraphs (and the third paragraph, which supports the thesis) effective.

The fourth paragraph is something of a transition between what the writer has already established (Montresor is insane) and the extremely interesting idea that Montresor's insanity is understandable and interesting because it is based on his concept of family honor, a concept that allows him to think that killing Fortunato is a solemn sacrifice, an "immolation." A colleague thinks that Geraghty makes too much of the word "immolation," but one might say the same of almost any interpretation of any work; that is, in focusing on one point one almost inevitably overemphasizes it.

CHAPTER 8

Two Fiction Writers in Depth: Flannery O'Connor and Raymond Carver

FLANNERY O'CONNOR

A Good Man Is Hard to Find (p. 128)

In the early part of this story the grandmother is quite as hateful as the rest of the family—though students do not always see at first that her vapid comments, her moral clichés, and her desire to be thought "a lady" are offensive in their own way. Her comment, "People are certainly not nice like they used to be," can be used to convince students of her mindlessness and lack of charity.

The Misfit, like Jesus, was "buried alive"; he believes that "Jesus thrown everything off balance," and he finds no satisfaction in life (i.e., his life without grace). Life is either a meaningless thing in which all pleasure is lawful (and, ironically, all pleasure turns to ashes), or it derives its only meaning from following Jesus. The Misfit, though he does not follow Jesus, at least sees that the materialistic view of life is deficient. Confronted by the suffering of The Misfit, the nagging and shallow grandmother suddenly achieves a breakthrough and is moved by love. She had earlier recognized The Misfit (" 'You're The Misfit!' she said. 'I recognized you at once' "), and now she has a further recognition of him as "one of her own children," that is, a suffering fellow human. Faced with death, she suddenly becomes aware of her responsibility: her head clears for an instant and she says, "You're one of my own children." This statement is not merely an attempt to dissuade The Misfit from killing her; contrast it with her earlier attempts, when, for example, she says, "I know you come from nice people! Pray! Jesus, you ought not to shoot a lady. I'll give you all the money I've got." Rather, at last her head is "cleared." This moment of grace transfigures her and causes her death. The Misfit is right when he says, "She would of been a good woman if it had been somebody there to shoot her every minute of her life."

On the "moment of grace" in O'Connor's fiction, see *College English* (27, December 1965): 235-39, and R. M. Vande Kiefte in *Sewanee Review* 70 (1968): 337-56. Vande Kiefte notes that the description of the dead grandmother ("her legs crossed under her like a child's and her face smiling up at the cloudless sky") suggests that death has jolted the grandmother out of her mere secular decency into the truth of eternal reality. See also Martha Stephens, *The Question of Flannery O'Connor.*

For Flannery O'Connor's comments on this story, see our text. In her collected letters, entitled *The Habit of Being,* O'Connor says (letter to John Gawkes, Dec. 26, 1959) that she is interested in "the moment when you know that Grace has been offered and accepted—such as the moment when the Grandmother realizes The Misfit is one of her own children" (367).

O'Connor's letters, fiction, and essays are included in the volume of her work in the Library of America series (1988). See also *Conversations with Flannery O'Connor,* ed. Rosemary M. Magee (1987). Good points of departure for further study include: *Critical Essays on Flannery O'Connor,* ed. Melvin J. Friedman and Beverly Lyon Clark (1985); Suzanne Morrow Paulson, *Flannery O'Connor: A Study of the Short Fiction* (1988); and Miles Orvell, *Flannery O'Connor: An Introduction* (1972; rpt. 1991).

TOPICS FOR CRITICAL THINKING AND WRITING

1. Explain the significance of the title.
2. Interpret and evaluate The Misfit's comment on the grandmother: "She would of been a good woman if it had been somebody there to shoot her every minute of her life."
3. O'Connor reported that once, when she read aloud "A Good Man Is Hard to Find," one of her hearers said that "it was a shame someone with so much talent should look on life as a horror story." Two questions: What evidence of O'Connor's "talent" do you see in the story, and does the story suggest that O'Connor looked on life as a horror story?
4. What are the values of the members of the family?
5. Flannery O'Connor, a Roman Catholic, wrote, "I see from the standpoint of Christian orthodoxy. This means that for me the meaning of life is centered in our Redemption by Christ and what I see in the world I see in relation to that." In the light of this statement, and drawing on "A Good Man Is Hard to Find," explain what O'Connor saw in the world.

FLANNERY O'CONNOR

Revelation (p. 140)

This story, like "A Good Man Is Hard to Find," is concerned with a moment of grace, which most obviously begins when Mary Grace hurls a hook at Mrs. Turpin—an action somewhat parallel to The Misfit's assault on the grandmother. The doctor's office contains a collection of wretched human beings whose physical illnesses mirror their spiritual condition. There is abundant comedy ("The nurse ran in, then out, then in again"), but these people are treated sympathetically too. Mrs. Turpin's pitiful snobbery—especially her desperate effort to rank people in the eyes of God—is comic and horrible, but it at least reveals an uneasiness beneath her complacency, an uneasiness that finally compares well with the monumental hatred that characterizes Mary Grace. Yet Mary Grace, a pimply girl, is a messenger of grace. And so when the blow comes (from a book nicely called *Human Development*), it is not in vain. The girl's accusation ("Go back to hell where you came from, you old wart hog") strikes home, and later, among the pigs that Mrs. Turpin so solicitously cleans, the message produces a revelation, a revelation that forces upon her an awareness of the inadequacy of "virtue" (her horrible concept of respectability) as she has known it. Virtue is of as little value to fallen humanity as a hosing-down is to a pig; in her vision she sees that even virtue or respectability is burned away in the movement toward heaven.

On the one hand, some students have difficulty seeing that Mrs. Turpin is not simply a stuffy hypocrite; on the other, some students have difficulty seeing that her respectability is woefully inadequate and must be replaced by a deeper sympathy. But perhaps students have the greatest difficulty in reconciling the comic aspects of the story with its spiritual depth, and here the instructor can probably not do much more than read some passages and hope for the best.

In O'Connor's writings the sun is a common symbol for God. Here, the light of the sun transforms the hogs, so that they appear to "pant with a secret life," a parallel to the infusion of grace into Mrs. Turpin, which causes her to see the worthlessness of her earlier "respectable" values.

The story is deeply indebted to the Book of Revelation, traditionally attributed to St. John the Evangelist and probably written at the end of the first century A.D. (A revelation is, etymologically, an "unveiling," just as an apocalypse is, in Greek, an unveiling. What is unveiled in the Book of Revelation is the future.) Numerous details in O'Connor's story pick up details in the biblical account: O'Connor's "red glow" in the sky echoes the fiery heaven of Revelation; the "watery snake" that briefly appears in the air echoes the water-spewing "serpent" of Revelation (12:15), and even the "seven long-snouted bristling shoats" echo the numerous references to seven (angels, churches, seals, stars) in Revelation. But the details should not be pressed too hard; what matters most is the apocalyptic vision of the oppressed rejoicing and shouting hallelujah at the throne of God.

The story is not difficult, and no published discussions of it are essential reading, though it is of course discussed in books on O'Connor and in general comments on her work, such as A. R. Coulthard, "From Sermon to Parable: Four Conversion Stories by Flannery O'Connor" *American Literature* 55 (1983): 55-71. Two essays devoted entirely to "Revelation" are "'Revelation' and the Book of Job" by Diane Rolmedo, *Renascence* 30 (1978): 78-90, and Larue Love Slone's "The Rhetoric of the Seer: Eye Imagery in Flannery O'Connor's 'Revelation,'" *Studies in Short Fiction* 25 (1988): 135-145.

TOPICS FOR CRITICAL THINKING AND WRITING

1. Why does Mary Grace attack Mrs. Turpin?
2. Characterize Mrs. Turpin before her revelation. Did your attitude toward her change at the end of the story?
3. The two chief settings are a doctor's waiting room and a "pig parlor." Can these settings reasonably be called "symbolic"? If so, symbolic of what?
4. When Mrs. Turpin goes toward the pig parlor, she has "the look of a woman going single-handed, weaponless, into battle." Once there, she dismisses Claud, uses the hose as a weapon against the pigs, and talks to herself "in a low fierce voice." What is she battling, besides the pigs?

FLANNERY O'CONNOR

Parker's Back (p. 154)

This is O'Connor's last story. Much of it was written in the hospital a few weeks before her death.

Like many of her other stories, and especially like "Revelation" (written at almost the same time as " Parker's Back"), this story is about conversion, which is literally a "turning" or "returning," that is, toward God. And as in many of her other stories, the turning is brought about through a violent act of grace.

Parker, earlier "as ordinary as a loaf of bread," discovers "wonder" at a sideshow, when he sees a tattooed man:

> The man, who was small and sturdy, moved about on the platform, flexing his muscles so that the arabesque of men and beasts and flowers on his skin appeared to have a subtle motion of its own. Parker was filled with emotion, lifted up as some people are when the flag passes.
>
> Parker had never before felt the least motion of wonder in himself. Until he saw the man at the fair, it did not enter his head that there was anything out of the ordinary about the fact that he existed. Even then it did not enter his head, but a peculiar unease settled in him. It was as if a blind boy had been turned [here we get a clear reference to conversion] so gently in a different direction that he did not know his destination had been changed.

This "unease," which now alters Parker's being, proves to be of the sort, we can surely say, that St. Augustine spoke of when he said, "Restless I am until I rest in Thee."

So Parker begins his quest for tattoos. Each new tattoo, however, brings him only brief comfort; he is driven to seek another, and another, and still he is dissatisfied:

> The effect was not of one intricate arabesque of colors but of something haphazard and botched. A huge dissatisfaction would come over him and he would go off and find another tattooist and have another space filled up.

He is, apparently, trying to transform his body, but it is his soul that needs to be transformed. (It may be noted parenthetically that the impulse to acquire a tattoo presumably arises from a discontent with the natural body; this discontent—however grotesque tattooing may seem as an image of the human craving for a higher life—is the basis of O'Connor's story.)

Parker's second great perception occurs when he cries out, "God above," drives his tractor into a tree, sets the tree afire, and is knocked out of his shoes. Perhaps this episode is meant to remind us of Moses and the burning, in Exodus 32:1-6, where God appears in a burning bush and tells Moses to remove his shoes, "for the place whereon thou standest is holy ground." A passage from the New Testament is also relevant; although Parker himself says, "God above," the conjunction of sudden light and the words Parker utters may put a reader in mind of St. Paul's conversion, which was accompanied by a blinding light and by voices in heaven. Even without associating the episode of the tractor with any particular episode in the Bible, we must feel that when he is knocked out of his shoes, Parker—now barefoot—is reborn:

> Parker did not allow himself to think on the way to the city. He only knew that there had been a great change in his life, a leap forward into a worse unknown, and that there was nothing he could do about it. It was for all intents accomplished.

Given the decisiveness of this experience, it may not be fanciful to suggest that the words "It was for all intents accomplished" deliberately echo *Consummatum est,* the words of Christ on the Cross (see John 19:30). (The usual translation is "It is finished," or " It is fulfilled.")

At the tattooist's office Parker looks through a book with the images of God. Because the tattooist tells him that "The up-to-date ones are in the back," he begins at the back, where he encounters images of the Good Shepherd, the Smiling Jesus, and Jesus the Physician's Friend—that is, sentimental images that suit modern taste. These cozy images are of a God who demands nothing, and they are therefore of no interest to Parker, who, as he moves toward the front of the book, encounters pictures that are "less and less reassuring," old fashioned images of a God almost forgotten today. A pair of "all-demanding eyes" (the Byzantine Christ) arrests his attention.

His back adorned with the tattoo of Christ—with, we might say, Christ not merely on his back but literally under his skin—Parker nevertheless denies to the tattooist and later to his cronies in the pool hall that he has "gone and got religion." He is still resisting the workings of grace. An allusion to Jonah (the pool hall from which Parker is ejected is compared to "the ship from which Jonah had been cast into the sea") emphasizes the idea that Parker is a man struggling (unsuccessfully, like Jonah) to evade God's demand of total obedience. "Examining his soul" in the alley behind the pool hall, Parker sees that "the eyes that were now forever on his back were eyes to be obeyed."

The emphasis on Christ's eyes reminds a reader of the emphasis on Sarah Ruth's "ice pick eyes." In the first paragraph of the story, for instance, we are told that her eyes were "sharp like the points of two ice picks." Though Parker's marriage to Sarah Ruth remains something of a mystery, it's safe to assert that he marries her partly because of these eyes; she is mysterious, demanding, different from himself. She humiliates him, and thus is an agent of grace. Now, when Parker returns to her, hoping to gain her approval, she further humiliates him, alleging that she does not know him. O'Connor emphasizes the immense importance of this moment by giving us a mysteriously illuminated landscape:

> The sky had lightened slightly and there were two or three streaks of yellow floating above the horizon. Then as he stood there, a tree of light burst over the skyline.

The next sentence in the story, a paragraph by itself, is especially important:

> Parker fell back against the door as if he had been pinned there by a lance.

Surely this passage is meant to remind us of the Crucifixion. Sarah Ruth persists in asking Parker who he is, until he finally whispers "Obadiah." And at this moment

> he felt the light pouring through him, turning his spider web soul into a perfect arabesque of colors, a garden of trees and birds and beasts.

We recall that the tattooed man at the fair wore an "arabesque of men and beasts and flowers on his skin," but Parker's "arabesque," O'Connor specifies, is not of the skin but of the "soul." At this moment, when perhaps the idea of Eden flits through a reader's mind, Parker whispers the Biblical name (Obadiah Elihue) that he has long disguised by using only his initials.

What does one make of the ending, when Sarah Ruth beats Obadiah with a broom, just as she had done when she first met him? There is something comic, of course, in such a line as "She stamped the broom two or three times on the floor and went to the window and shook it out to get the taint of him off it," but there is more. When she thrashes Obadiah across the shoulders, and raises "large welts... on the face of the tattooed Christ," surely we see a repetition of the Crucifixion Which is not to say that Parker is Christ. Of course he is not. He is Parker, the broken man, "crying like a baby" (the last words of the story)—and therefore at last (one may guess) he is fully humiliated and capable of salvation.

The fullest discussion of the story is Preston Browning, Jr., "'Parker's Back': Flannery O'Connor's Iconography of Salvation and Profanity," *Studies in Short Fiction* 6 (1968–69): 525-35.

TOPICS FOR CRITICAL THINKING AND WRITING

1. What is the meaning of the title? (Three points come to mind. First, of course, one thinks of that part of Parker's body on which the image of Christ is tattooed, or perhaps of the image itself. Second, one may think of Parker's return to God: his early vague dissatisfaction leads him ultimately not simply to acquire an image of Christ but to admit his Biblical name, and to accept a scourging by the world. He is, so to speak, back with God.)
2. Why does Parker keep adding tattoos?
3. Why does Parker, who had promised himself never to get "caught," marry, and marry a woman whose values are so different from his own?
4. Putting aside the problem of the "meaning" of the story, are there characters or actions or episodes that you especially enjoyed reading about? If so, cite

two or three, and explain what you found especially engaging about them.
5. Do you think "Parker's Back" is saying something about idolatry and about religion? If so, what?

RAYMOND CARVER

Popular Mechanics (p. 175)

The usual characteristics of Minimalism are alleged to be:

- lower-middle-class characters, who are relatively inarticulate and out of touch with others and with themselves
- little if any setting
- little action of any apparent importance
- little if any authorial comment, i.e., little interpretation of motive
- a drab style—fairly simple sentences, with little or no use of figurative language or allusions

Almost no story perfectly exemplifies this textbook paradigm. In fact, "Popular Mechanics" is an excellent way of seeing the *in*adequacy of such a view of minimalism.

Let's look at this very short story—certainly minimal in terms of length—from beginning to end, though for the moment we'll skip the title. Here is the first paragraph:

> Early that day the weather turned and the snow was melting into dirty water. Streaks of it ran down from the little shoulder-high window that faced the backyard. Cars slushed by on the street outside, where it was getting dark. But it was getting dark on the inside too.

If you read the paragraph aloud in class, students will easily see that Carver very briefly establishes an unpleasant setting ("dirty water," "streaks," "cars slushed by"), giving us not only a sense of what we see but also the time of day ("dark"). But of course Carver is *not* giving us mere landscape and chronology. When we read "But it was getting dark on the inside too," we anticipate dark passions. A reader can't be sure that such passions will materialize, or how the story will turn out; the darkness may dissipate, but at this stage a reader is prepared for a story that fits the rotten weather. (Another way of putting it is to say that Carver is preparing the reader, i.e., is seeking to control our responses.) Perhaps, then, it is incorrect to say that minimalists do not use figurative language; surely the dark weather is figurative. And on rereading the story a reader may feel that the metamorphosis of snow into dirty water is an emblem of the history of this marriage.

The second question printed at the end of this discussion asks students to compare the opening paragraph with an earlier version. Perhaps the chief differences are the elimination of the sun from the revised version—there is no sunshine in this world—and the emphasis, in the last sentence of the revised paragraph, on the internal darkness. In the earlier version, "It was getting dark, outside and inside;" in the later version, the inside darkness gets a sentence to itself: "But it was getting dark on the inside too." The real point of asking students to look at the revisions "to account for the changes" is to help them to look closely at what Carver has written, so that they will give his words a chance to shape their responses.

As we read the story, we never get inside the heads of the characters. The author tells us nothing about them, other than what they say and what they do. We don't know why they behave as they do. We know very little about them, not even their names, since Carver calls them only "he" and "she." The first line of dialogue is angry, and all of the remaining dialogue reveals the terrific hostility that exists between the two speakers. As the author presents them to us, the alienation of these characters does seem to fit the textbook description of minimalist writing.

The quarrel about the picture of the baby leads (because Carver is an artist, not a mere recorder) to the quarrel about the baby. (These people may hate each other, but apparently they both love the baby, although of course it is possible that each wants to possess the picture and the baby simply in order to hurt the other. Again, the author gives no clues.) The adults' angry passions contaminate the baby, so to speak, for the baby begins to cry and soon is "red-faced and screaming."

Even a little detail like the flowerpot is relevant. In the fight, the adults could have knocked over some other object, for example a kitchen chair. But it is a flowerpot—a little touch of life and presumably a small attempt at beautifying the house—that is upset. Norman German and Jack Bedell, *Critique* 29 (1988): 257-60 make the interesting point that no plant is mentioned, only a pot. "The empty pot," they suggest, "is like the house, a lifeless hull." Carver isn't just recording; he is choosing what he wishes to record, because he wants to evoke certain responses.

We can't tell what ultimately happened to the baby, but there is every reason to believe that he is physically harmed, possibly even killed, and this point gets back to the title, a topic raised below, in question 4. Why did Carver change the title from "Mine" to "Popular Mechanics"? The new title of course summons to mind the magazine of that name, but the magazine is never mentioned. What then, is the relevance of the title? First, it probably calls to mind the male blue-collar world, the chief readership of *Popular Mechanics.* Second, by the time one finishes the story and thinks about the title, one sees a sort of pun in "popular," one of whose meanings is "Of or carried on by the common people" (*Webster's New World Dictionary).* And in "mechanics" we see the forces at work—the physical forces operating on the baby as the two adults each pull him.

The last sentence surely is worth discussing in class: "In this manner, the issue was decided." The language seems flat, unadorned, merely informative. But "decided" is monstrously inappropriate. The word suggests thought rather than sheer violence; even if, say, we decide an issue by tossing a coin, the decision to toss a coin is arrived at by thinking and by common consent. Perhaps the word "issue," too, is significant; German and Bedell find in it a pun (offspring as well as argument). To find a parallel for Carver's last sentence we probably have to turn to the world of Swiftian irony.

Question 3, below, invites students to compare the last line with Carver's earlier version, "In this manner they decided the issue." In the revision, by means of the passive, Carver makes the sentence even flatter; the narrator seems even more effaced. But he is therefore, to the responsive reader, even more present. As Tobias Wolff puts it, in the introduction to *Matters of Life and Death,* "Irony offers us a way of talking about the unspeakable. In the voices of Swift and Nabokov and Jane Austen we sometimes hear what would have been a scream if irony had not subdued it to eloquence."

The circumstances and the word "decided" may remind the reader of another decision concerning a disputed child, the decision Solomon made (1 Kings 3:16-27) when confronted with two prostitutes who disputed over which was the true mother of the child. One woman, you'll recall, was even willing to murder the child in order to settle the dispute.

In short, Carver's language is not so drab as it sometimes appears to be, which disputes the contention that his stories—especially the early ones—are "thin." As the three stories in this book indicate, he changed as a writer, but in some ways the body of his work is consistent. Late in his life, in the preface to *The Best American Short Stories 1986,* he described his taste:

> I'm drawn toward the traditional (some would call it old-fashioned) methods of storytelling: one layer of reality unfolding and giving way to another, perhaps richer layer; the gradual accretion of meaningful detail; dialogue that not only reveals something about character but advances the story.

In interviews shortly before his death he freely admitted that his view of life had changed; he was in love, and things didn't seem as bleak as they had seemed earlier. But this does not mean that his early stories are less skillfully constructed than are his later, more tender stories.

There is now a body of critical and biographical work on Carver, and it continues steadily to grow. The following are helpful: Arthur M. Saltzman, *Understanding Raymond Carver* (1988); *Conversations with Raymond Carver,* ed. Marshall Bruce Gentry and William L. Stull (1990); Ewing Campbell, *Raymond Carver: A Study of the Short Fiction* (1992); and Sam Halpert, *Raymond Carver: An Oral Biography* (1995).

TOPICS FOR CRITICAL THINKING AND WRITING

1. Some readers object to "minimalist" writings on the grounds that the stories (1) lack ideas, (2) do not describe characters in depth, and (3) are written in a drab style. Does Carver's story seem to you to suffer from these alleged weaknesses?

2. When Carver first published the story, the opening paragraph was slightly different. Here is the earlier version:

> During the day the sun had come out and the snow melted into dirty water. Streaks of water ran down from the little, shoulder-high window that faced the back yard. Cars slushed by on the street outside. It was getting dark, outside and inside.

Which version do you prefer? Why?

3. The last line—"In this manner, the issue was decided"—in the original version ran thus: "In this manner they decided the issue." Do you consider the small change an improvement? Why, or why not?
4. The original title was "Mine." Again, what do you think of the change, and why?

RAYMOND CARVER

What We Talk About When We Talk about Love (p. 176)

This story is Carver's dark version of Plato's *Symposium*, even though there are no direct echoes beyond the situation (people talking and drinking) and the subject (love). Carver's story begins in daylight and moves into darkness, with the talk seeming (at least on the surface) to clarify nothing, whereas Plato's dialogue moves from late afternoon or evening through the night and into the daylight. True, at the end of *The Symposium* we are told that some of the participants have fallen asleep and others are drowsy and unable to follow the argument that Socrates is presenting, but presumably the reader has been persuaded by Socrates's words (Socrates modestly attributes them to the priestess Diotima) concerning the nature of love.

In ordinary talk, love means many things, ranging from (say) a passion for the movies or for shopping to more serious things, such as love of one's country, love of God, love of humanity, love of parents for children, and erotic love of human beings. Even if we confine our attention to erotic love—the only kind of love discussed in Carver's story—we probably can hardly come up with a narrow definition; rather, when we think about what love is, we think of three things. First, we think of our own experiences; second, we think of the lovers around us, whose secrets we don't know but whose relationships we can guess to be widely (and wildly) varied, and, third—or perhaps really first—we think of famous stories of love, for it probably is these (e.g. Romeo and Juliet, Othello and Desdemona, Beatrice and Benedict, Petruchio and Kate, Tristan and Isolde, perhaps even Edward VIII and Wallace Simpson) that give us our clearest and most memorable ideas about what love is. These fictions help to create life. (Someone—maybe La Rochefoucauld—said that people would not fall in love if they had not read about it in a book.) In *The Symposium*, too, there is a range of kinds of love, though it is clear that for Plato the highest is love of wisdom.

Carver's story resembles Plato's *Symposium* not only in the setting and in the topic of discussion, but in form. We say that "What We Talk About" is a short story, but perhaps we ought to call it (following Northrop Frye) an anatomy, a prose fiction characterized by debates or dialogues. Frye used the word to distinguish such long prose fictions as *Gulliver's Travels* and *Point Counterpoint* from the novel; he pointed out that it was not very useful to discuss all long prose fictions as though they are novels, with realistic characters and plots that moved to resolutions. Similarly, we can say that not all short works of fiction need be short stories, if by "short story" we mean, again, a work with realistic characters participating in a plot that is resolved. Frye himself saw some short prose fictions as *tales* (narratives with the emphasis on the improbable), and perhaps we can see others—those that explore ideas and that do not come to a resolution—as anatomies.

In any case, it is evident that we can distinguish between literature of *resolution* and literature of *revelation*, that is, between (1) literature that stimulates us to ask, "And what happened next?" and that finally leaves us with a settled state of affairs, and (2) literature that causes us to say, "Ah, I understand what they mean." But we should add that in Carver, and, for that matter, in *The Symposium* too, the more the characters talk, the more mysterious the topic becomes. Doubtless one reason Socrates attributed to the priestess Diotima his vision of the love of the ideal was to make it unearthly, mysterious, overpowering—in short, to make it emotionally appealing.

In the case of "What We Talk About When We Talk about Love," we can— by "consistency-building," to use a term from reader-response criticism—try to make some sense of the characters. There is, for instance, Mel, the cardiologist who had been a seminarian and who "would like to come back again in a different life, a different time and all, . . . as a knight." Yet this knight—if we have stock ideas we think of chivalry—fantasizes killing his wife by releasing a swarm of bees in her home. We can put together all that we see and hear of each character, and can try to make sense of the bundle, but the characters remain elusive. Terri, for instance, insists that the man who beat her up and who tried to kill her *did* love her, and though Mel can say, "I just wouldn't call Ed's behavior love," *we* are hardly in a position to pass judgment. The reader can only say what the narrator says: "I'm the wrong person to ask. . . . I didn't even know the man. . . . I wouldn't know. You'd have to know the particulars." Terri *did* know the particulars, and she says that Ed—a suicide—died for love (paragraph 37), to which Mel replies, "If that's love, you can have it."

That is, the characters are insulated from each other just as we are insulated from the characters. The extreme example is the old couple in the hospital, swathed in bandages with only "little eye-holes and mouth-holes. . . . The man's heart was breaking because he couldn't turn his goddam head and *see* his goddam wife." These two characters are probably pretty clear to the reader, and they are clear to Mel, too, but (given his experience with his former wife) he can hardly believe what he knows is true. In any case, the image of the elderly swathed lovers, unable to communicate, is connected with the image of knights in heavy armor—protective but also suffocating—and with the image of the beekeeper wearing "a helmet with the plate that comes down over your face, the big gloves, and the padded coat." A moment after he gives us this description, Mel decides not to telephone his children (by his first marriage), again emphasizing the gaps between people. Immediately after Mel makes this decision, the narrator speaks of heading "out into the sunset," to which the narrator's wife asks, "What does that mean, honey?" "It just means what I said," the narrator curtly replies, "That's all it means." This communication that does not communicate is immediately paralleled by words that do not lead to actions or, more precisely, by words that are not accompanied by the appropriate action: Terri offers to get some cheese and crackers but in fact she makes no move to do so, and the characters remain sitting in the dark room, their heartbeats audible.

We can, of course, chart some patterns. There is the bandaged couple (old, devoted lovers); Mel and Terri (lovers for a considerable time, but not old); the narrator and Laura ("going on a year and a half"); but these characters are not set within a traditional plot, and nothing in the way of obvious action happens. Nothing is resolved, but (paradoxically) something is revealed in the darkness; readers may feel that Carver has drawn them more deeply into the mystery of love—perhaps even given them one more picture of lovers, to add to the literary gallery that helps to give us an idea of what love is.

TOPICS FOR CRITICIAL THINKING AND WRITING

1. Terri believes Ed's dealings with her and (as well as his suicide) show that he loved her. How else might his actions be interpreted? And in your opinion why does she interpret his actions the way that she does?
2. Mel says that if he could come back in a different life, he would come back as a knight. What does this tell us about Mel?
3. What *kinds* of love get discussed? Sexual attraction, of course, but what other kinds of love?
4. We usually expect something to *happen* in a story, an action to reach some sort of completion. What, if anything, happens in this story? For instance, can we say that such-and-such a character changes?
5. Mel asks his companions, "What do any of us really know about love?" What is *your* response?

RAYMOND CARVER

Cathedral (p. 184)

You might begin by asking students to indicate what sort of impression the narrator makes on them in the first paragraphs. (You may want to assign a short writing requirement of this sort along with the story. If students come to class with a paragraph or two on the topic, the discussion is usually good.)

Probably no single word adequately describes the narrator at this stage, but among the words that students have suggested in their paragraphs are "mean," "cynical," "bitter," "sullen," (this seems especially apt), "unfeeling," "cold," and "cruel"; all of these words are relevant. He is also (though fewer students see this at first) jealous, jealous both of the blind man and of the officer who was his wife's first husband. His jealousy of the officer emerges in his wry reference to "this man who'd first enjoyed her favors." (Later in the story his hostility to the officer is more open, for instance, in this passage: "Her officer—why should he have a name? he was the childhood sweetheart, and what more does he want?—came home from somewhere, found her, and called the ambulance.")

With the blind man, too, the narrator's characteristic form of aggression is the ironic or mocking comment, as when he tells his wife that he will take the blind man bowling. His jealousy of the affectionate relationship between his wife and Robert is understandable if unattractive, and equally unattractive is the way in which he at last reveals that he does not fear this intruder into his house, when he flips open her robe, thus "exposing a juicy thigh." Still, this action is a step toward his accepting Robert and ultimately responding to Robert's influence. One other characteristically aggressive response also should be mentioned: Only rarely does he call Robert by his name. In speaking about him, as early as the first sentence of the story but pretty much throughout the story, he usually calls him "the blind man," a way of keeping him at a distance. (Not surprisingly, we soon learn that the narrator has no friends.) Late in the story, when Robert asks the narrator if he is "in any way religious," the narrator replies, " I guess I don't believe in it. In anything." This reply is not surprising; all of his behavior has shown that he doesn't believe "in anything."

The narrator seems to us, until near the end, to be a thoroughly unattractive figure. His irony is scarcely witty enough to make us deeply interested in him, so why do we continue reading the story after we have read the first few paragraphs? Mark A. R. Facknitz interestingly suggests in *Studies in Short Fiction* (Summer 1986) that "perhaps what pushes one into the story is a fear of the harm [the narrator] may do to his wife and her blind friend" (293).

Despite the narrator's evident aggressiveness, fairly early in the story he does profess some sympathy for Robert and especially for Robert's late wife, who died without her husband

> having ever seen what the goddamned woman looked like. It was beyond my under-standing. Hearing this, I felt sorry for the blind man for a little bit. And then I found myself thinking what a pitiful life this woman must have led. A woman whose hus-band could never read the expression on her face, be it misery or something better. Someone who could wear makeup or not—what difference to him?... And then to slip off into death, the blind man's hand on her hand, his blind eyes streaming tears—I'm imagining now—her last thought maybe this: that he never even knew what she looked like, and she on the express to the grave. Robert was left with a small insurance policy and half of a twenty-peso Mexican coin. The other half of the coin went into the box with her. Pathetic.

But to say that the narrator displays "sympathy" here is, obviously, to use the word too loosely. What is displayed, again, is his bitterness, cynicism, and (despite his "imagining") his utter inability to understand the feelings of others. (Later, when the blind man's hand rests on the narrator's as the narrator draws a box—like his house—that turns into a cathedral, he will presumably come close to the experience that here he so ineptly imagines.)

Almost by chance the blind man enters into the narrator's life and thaws the ice frozen around his heart, or better, the blind man enables the narrator to see. As Facknitz puts it,

> Carver redeems the narrator by releasing him from the figurative blindness that results in a lack of insight into his own condition and which leads him to trivialize human feelings and needs. Indeed, so complete is his misperception that the blind man gives him a faculty of sight that he is not even aware that he lacks. (293)

The narrator so dominates the story that there is a danger in class that no other matters will get considered, but it's worth asking students to characterize the wife and also Robert. Carver has taken care not to make Robert too saintly a fellow, full of wisdom and goodness and all that. True, Robert does have an uncanny sense of the difference between a black-and-white television set and a color set, but Carver nicely does not dwell on this; he just sort of lets it drop. Further, Robert's use of "bub" is maddening, and his confidence that he has "a lot of friends" in "Guam, in the Philippines, in Alaska, and even in Tahiti" suggests that he takes quite a bit for granted. It is easy, in fact, to imagine that one wouldn't much like Robert. The man who brings the narrator to a new consciousness is not sentimentalized or etherealized.

The story also invites comparison with Flannery O'Connor's "Revelation," which is about unearned grace, although the word "grace" should be used metaphorically when talking about Carver, whereas O'Connor was literally concerned with the working of the Holy Spirit. Talking of several of Carver's stories (including "Cathedral"), Facknitz puts the matter thus:

> Grace, Carver says, is bestowed upon us by other mortals, and it comes suddenly, arising in circumstances as mundane as a visit to the barber shop, and in the midst of feelings as ignoble or quotidian as jealousy, anger, loneliness, and grief. It can be represented in incidental physical contact, and the deliverer is not necessarily aware of his role. Not Grace in the Christian sense at all, it is what grace becomes in a godless world—a deep and creative connection between humans that reveals to Carver's alienated and diminished creatures that there can be contact in a world they supposed was empty of sense or love. Calm is given in a touch, a small, good thing is the food we get from others, and in the cathedrals we draw together, we create large spaces for the spirit. (295-96)

One last point: Obviously a cathedral is a more appropriate and richer symbol for what Carver is getting at than is, say, a gas station or shopping mall. Notice, too, that in the television program about cathedrals there is an episode in which devils attack monks; that is an assault is made on the soul. Presumably the narrator is unaware of morality plays, but some readers will understand that this scene introduces the possibility of a sort of spiritual change. A little later the inner change is further prepared for by the narrator's comments about a change in physical sensation. When he goes upstairs to get a pen so that he can draw a cathedral, he says, "My legs felt like they didn't have any strength in them. They felt like they did after I'd done some running."

TOPICS FOR CRITICAL THINKING AND WRITING

1. What was your impression of the narrator after reading the first five paragraphs?
2. Why does the narrator feel threatened by the blind man? Has he any reason to feel threatened?
3. What attitude does the narrator reveal in the following passage:

> She'd turned so that her robe slipped away from her legs, exposing a juicy thigh. I reached to draw her robe back over her and it was then that I glanced at the blind man. What the hell! I flipped the robe open again.

4. Why does the narrator not open his eyes at the end of the story?
5. The television program happens to be about cathedrals, but if the point is

to get the narrator to draw something while the blind man's hand rests on the narrator's, the program could have been about some other topic, for example, about skyscrapers or about the Statue of Liberty. Do you think that a cathedral is a better choice, for Carver's purposes, than these other subjects? Why?

6. In what ways does Carver prepare us for the narrator's final state of mind?

CHAPTER 9

A Collection of Short Fiction

A NOTE ON GENDER IN FICTION

Before we discuss each story in the chapter, we want to mention that students may be especially interested in thinking about certain stories partly in terms of gender. In Chapter 27 we discuss gender criticism along with some other kinds of criticism, but—given the fact that students can more easily practice gender criticism than, say, New Historicism—it seems appropriate (if one is going to encourage students to think about critical approaches) to begin with gender criticism rather than with some other approach. We therefore offer here two units on the topic—either or both of which you may want to photocopy and distribute to students. The first is a very brief introduction to the topic; the second is a series of questions that students can ask themselves when they read stories. Among the stories that lend themselves to a gender approach are:

Atwood, "Rape Fantasies"

Dark, "In the Gloaming"

Gilman, "The Yellow Wallpaper"

D. H. Lawrence, "The Horse Dealer's Daughter"

Lessing, "A Woman on a Roof"

Mason, "Shiloh"

Maupassant, "Mademoiselle"

Minot, "Lust"

Munro, "Boys and Girls"

Naylor, "The Two"

Steinbeck, "The Chrysanthemums"

Tallent, "No One's a Mystery"

Now for the material—a brief introduction to the topic, followed by some questions that students may find useful—that you may wish to distribute among students.

THINKING ABOUT GENDER

Most feminist critics—and now, following their lead, many others—make a distinction between sex and gender. *Sex* is physiological, the biologically fixed sex divisions between male and female (a matter of chromosomes, hormones, and anatomical differences). *Gender* is cultural, "the socially imposed dichotomy of masculine and feminine roles and character traits." These roles, it is now argued, are not "natural" or innate, but rather are "constructed" by the society in which we live. According to this view, society exaggerates the biological sexual difference (male, female), producing patterns of gender (masculinity, femininity) and of sexuality (for instance, the idea that heterosexuality is the only natural behavior). Thus, it is a biological fact (it is thought) that the female hormone estrogen inhibits aggression and the male hormone androgen influences aggression, but it is society that inculcates the idea that (for instance) young girls should be docile and young boys should be aggressive. Sayings such as "A woman's place is in the home," "*kinder, küche, kirche*" (German for "children, cooking, and the church"), and "*Fatti maschii, parole femine*" (Italian for "Manly deeds, womanly words," the preposterous motto of the State of Maryland), reflect what was once thought to be the obvious fact that biology determines one's identity, and that males should be strong, self-assured, rational, competitive, and so forth, and that women should be weak, dependent, emotional, and so forth. We can now see how sayings such as these are these *create social ideals and identity.* Against such statements that assume a fixed identity we can cite the now-famous words of Simone de Beauvoir in *The Second Sex* (1953), "One is not born, but rather becomes a woman."

As you read certain stories, you will want of course to reflect upon the technical points that you have been learning about—plot, character, point of view, setting, symbolism, style, theme. But for some stories, especially keep in mind the distinction we have just set forth, between physiological and social or cultural differences.

TOPICS FOR CONSIDERATION

You will find other stories in this volume that explore gender issues and themes, but we think that many of the stories in this chapter form an interesting group that can be studied with profit as a whole. After reading a story, you may find it stimulating to reread the following questions.

How does the author describe men and women? Is their behavior in the story meant to illustrate something typical about men's and women's beliefs, attitudes, values?

- Does it make a difference to the story whether its author is a man or a woman? If you did not know the identity of the author, could you tell whether a man or a woman wrote it? If so, how?
- Does the author suggest that men and women are simply "the way they are," or, instead, that their understanding of themselves is the result of social pressures and circumstances—that they act out the roles that their societies assign to them?
- Do you see moments in the story when men and women resist the gender roles to which they have been accustomed?
- Think about stories, such as Margaret Atwood's "Rape Fantasies" and Doris Lessing's "Woman on a Roof," which touch on similar themes, and examine the similarities and differences between the authors' perspectives on gender.
- The study of gender also involves attention to gay and lesbian identities and to the special social and personal situations that same-sex lovers face, illustrated here by Gloria Naylor's "The Two." Can this story be connected, in the feelings about love and sexual desire it depicts, to the stories gathered here about heterosexual love?
- The stories in this chapter are arranged chronologically. After you have read several of the stories, review and re-read them according to their dates of publication, beginning with Guy de Maupassant's "Mademoiselle" and Gilman's "The Yellow Wallpaper." Do you see signs of a development or evolution in the treatment of gender?
- Does fiction strike you as a good means for exploring gender? What can a short story accomplish that a prose essay cannot? Can you imagine instances in which an essay or an autobiography might be more effective?
- In *On Deconstruction* (1982), a study of contemporary literary theory, Jonathan Culler remarks that feminist criticism has often stressed "reading as a woman." This concept, Culler states, affirms the "continuity between women's experience of social and familial structures and their experiences as readers." Do you agree with Culler's suggestion that men and women often interpret characters and incidents in stories differently? Locate moments in these stories when you think that men and women readers might differ in their responses.

LEO TOLSTOY

The Death of Ivan Ilych (p. 201)

No author need apologize for writing about death, a topic of such enormous interest that it is rivaled only by sex. But if we think for a moment about "The Death of Ivan Ilych," we realize that it is largely about the life of Ivan Ilych, or, more precisely about his deathbed realization that he has scarcely lived. Despite the recurrent references to Ivan Ilych's illness, the story reveals not a morbid interest in illness and dying but a heartening interest in living.

The first sentence of the second part of the story makes this clear: "Ivan

Ilych's life had been most simple and most ordinary and therefore most terrible." In the remainder of the story Tolstoy (clearly the narrator is Tolstoy, or someone so close to him that we need scarcely speak delicately of "the narrator") goes on to demonstrate the terribleness of this ordinariness. Superficially Ivan Ilych's life would seem to be unusual and successful: he climbs fairly high up the social ladder, achieves a substantial salary, has a wife, children, and an ample home, and he has some power which he savors even if he does not abuse it.

But the point, of course, is that after he falls ill and nears death, he becomes aware—as Tolstoy has kept the reader aware—that Ivan Ilych's interests are so narrow, and even his vices so trivial, that however he may be envied he can scarcely be said to have lived. He learns this through sickness, which forces intense awareness of oneself, as anyone realizes who has had even so trivial a sickness as a running nose. And one of the facts about us, which we are scarcely aware of until we become sick, is that some day we will die.

Tolstoy makes it clear that, in a way, Ivan Ilych knew this: in a logic text he had learned that "Caius is a man, men are mortal, therefore Caius is mortal," but, Tolstoy says, these words "had always seemed to him correct as applied to Caius, but certainly not as applied to himself." And here we can digress for a moment on one of the differences between literature and philosophy. Literature, it has long been recognized, has a concreteness or immediacy that at least in some considerable degree forces the reader to sense or experience the reality that is being presented: to some degree we believe in and understand the experiences of the characters in good literature (at least in realistic prose fiction such as this story). Why do we identify with such figures? Probably for at least two reasons: (1) We are given a fairly convincing detailed picture of their surroundings, and (2) we are given revelations of character or psychological insights whose truth we recognize from our own experiences. Each of these two points may be discussed a bit.

Most novels, long or short, carefully build up a picture of the characters' surroundings. Thus, "The Death of Ivan Ilych" begins with a reference to an apparently public event ("The Melvinsky trial") and to a public building (" the "Law Courts"), specifies the name of a particular person, and moves through other people's names to the name of a newspaper. We know, of course, that we are reading fiction, but it is fiction that insists on facts, rather than fiction that begins, "Once upon a time in a far-off country there lived a woodsman who had three sons." But it is not merely the specification of names of buildings, people, and newspapers that gives us a sense of a believable world. Tolstoy continually gives us a sense of the solidity of things. For example, describing the players beginning a card game Tolstoy mentions that "they dealt, bending the new cards to soften them." We need not look here for symbolism, we need not fancy that the cards, like Ivan Ilych, are being forced into a new shape; we can be content simply with our sense of the reality of this (fictional) card game. It is through such details, which pervade the story, that the writer gains our confidence.

Illustrations need not be multiplied, but we might look briefly at one other scene before proceeding to the second point, the author's psychological astuteness. In the first section of the story there is a highly comic scene in which Peter

Ivanovich sits "on a low pouffe, the springs of which yielded spasmodically under his weight." There again, most literally, is the sense of the weight of things. When Peter must get up to assist the widow in detaching a shawl that catches on the carved edge of a table (again, convincing even if apparently irrelevant detail) "the springs of the pouffe, relieved of his weight, rose also and gave him a push." It probably is not fanciful to see here, in the pouffe's mechanical behavior, satiric commentary on the mechanical (conventional, unspontaneous) behavior of Peter and the widow, but it would be wrong to neglect the fact that Tolstoy also sees the pouffe as a pouffe, a thing with a density of its own, and it is through a world of believable things that his characters move.

Now for the second point, the revelation of convincing characters. Possibly the presentation of convincing *things* is a sort of sleight of hand whereby authors win our confidence in their perceptions. After all, it does not follow that because a writer is perceptive enough to notice that card players bend new cards and that pouffes have springs, he or she is a shrewd perceiver of human nature. But in page after page Tolstoy does indeed give us shrewd perceptions of human nature. He catches the irritability and the hypersensitivity of a sick man, for example, in the scene when his partner "pushed the cards courteously and indulgently towards Ivan Ilych that he might have the pleasure of gathering them up without the trouble of stretching out his hand for them." Ivan Ilych's mental response is, "Does he think I am too weak to stretch out my arm?"

As we begin to read the story, perceiving the mutual insincerity that passes between Peter Ivanovich and the widow he is supposed to be consoling, and perceiving Ivan Ilych's shallowness, we may feel superior to the characters, but it soon becomes evident that although these people are not very amiable, we can scarcely look down on them. Too much is revealed about them that we recognize in ourselves. We have been pushed by pouffes, we have experienced "the complacent feeling that, 'it is he who is dead and not I,'" we have said to widows what we believe we are supposed to say, and—most telling—we know from experience the truth of Tolstoy's assertion that after Peter pressed the widow's hand because it was "the right thing," "both he and she were touched." That hurts, this perception that we are moved by our own calculating gestures.

Most of all, of course, we are concerned with Ivan Ilych, not with his widow or his acquaintances, and here again, we are compelled to recognize that we cannot take a superior attitude. We simply find him too recognizable, too human, too much ourself, to take refuge in thoughts of our superiority. Interestingly, he is "not given much external characterization: he has a name, he is somewhat bald, he has a prominent nose and a graying beard, but he is not described in such detail as to become a "character" and therefore someone apart from us. The story, after all, is the story of Everyone: near the end of one's life one finds that death terrifies, and that one has not loved and therefore in any significant sense one has scarcely lived. Ivan Ilych very late and very painfully comes to an awareness of these things; his body racks him first into an awareness of physical existence and then into an awareness of spirit whereby he is at last able to recognize his lifetime of failure and to experience—terribly late—a compassion that banishes the fear of death.

In a very crude sense, then, the story has a happy ending; a man in his last couple of hours experiences a pity for others that is perhaps indistinguishable from love and dies without fear; but Tolstoy does not let us off that easily with a comforting message. We continue to remember the agony of Ivan Ilych's dying months and the waste of his life.

The discussion of Tolstoy's story is often one of the high points of any course in which it is taught. This is testimony to Tolstoy's art and intention, his desire to make his literary gifts serve the teaching of a compelling moral lesson. But instructors might use the students' responses here, more generally, to bring home to the class the powerful connection between literature and life. This is a truism that we frequently express but that perhaps is not always evident to students, who tend to compartmentalize their literary experiences, seeing them as separate from the lives they lead. Tolstoy shows that a literary work can directly engage us in reflecting on the choices by which we organize our lives from day to day. He addresses each reader: "Is this the way you should be living?" And what is wonderful, even breathtaking, we think, is the manner in which he asks this question through the highest form of narrative artistry. There is something essential here about the value of literature that instructors should talk about with their students.

Biographies of Tolstoy have been written by Ernest J. Simmons (1946), Henri Troyat (1967), and A. N. Wilson (1988). A good introduction to his literary career is R. F. Christian, *Tolstoy: A Critical Introduction* (1969). For commentary on "The Death of Ivan Ilych," see the relevant sections in Philip Rahv, *Image and Idea* (1949); *Tolstoy: A Collection of Critical Essays*, ed. Ralph E. Matlaw (1967); and E. B. Greenwood, *Tolstoy: The Comprehensive Vision* (1975).

TOPICS FOR CRITICAL THINKING AND WRITING

1. What do you think of the way the story opens? Why, in your opinion does Tolstoy begin, not by telling us about Ivan's early years but by having Ivan's colleagues learn of his death during a pause in some business?
2. Tolstoy tells us a good deal about Ivan's house. What does the house tell us about its owner?
3. What, if anything, did you find comic in the story? And if you did find some comic passages, what do they contribute?
4. Summarize the change (and the reasons for the change) in Praskovya, from a bright and attractive woman to the woman we meet early in the story.
5. Of Ivan's death, the narrator says, near the very end of the story, "He tried to add 'forgive me,' but he said,'forgo.'" Why did Ivan say "forgo"? Is the word relevant to the story?

GUY DE MAUPASSANT

Mademoiselle (p. 241)

Anthologists who want to include a story by Maupassant surely have a duty to find something other than the grotesquely over-anthologized "Necklace." We browsed through his stories and came upon "Mademoiselle," a story that we find both moving and puzzling. To the best of our knowledge this story about gender-identity has not been anthologized in any book comparable to ours.

What do we make of the story? We are inclined to think that the chief point is this:society (beginning with the boy's mother) has made him into what at first sight might seem to he a cross-dresser. That is, the family has dressed this delicate, weak boy in girl's clothing, and the rest of society follows, giving him approval in this guise. The boy accepts the role, perhaps partly because he is simple, but chiefly, we imagine, because the role provides him with the warmth (approval and affection) that he needs. He accepts this role, and so does society (the family, and the whole village). Why does society accept it? The boy is mentally and perhaps physically unusual for a male, and society therefore finds it convenient to treat him as something other than a male. Those around him give him a feminine identity, and, to repeat, he responds by acting out a feminine gender role. Notice, however, that in the middle of the story we are told that "he thought more of his nickname than he did of his dress." The story clearly is not about someone who is sexually excited by wearing clothes of the opposite sex, but rather is (up to this point) about a young man who finds apparent satisfaction in a role society creates for him.

By accepting the role that society has given to him, he gets the warmth that a human being requires. When, however. he dresses like a boy, society rejects him. His use of male clothing

> created quite a disturbance in the neighborhood, for the people who had been in the habit of smiling at him kindly when he was dressed as a woman, looked at him in astonishment and almost in fear, while the indulgent could not help laughing, and visibly making fun of him.

The distress of the community when it sees male clothing on a female-like person is paralleled by the distress of the boy: "Suppose that, after all, I am a girl?" The how knew before that he was not a girl, and that he was "in disguise," but he did not fully understand what the disguise consisted of. He thought it was a matter only of clothing, yet when he wears male clothing the disguise does not end: "He had totally lost all masculine looks and ways."

Later in the story he makes a second attempt to assert his maleness, this time when he tries to have sex with Josephine. She screams (understandably), and he is seized (again understandably). Society for a second time will not let him assert or express his masculinity. And in fact, this attempt to confirm his sex is no more successful than was the exchange of female clothes for male clothes. Each of his attempts to declare his biological nature encounters difficulty:Society is angry when he prances in male garb, and society is angry when he attacks Josephine. Both events imply a tragic side to the old collusion between the boy and the world around him, to call him "Mademoiselle." That is, it robbed him of the ability to bring his behavior in line with his biological nature.

In our view, the story is largely about the way in which society establishes gender (masculine or feminine behavior). Gender usually corresponds with external genitals, hut in this case society has (for its own reasons) preferred to see the boy as feminine, and the boy for a while has acquiesced. After he finds (by observing couples, and in the encounter with Josephine) his erotic orientation, he learns that he is locked into the wrong gender.

We offer this reading with some hesitancy (and only after we have modified it in line with discussions with Professor Donald Stone, a specialist in French literature), since we don't quite know what to make of certain passages in the story. For instance, although the boy says that he dresses like a girl "only... for a joke," he also says, "But if I dress like a lad, I shall no longer be a girl; and then, *I am a girl*"(our italics). Still, although we find a contradiction between these passages, we think that the statement (already quoted) that he values his nickname more than his dress clearly indicates that the dress itself is of only minor importance to him; it does not in itself give him pleasure, but it is the means whereby he gets approval from the community.

The story ends with the boy asserting his maleness. It does not tell us what happened thereafter, that is, whether (for example) from that time onward he refused to wear female clothing, or (again, for example) whether society continued to treat him as a girl. Donald Stone finds the dark irony thoroughly in Maupassant's vein. He points out that there is even a similarity with Maupassant's "Necklace," in which a woman, eager to shine (see also the boy's quest for affection), borrows a diamond necklace, loses it, spends much of the rest of her life in efforts to pay for it, and at last finds out that the necklace was of no value.

Students might be invited to write a paragraph to be added to the ending, or to write an essay explaining why the present ending is preferable.

Developing an insight of Henry James's, the novelist Wallace Stegner has noted: "Maupassant saw with great clarity the small characteristic, the tiny episode, the telling relationship, the perverted motive, and he focused on it—wrung it, as James said, 'either until it grimaces or until it bleeds.'"

Much of the best critical work on Maupassant's stories and novels is in French—for example, A. Vial, *Guy de Maupassant et l'art du roman* (1954); but Edward D Sullivan, *Maupassant the Novelist* (1972) is helpful. For biography: Francis Steegmuller, *Maupassant: A Lion in the Path* (1949). Henry James's keen study of Maupassant is included in *Partial Portraits* (1888), and has been reprinted, along with a second, shorter piece, in the Library of America's two-volume collection of James's critical writings (1984).

CHARLOTTE PERKINS GILMAN

The Yellow Wallpaper (p. 245)

In this story the wife apparently is suffering from postpartum depression, and her physician-husband prescribes as a cure the things that apparently have caused her depression: isolation and inactivity. Victorian medical theory held that women—more emotional, more nervous, more fanciful than men—needed special protection if they were to combat lunacy. As Gilman tells us in her autobiography, *The Living of Charlotte Perkins Gilman* (1935), the story (published in 1892) is rooted in the author's experience: After the birth of her child, Gilman became depressed and consulted Dr. S. Weir Mitchell (physician and novelist, named in the story), who prescribed a rest cure: "Live as domestic a life as possible. Have your child with you all the time. Lie down an hour after each meal. Have but two hours intellectual life a day. And never touch pen, brush or pencil as long as you live." Gilman in fact tried this routine for a month, then took a trip to California, where she began writing, and recovered nicely. Thinking about Mitchell's plan later, Gilman concluded that such a way of life would have driven her crazy.

Although the prescribed treatment in the story is not exactly Mitchell's, it does seem clear enough that the smug husband's well-intended treatment is responsible for the wife's hallucinations of a woman struggling behind the wallpaper. The narrator is mad (to this degree the story resembles some of Poe's), but she is remarkably sane compared to her well-meaning husband and the others who care for her. Elaine R. Hedges, in the afterword to the edition of *The Yellow Wallpaper* published by the Feminist Press (1973) comments on the narrator:

> At the end of the story the narrator both does and does not identify with the creeping women who surround her in her hallucinations. The women creep through the arbors and lanes along the roads outside the house. Women must creep. The narrator knows this. She has fought as best she could against creeping. In her perceptivity and in her resistance lie her heroism (or heroineism). But at the end of the story, on her last day in the house, as she peels off yards and yards of wallpaper and creeps around the floor, she has been defeated. She is totally mad. But in her mad sane way she has seen the situation of women for what it is. (53)

Judith Fetterley offers a thoughtful interpretation of Gilman's story in "Reading about Reading" in *Gender and Reading: Essays on Readers, Texts, and Contexts*, edited by Elizabeth A. Flynn and Patrocinio P. Schwieckart (1986), pp. 147-64). Here (in direct quotation) are some of Fetterley's points, but the entire essay should be consulted:

> Forced to read men's texts [i.e. to interpret experience in the way men do], women are forced to become characters in those texts. And since the stories men tell assert as fact what women know to be fiction, not only do women lose the power that comes from authoring: more significantly, they are forced to deny their own reality and to commit in effect a kind of psychic suicide. (159)
>
> The nameless narrator of Gilman's story has two choices. She can accept her husband's definition of reality [that his version is sane and that her version is mad] . . . or she can refuse to read his text, refuse to become a character in it, and insist on writing her own, behavior for which John will define and treat her as mad. (160)
>
> Despite the narrator's final claim that she has, like the women in the paper, "got out," she does not in fact escape the patriarchal text. Her choice of literal madness may be as good as or better than the "sanity" prescribed for her by John, but in going mad she fulfills his script and becomes a character in his text. Still, going mad gives the narrator temporary sanity. It enables her to articulate her perception of reality and, in particular, to cut through the fiction of John's love. (163)
>
> The narrator's solution finally validates John's fiction. In his text, female madness results from work that engages the mind and will; from the recognition and expression of feelings, and particularly of anger; in a word, from the existence of a

subjectivity capable of generating a different version of reality from his own. (164-65)

> More insidious still, through her madness the narrator does not simply become the character John already imagines her to be as part of his definition of feminine nature; she becomes a version of John himself. Mad, the narrator is manipulative, secretive, dishonest; she learns to lie, obscure, and distort. (164)
>
> This desire to duplicate John's text but with the roles reversed determines the narrator's choice of an ending. Wishing to drive John mad, she selects a denouement that will reduce him to a woman seized by a hysterical fainting fit. Temporary success, however, exacts an enormous price, for when John recovers from his faint he will put her in a prison from which there will be no escape. (164)

Of the many feminist readings of the story, perhaps the most widely known is that of Sandra M. Gilbert and Susan Gubar, *The Madwoman in the Attic* (1979). For Gubar and Gilbert, the wallpaper represents "the oppressive structures of the society in which [the narrator] finds herself" (p. 90). The figure behind the wallpaper is the narrator's double, trying to break through. But Jeanette King and Pam Morris, in "On Not Reading Between the Lines: Models of Reading in 'The Yellow Wallpaper,'" *Studies in Short Fiction* 26 (1989): 23-32, raise questions about this interpretation. Their essay, influenced by Lacan, is not easy reading (one finds such terms as "decentered subject," "signified and signifier," "a polysemic potential"), but they present some impressive evidence against the widespread view that the woman behind the paper is "the essential inner psyche which has been trapped by repressive social structures" (25). First, they argue that if the woman indeed is the essential inner psyche, "the breaking free, even if only in the hallucination of madness, ought surely to indicate a more positive movement than the chilling conclusion of the tale suggests" (25). They point out that the wallpaper is not described in terms of "a controlling order"; rather, the narrator says it has "sprawling flamboyant patterns," and it resembles "great slanting waves" that "plunge off at outrageous angles. . . in unheard-of contradictions." For King and Morris, the wallpaper's "energy and fertility are anarchic and lawless, at times aggressive. It displays, that is, an assertive creativity and originality that have no place in the wifely ideal constructed by patriarchal ideology" (29). They therefore interpret it not as a metaphor of a repressive society but as a metaphor of the "forbidden self" (29), "the repressed other" (30). The narrator, seeking to comply with the male ideals, is thus threatened by the wallpaper, and her "attempts to tear down this obdurate wallpaper are not intended. . . to free her from male repression. . . but to eliminate the rebellious self which is preventing her from achieving ego-ideal" (30). That is, she wishes to remove the paper (the image of her secret self, which she strives to repress) in order to gain John's approval. "When the woman behind the paper 'gets out,' therefore, this is an image not of liberation but of the victory of the social idea." We get a "grotesque, shameful caricature of female helplessness and submissiveness—a creeping woman." Nevertheless, King and Morris argue, the narrator does indeed have "a desperate triumph. . . : she crawls over her husband" (31).

King and Morris assume that "Jane" (mentioned only near the end of the story) is the narrator, but, like most earlier critics, they do not greatly concern themselves with arguing this point. William Veeder, in "Who Is Jane?," *Arizona Quarterly* 44 (1988): 41-79, does argue the point at length. He writes "By defining a context beyond Poesque horror and clinical case-study, Kolodny, Hedges, and others have convincingly described the heroine's confrontation with patriarchy. What remains to be examined is another source of the heroine's victimization. Herself" (41). Veeder discusses Gilman's difficult childhood (an absent father and a "strict and anxious mother"), and, drawing on Freud and Melanie Klein, argues that the history is not only about a repressive marriage but also about "the traumas wrought by inadequate nurturing in childhood" (71). To escape bondage to men, "Jane moves not forward to the egalitarian utopia of *Herland* but back into the repressive serenity of the maternal womb" (67).

We've had good luck recently with a paper assignment keyed to the final paragraphs of Gilman's story. It takes as its point of departure an observation by Edith Wharton, a contemporary of Gilman's and the author of *The House of Mirth* (1905) and *The Age of Innocence* (1920), who said that in structuring her novels she sought to "make my last page latent in my first."

Wharton wanted her readers, after they had completed the final page, to be able to return to the first chapter and see the sources for the conclusion there: the novel would have a logic that would be developed throughout the story, which would give the whole work its effectiveness and coherence. Ask the class to apply Wharton's statement to the conclusion of "The Yellow Wallpaper" where the narrator "creeps" over her husband. Is Gilman's last page "latent in her first?"

TOPICS FOR CRITICAL THINKING AND WRITING

1. Is the narrator insane at the start of the story, or does she become insane at some point during the narrative? Or can't we be sure? Support your view with evidence from the story.
2. How reliable do you think the narrator's characterization of her husband is? Support your answer with reasons.
3. The narrator says that she cannot get better because her husband is a physician. What do you take this to mean? Do you think the story is about a husband who deliberately drives his wife insane?
4. In the next-to-last paragraph the narrator says, "I've got out at last." What does she mean, and in what way (if any) does it make sense?

WILLA CATHER

Paul's Case (p. 256)

It's clear enough that in "Paul's Case" the conflict is not between two people but rather is between one person and his environment. But can one go on to say (as many people *do* say) that the conflict is between Paul and Pittsburgh? After all, to say that the conflict is between Paul and Pittsburgh is to suggest that everything would have been fine if Paul had been born in New York.

It is, of course, true that Cather establishes a clear conflict between Paul and Pittsburgh, a city in which the men "interspersed their legends of the iron kings with remarks about their sons' progress at school, their grades in arithmetic, and the amounts they had saved in the toy banks." Pittsburgh represents materialism, and it also represents an oppressive, joyless Christianity, as implied by the picture of Calvin in Paul's bedroom. (The picture of George Washington, in this context, also implies a patriarchal materialistic society.)

But if it is easy enough to say what Paul's home and Cordelia Street and Pittsburgh "stand for," what can we say about Paul? At first perhaps we see him as a boy with many "peculiarly offensive" ways, not the least of which is his habit of lying. (The first four paragraphs might be read aloud in class, and students might be invited to summarize their responses after each paragraph. Most students—but not all—find Paul extremely unsympathetic.) As we get to know more about Paul—as we enter further into his consciousness—does he become more sympathetic? Many students, on finishing the story, find him sufficiently sympathetic that they blame Paul's father and Paul's teachers for Paul's suicide. A variation is to attribute the suicide partly to the absence of Paul's mother. The first question printed at the end of this discussion, concerning Paul's character and the ways in which he is made sympathetic or unsympathetic, usually generates, for a start, two opposed responses:

> He is sympathetic because he does not have a mother, and because he lives in a gray and mercenary world;

> He is unsympathetic because he lies and steals, and because he lives in a dream world.

For the drabness of home, Cordelia Street, and Pittsburgh, Paul substitutes the world of art, or, more precisely, visits to art galleries and to Carnegie Hall. Does the story, then, show the conflict between an artist and a materialistic society?

Surely it is clear that Paul is not an artist. He imagines, but he creates nothing:

> He needed only the spark, the indescribable thrill that made his imagination master of his senses, and he could make plots and pictures enough of his own. It was equally true that he was not stage struck—not, at any rate, in the usual acceptation of that expression. He had no desire to become an actor, any more than he had to become a musician. He felt no necessity to do any of these things; what he wanted was to see, to be in the atmosphere, float on the wave of it, to be carried out, blue league after blue league, away from everything.

Clearly Paul is *not* an artist. But does he have an artistic temperament? If he does, it apparently is in the sense that G. K. Chesterton had in mind when he said that one of the tragedies of the "artistic temperament" is that it cannot create art. Many critics strongly denigrate Paul's interest in the arts; they remind us so vigorously of his escapist desires that a reader of such criticism is forced to conclude that these critics regularly turn to the arts—tragic drama, long novels, or museum exhibitions—for only the most exalted reason, that is, in order to have their own sense of reality heightened. Still, one knows what they mean. Paul chiefly wants to "lose himself," and for this anything from an "orchestra to a barrel organ" will serve.

David A. Carpenter, in an interesting article in *American Literature* 59 (1987): 590-608, suggests that Paul's response to art "is not an artist's 'genuine' feeling for art." Carpenter supports his case thus: Paul goes to the art gallery because there really is nothing else he can do; it is too early for him to usher at Carnegie Hall, he does not want to go home for supper, and it is "chilly outside." Cather tells us that in the gallery there were "some of Raffelli's gay studies of Paris streets and an airy Venetian scene or two that always exhilarated him. After a while he sat down before a blue Rico and lost himself." When he leaves the gallery we see Paul "making a face at Augustus Caesar, peering out from the cast-room, and an evil gesture at the Venus of Milo as he passed her on the stairway." Carpenter is very stern about all of this; Cather, he tells us, added this "irreverent and infantile" behavior (the words are Carpenter's) so that we will realize that Paul does not really have any "feeling for art." One might reply that at least Paul responds to the works of art; he notices them and they stimulate him.

Carpenter goes on: "If [Cather] had intended to relate Paul to art in any significantly genuine way, she might have had him focus upon the paintings there in the gallery a bit more carefully, might have at least permitted him to notice a title of one of Rico's or Raffelli's paintings." Cather explicitly tells us that Raffelli's pictures "always exhilarated" Paul. What more can we demand in the way of a response to a work of art? Would, as Carpenter claims, noticing the title of the picture suggest a deeper aesthetic response? Further, does one really expect a schoolboy—even one who may become an artist—to have highly developed artistic tastes? Most English teachers will agree that in an adolescent, a taste for, let's say, Poe's "The Bells" is a very good thing; one hopes the adolescent will go on to Shakespeare and Whitman and Dickinson, but a young person's delight in "The Bells" is nothing to brush off. If Paul "loses himself" in a work of art, or is "exhilarated" by it, that may be a very good thing, given his age and his surroundings. (It's the adolescents who don't respond to even the most obvious arts who are cause for worry.)

This brief defense of Paul—the suggestion that we need not deride his interest in the arts—is not meant to say that Paul represents the artist (or the artistic temperament) in its conflict with bourgeois society. Cather shows the shallowness of his interest quite well, for example in this passage:

> It was not that symphonies, as such, meant anything in particular to Paul, but the first sigh of the instruments seemed to free some hilarious spirit within him; something that struggled like the Genius in the bottle found by the Arab fisherman.

Cather tells us too (as Carpenter points out) that Paul "scarcely ever read at all." Music was quicker:

> He got what he wanted much more quickly from music; any sort of music, from an orchestra to a barrel-organ.

Again, though, we might think twice before we say that this indiscriminateness is a bad thing in a youngster.

What does seem fairly clear, though, is that Paul's desire to escape from reality is, in the words of Sharon O'Brien, *Willa Cather* (1987), p. 284, "the child's regressive yearning to regain the preoedipal union with the mother."

In 1975 Larry Rubin published an article in *Studies in Short Fiction* 12 (1975): 127-31, in which he said what many people must earlier have thought but had hesitated to say. The title of his article makes the point: "The Homosexual Motif in Willa Cather's 'Paul's Case.'" Rubin says that "Paul is very probably homosexual by nature and temperament," and that "Cather is trying to show us the tragic consequences of the conflict between a sensitive and hence alienated temperament, on the one hand, and a narrowly 'moral,' bourgeois environment, on the other." Rubin's chief evidence is:

1. Cather's comment that Paul used his eyes "in a conscious, theatrical sort of way, peculiarly offensive in a boy".
2. Paul uses violet water, which he feels compelled to hide from his father, presumably because it suggests effeminacy.
3. Paul's only social relationships are with boys of his own age, or perhaps a little older: (a) the young actor; (b) the Yale freshman—a relation that ends coolly. Why? Rubin suggests that perhaps "Paul wanted something from his companion that the latter was unprepared to give."

Rubin does not claim that to have proved the point conclusively; he says only that Paul is *very probably* homosexual.

A word about the point of view in "Paul's Case." The point of view is omniscient, though at first we see Paul chiefly through the eyes of the adults around him (the principal and the teachers). Later we get inside Paul's mind, and he may become more sympathetic, but Cather presumably does not want us to sympathize fully; thus she lets us see him through other eyes and also, so to speak, under the aspect of eternity. She certainly distances him in the final paragraph:

> He felt something strike his chest, and that his body was being thrown swiftly through the air, on and on, immeasurably far and fast, while his limbs were gently relaxed. Then, because the picture making mechanism was crushed, the disturbing visions flashed into black, and Paul dropped back into the immense design of things.

Here is naturalism—a materialistic, deterministic view—of the sort that we usually associate with Thomas Hardy and Stephen Crane. (Cather's earliest stories in fact have much in common with Crane's bitterly ironic stories.) Paul is reduced to a "picture making mechanism," a mere part of "the immense design of things." But what tone do we hear in the narrator's voice? The overt content of the paragraph diminishes Paul, but don't we hear, beneath this apparently cool, impartial, scientific account, a voice calling us to pity Paul, somewhat as one hears pity (as well as indignation) in Hardy's famous outburst: "Justice was done, and the President of the Immortals (in the Aeschylean phrase) had finished his sport with Tess"? Granted, Cather's passage does not express the indignation and immense pain evident in Hardy's words, but doesn't the passage in effect ask the reader to protest against this bald assertion, and to say that Paul was—for all of his unpleasant traits—much more than a "picture making mechanism"?

The question of Cather's point of view is connected to how much or how little Cather means us to perceive Paul as homosexual. It is connected, too, to the debates among Cather's biographers about whether she was or wasn't lesbian, and, if she was, the extent to which her sexual identity influences and shapes her novels and stories. Sharon O'Brien, in *Willa Cather: The Emerging Voice* (1987), focuses on lesbianism as a powerful current in Cather's life and work. Hermione Lee, in *Willa Cather: Double Lives* (1989), acknowledges its importance, but is skeptical about its primacy as a key to interpreting Cather's fiction. This critical controversy has been surveyed by Joan Acocella, in "Cather and the Academy," *The New Yorker*, November 27, 1995.

In *Willa Cather: A Literary Life* (1987), James Woodress has stated:

> If one defines a lesbian as a woman who has sexual relations with another woman, Cather cannot be called a lesbian on the basis of available records. On the other hand, if a lesbian is a woman whose primary emotional attachments are to other women, regardless of sexual relations, the definition adopted by some feminists, then Cather was most certainly a lesbian. There is no disputing that her closest friends were women. (141)

There is something to be said for the tact and balance of this approach.

We do think it is important to explore this biographical and thematic issue when studying "Paul's Case," but we have not been satisfied so far by our work on it in the classroom. The discussions have been lively, yet have also felt reductive, as though the experience of Cather's story ultimately hinged solely on the presence or absence of homosexuality in it. Is Paul "really" gay? Does he know this about himself? Does *Cather* know this about her character? These are provocative questions, but if they are not handled well, they can make some students—who haven't "seen" homosexuality in the story at all—feel that they have missed the point altogether and badly misunderstood Cather's work. They might have found the story absorbing and moving, yet then conclude, when the secret is revealed to them, that they were wrongheaded, missing something that was obvious to others.

The next time we teach "Paul's Case," we'd like to begin by treating the story in the traditional way, as a story about an alienated young man in a grim environment and the function that art and imagination serve for him. Then we would zero in on details in the text that lend themselves to a gay reading, such as those that Rubin has noted. Without discounting such a reading, we then might return to the question of what the story offers to readers—*continues* to offer to them—even if they are unaware of the interpretive possibilities that Rubin and O'Brien have outlined, The story is, we believe, all the more interesting and affecting when read as a story with a gay subject-matter and theme, but not perhaps when this overrules everything else in it. "Paul's Case" succeeds on multiple levels, and it is that point that we would want to help students to recognize.

TOPICS FOR CRITICAL THINKING AND WRITING

1. Characterize Paul. In your response, try to indicate in what ways (if any) he is made sympathetic and in what ways (if any) he is made unsympathetic.
2. What values do the arts have for Paul? Does Cather suggest that Paul is

"artistic"? Is the story about the difficulties of a refined sensibility in a crude world?

3. Whom do you blame (if anyone) for Paul's character and for what happens to him—Paul, or the people and the conditions surrounding him? How does your sorting out of blame help you to settle on the meaning of the story?

4. Cather uses an omniscient point of view, rather than a third-person limited omniscient point of view with Paul as the central intelligence. Why do you suppose she chose an omniscient point of view? How would the meaning of the story be different if it were told from the point of view of Paul's father or of the young man with whom Paul spends an evening?

JAMES JOYCE

Araby (p. 271)

Probably the best discussion of "Araby" remains one of the earliest, that of Cleanth Brooks and Robert Penn Warren in *Understanding Fiction*. Among more recent discussions, L. J. Morrissey, "Joyce's Narrative Strategies in 'Araby'" *Modern Fiction Studies* 28 (1982): 45-52, is especially good.

Students have difficulty with the story largely because they do not read it carefully enough. They scan it for what happens (who goes where) and do not pay enough attention to passages in which (they think) "nothing is happening." But when students read passages aloud in class, for instance the first three paragraphs, they *do* see what is going on (that is, they come to understand the boy's mind) and enjoy the story very much. To help them hear the romantic boy who lives in what is (from an adult point of view) an unromantic society, it is especially useful to have students read aloud passages written in different styles. Compare, for instance, "At night in my bedroom and by day in the classroom her image came between me and the page I strove to read" with "I asked for leave to go to the bazaar on Saturday night. My aunt was surprised and hoped it was not some Freemason affair."

That the narrator is no longer a boy is indicated by such passages as the following:

> her name was like a summons to all my foolish blood.

> Her name sprang to my lips at moments in strange prayers and praise which I myself did not understand. My eyes were often full of tears (I could not tell why).

> What innumerable follies laid waste my waking and sleeping thoughts. . . .

Morrissey points out that in addition to distancing himself from his past actions by such words as "foolish" and "follies" (and, at the end of the story, "vanity"), the narrator distances himself from the boy he was by the words "imagined" and "seemed," words indicating that his present view differs from his earlier view.

The narrator recounts a story of disillusionment. The first two paragraphs clearly establish the complacent middle-class world into which he is born—the houses "conscious of decent lives within them" gaze with "imperturbable faces." This idea of decency is made concrete by the comment in the second paragraph that the priest's charity is evident in his will: he left all of his money to institutions and his furniture to his sister. (Probably even the sister was so decent that she too thought this was the right thing to do.) Morrissey, interpreting the passage about the priest's will differently, takes the line to be the boy's innocent report of "what must have been an ironic comment by adults."

As a boy he lived in a sterile atmosphere, a sort of fallen world:

· The house is in a "blind" or dead-end street.
· The rooms are musty.
· The priest had died (religion is no longer vital?).
· A bicycle pump, once a useful device, now lies rusty and unused under a bush in the garden.
· An apple tree in the center of the garden in this fallen world.
· Nearby are the odors of stable and garbage dumps.

Nevertheless the boy is quickened by various things, for instance by the yellow pages of an old book, but especially by Mangan's sister (who remains unnamed, perhaps to suggest that the boy's love is spiritual). He promises to visit " Araby" (a bazaar) and to return with a gift for her.

The boy for a while moves through a romantic, religious world:

· He sees her "image".
· He imagines that he carries a "chalice."
· He hears the "litanies" and "chanting" of vendors. He utters "strange prayers."

Delayed by his uncle, whose inebriation is indicated by the uncle's "talking to himself" and by "the hall-stand rocking" (his parents seem not to be living; notice the emphasis on the boy's isolation throughout the story, e.g., his ride alone in the car of the train), he hears the clerks counting the days' receipts—moneychangers in the temple.

"The light was out. The upper part of the hall was now completely dark." The darkness and the preceding trivial conversations of a girl and two young men reveal—Joyce might have said epiphanize—the emptiness of the world. The boy has journeyed to a rich, exotic (religious?) world created by his imagination and has found it cold and trivial, as dead as the neighborhood he lives in.

The boy's entry through the shilling entrance rather than through the sixpenny (children's) entrance presumably signals his coming of age.

This brief discussion of "Araby" of course seems reasonable to its writer, even the remarks that the rusty bicycle pump suggests a diminished world, and that the entry through the shilling entrance rather than the sixpenny entrance suggests, implies, or even—through one hesitates to use word—symbolizes (along with many other details) his initiation into an adult view. But how far can (or should) one press the details? An article in *James Joyce Quarterly* 4 (1967): 85-86 suggests that the pump under the bushes stands for the serpent in the garden. Is there a difference between saying that the rusty pump—in the context of the story—puts a reader in mind of a diminished (deflated) world, and saying that it stands for the serpent? Is one interpretation relevant, and the other not? Students might be invited to offer their own views on how far to look for "meaning" or "symbols" in this story, or in any other story. They might also be advised to read—but not necessarily to swallow—the brief discussions of symbolism in the text and in the glossary.

When teaching Joyce's stories, we turn often to the textual glosses in *Dubliners: Text, Criticism, and Notes,* ed. Robert Scholes and A. Walton Litz (1969); Don Gifford, *Joyce Annotated: Notes for Dubliners and A Portrait of the Artist as a Young Man* (2nd ed., 1982); and, especially, John Wyse Jackson and Bernard McGinley, *James Joyce's Dubliners: An Illustrated Edition* (1993), which includes many helpful drawings, maps, and photographs.

An audio cassette of James Joyce reading is available from Longman.

TOPICS FOR CRITICAL THINKING AND WRITING

1. What do the first two paragraphs tell us about the boy's environment? What does the second paragraph tell us about his nature?
2. Of course none of us can speak authoritatively about what life was *really* like in Dublin around 1900, but would you say that Joyce gives—insofar as space allows—a realistic picture of Dublin? If so, was his chief aim to give the reader a slice of Dublin life? What do you think Joyce wants us to believe that life in Dublin was like?
3. The boy says that when his uncle returned he heard his uncle talking to himself, and he heard the hallstand (coattree) rocking. Then he says, "I could interpret these signs." What do "these signs" mean? How is the uncle's behavior here consistent with other details of life in Dublin?
4. Reread the story, underlining or highlighting religious images. What is the point of these images?

D.H. LAWRENCE

The Horse Dealer's Daughter (p.275)

Despite the title, the story is about Dr. Fergusson as well as about Mabel. The deadness that characterizes her at the outset is later seen to be relevant to him as well, though he has managed to retain some vitality by keeping in touch with "the rough strongly-feeling people."

Mabel's lifelessness, consequent upon the breakup of the family, brings her to her dead mother's tomb (she feels secure in the churchyard); the "gray," "deadening" landscape contributes to the bleakness. Her devotion to her mother suggests not only a spiritual death but also a deep capacity for love, and it is therefore fitting that her attempt to commit suicide by drowning herself in the mucky winter pond turns out to lead to rebirth; the doctor, though he cannot swim, enters the pond to rescue her, goes over his head, and yet saves her. Both rise out of the foul water changed persons, having undergone a sort of baptism or rebirth from a womb. In short, character *evolves* and is not simply revealed.

The change is also suggested by the change of clothing and in the references to fire and light. Their new love is passionate and frightening, but that is (presumably) a sign of its vitality. (Lawrence originally called the story "The Miracle.") Kate Chopin's "The Story of an Hour" deals somewhat similarly with a sort of rebirth and can be compared usefully.

Donald Junkins, in *Studies in Short Fiction* [6 (1968-1969), 210-212], points out that:

> [r]itual overtones pervade the action: the silence, the solemn purification rite at her mother's grave, the personal ritual washing, the dedicatory vows, the commitment to water and death. The resuscitation of Mabel's flesh prefigures the resurrection of her spirit.

Junkins also calls attention to fairy tale or "mythological motifs: there are three brothers; the real mother has died and the father married again... the girl experiences a death-like unconsciousness; the hero braves death to rescue the maiden; there is a kiss of recognition remembered." (Again, it should be remembered that Fergusson too evolves and comes to life.)

Other useful discussions of the story can be found in T. H. McCabe, *PMLA* [87 (1972): 64-68], and Steven R. Phillips, *Studies in Short Fiction* [10 (1973): 94-97].

We don't hesitate to say to our students that we think that *The Rainbow* (1915) and *Women in Love* (1920) stand among the very best novels of the twentieth century. We also believe that Lawrence is one of the masters of the short story; see his *Collected Stories* (1994). For a biography see *The Priest of Love* by Harry T. Moore (1974). Older important critical books that are still useful include Mark Spilka, *The Love Ethic of D. H. Lawrence* (1955); F. R. Leavis, *D. H. Lawrence, Novelist* (1955); George Ford, *Double Measure: A Study of the Novels and Stories of D. H. Lawrence* (1965); and David Cavitch, *D.H. Lawrence and the New World* (1969). See also Janice Hubbard Harris, *The Short Fiction of D. H. Lawrence* (1985).

TOPICS FOR CRITICAL THINKING AND WRITING

1. In the opening scene, what is the attitude of the men toward Mabel? What was it like to be a daughter in this family? In the context of the entire story why is it important that the family is breaking up?
2. Briefly characterize each of Mabel's brothers, and then, more fully, characterize Mabel, pointing out the ways in which she differs from them. You may want to emphasize the ways in which her relations with her mother and father help to differentiate her from them.
3. During what season is the story set? How is this setting relevant?
4. Many psychologists and sociologists say that love is not an instinct but a

learned behavior. Basing your views on "The Horse Dealer's Daughter," indicate whether or not, in your opinion, Lawrence would have subscribed to such a view.

5. The uses of point of view in "The Horse Dealer's Daughter."
6. In a letter to Ernest Collings (Jan. 17, 1913) Lawrence says: "My great religion is a belief in the blood, the flesh, as being wiser than the intellect. We can go wrong in our minds. But what our blood feels and believes and says is always true." In an essay of 500 to 750 words, discuss the degree to which "The Horse Dealer's Daughter" illustrates this view.
7. Lawrence originally entitled this story "The Miracle." In a paragraph or two, set forth what you conjecture to be his reasons for changing it to "The Horse Dealer's Daughter." (You will probably briefly want to mention what "the miracle" in the story is.)
8. In an essay of 500 to 750 words, evaluate the thesis that Dr. Fergusson saves not only Mabel but also himself.

WILLIAM FAULKNER

A Rose for Emily (p. 287)

The chronology of the story—not very clear on first reading—has been worked out by several writers. Five chronologies are given in M. Thomas Inge, *William Faulkner: "A Rose for Emily"*; a sixth is given in Cleanth Brooks, *William Faulkner: Toward Yoknapatawpha and Beyond* (382-84). Brooks conjectures that Miss Emily is born in 1852, her father dies around 1884, Homer Barron appears in 1884 or 1885, dies in 1885 or 1886, the delegation calls on Miss Emily about the smell in 1885/86. In 1901 or 1904 or 1905, Miss Emily gives up the lessons in china-painting. Colonel Sartoris dies in 1906 or 1907, the delegation calls on her about the taxes in 1916, and Miss Emily dies in 1926.

The plot, of course, is gothic fiction: a decaying mansion, a mysteriously silent servant, a corpse, necrophilia. And one doesn't want to discard the plot in a search for what it symbolizes, but it is also clear that the story is not only "about" Emily Grierson but also about the South's pride in its past (including its Emily-like effort to hold on to what is dead) and the guilt as well as the grandeur of the past. Inevitably much classroom discussion centers on Miss Emily's character, but a proper discussion of her character entails a discussion of the narrator.

(This next paragraph summarizes an essay on this topic by John Daremo, originally printed in S. Barnet, *A Short Guide to Writing about Literature*.) The unnamed narrator is never precisely identified. Sometimes he seems to be an innocent eye, a recorder of a story whose implications escape him. Sometimes he seems to be coarse: he mentions "old lady Wyatt, the crazy woman," he talks easily of "niggers," and he confesses that because he and other townspeople felt that Miss Emily's family "held themselves a little too high for what they really were," the townspeople "were not pleased exactly, but vindicated" when at thirty she was still unmarried. But if his feelings are those of common humanity (e. g., racist and smug), he at least knows what these feelings are and thus helps us to know ourselves. We therefore pay him respectful attention, and we notice that on the whole he is compassionate (note especially his sympathetic understanding of Miss Emily's insistence for three days that her father is not dead). True, Miss Emily earns our respect by her aloofness and her strength of purpose (e.g., when she publicly appears in the buggy with Homer Barron, and when she cows the druggist and the alderman), but if we speak of her aloofness and her strength of purpose rather than of her arrogance and madness, it is because the narrator's imaginative sympathy guides us. And the narrator is the key to the apparently curious title: presumably the telling of this tale is itself the rose, the community's tribute (for the narrator insistently speaks of himself as "we") to the intelligible humanity in a woman whose unhappy life might seem monstrous to less sympathetic observers. Another meaning, however, may be offered (very tentatively) for the title. In the story Faulkner emphasizes Miss Emily's attempts to hold on to the past: her insistence, for example, that her father is not dead, and that she has no taxes to pay. Is it possible that Homer Barron's corpse serves as a sort of pressed or preserved will, a reminder of a past experience of love? If so, the title refers to him.

For a feminist reading, see Judith Fetterley, in *The Resisting Reader: A Feminist Approach to American Fiction* (1978), reprinted in *Literary Theories in Praxis*, edited by Shirley F. Staton (1987). Fetterley sees the story as revealing the "sexual conflict" within patriarchy (whether of the South or the North, the old order or the new). Emily's confinement by her father represents the confinement of women by patriarchy, and the remission of her taxes reveals the dependence of women on men. Emily has been turned into a "Miss," a lady, by a chivalric attitude that is "simply a subtler and more dishonest version of her father's horsewhip." The narrator represents a subtle form of this patriarchy. According to Fetterley, the narrator sees her as "'dear, inescapable, impervious, tranquil, and perverse'; indeed, anything and everything but human."

Fetterley—the "resisting reader" of her title, that is the reader who refuses to accept that text—argues that the story exposes "the violence done to a woman by making her a lady; it also explains the particular form of power the victim gains from this position and can use on those who enact their - violence. . . . Like Ellison's invisible man, nobody sees *Emily*. And because nobody sees *her*, she can literally get away with murder."

Biographies of Faulkner have been written by Joseph Blotner (2 vols., 1974); Judith Wittenberg (1979); David Minter (1980); Frederick Karl (1989); and the historian Joel Williamson (1993). For undergraduates, the best studies are some of the earliest: Michael Millgate, *The Achievement of William Faulkner* (1966); Cleanth Brooks, *William Faulkner: The Yoknapatawpha Country* (1963); and Irving Howe, *William Faulkner* (1952; rev. ed. 1991).

An audio cassette of William Faulkner reading is available from Longman.

TOPICS FOR CRITICAL THINKING AND WRITING

1. How valid is the view that the story is an indictment of the decadent values of the aristocratic Old South? Or a defense of these values (embodied in

Emily) against the callousness (embodied in Homer Barron) of the North?

2. Suppose Faulkner had decided to tell the story from Miss Emily's point of view. Write the first 200 or 300 words of such a version.

3. Characterize the narrator.

JOHN STEINBECK

The Chrysanthemums (p. 294)

Because most students find this story accessible, it can be effectively taught early in the semester. To say that most students find it accessible, however, is not to say that they see all its workings. Some class discussion can be devoted to the opening paragraph on the setting: "a closed pot" suggests that there may be an explosion, and the flaming leaves similarly prepare one for violence. The first description of Elisa, too, can be studied, with an eye toward the implications of the fact that she wears a man's hat and almost completely covers her "figured print dress." Like the winter fog that has "closed off the Salinas Valley from the sky and from all the rest of the world," Elisa's clothing seems to suppress her femininity.

One can go on to talk about her energy, which turns out to be devoted not to any children but to the "neat white farm house" and to her flowers. The flowers are an expression of her vitality, or of her otherwise unexpressed drive to procreate. The shrewd traveling repairman brings out her femininity ("she tore off the battered hat and shook out her dark pretty hair") and her generosity or creativity. The story becomes strongly sexual in Elisa's comment about the pointed stars driven into her body, and in the narrator's report that "her hand went out toward his legs," but as soon as the man receives the saucepans his manner changes; he becomes "professional." Elisa, however, remains in a state of excitement (the hot bath, the vigorous scrubbing, the look at her body in the mirror, the ritual of putting on feminine clothing and makeup); her womanliness revived, she confronts a husband who is somewhat puzzled by her new, attractive vitality. Then comes her disillusionment when she perceives that the tinker wanted only some work and the pot, not her gift of flowers, a disillusionment that at first finds an outlet in her thoughts of drinking wine, and of seeing men pummeled (i.e., of vicariously pummeling a male), and finally in tears.

There is, however, another angle from which the story may be viewed, for one can also see "The Chrysanthemums" as a story of two ways of life, that of the solid, rooted citizen (here the farmer) versus the amoral wanderer who scratches out a living. The wanderer's treatment of Elisa is despicable, but it is part of a way of life that Steinbeck implies is not without its strengths. Like his mismatched team, he gets along; and like his dog—who wisely refrains from taking on two shepherds—he knows how to survive as an outsider. The story is not the tinker's—it is chiefly Elisa's—but he is worth attention. During the course of class discussion, students may come to feel that he is not the villain they may at first have taken him to be.

One other point: judging from the published criticism of the 1960s and early 1970s many readers saw in Elisa's gardening a sublimation of her maternal instincts. Today perhaps readers are more likely to see Elisa's gardening as a woman's effort to established a creative role in a man-dominated society.

As social records of the 1930s, Steinbeck's novels In *Dubious Battle* (1936) and *The Grapes of Wrath* (1939) are still valuable. The standard biography is Jackson J. Benson, *The True Adventures of John Steinbeck, Writer* (1984). Critical studies include: Warren French, *John Steinbeck* (1961; rev. ed., 1975); Peter Lisca, *John Steinbeck, Nature and Myth* (1978); J. Timmerman, *John Steinbeck's Fiction: The Aesthetics of the Road Taken* (1986); and R. S. Hughes, *Beyond the Red Pony: A Reader's Guide to Steinbeck's Complete Short Stories* (1987).

TOPICS FOR CRITICAL THINKING AND WRITING

1. In the first paragraph of the story, the valley, shut off by fog, is said to be "a closed pot." Is this setting significant? Would any other setting do equally well? Why, or why not?
2. What physical descriptions in the story—literal or figurative—suggest that Elsa is frustrated?
3. Describe Elisa's and Henry's marriage.
4. Evaluate the view that Elisa is responsible for her troubles.

FRANK O'CONNOR

Guests of the Nation (p. 302)

We once began teaching this story by asking, "What is this story about?" The first answer, "War," brought the reply, "Yes, but what about war? Is it, for example, about the heroism that war sometimes stimulates?" Another student replied, "No, it's about the cruelty of war." The point: Though it is obvious to all instructors that the story is Bonaparte's, specifically about his growing up or initiation or movement from innocence to experience, this movement is not so evident to inexperienced readers.

This is not to say, of course, that it is not also about the conflict between the ideas of society and the ideals of the individuals. Jeremiah Donovan, though he thinks of himself as experienced, seems never to have grown up, never to have come to any sorrowful awareness of human loneliness. The bickering between Noble and Hawkins is, however, not a sign of enmity but a sort of bond. They may quarrel, but at least they share a relationship. Hawkins's offer to join the Irish cause indicates not so much his cowardice as his intuitive awareness that life and fellowship are more important than blind nationalism that excuses murder by an appeal to "duty."

Question 4, below, lends itself well to a theme. The old woman is a "simple... countrywoman," but she knows (as the narrator finds out) that "nothing but sorrow and want can follow the people that disturb the hidden powers." An interview with O'Connor in *Writers at Work*, edited by Malcolm Cowley, reveals some of O'Connor's ideas about fiction. Asked why he chose the short story as his medium, O'Connor said, "Because it's the nearest thing I know of to lyric poetry.... A novel actually requires far more logic and far more knowledge of circumstances, whereas a short story can have the sort of detachment from circumstances that lyric poetry has." O'Connor's ideas about the short story are expressed at some length in his book on the topic, *The Lonely Voice.*

TOPICS FOR CRITICAL THINKING AND WRITING

1. Although the narrator, Noble, and Donovan are all patriotic Irishmen, Donovan's attitude toward the English prisoners is quite different from that of the other two. How does that difference in attitude help point up the story's theme?

2. When he hears he is about to be shot, Hawkins, to save his life, volunteers to join the Irish cause. Is his turnabout simply evidence of his cowardice and hypocrisy? Explain.

3. Throughout most of the story Belcher is shy and speaks little; just before his execution, however, he suddenly becomes quite loquacious. Is he trying to stall for time? Would it have been more in character for Belcher to have remained stoically taciturn to the end, or do the narrator's remarks about Belcher's change make it plausible?

4. Does the old woman's presence in the story merely furnish local color or picturesqueness? If so, is it necessary or desirable? Or does her presence further contribute to the story's meaning? If so, how?

5. The following is the last paragraph of an earlier version. Which is the more effective conclusion?

> So then, by God, she fell on her two knees by the door, and began telling her beads, and after a minute or two Noble went on his knees by the fireplace, so I pushed my way past her, and stood at the door, watching the stars and listening to the damned shrieking of the birds. It is so strange what you feel at such moments, and not to be written afterwards. Noble says he felt he seen everything ten times as big, perceiving nothing around him but the little patch of black bog with the two Englishmen stiffening in it; but with me it was the other way, as though the patch of fog where the two Englishmen were was a thousand miles away from me, and even Noble mumbling just behind me and the old woman and the birds and the bloody stars were all far away, and I was somehow very small and lonely. And nothing that ever happened to me after I never felt the same about again.

6. How does the point of view help to emphasize the narrator's development from innocence to awareness? If the story had been told in the third person, how would it have affected the story's impact?

ISAAC BASHEVIS SINGER

The Son from America (p. 310)

The first question given below invites students to formulate their attitudes

toward Berl and Berlcha. Responses will of course vary, from respect to conde-
scension and perhaps even contempt, but many students probably will offer a
response along this line: they are good but rather stupid people. If something
like this is said, you may want to begin by asking students to distinguish
between stupidity and ignorance. That the peasants are ignorant is beyond
doubt, but that they are stupid is less certain. They share the values of the village (although they don't go for newfangled kerosene lamps), and by the end of
the story the reader sees that these values—rooted in piety—bring contentment,
and are life-sustaining. Yes, if Berl and Berlcha were a bit more adventurous
they would at least have bought eyeglasses so that they could see better—
although, when one thinks about it, except for being unable to make much out
of the photographs that Samuel sends, they can see as much as they have to.

Singer makes clear the ignorance of his peasants, for instance in the business about the people in America walking with "their heads down and their
feet up," and "since the teacher said so it must be true." Further, we smile at the
characters when, by taking us inside their minds, Singer delicately reveals their
uncomprehending views. For instance we know that Samuel is embracing his
mother, but Singer gives us Berl's view thus:

> At that moment Berl came in from the woodshed, his arms piled with logs. The goat
> followed him. When he saw a nobleman kissing his wife, Berl dropped the wood and
> exclaimed, "What's this?"

It is useful to discuss the point of view in the story. In "When [Berl] saw a
nobleman," Singer conveys the sight from Berl's naive point of view. Much of
the story, however, is told from a relatively objective point of view, though
surely even in the first paragraph a reader perceives the narrator's affection for
this fairy-tale like place:

> The village of Lentshin was tiny—a sandy marketplace where the peasants of the area
> met once a week. It was surrounded by little huts with thatched roofs or shingles
> green with moss. The chimneys looked like pots.

For the most part the narrator is content to report in what passes for an objective manner, but in the final paragraph, after the dialogue has convincingly
done its work, the narrator offers a judgment:

> But this village in the hinterland needed nothing.

Few American readers in the late twentieth century will envy the life of the villagers, but these readers may nevertheless see that the villagers do not need
what Samuel can give. Which is not to say that Samuel has become corrupted.
From all that we can see, he is a dutiful son and a generous man. He is, moreover,
a man who has kept the faith. But (as the last paragraph makes clear), some of
the things that give him his identity—"his passport, his checkbook, his letters of
credit"—are not needed in Lentshin.

For us, *The Collected Stories of Isaac Bashevis Singer* (1982) is a source of
much wisdom and delight.

TOPICS FOR CRITICAL THINKING AND WRITING

1. What is your attitude toward Berl and Berlcha? Admiration? Pity? Or what? (Of course you need not limit your answer to a single word. You may find that your response is complex.) What is your attitude toward Samuel?

2. Compare Samuel's values with those of his parents. What resemblances do you find? What differences?

NAGUIB MAHFOUZ

The Answer Is No (p. 315)

Mahfouz is said to be familiar with much European writing, and especially with Proust, but all of Mahfouz's stories—or at least the ones that have been translated into English—are set in Cairo and most of them seem to an American to deal with a culture that in some ways differs significantly from modern Western cultures. The story we have chosen is perhaps the most accessible, but even this story may contain elements that will puzzle most American readers.

Probably a reader's chief question has to do with the consequences of the unnamed woman's rejection of Badran Badawi's offer of marriage. When the narrator says, "She had either to accept or to close the door forever," is the narrator drawing on an Egyptian code of behavior, or on the other hand is he simply reporting the feelings of this particular woman? Readers may wish that they knew more about Egyptian traditions, but they nevertheless may feel that the woman's response is in itself psychologically clear: she has been violated by her teacher, and she now rejects not only him but all other potential suitors. Perhaps she decides "to close the door forever" because she feels it would be immoral for her to give herself to an unsuspecting husband, or perhaps she makes the decision because she now abhors sexuality. We are not sure whether for an Egyptian reader there are indeterminacies in the text, but in any case we think there is plenty of room here for American students to offer various responses.

We have spoken of indetermanacies, but perhaps Mahfouz does provide some guidance. He tells us that "She had welcomed being on her own, for solitude accompanied by self-respect was not loneliness." The explanation here seems psychological, not a matter of Egyptian social conventions. Toward the end of the story we find, however, that her feelings have changed: "She avoids love, fears it." When the narrator tells us that "she goes on persuading herself that happiness is not confined to love and motherhood," we probably feel (because of the unconvincing ring of "persuading herself") that she herself must unconsciously sense that she is unhappy. Nevertheless, she behaves with dignity, and probably the reader is pleased by her final response, "I told you, I'm fine." But we are offering conjectures about the responses of other readers. It will be interesting to hear the responses of students.

Of the work by Mahfouz we have read, we recommend *The Cairo Trilogy* (1956-57), three volumes which explore the lives of a Cairo family from 1918 to 1944.

Helpful studies include: *Critical Perspectives on Naguib Mahfouz*, ed. Trevor le Gassick (1991); *Naguib Mahfouz*, ed. Michael Beard and Adnan Haydar (1993); *Naguib Mahfouz: The Pursuit of Meaning*, ed. Rasheed El-Enany (1993); and Nadine Gordimer, *Writing and Being* (1995). For an overview that includes commentary on Mahfouz, see Roger M. A. Allen, *The Arabic Novel: An Historical and Critical Introduction* (1982).

TOPICS FOR CRITICAL THINKING AND WRITING
1. What is the effect on you of knowing the name of the man but not the name of the woman?
2. In the paragraph that begins the last section of the story ("Day by day she becomes older") Mahfouz uses the historical present, though in the final lines of the story he shifts to the past. Why do you suppose he did this?

RALPH ELLISON

Battle Royal (p. 318)

The term "battle royal" has two chief meanings: (1) a fight involving several or many contestants, and (2) a bitterly fought battle. Both meanings are relevant to this story, most obviously in the contest between the boys in the ring, and almost as obviously in the battle between blacks and whites.

The battle between blacks and whites in many ways is evident enough to all of the participants, but in two important ways it is not evident to some of them. First, the whites presumably did not perceive that the narrator's grandfather was a traitor and a spy; presumably they mistakenly accepted his feigned acquiescence as genuine submission, not realizing that in fact he was an enemy, maintaining his ideals in the only way available to him. Second, the narrator, who in his youth accepted the traditional answers, did not understand that a war was going on, or ought to be going on. In his immaturity he sought to please the whites, subjecting himself to all sorts of indignities—not only by fighting against blacks for the amusement of whites and grabbing for counterfeit coins on an electrified rug, but also by giving a speech that he thinks is impressive but reduces him to a puppet mouthing ideas that lend support to his enemy. He is so unaware of his plight that even during the fisticuffs he wonders if his speech will impress his audience. (Ellison emphasizes the point a little later in various ways, for instance when the M.C. introduces the boy as someone who "knows more big words than a pocket-sized dictionary," and when the narrator tells us that he was swallowing his own blood while giving his speech to the amused audience.) As the narrator says at the beginning of the story, it took him a long time to realize that he must be himself—not the creature that white society wants him to be—and that as far as white society goes, a black is an invisible man, i.e. a person of no identity.

As long as he accepts the role the whites give him, he serves the purpose of whites. In fact, because he is verbally talented, he is extremely useful to whites; he will persuade other blacks to perceive themselves as the whites perceive them. As the school superintendent puts it, the boy will "lead his people in the proper paths." Thus the scholarship is used by the whites to strengthen their army by recruiting a man who betrays the blacks. If the narrator had not ultimately come to understand this, he would have become a traitor of a sort very different from his grandfather. Fortunately, however, the nightmarish experience of the battle and the subsequent speech are balanced by another sort of nightmare, a dream (presided over by his grandfather) in which the briefcase contains not a scholarship but a note: "Keep This Nigger-Boy Running." (The message is rooted in a horrible practical joke, in which a white plantation owner would send an illiterate African-American to another plantation owner, with a letter supposedly recommending the bearer but which actually said, "Keep this Nigger-Boy Running." The second owner would say he could not offer a job, but would recommend that the bearer go to a third plantation, and so on.) The narrator's dream is as real as the battle, and more real than the scholarship, since the scholarship (though of course literally real) was not at all what the young man had thought it was.

"Battle Royal" became part of Ellison's novel, *Invisible Man* (1952). On this important book, see *New Essays on Invisible Man,* ed. Robert G. O'Meally (1988); and *Approaches to Teaching Ellison's Invisible Man,* ed. Susan Parr and Pancho Savery (1989).   All students of modern and contemporary American and African American literatures should explore *The Collected Essays of Ralph Ellison,* ed. John F. Callahan (1995).

TOPICS FOR CRITICAL THINKING AND WRITING

1. Now that you have read the entire story, the opening paragraph may be clearer than it was when you first read it. Briefly restate the paragraph, making it as clear as possible. For instance, "translate" into literal language such a statement as "I am an invisible man."

2. Do you recall your response to the opening paragraph? Did it puzzle you—perhaps so much that you anticipated a boring story with lots of abstract talk and with little action? Having finished the story, do you think the opening is appropriate? Why, or why not?

3. The narrator says of his grandfather's dying speech, "I could never be sure what he meant." What do you think the grandfather meant by calling himself a traitor and a spy in the enemy's country?

4. The narrator dreams that the briefcase contains a message: "Keep this Nigger-Boy Running." Why in maturity does he come to believe that the scholarship is a trick to keep him running?

5. What would the effect be if instead of being a white woman the dancer were a black woman? And, by the way, why is "a small American flag tattooed on her belly"?

DORIS LESSING

A Woman on a Roof (p. 328)

Although the story is called "A Woman on a Roof," most students will be able to see—especially if classroom discussion centers on point of view—that the story is Tom's. In the early part the narrator takes us equally into the minds of all three men ("they speculated," "they were all a bit dizzy," and so forth), but soon the narrator, entering only into Tom's mind, reveals the two other men and the woman by recording what they say or do, not by what they think. Thus Stanley's lust is presented by, for example, his comment that he would not allow his wife to sun on the roof, his whistling and screaming, and, more comically, by his suggestion when they are working in the basement that they take a break by going up to the roof. Similarly, after the first page or so, the narrator tells us little about Harry's mind. In fact, the fullest description of Harry's state of mind comes from a report of Tom's thoughts about Harry:

> Even Harry sounded aggrieved, Tom noted. The small, competent man, the family man with his grey hair, who was never at a loss, sounded really off balance.

If we get into the minds of Harry, Stanley, and the woman chiefly through reports of what they say and do rather than through editorial omniscience, we learn a good deal about Tom's fantasies. The narrator tells us that Tom thinks of the woman as a work of art ("Tom thought she looked like a poster, or a magazine cover"), then as someone made available to him by means of a crane that would "swing over and pick her up and swing her back across the sky to drop her near to him," and then as someone who invites him into her bedroom. Moved by her "tenderness" in his fantasy), he grins, finds her "romantic," and soon we are told that he "loved her."

Tom's romance is fleshly enough—like Tom in the Godiva story, this Tom can't keep his eyes off the woman—but Lessing's presentation of his fantasies is such that he retains our sympathy, at least when we compare him to the enraged Stanley, and even to the normally restrained Henry, who after a few days finds that the woman's presence knocks him off his usual balance. Doubtless readers will differ in their response to the woman's rebuff of Tom at the end, but probably most will understand (if not sympathize with) Tom's belief that "She hadn't understood him" and that she has been "unfair" to him. (Of course the woman knows nothing of the romantic fantasies that he has conjured up, and there is no reason why she should distinguish him from the other men.) Tom's "resentment," drunkenness, and "hatred of her" are not attractive, but they are understandable and (psychologically speaking) they may well strike many readers as correct. In so far as there is a narrative, it might be said to be (like Joyce's "Araby") a story of fantasy and then disillusionment. At the end of the story, Tom, like the other men, is eager to finish the job and get out, though his reason is not exactly the same as theirs.

In short, in "A Woman on a Roof" we get a story whose concern is with revealing states of mind, not with conveying a message about how we ought to behave, or how we ought to view the external world in a new way. Thus, to take an obvious example, Mrs. Pritchett is in the story for at least two reasons, neither of which has anything to do with a moral. Her presence allows Stanley a little release in "badinage," which, we are told, has the effect of leaving Tom's romance with the woman on the roof "safe and intact." Second, Mrs. Pritchett makes a contrast with the woman on the roof (Mrs. Pritchett went up once, but found the roof too dirty and too hot), but it is probably safe to assume that the purpose of the contrast is not to make any sort of moral point about the woman on the roof.

Once when we taught this story, we asked the class to examine it not as a story about gender and sexuality but about work. You can enrich the discussion by examining Lessing's descriptions of the hot, demanding work that the men perform: how are their attitudes toward their jobs connected to their feelings (and their words) about the woman on the roof?

We might mention, on a related note, that one of us took a chance with an assignment here that led to good results. Students were presented with a maxim by Voltaire, "Work keeps at bay three great evils: boredom, vice, and need," and the students were then told to apply it to Lessing's story. We could have used a passage by Marx or Engels, but the advantage of Voltaire's passage is that it kept the students from too easily lapsing into generalities about the oppression of the workers, the conditions of the working class, etc. It's not that we didn't want them to think about these issues, but, rather, that we judged they might arrive at better, more independent formulations about work, as depicted in Lessing's text, if they approached the subject from a somewhat unfamiliar angle.

Students interested in Lessing might begin with *The Doris Lessing Reader* (1989), and also the essays on writers and writing gathered in Lessing's collection, *A Small Personal Voice* (1974). Recent books include: Betsy Draine, *Substance Under Pressure: Artistic Coherence and Evolving Form* (1983); Lorna Sage, *Doris Lessing* (1983); and Mona Knapp, *Doris Lessing* (1984).

TOPICS FOR CRITICAL THINKING AND WRITING

1. Is the story chiefly about one character? If so, which one?
2. Stanley mentions Lady Godiva. Do you recall the name of the man who peeped at her in the legend? How does his name fit in with Lessing's story?
3. What does Mrs. Pritchett contribute to the story?
4. The last line of the story is, "Because it was cool now, they would finish the job that day, if they hurried." Do you assume that they hurried? Why or why not?

SHIRLEY JACKSON

The Lottery (p. 335)

This story is based on fertility rituals of the sort described in Sir James Frazer's *The Golden Bough:* a community is purged of its evil, and fertility is ensured, by the sacrifice of an individual, that is, by killing a scapegoat. "Lottery in June, corn be heavy soon," Old Man Warner says. In "The Lottery," the method of execution is stoning, which Frazer reports was a method used in ancient Athens.

Until the last six paragraphs we think we are reading a realistic story about decent small-town life. Probably on rereading we notice that, despite all the realism, the time and the place are never specified; we may feel we are reading about a twentieth-century New England town, but we cannot document this feeling. On rereading, too, we pay more attention to the early references to stones, and to the general nervousness, and of course we see the importance of Tessie Hutchinson's outburst. (Consult Helen E. Nebeker, "'The Lottery': Symbolic Tour de Force," *American Literature* 46 [1974]: 100-107.) With the last six paragraphs the horror comes, and it is described in the same matter-of-fact, objective tone used in the earlier part of the story.

Inevitably a discussion turns to the question, "Does the story have any meaning for a modern society?" Students in the 1990s may have to be reminded that a lottery was used as recently as the Vietnam War to pick the people who would be subject to slaughter.

In *Come Along With Me,* Shirley Jackson discusses the furor "The Lottery" evoked after its original publication in the *New Yorker* in 1948. Lenemaja Friedman, in *Shirley Jackson* (1975) reports that Jackson said of the theme: "Explaining just what I hoped the story to say is very difficult. I suppose I hoped, by setting a particularly brutal ancient rite in the present and in my own village, to shock the story's readers with a graphic demonstration of the pointless violence and general inhumanity in their own lives." On the other hand, Jack O'Shaughnessy in *The New York Times Book Review* (August 18, 1988, 34), said that after reading the story in the *New Yorker* he wrote to Jackson, asking, "What does it mean?" He says that Jackson replied, on a postcard, "I wish I knew. Shirley Jackson."

Perhaps this story should not be pressed for its meaning or theme. Formulations such as "Society engages in ritualized slaughter," or "Society disguises its cruelty, even from itself," or "Even decent people seek scapegoats" do not quite seem to fit. Isn't it possible that the story is an effective shocker, signifying nothing? As many people have pointed out, much of the effect of the story depends on the contrast between the objective narration and the horrifying subject. The story is clever, a carefully wrought thriller, but whether it is an allegory—something about the cruelty of humanity, a cruelty which is invisible to us because it is justified by tradition—is a matter that may be reasonably debated.

The date of the story is significant, June 27, close to the summer solstice, and the season for planting. Some of the names, too, are obviously significant: the ritual is presided over by Mr. Summers, the first man to draw a lot is Mr. Adams, and conservative warnings are uttered by Mr. Warner. Note, too, that the leaders of the attack on Mrs. Hutchinson are Adams (the first sinner) and Graves (the result of sin was death).

One last point about the ritual: Clyde Dunbar, at home with a broken leg, does not participate. Why? Because a sacrificial victim must be unblemished.

For biography: Judy Oppenheimer, *Private Demons: The Life of Shirley Jackson* (1988).

TOPICS FOR CRITICAL THINKING AND WRITING
1. Is "The Lottery" more than a shocker?
2. What is the community's attitude toward tradition?
3. Doubtless a good writer could tell this story effectively from the point of

view of a participant, but Jackson chose a nonparticipant point of view. What does she gain?

4. Let's say you were writing this story, and you had decided to write it from Tessie's point of view. What would your first paragraph, or your first 250 words, be?

5. Suppose someone claimed that the story is an attack on religious orthodoxy. What might be your response? (Whether you agree or disagree, set forth your reasons.)

GRACE PALEY

A Conversation with My Father (p. 341)

The first sentence is direct, present tense, and plainly descriptive: "My father is eighty-six years old and in bed." This, one could say, is a sentence anyone could write. But not just anyone could write the next sentence, which begins, "His heart, that bloody motor." This vivid image startles the reader and shows the verbal command of the writer. It takes a special gift of the imagination, an authoritative way with words, to fix on an image of this striking kind, with its keen, wounding incongruity of body and machine. (Metaphor, Aristotle shrewdly observed, is the gift of the imaginative writer.)

Students might be told that Paley was first a poet, but then turned in the 1950s to writing short stories. We'd encourage students to linger over Paley's poetic, attention-seizing effect in "bloody motor" because the burden of the story is to *raise questions* about the narrator-writer's authority, as she engages in a conversation with her father, who grumbles about the stories she produces and prods her to do something different (and better) for a change.

Indeed, this is a story with additional stories contained within it, as the writer seeks to please her father, doing better on the second attempt than on the first. In a sense this story about a "conversation" between father and daughter is also a conversation between the writer and herself, as she thinks about other forms that her stories might take, and acts as an audience for them: what do I sound like when I write like that?

Is this a story, or a non-fictional account? Would it make any difference to our experience of this piece of writing if Paley said, "Well, yes, I have called it a story, but it's really about me and my real-life father?" Perhaps such a question seems off the point—this *is* a short story, we know. But students often have asked us if Paley really had an eighty-six year old father, with a bad heart, etc. The question is so common, in fact, that we wonder if Paley might have intended it as a part of the work's perplexing, ironic effects, as yet another reflection on the status of "story."

Another question that students sometimes raise is whether the story becomes too overtly serious at the end, when the father starts to talk about life as, ultimately, a tragedy. Ask the class if these comments that he makes seem "in character" or not. Is Paley striving too hard to give a large significance to her story as it concludes, or do these important-sounding words about tragedy and hopelessness follow organically from what has preceded them?

Henry James on Turgenev, to whom Paley refers in her story: "No one has had a closer vision, or a hand at once more ironic and more tender, for the individual figure. He sees it with its minutest signs and tricks—all its heredity of idiosyncrasies, all its particulars of weakness and strength, of ugliness and beauty, or oddity and charm; and yet it is of his essence that he sees it in the general flood of life, steeped in its relations and contacts, struggling or submerged, a hurried particle in the stream" ("Turgenev and Tolstoy," 1897).

On Paley, see N. Isaacs, *Grace Paley, A Study of the Short Fiction* (1990); J. Taylor, *Grace Paley, Illuminating the Dark Lives* (1990); and Judith Arcana, *Grace Paley's Life Stories: A Literary Biography* (1993).

GABRIEL GARCÍA MÁRQUEZ

A Very Old Man with Enormous Wings: A Tale for Children (p. 346)

A neighbor is the first to call the winged man an angel, and then other characters call him an angel—maybe he is, but maybe he is just a winged old man. That is, despite the references to an angel, and even to the somewhat biblical sounding start with its "third day," its torrent of rain (in the Old Testament such a torrent is symbolic of God's power), and its "newborn child," we need not assume that the story is about the human response to the divine.

Most of our students, like most of our colleagues, argue that the story satirizes the inability of people to perceive the spiritual. Thus the angel attracts attention only briefly and is, when not abused, finally neglected. All of this, in the common view, constitutes a satire on humanity, an attack that suggests we are like those contemporaries of Jesus who saw in him only a troublemaker.

But this is to assume that García Márquez, like Flannery O'Connor, subscribes to a Christian view of reality. Such an assumption is highly doubtful. Moreover, the assumption that in this story García Márquez is talking about our inability to perceive and revere the miraculous neglects the fact that he deals in fantasy or, perhaps more precisely, that he employs fantasy in order to write about the individual's isolation in an unintelligible world. Such worlds as he gives us in his stories and novels are, he would say, projections of his mind rather than pictures of objective reality.

In short, we doubt that the story is about the ways in which human beings ignore, domesticate, or in other ways maltreat the divine. Of course, there is some satire of churchgoers and of the church: the old lady who thinks angels live on meatballs, the inappropriate miracles, and especially the correspondence with the authorities in Rome and the business about the priest who suspects that the winged man is an impostor because he doesn't speak Latin. But satire in this story is directed less at religious faith than at exploitative capitalism—selfishness, gullibility, etc.

To say that the story is satiric is to say also that it is comic. One ought not to be so concerned with creating a religious allegory that one fails to see the humor, for instance, in the comments on the priest, the mail from Rome, and the "lesson" taught by the spider-woman. (In this last we hear a jibe at the conventional morality of fairy tales and of bourgeois standards.) As in other satire, the vision of human stupidity and cruelty is as unnerving as it is amusing. And what perhaps is especially unnerving is the fact that Pelayo and Elisenda are, at least when they discover the man, not particularly villainous. "They did not have the heart to club him to death," and so they at first (kindly, by their standards) plan to set him adrift on a raft for three days and "leave him to his fate on the high seas." Such is the depth, or rather the shallowness, of decency.

For a good discussion of the story, see John Gerlach, "The Loss of Wings," in *Bridges to Fantasy*, ed. George E. Slusser et al. (1982). Rejecting the fairly common view that the story of a feeble old flyer is meant to explode our taste for antiquated myths, Gerlach points out that many passages are puzzling. For instance, a line such as "He answered in an incomprehensible dialect with a strong sailor's voice" makes the careful reader wonder what a "sailor's voice" is. Or take, for instance, the last sentence of the story, which says that the old man "was no longer an annoyance in [Elisenda's] life, but an imaginary dot on the horizon of the sea." First, there is the odd contrast between an "annoyance" (an abstraction) and a "dot" (something barely visible); Gerlach calls the sentence grammatically uncomfortable. Second, Gerlach points out that an "imaginary dot" is strange; Elisenda is simultaneously seeing and imagining. Briefly, Gerlach's gist is that although the world of myth seems to be demeaned by this story about a winged old man who looked "like a huge decrepit hen," the story gives us a world of mystery, partly in the almost miraculous patience of the old man and partly in its puzzling statements. One mystery is that the mysterious, winged old man seems more real (in his behavior) than the others in the story. Drawing heavily on Tzvetan Todorov's *The Fantastic,* Gerlach's overall point is that this story, like other works of fantasy, evokes "hesitation" (we'd say uncertainty). In Todorov's view, fantasy is not simply a matter of improbable happenings. The happenings in an allegory are usually improbable, but allegories are not fantasies, Todorov says, because the supernatural events can be interpreted on a naturalistic level. But in "A Very Old Man," there remains a strong sense of uncertainty, an uncertainty that survives such an allegorical interpretation as "There is a winged aspect of man that can fly despite the lack of appreciation of others."

García Márquez's best novels are *One Hundred Years of Solitude* (1967; trans. 1970) and *The Autumn of the Patriarch* (1975; trans. 1975). There have been a number of scholarly studies, including Kathleen McNerney's *Understanding Gabriel García Márquez* (1989); but for the stories, we suggest Raymond Williams, *Gabriel García Márquez* (1984).

TOPICS FOR CRITICAL THINKING AND WRITING

1. The subtitle is "A Tale for Children." Do you think that the story is more suited to children than to adults? What in the story do you think children would especially like, or dislike?
2. Is the story chiefly about the inability of adults to perceive and respect the miraculous world?
3. Characterize the narrator of the story.
4. Characterize Pelayo, Elisenda, their son, and the man with wings.

CHINUA ACHEBE

Civil Peace (p. 350)

This story is told with a directness that suits the chief character. It begins, "Jonathan Iwegbu counted himself extraordinarily lucky." Nevertheless, the story is complex. After all, the first paragraph goes on to tell us that he lost one of his children. So we are in a world in which a person who loses only one child is "extraordinarily lucky." And, in fact, given the war-torn condition of the country, the assertion is true.

It is a world in which "Happy survival" is the current greeting, and although these words apparently have become a formula for some people (as, for example, "good morning" can be said on an unpleasant morning), for Jonathan the words "went deep to his heart."

Classroom discussion might begin with talk about what sort of person Jonathan is. Most students will see that if he seems simple or naive, he is in fact something else. The second paragraph is especially important in establishing Jonathan's character. We are told that when a man in uniform sought to commandeer Jonathan's bicycle, Jonathan "would have let it go without a thought"—even though the loss would be great—but Jonathan

> had some doubts about the genuineness of the officer. It wasn't his disreputable rags, nor the toes peeping out of one blue and one brown canvas shoe, nor yet the two stars of his rank done obviously in a hurry in biro that troubled Jonathan; many good and heroic soldiers looked the same or worse. It was rather a certain lack of grip and firmness in his manner.

Especially if the passage is read aloud in class, students will see that Jonathan is a sharp observer of character. They will see also that Jonathan is a decent man, a man who would give up an important possession for a worthy cause.

His astuteness and capacity for hard work enable him to patch up his house and save a little money. True, at his bar he is not above diluting the wine with water, but Achebe defuses any moral objection we might have by telling us that the palm wine was "generously" mixed with water. Achebe thus jokingly makes the deception sound almost virtuous.

Doubtless, Jonathan likes money, and surely he needs it, but he is astute enough to yield it when the thieves arrive. Life is worth much more than money. It's interesting to notice, too, that although the thieves demand one hundred pounds, when Jonathan tells them (truthfully) he has only twenty pounds the leader accepts his word unquestioningly and effectively silences the "loud murmurs of dissent among the chorus." The leader is as acute and (though a thief) as reasonable as Jonathan is.

Jonathan's last speech is surely sincere, and worthy of admiration. He has endured the losses of civil war, and (given the horrors of war) has come out fairly well. (The loss of one child is dreadful, but Achebe makes it clear that things could have been much worse.) And now he endures the losses of "civil peace," an odd phrase that of course puts us in mind of "civil war." War and peace in Jonathan's world are not much different. He still has his strength and acuity; he survived the war, and now, sustained by faith in God, he will survive the peace. Human beings are (quite rightly) puzzled by the ways of the world— deaths, the destruction of homes, the closing of the mine, the failure of the police to provide protection—but "nothing puzzles God." If Jonathan's life had been easy, his faith and stoicism might be unconvincing and even offensive, but the faith and stoicism of a person who has undergone what he has under- gone is not something that the comfortably-seated reader can easily dismiss.

Achebe has written a number of books, the most important of which are his novel, *Things Fall Apart* (1958), and a collection or prose pieces on literature and culture, *Hopes and Impediments: Selected Essays, 1965-87* (1988). In our casebook on Conrad's *Heart of Darkness* we include an extract from one of Achebe's essays.

For analyses of Achebe's work: C. L. Innes, *Chinua Achebe* (1990); and Simon Gikandi, *Reading Chinua Achebe: Language and Ideology in Fiction* (1991). Also helpful: Robert M. Wren, *Achebe's World: The Historical and Cultural Context of the Novels of Chinua Achebe* (1981). Instructors will also benefit from *Approaches to Teaching Achebe's Things Fall Apart*, ed. Bernth Lindfors (1991)

TOPICS FOR CRITICAL THINKING AND WRITING
1. Why does Achebe begin with the story of the bicycle?
2. In the last paragraph Jonathan says of *egg-rasher*, "I count it as nothing." Do you believe him?
3. Characterize Jonathan. What do you think of him? Do you assume that the author regards him as you do? Why, or why not?

ALICE MUNRO

Boys and Girls (p. 354)

A good way to begin the discussion of this story is to have a student read the first paragraph aloud, and then ask if the sentences about the calendar have any relevance to the rest of the story. Of course this passage would be justified if it did no more than give a glimpse of the sort of decorations that might be found on a Canadian fox farm, and one doesn't want to press too hard for a deep meaning, but surely the picture of "plumed adventurers" (male, naturally) who use "savages" as pack animals introduces, however faintly, a political note that can be connected with the treatment of distinctions between the sexes.

This is not to say that the story suggests that women are comparable to the Indians who bend their backs in service to the whites. The wife works hard, but so does the husband. And the early part of the story indicates that the female narrator, when a child, eagerly engaged in what the mother must have thought was "man's work." Certainly the girl, feeling quite superior to her little brother, had no sense that she was oppressed. She came to learn, however, that she must "become" a girl. If we hear a note of protest in this statement that society expects us to assume certain roles, the story nevertheless seems also to suggest that females are, by nature rather than by nurture, mentally or emotionally different from males. Despite the narrator's early enthusiasm for her father's work, and despite her sense of superiority to her brother (she can handle the wheelbarrow used for watering the foxes, whereas Laird, carrying a "little cream and green gardening can," can only play at watering), she is more shaken by the killing of Mack than she will admit. "My legs were a little shaky," she says, and later she adds that she "felt a little ashamed," but for the most part she deals with her response by talking about another episode, the time when she endangered Laird's life, and afterwards felt "the sadness of unexorcised guilt." Of course we may think that anyone—male or female—might feel shaky and guilty upon first witnessing the death of a harmless animal, but in fact Laird does not seem even mildly disturbed. Rather, after witnessing the shooting of Mack, Laird is "remote, concentrating."

The guilt engendered by watching Mack die prompts the narrator to let Flora escape. (A question: If the first horse killed had been a female, would the narrator have let the second horse, a male, escape? One answer: The story is right as it is. Don't monkey with it. If the horses were reversed, the story would be less coherent.) The narrator is irretrievably female. (Notice too the passage recounted after the episode with Flora, about the narrator's attempt to prettify her part of the bedroom and, in the same paragraph, the discussion of her new fantasies, in which she no longer performs heroic rescues but is now the person rescued, and is wondering about her hairstyle and her dress.) Having let Flora escape, she of course has no desire to join in the chase, but Laird does, and when he returns, daubed in blood (this passage, however realistic, seems almost a parody of Hemingway and Faulkner on rituals of initiation), he is quite casual about what happened: "'We shot old Flora,' he said, 'and cut her up in fifty pieces.'" Laird, no longer his sister's partner but now firmly aligned with the men, soon betrays the narrator, reducing her to tears. Her father means well in absolving her ("She's only a girl"), but, as the narrator says, the words not only absolve but also "dismiss" her. On the other hand, the narrator recognizes that the father's words may be "true."

In teaching this story, one might get around to making the point that a work of literature doesn't "prove" anything. *Hamlet* doesn't prove that ghosts exist, or that one should not delay, or that revenge is morally acceptable. Similarly, Munro's story doesn't prove that girls are by nature more sensitive to the killing of a horse than boys are. We won't attempt here (or anywhere) to say what a work of fiction does do, but the point is worth discussing—probably early in the course and again near the end, after students have read a fair amount of literature.

Among Munro's books, we remain partial to her first two collections of stories: *Dance of the Happy Shades* (1968), and *Lives of Girls and Women* (1971).

TOPICS FOR CRITICAL THINKING AND WRITING

1. What does the narrator mean when she says, "The word *girl* had formerly seemed to me innocent and unburdened, like the word *child;* now it appeared that it was no such thing. A girl was not, as I had supposed, simply what I was; it was what I had to become."

2.   The narrator says that she "could not understand" why she disobeyed her father and allowed the horse to escape. Can you explain her action to her? If so, do so.

3.   Characterize the mother.

JACK FORBES

Only Approved Indians Can Play: Made in USA (p. 364)

One way to begin a discussion of this story is to ask students what kind of story they anticipated from the title. What did they expect, and why? (Consider especially "Approved Indians," and "Made in USA.") Sooner or later, of course, the discussion will shift to the narrator's tone. Recited in a matter-of-fact colloquial voice ("Excitement was pretty high," " A lot of people were betting"—both in the first paragraph), the story for the most part is a goodhearted, farcical, wry narrative, but with the last line (the white BIA official tearfully says, "God Bless America. I think we've won") it becomes evident that the irony is scathing.

By the way, the Bureau of Indian Affairs really does concern itself with "official" Indians. For instance, the Indian Arts and Crafts Law of 1990 defines an Indian as a person of at least one-quarter Indian blood. Only such persons (in the BIA view) can sell their work as a Native American product. Many Native Americans, however, refuse to acknowledge the authority of the BIA and therefore don't seek enrollment in its records.

JOYCE CAROL OATES

Where Are You Going, Where Have You Been? (p. 366)

The title seems to be derived from Judges 19:17 ("So the old man said, 'Where are you going, and where do you come from?'"), a point made in a rather strained discussion of the story in *Explicator* (Summer 1982).

Tom Quirk in *Studies in Short Fiction* 18 (1981): 413-19 pointed out that the story derives from newspaper and magazine accounts (especially one in *Life*, Mar. 4, 1966) of the activities of a psychopath known as "The Pied Piper of Tucson," who drove a gold-colored car and seduced and sometimes murdered teenage girls in the Tucson area. Because he was short, he stuffed his boots with rags and flattened tin cans, which caused him to walk unsteadily. Oates herself has confirmed, on various occasions, her use of this material (e.g., *New York Times*, Mar. 23, 1986, reprinted in our text).

According to Oates, in an early draft of her story "Death and the Maiden" (she is fond of a type of fiction that she calls "realistic allegory"), "the story was minutely detailed yet clearly an allegory of the fatal attractions of death (or the devil). An innocent young girl is seduced by way of her own vanity: she mistakes death for erotic romance of a particularly American/trashy sort." The story went through several drafts. Oates has said she was especially influenced by Bob Dylan's song, "It's All Over Now, Baby Blue." One line of Dylan's song ("The vagabond who's standing at your door") is clearly related to the story, and note that in the story itself Connie wishes "it were all over."

In speaking of the revisions, Oates writes that "the charismatic mass murderer drops into the background and his innocent victim, a 15-year-old, moves into the foreground. She becomes the true protagonist of the tale. . . . There is no suggestion in the published story that Arnold Friend has seduced and murdered other girls, or even that he necessarily intends to murder Connie." Oates goes on to explain that her interest is chiefly in Connie, who "is shallow, vain, silly, hopeful, doomed—perhaps as I saw, and still see, myself?—but capable nonetheless of an unexpected gesture of heroism at the story's end. . . . We don't know the nature of her sacrifice [to protect her family from Arnold], only that she is generous enough to make it." Instructors who are interested in discussing the intentional fallacy (and is it a fallacy?) will find, if they use this passage, that students have strong feelings on the topic.

The story has abundant affinities with the anonymous ballad called "The Demon Lover." The demon lover has "music on every hand," and Connie "was hearing music in her head"; later, Arnold and Ellie listen to the same radio station in the car that Connie listens to in the house; the demon lover's ship has "masts o' the beaten gold," and Arnold's car is "painted gold."

The first sentence tells us that Connie "had a quick nervous giggling habit of craning her neck to glance into mirrors." Her mother attributes it to vanity, and indeed Connie does think she is pretty, but a more important cause is insecurity. Connie's fear that she has no identity sometimes issues in her a wish that "she herself were dead and it were all over with." "Everything about her had two sides," which again suggests an incoherent personality.

Arnold Friend has a hawklike nose, thick black lashes, an ability to see what is gong on in remote places, a curious (lame) foot, a taste for strange bargains, incantatory speech, an enchanted subordinate, and a charismatic personality; all in all he is a sort of diabolical figure who can possess Connie, partly because he shows her an enormous concern that no one else has shown her. (The possession—"I'll come inside you, where it's all secret"—is possession of her mind as well as of her body.) Notice, too, that like a traditional evil spirit, Arnold Friend cannot cross the threshold uninvited.

The dedication to Dylan has provoked considerable comment. Marie Urbanski, in *Studies in Short Fiction* 15 (1978): 200-203, thinks it is pejorative, arguing that Dylan made music "almost religious in dimension among youth." Tom Quirk, on the other hand, says it is "honorific because the history and effect of Bob Dylan's music had been to draw youth away from the romantic promises and frantic strains of a brand of music sung by Buddy Holly, Chuck Berry, Elvis Presley, and others." A. H. Petry *Studies in Short Fiction* 25 (1988), 155-57 follows Quirk, and goes on to argue that Ellie is meant to suggest Elvis Presley (lock of hair on forehead, sideburns, etc.). According to Petry, Oates is seeking "to warn against the dangerous illusions and vacuousness" generated by Elvis's music, in contrast to Bob Dylan's.

Perhaps the most astounding comment is by Mike Tierce and John Michael Crafton *(Studies in Short Fiction* 22 [1985]: 219-24), reprinted in our text. Tierce and Crafton argue that Arnold Friend, the mysterious visitor, is not satanic but rather a savior, and that he is (as his hair, hawklike nose, unshaved face, and short stature suggest) an image of Bob Dylan. Arnold's visit, in their view, is a fantasy of Connie's "overheated imagination," and it enables her to free herself "from the sense of confinement she feels in her father's house. . . . She broadens her horizons to include the 'vast sunlit reaches of the land' all around her."

Many readers find resemblances between the fiction of Oates and Flannery O'Connor, but in an interview in *Commonweal* (Dec. 5, 1969), Oates said that although she at first thought her fiction was indebted to Flannery O'Connor, she came to see that in O'Connor there is always a religious dimension whereas in her own fiction "there is only the natural world."

The story has been made into a film called *Smooth Talk* (Spectra Films, 1986). The essay in *The New York Times* in which Oates discusses the film is reprinted in a volume of her essays entitled (*Woman*)*Writer*, and reprinted in our text.

TOPICS FOR CRITICAL THINKING AND WRITING

1. Characterize Connie. Do you think the early characterization of Connie prepares us for her later behavior?
2. Is Arnold Friend clairvoyant—definitely, definitely not, maybe? Explain.
3. Evaluate the view that Arnold Friend is both Satan and the incarnation of Connie's erotic desires.
4. What do you make of the fact that Oates dedicated the story to Bob Dylan? Is she perhaps contrasting Dylan's music with the escapist (or in some other way unwholesome) music of other popular singers?
5. If you have read Flannery O'Connor's "A Good Man is Hard to Find" (text), compare and contrast Arnold Friend and the Misfit.

TONI CADE BAMBARA

The Lesson (p. 377)

It would be hard to find a less strident or more delightful story preaching revolution. At its heart, "The Lesson" calls attention to the enormous inequity in the distribution of wealth in America, and it suggests that black people ought to start thinking about "what kind of society it is in which some people can spend on a toy what it would cost to feed a family of six or seven" for a year. That the young narrator does not quite get the point of Miss Moore's lesson—and indeed steals Miss Moore's money—is no sure sign that the lesson has failed. (Presumably, Miss Moore doesn't much care about the loss of her money; the money is well lost if it helps the narrator, who plans to spend it, to see the power of money.) In any case, the narrator has been made sufficiently uneasy ("I sure want to punch somebody in the mouth") so that we sense she will later get the point: "I'm goin. . . to think this day through." The last line of the story seems to refer to her race to a bakery, but it has larger implications: "Ain't nobody gonna beat me at nuthin."

The difference between Sylvia's response and Sugar's response to Miss Moore's lesson is worth discussing in class. As Malcolm Clark, of Solano Community College, puts it, "The obvious question of the story is, 'What is the lesson?... It's clear that Miss Moore is trying to teach these children a lesson in economic inequity.... Sugar learns this lesson, as her comments to Miss Moore indicate. However, Sylvia has also learned this lesson, though she does not reveal her understanding to Miss Moore." As Clark goes on to point out, Miss Moore's lesson is not simply that some people are rich and others are not. She wants to bring the children to a state where they will demand their share of the pie.

> And it is in learning this part of the lesson that Sylvia and Sugar part company. Despite Sugar's obvious understanding of the lesson and her momentary flash of anger— strong enough to make her push Sylvia away— her condition is only temporary.
>
> At the end of the story she is unchanged from the little girl she was at the beginning. It is she who wants to go to Hascomb's bakery and spend the money on food, essentially the same thing they intended to do with the money before the lesson began.... Sylvia, however, is greatly changed. She does not intend to spend the money with Sugar; instead, she plans to go over to the river and reflect upon the lesson further.

Students always enjoy reading and discussing "The Lesson," and thus are grateful when told of other books by Bambara they might read: *Gorilla My Love* (short stories, including "The Lesson," 1972); *The Sea Birds Are Still Alive: Collected Stories* (1977); and *The Salt Eaters* (a novel, 1980).

We often use the occasion of teaching "The Lesson" to highlight for students the prominent place today of African-American women writers, including Bambara, Alice Walker, Gloria Naylor, Toni Morrison, and Terry McMillan. For background and critical discussion, students might turn to: *Sturdy Black Bridges: Visions of Black Women in Literature*, ed. Bettye J. Parker and Beverly Guy-Sheftall (1979); *Black Women Writers at Work*, ed. Claudia Tate (1983); *Black Women Writers, 1950-1980: A Critical Evaluation*, ed. Mari Evans (1984); and *Dictionary of Literary Biography: Afro-American Writers Since 1955*, ed. Trudier Harris and Thadious Davis (1985).

TOPICS FOR CRITICAL THINKING AND WRITING

1. In a paragraph or two, characterize the narrator.
2. Let's suppose Bambara had decided to tell the story through the eyes of Miss Moore. Write the first 250 words of such a story.
3. What is the point of Miss Moore's lesson? Why does Sylvia resist it?
4. Describe the relationship between Sugar and Sylvia. What is Sugar's function in the story?
5. Miss Moore says, "Imagine for a minute what kind of society it is in which some people can spend on a toy what it would cost to feed a family of six or seven. What do you think?" In an essay of 500 words, tell a reader what you think about this issue.

MARGARET ATWOOD

Rape Fantasies (p. 383)

Responses to this story will vary, of course—from the view that rape is not a fit subject for humor, or that the story is not at all humorous, to the view that the story is humorous and a great deal more. In any case, most readers find amusing the would-be rapist whose zipper gets stuck, and the would-be rapist who talks funny because he has a cold. It's worth asking those who find the story funny *why* they think it is funny. Among the points that probably will come up are these:

1. The rapists whom Estelle describes are all—as she describes them—weak and unthreatening; in fact, none of the fantasies ends with rape. (Again, one thinks of the man whose zipper is stuck, and of the man who has a bad cold; earlier in the story there is the man who politely holds the junk from her bag until she finds the plastic lemon with which to squirt him.)
2. The rapists are not only unthreatening; they are also in varying degrees sympathetic and pathetic. The last of them, for instance, is imagined as having leukemia.
3. They are sympathetic—that is, we regard them with some sympathy—because the narrator regards them thus. Of course, in fiction the reader does not always see things the way the narrator does, but in this story, where the narrator is frankly inventing stories (fantasies), and is not an innocent eye recounting what the reader is supposed to take to be a real event, the narrator is rather like an author, that is, is an inventor of stories, and probably we do in large measure regard her fantasies the way in which she regards them. And since she is a decent person—superficially tough, but fundamentally kind—we don't have a great deal of trouble accepting her point of view. Her fantasies chiefly describe scenes not of violence but of vulnerability and, in response to this awareness of vulnerability, a sense of fellowship and support.
4. Another reason that the story is not fundamentally disturbing, despite the title, is that the rape fantasies of Estelle's friends (at the beginning of the story) are not, as Estelle sharply points out, rape fantasies. "I mean, you aren't getting *raped*, it's just some guy you haven't met formally."

Under the apparently playful story of fantasies that reveal human kinship, is there, however, a darker story? Is the narrator talking to a man, and, if so, are we to assume that this man may later rape her, or at least try to rape her?

The sexual identity of the hearer is never clearly established. Some students focus on two passages that, they say, sound as though Estelle must be talking to a man. The first occurs two-thirds through the story:

> I'm telling you, I was really lonely when I first came here; I thought it was going to be such a big adventure and all, but it's a lot harder to meet people in a city. But I guess it's different for a guy.

The second occurs in the fourth paragraph from the end:

> But maybe it's different for a guy.

These two passages, in which Estelle conjectures that men may hold a different view, are sometimes taken to indicate that Estelle is chatting with a man and is in some degree sounding him out. Other readers disagree. It's worth asking a student to read the passages aloud in class, and then discussing them.

The sex of the auditor is a matter of importance if, as some readers suggest, we are to understand that the rape fantasies may be replaced by a real rape, or at least by an attempted rape. For these readers, the story is essentially ironic; Estelle is chatting away about rape fantasies that are, first, amusing, and, second, rather sad in that they reveal pitiful creatures, but we are given clues that her auditor will seek to rape her. To say that we are given clues, however, is to overstate the matter. The evidence adduced is (1) the passages already indicated which are said to suggest that the listener is a male, and (2) the next-to-last paragraph, which begins thus:

> The funny thing about these fantasies is that the man is always someone I don't know, and the statistics in the magazines, well, most of them anyway, they say it's often someone you do know, at least a little bit.

Toward the end of this paragraph Estelle says

> I don't know why I'm telling you all this, except I think it helps you get to know a person, especially at first, hearing some of the things they think about. At work they call me the office worry wart, but it isn't so much worrying, it's more like figuring out what you should do in an emergency, like I said before.

Are we being told that Estelle will soon find herself confronted by an "emergency?" None of the passages already quoted will convince a skeptic that the story is about an attempt at rape that takes place after the last sentence of the story, but there can be no doubt that the exuberant comedy of the rape fantasies is no longer present in the last two paragraphs.

Atwood and Alice Munro are Canadian, and when teaching their stories, we have often noted for students the range and high quality of Canadian writers—e.g., the literary critic Northrop Frye; the poets Irving Layton and Jay MacPherson; the novelist Robertson Davies; the novelist Joy Kogawa, author of *Obasan* (1981), which describes the internment of Canadians of Japanese ancestry during World War II; and the poet and novelist Michael Ondaatje, author of the prize-winning novel *The English Patient* (1992). Canadians have produced a body of work that many students know little about. Atwood's best novels include *Surfacing* (1972), *Lady Oracle* (1976), and *The Handmaid's Tale* (1985).

TOPICS FOR CRITICIAL THINKING AND WRITING

1. In the next-to-last paragraph we learn that the narrator is speaking to someone in a bar, but we don't know—at least not for sure—the sex of the listener. Do you assume the listener is a man? If so, why do you make this assump-

tion, and does it color your view of the narrator?

2. Do you assume that the fantasies reported by the narrator's friends are indeed their fantasies, or are these reports inventions meant to interest the listener?

3. Did you find the story, or at least parts of it, funny? If so, what is funny, and why?

BOBBIE ANNE MASON

Shiloh (p. 390)

Writers in all periods have occasionally used the historical present in telling stories (Katherine Anne Porter, for example, used it for "Flowering Judas"), but in America in our century—until the early 1970s—few storytellers used it, except for melodramatic historians eager to convey a sense of immediacy: "The German armies march into Paris...." At first glance it seems that Updike uses the present in "A & P," a story whose opening line is this: "In walks these three girls in nothing but bathing suits " But Updike uses a first person narrator, who occasionally talks in a sort of "So he says to me... and I says to him" manner.

Exactly why so many writers in the 1970s and 1980s used the present tense (Mason wrote her story in 1982) is not clear, but some explanations attribute its widespread use to television, film, the new journalism, and drugs. But what sort of useful generalization can one make about the effect of this device? Usually it is said that the present adds realism and immediacy, but such an assertion is dubious.

Still, it seems true that contemporary writers who narrate in the present usually write in what can be called a plain style; i.e., they use (for instance) little subordination, few words with strong connotations, and few figures of speech. (In fact, in "Shiloh" Mason uses more figures than are commonly found in fiction of its type.) Such writing often seems "flat," lacking in energy, free from value judgments, uninvolved. Sample:

> When Leroy gets home from the shopping center, Norma Jean's mother, Mabel Beasley, is there. Until this year, Leroy has not realized how much time she spends with Norma Jean. When she visits, she inspects the closets and then the plants, informing Norma Jean when a plant is droopy or yellow. Mabel calls the plants "flowers," although there are never any blooms. She always notices if Norma Jean's laundry is piling up.

The narrator is just reporting on what passes before his or her eyes, not responding or evaluating. In "Shiloh," after the first surprising sentence ("Norma Jean is working on her pectorals"), almost no sentence seems to have been written to give the reader a special little thrill. But this is only to say that Mason writes the story in an appropriate style, since the story is about confused, almost numbed people, people whose lives (like their child) seem to have died, people who can't make out who they are, what they are, or even where they are:

Now that Leroy has come home to stay, he notices how much the town has changed. Subdivisions are spreading across western Kentucky like an oil slick. The sign at the edge of town says "Pop: 11,500"—only seven hundred more than it said twenty years before. Leroy can't figure out who is living in all the new houses. The farmers who used to gather around the courthouse square on Saturday afternoons to play checkers and spit tobacco juice have gone. It has been years since Leroy has thought about the farmers, and they have disappeared without his noticing.

Perhaps when storytellers customarily used the past tense they were (to some degree) implying that something had happened, was over and done with, and they were reporting on it because they thought they had made something out of it; further, they thought that what had happened and what they had made out of it were worth reporting. Perhaps when writers use the present tense they are (to some degree) implying that "such-and-such is passing in front of my eyes, I'm telling you about it, but I am not able to interpret it any more than the participants themselves are able to." In any case, "Shiloh" is obviously a story about a man and wife who don't know what to make of each other or of themselves. Leroy has his kits and his hope of building a real log cabin, and Norma Jean has her weights, her music, her cooking, and her English composition course, but none of these things provides a center. There was once a marriage, and there was once a baby, but the baby died and the marriage has fallen apart. This is not at all the world that existed when Leroy and Norma Jean got married; it's a new world, a world in which women engage in weight-lifting, men engage in needlepoint, and a doctor's son pushes dope. It's all very confusing, especially to Leroy.

Mabel, Norma Jean's mother, thinks things can be as they were in the past (Norma Jean should be a dutiful daughter and not smoke, Leroy and Norma Jean should go on a second honeymoon—to Shiloh, where Mabel went on her honeymoon), but of course there is no going back to the way things were. The trip to Shiloh proves to be a disaster. Norma Jean walks away from Leroy, leaving him to realize that he doesn't understand his wife, himself, or their marriage. He remembers some events, but

> he knows he is leaving out a lot. He is leaving out the insides of history. History was always just names and dates to him. It occurs to him that building a house out of logs is similarly empty—too simple.

Early in the story, when we first hear about Leroy's interest in kits, we are told that "Leroy has grown to appreciate how things are put together" (that's the way he sees it, of course), but at the end of the story we see that he has no idea of how the pieces of his life can be put together.

A few words about the names "Leroy" and "Norma Jean." Some readers suggest that Leroy (French for "the king") puts us in mind of Elvis Presley. Further, they say, the name evokes an image of a romantic knight errant, now reduced to a maimed man who does needlepoint of a scene from *Star Trek* while his truck rusts. Norma Jean of course evokes Marilyn Monroe.

For Mabel, Shiloh has the pleasant associations of a honeymoon, and she thinks that the happiness she experienced at Shiloh can now be transferred to

Leroy and Norma Jean. But Shiloh, though now a site for picnics, was a scene of vast destruction, and it is at Shiloh that Leroy sees that his marriage has come apart.

(The Battle of Shiloh took its name from Shiloh Church, a meeting house at the site. The church was named for the ancient Hebrew sanctuary about ten miles north of Bethel. It is thought that the word means "tranquility," so the name adds irony to the story.)

We admire Mason's novels, *In Country* (1985) and *Spence and Lila* (1988), but value her short stories, in *Shiloh and Other Stories* (1982) and *Love Life: Stories* (1989), even more. For studies of "Shiloh": Leslie White, "The Function of Popular Culture in Bobbie Ann Mason's *Shiloh and Other Stories* and *In Country*," *Southern Quarterly* 26 (Summer 1988), 69-79; and Barbara Henning, "Minimalism and the American Dream: 'Shiloh' by Bobbie Ann Mason and 'Preservation' by Raymond Carver," *Modern Fiction Studies* 35 (Winter 1989), 689-98.

TOPICS FOR CRITICAL THINKING AND WRITING

1. Whose feelings—Leroy's or Norma Jean's—are more fully presented in the story? Do we know exactly what Norma Jean wants? Do you think that she herself knows?
2. The story is written in the present tense, for instance, "Leroy Moffitt's wife, Norma Jean, is working on her pectorals," rather than (as would be more common in fiction) "... was working on her pectorals." What is gained by using the present in this story?
3. Why is Leroy preoccupied with kits, and why is Norma Jean so eagerly attempting to improve her body and her mini?
4. When we first meet Mabel, Norma Jean's mother, we learn that she has made "an off-white dust ruffle for the bed." Leroy jokes about it, and Mason refers to it in the last line of the story, a place of great emphasis. Why this business about a dust ruffle for a bed?
5. Why does Norma Jean leave Leroy?
6. Do you think "Shiloh" is a good title? Why?

ANNE TYLER

The Artificial Family (p. 510)

It's striking that when Toby first meets Mary, he is so smitten by her that he "clutch[es] the scrap of paper in his pocket" on which she has written her address, "for fear of losing it." The main "artificial family" in this story is, of course, the one that consists of Toby, Mary, and her daughter Samantha. But there's a second family, too, that we learn a little about along the way, the family includes Toby and his parents, the Scotts. They disapprove of Toby's marriage, and speak in irritating ways about Samantha (whom Toby loves and showers with affection) because they cannot imagine he could ever really love as his own a child from Mary's first marriage. It's conceivable that Toby's powerful, and somewhat over-zealous, devotion to his new family derives from the limited relationship he knew with his parents. That one is more real on one level, but ultimately is also "artificial" or least inadequate, not really authentic in its bonds.

Students, understandably, tend to be judgmental toward this story's characters. Some of them find Toby to be a decent young man struggling to hold on to persons whom he loves, whereas others conclude he is too possessive and is insensitive toward Mary, not seeing that Samantha is more her child than his. Mary, too, has both critics and defenders: is she detached and cruel, or is she someone who insists on her freedom, who moves away when she feels unduly controlled?

There's nothing wrong with basing the discussion of Tyler's story on these competing assessments. But it's a good idea to keep returning to specific details in the language, so that the students remember that their judgments must follow from the organization of the words on the page. Tyler is a witty, clever, savvy writer, as when at the outset she notes that Mary and Samantha looked like "they might have been about to climb onto a covered wagon"—a phrase that makes its comic point about their appearance and yet that also prophesies the ending of the story, when mother and child, always on the move, travel away from Toby. Lots of other details do their suggestive work well, too, such as the "cold water" that Mary uses to clean the potatoes, which concretely enforces the sense of fading affection and cool distance between her and Toby.

Students might be directed to Tyler's *Dinner at the Homesick Restaurant* (1983) and *The Accidental Tourist* (1985). We recommend: Joseph C. Voelker, *Art and the Accidental in Anne Tyler* (1989); and Alice Hall Petry, *Understanding Anne Tyler* (1990). For Tyler on her craft, see "Still Just Writing," in *The Writer on Her Work: Contemporary Women Reflect on Their Art and Situation*, ed. Janet Sternburg (1980), 3-16.

LILIANA HEKER

The Stolen Party (p. 405)

This short, easy story can be effectively taught early in the semester; it can even be used as a sort of textbook model to illustrate principles of irony, foreshadowing, character, plot, conflict, and symbolism.

The story begins with a conflict between the mother and the daughter; the mother proves to be right (not about the monkey but about a more important matter, the way in which rich people perceive their servants), but the point of the story is neither to vindicate the mother nor to emphasize the opposition between mother and daughter. Midway in the story we are sure that the mother in fact is fond and proud of her daughter, and by the end we find ourselves responding very sympathetically to the mother.

Señora Ines bothers some of the students, who say that she snobbishly puts Rosaura in her place. But one may doubt that there is any malice, and one may even argue that Señora Ines is courteous, charming, and sincere. She just can't help thinking of Rosaura as part of "the help." It is not surprising that Señora Ines offers Rosaura money; probably she is right in assuming that the family can use a little extra cash. True, a more imaginative woman might at the outset have understood that the child would like a gift comparable to (or better than!) the gifts given to the other children, whereas Señora Ines comes to that understanding only when Rosaura's arms stiffen. Still, Señora Ines *does* come to this understanding; a less intelligent or less sympathetic person would not have understood or even noticed the child's response. Señora Ines is guilty, then, of a lack of insight, a lack of sympathetic imagination that would take her beyond social distinctions, but nothing in the story suggests that she is not well-intentioned.

What of Señora Ines's evaluations of Rosaura, such as "What a marvelous daughter you have, Herminia," and "You really and truly earned this"? Of course, having seen Rosaura carry a jug of juice, and serve cake, Señora Ines is impressed with Rosaura as a domestic servant, but Rosaura had won Señora Ines's praise even before performing these tasks: "How lovely you look today, Rosaura." And if Señora Ines allows Rosaura to enter the kitchen, where the monkey is, we can conjecture that permission is granted not just for one reason but for two reasons: Rosaura, as "the daughter of the employee," is familiar with the kitchen, but second, Rosaura *is* (as Señora Ines says) better behaved than the "boisterous" children. Rosaura's superior nature soon is confirmed when she is contrasted with the fat boy who drops the monkey. Presumably her virtues are evident to all—except to the snobbish girl with the bow.

The point of these remarks is this: although Señora Ines destroys the day by offering Rosaura money—i.e., by revealing that Rosaura doesn't quite belong among the guests—she need not be thought of as cruel or even as stupid. She seems to us to be a person of intelligence and good will, but she cannot quite go beyond the way persons of her class think.

What is a reader to make out of the comment that Rosaura "had always loved. . . having power of life or death?" This remark, which might surprise some readers, might well characterize a wicked queen in a fairy tale. Still, readers do not judge her severely; despite the unexpected revelation, Rosaura remains attractive. Or, possibly, there is nothing at all sinister in the remark. It might characterize a precocious child, already better educated than her mother, who smarts at her mother's position, language, and distrust of the people whom the child loves and seeks to emulate (the people "who live in the big house"). That is, in this view it is both psychologically and politically sound for her to wish for power—and indeed she is a forceful figure, the winner of the sack race and a person whom the boys want on their side.

TOPICS FOR CRITICAL THINKING AND WRITING

1. The first paragraph tells us, correctly, that Rosaura's mother is wrong about the monkey. By the time the story is over, is the mother right about anything? If so, what?
2. Characterize Señora Ines. Why does she offer Rosaura money instead of a yo-yo or a bracelet? By the way, do you assume she is speaking deceptively when she tells Rosaura that she bars other children from the kitchen on the

grounds that "they might break something"? On what do you base your view?

3. What do you make of the last paragraph? Why does Señora Ines stand with her hand outstretched, "as if she didn't dare draw it back"? What "infinitely delicate balance" might be shattered?

ALICE WALKER

Everyday Use (p. 409)

The title of this story, like most other titles, is significant, though the significance appears only gradually. Its importance, of course, is not limited to the fact that Dee believes that Maggie will use the quilts for "everyday use"; on reflection we see the love, in daily use, between the narrator and Maggie, and we contrast it with Dee's visit—a special occurrence—as well as with Dee's idea that the quilts should not be put to everyday use. The real black achievement, then, is not the creation of works of art that are kept apart from daily life; rather, it is the everyday craftsmanship and the everyday love shared by people who cherish and sustain each other. That Dee stands apart from this achievement is clear (at least on rereading) from the first paragraph, and her pretensions are suggested as early as the fourth paragraph, where we are told that she thinks "orchids are tacky flowers." (Notice that in the fifth paragraph, when the narrator is imagining herself as Dee would like her to be on a television show, she has glistening hair—presumably because the hair has been straightened—and she appears thinner and lighter-skinned than in fact she is.) Her lack of any real connection with her heritage is made explicit (even before the nonsense about using the churn top as a centerpiece) as early as the paragraph in which she asks if Uncle Buddy whittled the dasher, and Maggie quietly says that Henry whittled it. Still, Dee is confident that she can "think of something artistic to do with the dasher." Soon we learn that she sees the quilts not as useful objects, but only as decorative works; Maggie, on the other hand, will use the quilts, and she even knows how to make them. Dee talks about black "heritage" but Maggie and the narrator embody this heritage and they experience a degree of contentment that eludes Dee.

Many white students today are scarcely aware of the Black Muslim movement, which was especially important in the 1960s, and they therefore pass over the Muslim names taken by Dee and her companion, the reference to pork (not to be eaten by Muslims), and so on. That is, they miss the fact that Walker is suggesting that the valuable heritage of American blacks is not to be dropped in favor of an attempt to adopt an essentially remote heritage. It is worth asking students to do a little work in the library and to report on the Black Muslim movement.

Houston A. Baker, Jr. and Charlotte Pierce-Baker discuss the story in *Southern Review* (new series 21 [Summer 1985]), in an issue that was later published as a book with the title *Afro-American Writing Today*, ed. James Olney (1989). Their essay is worth reading, but it is rather overheated. Sample:

> Maggie is the arisen goddess of Walker's story; she is the sacred figure who bears the scarifications of experience and knows how to convert patches into robustly patterned and beautifully quilted wholes. As an earth-rooted and quotidian goddess, she stands in dramatic contrast to the stylishly fiery and other-oriented Wangero. (131)

The essay is especially valuable, however, because it reproduces several photographs (in black and white only, unfortunately) of quilts and their makers. Lots of books on American folk art have better reproductions of quilts, but few show the works with the artists who made them. It's worth bringing to class some pictures of quilts, whether from the essay by the Bakers or from another source. Even better, of course, is (if possible) to bring some quilts to class.

Walker is best known for *The Color Purple* (1982), but her non-fiction, collected in *In Search of Our Mother's Gardens: Womanist Prose* (1983) and *Living by the Word: Selected Writings. 1973-1987* (1988), has also proven influential.

For secondary sources: Barbara Christian, *Black Women Novelists: The Development of a Tradition. 1892-1976* (1980); and Elliott Butler-Evans, *Race, Gender, and Desire: Narrative Strategies in the Fiction of Toni Cade Bambara, Toni Morrison, and Alice Walker* (1989).

TOPICS FOR CRITICAL THINKING AND WRITING

1. "Everyday Use" is by a black woman. Would your response to the story be the same if you knew it were written by a white woman? Or by a man? Explain.
2. How does the narrator's dream about her appearance on the television program foreshadow the later conflict?
3. Compare "Everyday Use" with Bambara's "The Lesson." Consider the following suggestions: Characterize the narrator of each story and compare them. Compare the settings and how they function in each story. What is Miss Moore trying to teach the children in "The Lesson?" Why does Sylvia resist learning it? In "Everyday Use," what does Dee try to teach her mother and sister? Why do they resist her lesson? How are objects (such as quilts, toys) used in each story? How in each story does the first-person narration enlist and direct our sympathies?

TOBIAS WOLFF

Powder (p. 416)

The first paragraph provides the necessary background: the parents are separated, the mother is sensible, and the father is irresponsible—but even at this stage one may wonder if perhaps there isn't something especially engaging about a father who sneaks his young son into a nightclub in order to see Thelonious Monk.

The father's irresponsibility is underlined in the second paragraph. He promised to get the boy home to the mother for Christmas Eve dinner, but "he observed some quality [in the snow] that made it necessary for us to get in one last run. We got in several last runs." The father tries to be reassuring at the diner, but the boy, a worrier, is distressed. He's a strange kid, as he himself knows, someone who bothers "teachers for homework assignments far ahead of their due dates" so he can make up schedules. But with a father like his, and a mother who clearly is not sympathetic to the father's adventurous (or child-ish?) enthusiasms, who can blame the boy? And though the boy in his orderli-ness is his mother's son, the last paragraph of the story validates the father. Although the father is "bankrupt of honor," the ride (or the boy's experience of the ride) is something so special that it is "impossible to describe. Except maybe to say this: if you haven't driven fresh powder, you haven't driven."

One detail may escape some readers: When the father makes a phone call from the diner, the boy quite reasonably thinks the father must be calling the mother, but this man-child in fact is calling the police, with some sort of bull that causes the officer to drive away and thus gives the father a chance to put aside the barrier and to drive home. The evidence? After making the call, the father stares through the window, down the road, and says, "Come on, come on." (He is impatiently waiting for the result of his call.) As soon as the trooper's car passes the window, the father hurries the boy out of the diner. When the boy asks the father where the policeman may have gone, the father ignores the question.

"Bankrupt of honor," yes, and one can easily imagine the impossibility of being married to such a man. But the father desperately wants to keep the fam-ily intact, and he wants to get the boy home for dinner with the mother in an effort to buy "a little more time," though we are not surprised to learn that the mother decides "to make the split final."

TOPICS FOR CRITICAL THINKING AND WRITING
How does the boy feel about his father? (Our own brief answer: He distrusts him—but he also enjoys and admires the father, even to the point of hero-wor-ship for his father as a driver.)

TIM O'BRIEN

The Things They Carried (p. 419)

A few words should be said about the movement away from the highly anec-dotal story of, say, the Middle Ages and even of the late nineteenth century (e.g., Maupassant)—a movement toward what has been called the lyric style of, say, Chekhov and Joyce.

Most stories, even those of the twentieth century, retain something of the anecdotal plot, a fairly strong element of conflict and reversal. Howard Nemerov offers a satirical summary in *Poetry and Fiction* (1963):

Short stories amount for the most part to parlor tricks, party favors with built-in snap-pers, gadgets for inducing recognitions and reversals; a small pump serves to build up the pressure, a tiny trigger releases it, there follows a puff and a flash as freedom and necessity combine; finally a celluloid doll drops from the muzzle and descends by parachute to the floor. These things happen, but they happen to no one in particular.

Some writers, however, have all but eliminated plot, and it's not unusual for twentieth-century writers of stories to disparage narrative (especially the novel) and to claim some affinity with poets. As we point out in our discussion of "Guests of the Nation," Frank O'Connor, in an interview in *Paris Review* (reprinted in *Writers at Work*, edited by Malcolm Cowley), said that the short story was his favorite form

> because it's the nearest thing I know to lyric poetry—I wrote lyric poetry for a long time, then discovered that God had not intended me to be a lyric poet, and the nearest thing to that is the short story. A novel actually requires far more logic and far more knowledge of circumstances, whereas a short story can have the sort of detachment from circumstances that lyric poetry has.

In his book on the short story, *The Lonely Voice*, O'Connor amplifies this point.

Faulkner makes pretty much the same point in another *Paris Review* interview that is reprinted in the same collection. Faulkner says:

> I'm a failed poet. Maybe every novelist wants to write poetry first, finds he can't, and then tries the short story, which is the most demanding form after poetry. And failing at that, only then does he take up novel writing.

Doubtless, Faulkner is being at least somewhat facetious, but we can't quite dismiss his implication that the short story is allied to the poem—by which he must mean the lyric.

If the course is being taught chronologically, students probably have already encountered Chekhov, Joyce, and Hemingway; if, for instance, they have read "Araby" they have read a story in which (many of them think) "nothing happens." In the "lyric story" (if there is such a species) the emphasis is not on telling about a change of fortune, marked by a decisive ending, but rather is on conveying (and perhaps inducing in the reader) an emotion—perhaps the emotion of the narrator. There is very little emphasis on plot, that is, on "What happened next?" (Chekhov said, "I think that when one has finished writing a short story one should delete the beginning and the end"), though of course there is a good deal of interest in the subtle changes or modulations of the emotion.

Certainly in "The Things They Carried"—a story set in a combat zone—there is none of the suspense and catastrophic action that one would expect in a war story of the nineteenth century, say a story by Ambrose Bierce or Stephen Crane. In "The Things They Carried" we learn fairly early that Ted Lavender got killed; because no one else gets killed, an inexperienced reader may conclude that nothing much happens in the story.

Of course, as far as plot is concerned, what "happens" is that Lieutenant Cross, feeling that his thoughts of Martha have led him to relax discipline with the result that one of his men has been killed, determines to pay attention to his job as a military leader, and he therefore burns Martha's letters and photographs. But this narrative could scarcely sustain a story of this length; or, to put it another way, if that's what the story is about, much of the story seems irrelevant.

Even inexperienced readers usually see that "The Things They Carried" is not to be judged on its plot, any more than is (say) "Born in the U.S.A." If some passages are read aloud in class, even the least-experienced readers—who may miss almost all of the subtleties when they read the story by themselves—will see and hear that O'Brien interestingly varies "the things they carried," from physical objects (chewing gum, and the latest gear for killing) to thoughts and emotions. In short, he uses verbal repetition (which creates rhythm) and metaphor to a degree rarely if ever found in the novel.

Not least of " the things they carried" are themselves and their minds. "For the most part they carried themselves with poise, a kind of dignity." "For the most part" is important. O'Brien doesn't sentimentalize the soldiers; they can be afraid and they can be wantonly destructive. He tells us, fairly late in the story, that "They shot chickens and dogs, they trashed the village well." He tells us, too, that "They carried the soldier's greatest fear, which was a fear of blushing." "They carried all the emotional baggage of men who might die." "They carried shameful memories." This insistent repetition, rather like the incremental repetition in the old popular ballads (e.g., "Edward," "Lord Randall," "Barbara Allen"), serves less to record a sequence of events than to deepen our understanding of a state of mind.

Still, there is, as has already been said, something of the traditional narrative here: Lieutenant Cross at last does something overt (burns Martha's letters and photographs). He thus "carries" less, literally, since the first line of the story is "First Lieutenant Jimmy Cross carried letters from a girl named Martha." Whether by burning the letters and photos he will in fact lighten his load—his guilt—is something about which readers may have different opinions. He may indeed impose stricter discipline, but it's hard to imagine that he will think less of Ted Lavender. Cross himself seems skeptical. "Lavender was dead. You couldn't burn the blame." One may lighten one's load by shooting off fingers and toes, and thus gain release from combat, and one can dream of flying away ("the weights fell off; there was nothing to bear"), but a reader may doubt that when Cross lightens his physical load he will find that the weights will fall off, and that he will have nothing, or only a little, to bear. He will still be a participant in a war where "men killed and died, because they were embarrassed not to." One may wonder, too, if Cross will be able to forget about Martha, or, so to speak, to keep her in her place. He thinks he will be able to do so, but the matter is left unresolved:

> Henceforth, when he thought about Martha, it would be only to think that she belonged elsewhere. He would shutdown the daydreams This was not Mount Sebastian, it was another world, where there were no pretty poems or midterm exams, a place where men died because of carelessness and gross stupidity. Kiowa was right. Boom-down, and you were dead, never partly dead.

This quotation, however, raises yet another question, and perhaps a central question if one takes the story to be about Cross rather than about the soldiers as a group. Cross here seems to assume that death comes only to those who are careless or stupid. He thinks, presumably, that it is his job as an officer to prevent the carelessness and the stupidity of his men from getting them killed. But of course we know that in war even the careful and the bright may get killed. Further, nothing in the story tells us that Lavender was careless or stupid. He was killed while urinating, but even the careful and the bright must urinate. We are told that he was shot in the head, and perhaps we are to understand that, contrary to standard operating procedure, he was not wearing his helmet, but the point is not emphasized. When we first hear of Lavender's death we are told that Cross "felt the pain" and that "he blamed himself," although the reader does not know exactly why the lieutenant is blameworthy. Later perhaps a reader concludes (though again, this is not made explicit) that it was Cross's job to insist that the men wear their helmets. In any case, the reader is probably much easier on Cross than Cross is on himself.

To the extent that the story is about Cross's isolation—and, as Kiowa knows, Cross is isolated—it fits Frank O'Connor's remark (in *The Lonely Voice*) that a short story is "by its very nature remote from the community—romantic, individualistic, and intransigent." But, to repeat, it's probably fair to say that O'Brien is as much concerned with celebrating the state of mind of all the "legs or grunts" as he is with recording the sequence of actions that constitutes Lieutenant Cross's attempts to deal with his sense of guilt.

This story has been reprinted in a book called *The Things They Carried*, where it is one of twenty-two related but discontinuous pieces ranging from 2 to 20 pages. The book is dedicated to "the men of Alpha Company," and the names in the dedication correspond to the names in the stories. Further, in the book the narrator identifies himself as Tim O'Brien. A question thus arises: Is *The Things They Carried* a collection of stories, or is it biography, history, or whatever? Perhaps one's first thought, given the dedication and the name of the narrator, is that the book reports what O'Brien experienced—and yet in an interview in *Publisher's Weekly* O'Brien said, "My own experience has virtually nothing to do with the content of the book." He claims he used his own name for that of the narrator merely because he thought it would be "neat." (In another interview, he said the use of his own name was "just one more literary device.") If we believe what he told the interviewer, the book is fiction. But perhaps O'Brien is toying with the interviewer. Or perhaps he is behaving in accordance with a point made in the book: "In war you lose your sense of the definite, hence your sense of truth itself, and therefore it's safe to say that in a true war story nothing is ever absolutely true." Has O'Brien been infected by the "fact-or-fiction?" game of much recent writing? If so, should someone tell him that what we value in his writing is his ability to bring the Vietnam War home to us, rather than his philosophizing?

TOPICS FOR CRITICAL THINKING AND WRITING

1. What is the point of the insistent repetition of the words "the things the-carried?" What sorts of things does Lieutenant Cross carry?
2. We are told that "Kiowa admired Lieutenant Cross's capacity for grief." But

we are also told that although Kiowa "wanted to share the other man's pain," he could think only of "Boom-down" and of "the pleasure of having his boots off and the fog curling in around him and the damp soil and the Bible smells and the plush comfort of night." What might account for the different responses of the two men?

3. Near the end of the story, Lieutenant Cross "burned the two photographs." Why does he do this?

LESLIE MARMON SILKO

The Man to Send Rain Clouds (p. 432)

The church—especially perhaps the Roman Catholic Church—has often adapted itself to the old ways and beliefs of new converts, sometimes by retaining the old holidays and holy places but adapting them and dedicating them to the new religion. For instance, although the date of birth of Jesus is not known, from the fourth century it was celebrated late in December, displacing pagan festivals of new birth (e.g., the Roman Saturnalia, which celebrated the sowing of the crops on December 15-17, and the feast of the *Natalis Solis Invicti,* celebrating the renewal of the sun a week later).

Practices of this sort have facilitated conversion, but from the church's point of view the danger may be that the new believers retain too much faith in the old beliefs. In Silko's story the priest has every reason to doubt that his parishioners have fully accepted Christianity. The unnamed priest—he's just "the priest" or "the young priest," not anyone with a personal identity, so far as the other characters in the story are concerned—is kind and well-meaning, and he is even willing to bend the rules a bit, but he knows that he does not have the confidence of the people. He is disturbed that they didn't think the Last Rites and a funeral Mass were necessary, and he is not at all certain that they have given up their pagan ways: "He looked at the red blanket, not sure that Teofilo was so small, wondering if it wasn't some perverse Indian trick—something they did in March to ensure a good harvest. . . ." He is wrong in suspecting that Teofilo (the name means "beloved of God," from the Greek *theos* = God, and *philos* = loving) is not in front of him, but he is right in suspecting that a "trick" is being played, since the reader knows that the holy water is wanted not to assist Teofilo to get to the Christian heaven but to bring rain for the crops. In Part One we hear Leon say, "Send us rain clouds, Grandfather"; in Part Three we hear Louise express the hope that the priest will sprinkle water so Teofilo "won't be thirsty"; and at the very end of the story we hear that Leon "felt good because it was finished, and he was happy about the sprinkling of the holy water; now the old man could send them big thunderclouds for sure."

We aren't quite sure about what to make of the passage in which the water, disappearing as soon as it is sprinkled on the grave, "reminded" the priest of something, but the passage is given some emphasis and surely it is important. Our sense is that the priest vaguely intuits an archetypal mystery, something older and more inclusive than the Roman Catholic ritual he engages in.

During most of the story the narrator neither editorializes nor enters the minds of the characters; we are not told that the characters are reverential, and (for the most part) we are not allowed to hear their thoughts. Rather, we see them perform ceremonies with dignity, and, because the point of view is chiefly objective, we draw our own conclusions. Possibly, too, by keeping outside of the minds of the characters the narrator helps to convey the traditional paleface idea that Native Americans are inscrutable people, people of few words. Certainly Leon hoards words when, responding to the priest's admonition not to let Teofilo stay at the sheep camp alone, he says, "No, he won't do that any more now." But we do get into the priest's mind, notably in the passage in which he suspects trickery, and we get into Leon's mind at the end of the story when, in what almost seems like a thunderstorm of information, we are told his thoughts about the water.

Because the narrator, like the characters, is taciturn, some readers may think that Leon and his companions are callous. "After all," one student said, "don't they first round up the sheep before attending to the burial rites? And why don't they weep?" Class discussion can usually bring out the dignity of the proceedings here, and some students may be able to provide specific details about burial customs unfamiliar to other members of the class.

We do not know if the different colors of paint—white, blue, yellow, and green—have specific meanings, but perhaps blue suggests the sky and the water, yellow suggests corn meal, and green suggests vegetation. White is a fairly widespread sign of purity, but we have not been able to find out how Pueblo people regard it. (If you know about these things, we'll be most appreciative if you write to us, in care of the publisher.)

TOPICS FOR CRITICAL THINKING AND WRITING

1. How would you describe the responses of Leon, Ken, Louise, and Teresa to Teofilo's death? To what degree does it resemble or differ from responses to death that you are familiar with?
2. How do the funeral rites resemble or differ from those of your community?
3. How well does Leon understand the priest? How well does the priest understand Leon?
4. At the end of the story we are told that Leon "felt good." Do you assume that the priest also felt good? Why, or why not?
5. From what point of view is the story told? Mark the passages where the narrator enters a character's mind, and then explain what, in your opinion, Silko gains (or loses?) by doing so.

DIANA CHANG

The Oriental Contingent (p. 435)

The title comes from a remark in paragraph 15, when a voice—presumably belonging to Lisa's Caucasian husband—refers to the two Asian-American women as "the Oriental contingent." Is the remark offensive? The man sees two Asian-Americans together, and he (quite naturally?) sees them as a unit. The Asian-Americans, too, regard themselves (quite naturally?) as having something in common, although it turns out that Lisa, born in Buffalo, was not even brought up by Chinese parents.

It's hard to think of Lisa as Chinese in any significant way, other than that her biological parents were Chinese. And yet, of course, to Caucasians she will always be "Oriental," and when two people like Lisa are chatting they will (in Caucasian eyes) be "the Oriental contingent." And in their own eyes, too, they are not a hundred percent American; at one point Lisa thinks of her "American friends," and then remembers that she too is American. But if an American with Asian features, or, for that matter, with Indian features or black African features is in some degree an outsider to a Caucasian, such an individual is also in some degree—indeed, probably to a much greater degree—an outsider to persons with those features who were born in Asia, India, or Africa. Connie feels inferior to Lisa, who she mistakenly thinks is a more "authentic" Chinese than Connie, but it turns out that Lisa is so fearful of being insufficiently Chinese that she avoids visiting Asia.

One way to talk about the story is to talk about the degree to which any American—even someone from an Anglo background—feels an identity with some ethnic subgroup and therefore sees others as the Other. Of course the old idea was that all who came to the United States were turned into Americans, which more or less meant Anglos, or, let's say, Northern Europeans. America was a "melting pot," a term invented or at least popularized by Israel Zangwill in a play, *The Melting Pot* (1914): "America is God's crucible, the great Melting-Pot where all the races of Europe are melting and reforming." The idea was dominant in the late nineteenth century, and survived almost unchallenged into the middle of the twentieth century, but today the image of the melting pot has been replaced by other images, including "the salad bowl" and "the mosaic." These newer images emphasize the idea that each part retains its identity and also contributes to the whole. (You might ask students if they are familiar with other metaphors. In recent years we have noticed the occasional use of America as a kaleidoscope.)

Here are two relevant quotations:

Fortunately, the time has long passed when people liked to regard the United States as some kind of melting pot, taking men and women from every part of the world and converting them into standardized, homogenized Americans....Just as we welcome a world of diversity, so we glory in an America of diversity—an America all the richer for the many different and distinctive strands of which it is woven. (Hubert H. Humphrey, 1967)

And:

The crucial thing about the melting pot was that it did not happen: American politics and American social life are still dominated by the existence of sharply-defined ethnic groups. (Charles E. Silberman, 1964)

It would be easy to find many quotations in which African Americans call attention to their sense of having two identities as Americans, or call attention to the inadequacy of the image of the melting pot. Here is an example of each:

> One ever feels his twoness—an American, a Negro, two souls, two thoughts, two unreconciled strivings; two warring ideals in one dark body, whose dogged strength alone keeps it from being torn asunder. (W. E. B. Du Bois, 1903)

And:

> I hear that melting-pot stuff a lot, and all I can say is that we haven't melted. (Jesse Jackson, 1969)

Perhaps in class you may want to examine the following hasty generalizations. How much truth is in any of them?

1. It is probably true that, until some thirty years ago, most people who immigrated to this country wanted to enter the melting pot, i.e., wanted to put "the old country" behind them and to become "Americans."
2. Most African Americans, too, probably wanted to get into the pot, but they were excluded by whites.
3. Even immigrants who were or are eager to become 100% American probably retain a good deal of ethnic identity, perhaps unto the third and fourth generations (an idea implicit in Silberman's quotation).
4. Many recent immigrants emphasize their desire to retain their ethnic identity, but they too—or, rather, their children and grandchildren—will retain very little of the older generation's identity; they will, in fact, be like the Chinese Americans in Chang's story.

"The Oriental Contingent" provides an excellent opportunity for students to write—in journals, and then in essays and in their own fiction—about their ethnic backgrounds or about what they have seen in the behavior of second- and third-generation people of other backgrounds. (You may also want to refer students to Pat Mora's poem, "Immigrants" in Chapter 1, and to Martin Espada's poem, "Bully," in Chapter 20.

TOPICS FOR CRITICAL THINKING AND WRITING

1. In the first paragraph, a person (whose name we don't know) says "You must know Lisa Mallory." Why does she make that assumption?
2. During their first meeting Connie thinks "She recognized in herself that intense need to see, to see into fellow Orientals, to fathom them" and she waves "her hand in front of her eyes." Does she know what is she looking for?
3. What does Eric do in the story? What is his function? And "the American" (paragraph 40)?
4. In paragraph 85 we read: "'I'm so sorry,' Connie Sung said, for all of them. 'It's all so turned around.'" What does the writer mean by "for all of them"? And what does Connie mean by "It's all so turned around"?

JAMAICA KINCAID

Girl (p. 440)

Jamaica Kincaid, like her fictional heroine Annie John, lived in Antigua, a much doted-on only child, until she was seventeen, when she came to the United States to continue her education. In an interview in the *New York Times Book Review* (April 7, 1985, p. 6), she said, "I did sort of go to college but it was such a dismal failure. I just educated myself, if that's possible." She has published three collections of short stories based on her life in the West Indies.

In this story we meet a girl in her early adolescence, under the constant tutelage of her mother for her coming role as a woman. In today's terminology, we see the social construction of gender. The mother is a powerful presence, shrewd and spirited as well as overprotective and anxious about her daughter's burgeoning sexuality. The girl is attentive to her mother, and mostly submissive; we sense that it is through her reverie that we hear her mother's monologue, which the daughter twice interrupts briefly. But the repetition of instruction and correction in the monologue, especially of the incessant "this is how to," suggests the tension between the two that we know, from our own experience, will lead to a confrontation that will permanently alter the relationship. Despite the references to the island culture, which provide the story's rich, exotic texture, the central drama of coming of age could be happening anywhere.

A good way to teach the story is to have two students read it aloud in class. It's short, humorous, and in passages pleasantly rhythmical. The students will hear the shift in voices, and will want to discuss the characters and the conflict.

We especially admire Kincaid's novel, *Annie John* (1985), which consists of eight interrelated chapters (which were first published separately in *The New Yorker*) that explore a mother-daughter relationship.

See also: Selwyn R. Cudjoe, "Jamaica Kincaid and the Modernist Project: An Interview," *Callaloo* 12 (Spring 1989), 396-411; and Donna Perry, "An Interview with Jamaica Kincaid," in *Reading Black, Reading Feminist*, ed. Henry Louis Gates, Jr. (1990), 492-509.

A video cassette of Jamaica Kincaid reading "Girl" is available from Longman.

TOPICS FOR CRITICAL THINKING AND WRITING
1. What is the conflict in this story?
2. Is the girl naive? Explain.
3. Taking "Girl" as a model, write a piece about someone—perhaps a relative, teacher, or friend—who has given you more advice than you wanted.

GLORIA NAYLOR

The Two (p. 441)

Although instructors will be interested in matters of technique—especially the metaphors of the quilt and of the smell, and the shift in point of view from (at the start) the outside view of the two women to (midway) the inside view of Lorraine and Theresa—discussion in class is likely to center on the characterization of "the two" (we don't learn even their names until we have read about one-third of the story), their relationship to each other, and society's relationship to them.

The differences between the two women are clear enough—Lorraine is shy, soft, and in need of the approval of the community; Theresa is tougher (but "the strain of fighting alone was beginning to show")—but both are at first lumped together as "nice girls," and this point is worth discussing in class. Why, at first, does the community find them acceptable? Because they don't play loud music, they don't have drunken friends, and—the next most important point—they do not encourage other women's husbands to hang around, that is, they are not a threat to the married women. But it is precisely this "friendly indifference to the men on the street" that (when its source is detected) becomes "an insult to the [neighborhood] women."

By the way, we have fairly often encountered in the popular press articles with such titles as "Why Are Gay Men Feared?" (the usual answer is that men insecure about their own heterosexuality feel threatened by gay men, who, the theory goes, in effect tell the supposed straight men that maybe they aren't really so straight), but we don't recall ever encountering an article on the response of heterosexual women to lesbians. Perhaps some students will want to confirm or dispute Naylor's view of why the straight community resents "the two." As we understand the story, Naylor is suggesting that heterosexual women welcome other women who are not threats to their relationships with men, but then reject lesbians (who fit this category) because lesbians, by virtue of their indifference to or independence from males, seem to be a criticism of heterosexuality. (Can we go so far as to say that lesbians, in this view, upset straight women because lesbians make other women aware of their need for men?)

There are two stories in this story, the story of the relationship between the community and "the two," and the story of the relationship between Lorraine and Theresa. This second story, we take it, is about two women who (like the members of most straight couples) differ considerably in personality and who have their problems, but who are tied to each other by deep affection. The last we hear in the story is a bit of good-natured bickering that reveals Lorraine is doing her best to please Theresa. Lorraine, who had tried to talk Theresa into avoiding fattening foods, is preparing a (fattening) gravy for the chicken, and Theresa is pretending to disapprove.

"The Two" is included in Naylor's first and, we think, her best book, *The Women of Brewster Place* (1982). But students might be directed to her later novels: *Linden Hills* (1985); *Mama Day* (1988), which blends African-American folklore with stories derived from Shakespeare's *The Tempest;* and *Bailey's Cafe* (1992).

For background and context: Gloria Naylor and Toni Morrison, "A Conversation," *Southern Review* 21 (July 1985), 567-93; Gloria Naylor, "Love and Sex in the Afro-American Novel," *Yale Review* 78 (Autumn 1988), 19-31; and

Barbara Christian, "Gloria Naylor's Geography: Community, Class, and Patriarchy in *The Women of Brewster Place* and *Linden Hills*," in *Reading Black, Reading Feminist*, ed. Henry Louis Gates, Jr. (1990), 348-73.

TOPICS FOR CRITICAL THINKING AND WRITING

1. The first sentence says, "At first they seemed like such nice girls." What do we know about the person who says it? What does it tell us (and imply) about the "nice girls"?
2. What is Sophie's role in the story?
3. In the second part of the story, who is the narrator? Does she or he know Theresa's thoughts, or Lorraine's, or both?
4. How does the story end? What do you think will happen between Lorraine and Theresa?
5. Try writing a page or less that is the *end* of a story about two people (men, women, childre—but *people*) whose relationship is going to end soon, or is going to survive, because of, or despite, its difficulties.

AMY TAN

Two Kinds (p. 448)

It's not a bad idea to ask a student to read the first two paragraphs aloud, and then to invite the class to comment. What, you might ask them, do they hear besides some information about the mother's beliefs? Probably they will hear at least two other things: (1) the voice of a narrator who does not quite share her mother's opinion, and (2) a comic tone. You may, then, want to spend some time in class examining *what the writer has done* that lets a reader draw these inferences. On the first point, it may be enough to begin by noticing that when someone says, "My mother believed," we are almost sure to feel some difference between the speaker and the reported belief. Here the belief is further distanced by the fivefold repetition of "You could." The comedy—perhaps better characterized as mild humor—is evident in the naivete or simplicity of ambitions: open a restaurant, work for the government, retire, buy a house with almost no money down, become famous. Many readers may feel superior (as the daughter herself does) to this mother, who apparently thinks that in America money and fame and even genius are readily available to all who apply themselves—but many readers may also wish that their mother was as enthusiastic.

The second paragraph adds a sort of comic topper. After all, when the mother says, in the first paragraph, "you could be anything you wanted to be in America," the ambitions that she specifies are not impossible, but when in the second paragraph she says, "you can be prodigy too," and "you can be best anything," we realize that we are listening to an obsessed parent, a woman ferociously possessive of her daughter. (In another story in Tan's *Joy Luck Club* a mother says of her daughter, "How can she be her own person? When did I give her up?") Obsessions of, course, can be the stuff of tragedy—some students will be quick to talk about Macbeth's ambition, Brutus's self-confidence, and so forth—but obsessions are also the stuff of comedy; witness the lover who writes sonnets to his mistress's eyebrow, Harpo Marx in pursuit of a blonde, the pedant, and all sorts of other monomaniacs whose monomania (at least as it is represented in the work of art) is not dangerous to others.

The third paragraph, with its references to the terrible losses in China, darkens the tone, but the fourth restores the comedy, with its vision of "a Chinese Shirley Temple." The fifth paragraph is perhaps the most obviously funny so far: when Shirley Temple cries, the narrator's mother says to her daughter: "You already know how. Don't need talent for crying."

There's no need here to belabor the obvious, but students—accustomed to thinking that everything in a textbook is deadly serious—easily miss the humor. They will definitely grasp the absurdity of the thought that "Nairobi" might be one way of pronouncing Helsinki, but they may miss the delightful comedy of Auntie Lindo pretending that Waverly's abundant chess trophies are a nuisance ("all day I have no time to do nothing but dust off her winnings"), and even a deaf piano teacher may not strike them as comic. (Of course, in "real life" we probably would find pathos rather than comedy in a deaf piano teacher—and that's a point worth discussing in class.) So the point to make, probably, is that the story is comic (for example, in the mother's single-mindedness, and in the daughter's absurd hope that the recital may be going all right, even though she is hitting all the wrong notes) but is also serious (the conflict between the mother and the daughter, the mother's passionate love, the daughter's rebelliousness, and the daughter's later recognition that her mother loved her deeply). It is serious, too, in the way it shows us (especially in the passage about the "old Chinese silk dresses") the narrator's deepening perception of her Chinese heritage.

As a child, she at first shares her mother's desire that she be a "prodigy," but she soon becomes determined to be herself. In the mirror she sees herself as "ordinary" but also as "angry, powerful"; she is an independent creature, not an imitation of Shirley Temple. The question is, Can a young person achieve independence without shattering a fiercely possessive parent? Or, for that matter, without shattering herself? We can understand the narrator's need to defy her mother ("I now felt stronger, as if my true self had finally emerged"), but the devastating effect when she speaks of her mother's dead babies seems almost too great a price to pay. Surely the reader will be pleased to learn that the narrator and her mother became more or less reconciled, even though the mother continued to feel that the narrator just didn't try hard enough to be a genius. It's worth reading aloud the passage about the mother's offer of the piano:

> And after that, every time I saw it in my parents' living room, standing in front of the bay window, it made me feel proud, as if it were a shiny trophy that I had won back.

As a mature woman, the narrator comes to see that "Pleading Child" (which might almost be the title of her early history) is complemented by "Perfectly Contented." Of course, just as we have to interpret "Pleading Child" a bit freely— let's say as "Agitated Child"—so "Perfectly Contented" must be interpreted freely as, say, "Maturity Achieved." We get (to quote the title of the story) "two kinds" of experience and "two kinds" of daughter, in one.

See Marina Heung, "Daughter-Text/Mother-Text: Matrilineage in Amy Tan's *Joy Luck Club*," *Feminist Studies* 19 (Fall 1993), 597-616.

TOPICS FOR CRITICAL THINKING AND WRITING

1. Try to recall your responses when you had finished reading the first three paragraphs. At that point, how did the mother strike you? Now that you have read the entire story, is your view of her different? If so, in what way(s)?
2. When the narrator looks in the mirror, she discovers " the prodigy side," a face she "had never seen before." What do you think she is discovering?
3. If you enjoyed the story, point out two or three passages that you found particularly engaging, and briefly explain why they appeal to you.
4. Do you think this story is interesting only because it may give a glimpse of life in a Chinese-American family? Or do you find it interesting for additional reasons? Explain.

RITA DOVE

Second-Hand Man (p. 456)

In "real slow," in the first paragraph, we hear a voice that is speaking something other than Standard English, and discussion in class may well spend some time on the narrator. Technically the narrative point of view is editorial omniscience, but that seems like an awfully highfalutin' term for this folksy narrator who, admittedly, knows what is going on in everyone's mind ("All the girls loved James") but who surely seems to be a voice of common sense, speaking the idiom of the characters in the story. Thus, if the narrator knows what is going on in Virginia's mind (for instance, that she hated to be called *Ginny*), well, any sensible person in this part of the woods would know that. And if we want to say that Dove uses the technique known as editorial omniscience, one might add that only a very self-satisfied system of critical theory would apply so heavy-handed a term to a narrator who says, "It was time to let the dog in out of the rain, even if he shook his wet all over the floor." In any case, the narrator's voice surely is close to Virginia's, and the narrator's wisdom probably is close to hers too.

The story is very much in the oral tradition, not only in its occasional moralizing ("But people are too curious for their own good") but also in the narrator's concern that the hearer understand the way the characters feel:

"Virginia," he said. He was real scared. "How can you shoot me down like this?"

That gratuitous but thoroughly welcome "He was real scared" wonderfully catches the voice of the oral reporter.

And like much oral narrative, this story deals with archetypal material (though it is set in the 1920s)—a courting (briefly imperiled by a snake in the garden) that produces a happy marriage (the happiness is in this world proved by the production of a beautiful baby). The oral flavor is emphasized by the five passages of song. The story is told with great sobriety: ("No, he courted her proper"), and yet with humor too, as in the story about Virginia dumping hot water on an unwelcome suitor ("She only got a little piece of his pant leg"), or in pictures of the unsuccessful wooer, Sterling Williams, who "kept buying root beers [for Virginia] and having to drink them himself." And the narrator can value both ritual and common sense, as when he speaks approvingly of the formal courtship ("He courted her just inside a year, came by nearly every day"), and yet can say, of James Evans's proposing while kneeling on one knee, "There's a point when all this dignity and stuff get in the way of destiny." (James is so taken by his role as suitor that he can't believe the woman of his dreams has actually said *yes.*)

If the courting is both realistic and ritualistic, so is Virginia's threat to shoot James. She proceeds according to ritual (and the narrator emphasizes the ritual by using the same syntax in successive sentences):

> She took off her coat and hung it in the front closet. She unpinned her hat and set it in its box on the shelf. She reached in the back of the closet and brought out his hunting rifle and the box of bullets. She didn't see no way out but to shoot him.

She means it, or thinks she does, but, "No, she couldn't shoot him when he stood there looking at her with those sweet brown eyes, telling her how much he loved her." What to do? She'll wait until he sleeps. But "He didn't sleep for three nights." We are in the world of battling heroes—he won't sleep or run, and she won't put aside her standards—but fortunately she finds a way out. "Sitting there, Virginia had plenty of time to think." He had lied—but only to win her, so the lie is forgivable. She lays down the rifle, and lays down certain conditions that domesticate her man ("You will join the choir and settle down instead of plucking on that guitar at the drop of a hat"). She plans to bring James's child to Ohio, but we learn that the child had died some time before this episode. Why? Perhaps because we have to see that even the wonderful Virginia can't have everything her way, and perhaps because since James *did* lie—even though only for the perfectly good reason of gaining Virginia—in the world of folk tale he has to be punished. We think the point is worth discussing.

An interview with Rita Dove, and articles on her work, appear in the journal *Callaloo,* 12, no. 2 (1991).

LOUISE ERDRICH

Fleur (p. 461)

Except for the opening of Kafka's "The Metamorphosis" it's hard to think of a more striking opening than the words that begin this story, "The first time she drowned." By the end of the paragraph it is clear that we are in a mysterious world—which is not to say a world in which odd things happen arbitrarily. The gist of the first paragraph makes it clear that some sort of principle of cause and effect is at work, at least with reference to anyone who comes into contact with Fleur. The next four paragraphs develop the theme of magic, partly by describing Misshepeshu the waterman, but the focus soon returns to Fleur, who can become an owl if she wishes: "We know for sure because... we followed the tracks of her bare feet and saw when they changed, where the claws sprang out."

Several other passages further identify Fleur with animals. For instance, "her hips [were] fishlike, slippery, narrow," her braids were " thick like the tails of animals," and she grinned "the white wolf grin a Pillager turns on its victims." (On the other hand, animal imagery is not limited to Fleur; the loathsome Lily has "a snake's cold pale eyes.") In her green dress, Fleur seems to wear "a skin of lakeweed." These associations with nature help to prepare the reader for the larger connection, when the tornado destroys the men who violated her.

What is a reader to make of the narrator's view that magic is at work? There really is no problem, we think; a reader can dismiss the narrator as credulous in some matters, but the gist of the story puts no great strain on a reader's sense of reality. Notice, too, that the "magic" ranges from the sort of thing that a scientific mind would reject (e.g., that Fleur can turn into an owl) to things said to be magical but which would not disturb anyone, such as Pauline's assertion that she was invisible: "I was invisible, I blended into the stained brown walls." Later she says that she was invisible to the men, in effect meaning that they had no sexual interest in her and therefore paid no attention to her.

But the central point, of course, is the identification of Fleur with a mysterious, powerful, purposeful nature, and in particular with the storm that destroys the men who raped her. Fleur was earlier described partly in animal terms. Now the storm is described partly in human terms: "The whole place was shaking as if a huge hand was pinched at the rafters, shaking it"; "Clouds hung down, witch teats." Alternatively, a longish passage almost turns the storm into an animal:

> The odd cloud became a fat snout that nosed along the earth and sniffled, jabbed, picked at things, sucked them up, blew them apart, rooted around as if it were following a certain scent, then stopped behind me at the butcher shop and bored down like a drill.

It's worth noticing that at this point we are not told what the cloud is searching for, or what it found. Further, the tone changes here, introducing a different aspect of the storm, which should be mentioned especially because students often miss it when they first read the story. We are referring to the slightly comical touches, bits that come out of the tradition of the tall tale:

> A herd of cattle flew through the air like giant birds, dropping dung, their mouths open in stunned bellows. A candle, still lighted, blew past, and tables, napkins, garden tools, a whole school of drifting eyeglasses, jackets on hangers, hams, a checkerboard, a lampshade, and at last the sow from behind the lockers, on the run....

That herd of cattle (flying and defecating), that candle (which in a tornado was still lighted!), that school of eyeglasses, those jackets on hangers—all of these are magic, but magic with a humorous aspect. After this comic passage, however, we are told what the storm was looking for: "Of all the businesses in Argus, Kozka's Meats had suffered worst." There is still a hint of the tall tale here, for the narrator tells us that "The glass candy case went fifty [feet], and landed without so much as a cracked pane," but now the wonders are not so much comic as mysterious. "There were other surprises as well, for the back rooms where Fritzie and Pete lived were undisturbed." (The reader recalls that Fritzie and Pete were out of town when the men raped Fleur, so the storm—or is it Fleur?—spares their quarters.)

Is the mysterious Fleur (flower) a Pillager (plunderer)? Certainly she is dangerous to cross—but so, one might point out, is electricity, or the law of gravity. The last three paragraphs of the story emphasize her power, and her mystery.

TOPICS FOR CRITICAL THINKING AND WRITING
1. What significance do you find in the name Fleur Pillager?
2. In what ways is Fleur associated with nature?
3. In this story, what is the nature of nature? Mysterious? Cruel? Good? Amoral? Or what?
4. What is gained by telling the story from Pauline's point of view, rather than, say, from a third-person objective point of view?

SANDRA CISNEROS

One Holy Night (p. 470)

Some readers may feel that not much happens in this story; others may feel that there is indeed a sort of O. Henry story here, with an ironic ending (the boyfriend turns out to be a murderer), but it seems to us that the special pleasure of the story is in the narrator's voice, or, rather, voices, since the narrator lets us hear Chaq Uxmal Paloquín.

Take the epigraph. It is colloquial, almost Holden Caulfieldish in its diction ("About the truth, if you…") and at the same time it is powerfully resonant in its content. Similarly, the first paragraph of the story consists of rather simple assertions ("He said. That's what he told me. He was… This is what Boy Baby said"), but the content is richly evocative ("Chaq Uxmal Paloquín," "ancient line of Mayan kings," "Yucatan, the ancient cities"). Later we learn that Boy Baby is associated with mystery, with ancient rites—but the voice that tells us about these things, and about "the moon, the pale moon with its one yellow eye, the moon of Tikal, and Tulum, and Chichén," also tells us that the moon "stared through the pink plastic curtains."

In short, it seems to us that the story catches both the commonplaces of life (think, for instance, of the delightful bit about how "Abuelita chased [Boy Baby] away with the broom") and something of the mysteries of life. Thus, the sexual experience with Boy Baby was exotic ("So I was initiated beneath an ancient sky by a great and mighty heir—Chaq Uxmal Paloquín. I, Ixchel, his queen") and yet, "The truth is, it wasn't any big deal at all." Something of this multiple or paradoxical presentation given by a girl who has become a woman is evident in the comment that Boy Baby " seemed boy and baby and man all at once," and especially in the last three paragraphs, where we get three versions of what love is like. Students might be invited to try to put into other words these three versions of love.

Students might also be asked what they make of the title. Our own sense is that a reader is likely to begin with the expectation that the story will in some way be related to a Christian experience—maybe it will take place on a Christian holiday, or perhaps, given the early reference to Abuelita rubbing the speaker's " belly with jade," it will tell of some non-Christian ritual. The reader soon realizes, however, that what is holy is the mystery of ordinary existence.

What we have just said strikes even our ears as pretentious, false to the colloquial quality and the humor of the story (Abuelita wielding her broom, the lie about the pushcart, the frank appraisal that the sexual experience "wasn't a big deal"). The trick in teaching the story, we think, is to help the students see and enjoy Cisneros's skill in presenting mystery in an ordinary seeming way.

After we wrote the preceding material we were informed by Professor Maura Ives (Texas A&M) that in Mayan history Lord Chac was a tenth-century ruler of Uxmal. (There is also another Chaq, a rain god.) Ixchel (with whom the narrator identifies herself), a goddess associated with lakes, wells, and underground water, had a shrine in Cozumel. Ives went on to say that when she teaches the story she explains that:

> Cisneros is using Mayan mythology to create a character who can play upon the narrator's longing for romance and glamour, and to explore the theme of women's place in history. Boy Baby knows exactly what buttons to push with "Ixchel," a working-class Mexican-American girl who is excited and flattered by his invitation to participate in a glorious heritage and a heroic mission. For her part, Ixchel is eager to trade the harsh realities of barrio life for Boy Baby's romanticized version of Mexican history and mythology, in which she will assume a central historic role as "Ixchel, his queen." But Ixchel's commentary on her "holy night" with Boy Baby—"suddenly I became a part of history"—is ironic, because while she does end up repeating history, it is not in the way she had hoped. She is no Mayan queen; instead, like her mother before her, Ixchel takes on the age-old role of the seduced and abandoned woman, a role that transcends national and cultural boundaries. (Although Ixchel's Uncle Lalo blames her fate on the family's having left Mexico, he forgets that the family came to the United States to hide the pregnancy of Ixchel's unmarried Mexican mother.)

Betrayal seems to be the hallmark of Ixchel's introduction to "history," but it is clear that she is betrayed not only by Boy Baby but also (and more devastatingly) by her own myth of romance, through which she is led to repeat the pattern of her mother's life. The power and destructiveness of this myth are demonstrated in Ixchel's refusal to abandon her dream of love despite Boy Baby's deception. In the end, she is left with nothing else to hang on to but her place in the history of women who have loved and (inevitably?) lost.

Ives has also called to our attention an article by Luis Leal, "Without Borders: (De)mythologization in North American and Mexican Literature," *Mexican Studies/Estudios Mexicanos* 9.1 (Winter 1993), 95-118. Leal sees

Cisneros's story as an example of the tendency of contemporary Chicano literature both to create and to demythologize traditional Mexican myths.

HELENA MARIA VIRAMONTES

The Moths (p. 475)

Like most other stories with fantastic elements, "The Moths" has a good deal of highly realistic detail. Thus, for instance, the narrator is very specific when she tells us that she planted flowers, grasses, and vines in "red Hills Brothers coffee cans." Presumably humble details such as this help to establish the credibility of the narrator and thus serve to make the fantastic elements convincing.

Another way of making the fantastic acceptable is to cast doubt on it explicitly—that is, to say what the reader presumably thinks, and then to confirm the fantastic; thus the girl tells us that she was skeptical of the powers of Abuelita's potato slices, but they nevertheless seem to have cured her of scarlet fever: "You're still alive, aren't you?" Further, Viramontes begins with a relatively acceptable bit of fantasy, since most readers probably entertain the idea that folk medicines may (sometimes) work. Thus the improbable yet possible business about the potato slices helps to prepare us for the next (and much greater) improbability, Abuelita's shaping of the girl's hands by means of a balm of dried moth wings and Vicks. And this in turn helps to prepare us for the moths at the end of the story.

On the other hand, a skeptic can argue that the girl is an unreliable narrator: the death of her grandmother is so traumatic that the narrator imagines seeing the moths that her grandmother had told her "lay within the soul and slowly eat the spirit up." It's hard to argue against this view, though it seems excessively literal or materialistic in a story that is pretty clearly fantastic and symbolic.

Putting aside the moths, what are some of the other symbols? Perhaps the most obvious are the roots that "would burst out of the rusted coffee cans and search for a place to connect." During a discussion in class, students can relate these searching roots to the girl, who is not "pretty or nice" like her older sisters, and who finds little sympathy at home, where (doubtless partly because she is not "respectful") she is teased by her sisters and threatened by her father. She is also separated from the church, which she describes as cold and furnished with "frozen statues with blank eyes." However, she is connected to her grandmother, Abuelita, whose house provides a refuge from the "quarrels and beatings" of her own house. In short, the narrator is isolated from her immediate family, with which her harsh father is allied.

A second fairly obvious symbol is the sun, which in one paragraph is related to death and rebirth:

> ... [T]here comes an illumination when the sun and earth meet, a final burst of burning red orange fury reminding us that although endings are inevitable, they are necessary for rebirths, and when that time came, just when I switched on the light in the kitchen to open Abuelita's can of soup, it was probably then that she died.

The passage is fairly dense and complex; it's worth asking a student to read it aloud in class before discussing it.

Death and birth also meet in the bath, which is both a ritual cleansing of the dead grandmother and a baptism or rebirth of the girl. (Notice that the girl does not deposit the grandmother in the tub; rather, she enters the tub holding the grandmother.) In the tub, the girl is mother to the old lady ("There, there, Abuelita, I said, cradling her"); even as she sobs like a child she becomes a woman.

Finally, there are the moths. There is possibly some connection here with the butterfly, which in antiquity was a symbol of the soul leaving the body at death, and in early Christian art was a symbol of the resurrected soul. However, in the last paragraph we are explicitly informed that Abuelita had told the narrator "about the moths that lay within the soul and slowly eat the spirit up." The appearance of the moths at the end thus suggests that Abuelita is at last free (in death) from the pressures that consume the spirit of a human being (specifically from the types of oppression that we have seen operate in the narrator, an unconventional female in a highly traditional society that severely limits the role of women). The loss of Abuelita reduces the narrator to tears and to infancy ("I wanted to return to the waters of the womb with her"), but it also serves to make clear that she is now, more than ever before, alone. We are not told that the experience liberates her, but perhaps we can assume that this rebellious girl, who knew how to use a brick in a sock, knows that her life will not be easy.

TOPICS FOR CRITICAL THINKING AND WRITING

1. The narrator says that she was not "pretty or nice," could not "do. . . girl things," and was not "respectful." But what can she do, and what is she? How, in short, would you characterize her?

2. Elements of the fantastic are evident, notably in the moths at the end. What efforts, if any, does the author exert in order to make the fantastic elements plausible or at least partly acceptable?

3. Why do you suppose the author included the rather extended passages about the sprouting plants and (later) the sun?

4. We can say, on the basis of the description of the bathing of Abuelita in the final paragraph, that the narrator is loving, caring, and grief-stricken. What else, if anything, does this paragraph reveal about the narrator?

ELIZABETH TALLENT

No One's a Mystery (p. 479)

There is nothing in the story that will puzzle students—nothing that they will not understand—but responses to the two chief characters, and also to the unseen wife may vary widely. Some students may find the girl sympathetic, others may find her pitiful, and some may find her contemptible because of her easy disregard for Jack's wife. Similarly, responses to Jack may vary. Many students condemn him as immoral, especially since the narrator was obviously underage when the affair began, but some may argue that he therefore is not taking advantage of her.

One way of getting students to think about the characters—what they are and what they will become—is to ask them to imagine that they are the narrator, and to write entries in the diary for a year from now, two years, five years. You may also want to ask them if they think Jack keeps a diary, or if he ever kept one. Most will immediately say that he doesn't and never did, but it's worth asking them why they think that—and why, in fact, far fewer boys keep diaries than girls.

Two other points: What does one make of the title, and what does one make of the final line ("Her breath would smell like milk, and it's kind of a bittersweet smell, if you want to know the truth.")? The title seems pretty easily explained, or, rather, the actions of everyone (his wife, his girlfriend, himself) are easily predicted. Given the characters in the story, readers may agree—or they may argue that Jack may find, to his surprise, that he gets a divorce, marries the girl, and lives happily with his new wife. As for the last line of the story, we assume "bittersweet" is the operative word. The story is bittersweet, a story of happiness that can't last, and will be remembered (by Jack and by the girl) with affection and with sadness.

ALICE ELLIOTT DARK

In the Gloaming (p. 481)

We begin with a comment by the author, printed in *Best American Short Stories 1994,* ed. Tobias Wolff

> After "In the Gloaming" was published, I got a lot of letters asking if it was really fiction; apparently it seemed autobiographical. I suppose it is, in the sense that I see it as a story about a woman trying to be a decent mother, a subject that was very much on my mind at the time I wrote it. I had recently become a mother; and was having bouts of vertigo whenever I thought of the scope of this new relationship. There were so many contradictory feelings to cope with I wanted to encourage my son to have his own life, yet I hoped he would like me; I wanted to help him feel brave going out into the world, yet when I imagined it, I instantly feared harm that could come to him.
>
> The story was not conceived as being about any disease in particular. AIDS came in when Laird made a remark about his immune system, and I left it at that. I never thought of it as an AIDS story; from what I've seen of AIDS, the end of the disease is not as gentle as this, nor do most victims have situations as idyllic as Laird's. (333)

We agree that it is not "an AIDS story." The central issue, as we see it, is the mother's relation with her son—and the adjacent issue is her relation with her husband, hence we include the story in this chapter. To say this, however, is not to say that AIDS is peripheral to the story; the story as we have it is about such constructions as manliness and motherliness.

We begin with a few remarks about stereotypes, which may reveal that we are Politically Incorrect, or since these things have a way of changing almost overnight, Politically Correct. One hears that stereotypes are a Bad Thing, but one also hears about pride in ethnic identity, which assumes that individuals within groups have certain identities. Proud advocates of ethnic or racial or religious identity claim to have certain characteristics, lets say a sense of humor or some sort of special courage or love of nature, or whatever; almost all groups seem to claim to be special by virtue of having loving families, and by virtue of having strong mothers. To this degree they stereotype themselves, and they are proud of their stereotypes. On the other hand, they strongly object to outsiders imposing what seems to be negative stereotypes. About the only exception we can think of is the occasional Asian objection to the favorable stereotype of the Asian as the ideal immigrant. Some Asians argue that this favorable stereotype is damaging because it makes others expect too much of Asians.

But to get back to Dark's story: It is not a story about AIDS and it is not a gay story, but we do have some of the signs that are said (or used to be said) to mark gay relationships. A father who is "ambitious, competitive, self absorbed" (paragraph 74) and away too much; a mother who loves her son to the exclusion of the father; a boy who perhaps is too eager to please his mother (125) and who perhaps is a bit more attracted to sensuous pleasures (the cashmere lap blankets of paragraph 141) than a Real Man should be. We are not complaining that Dark's story is a tissue of stereotypes. Rather, we are saying that the characters are thoroughly believable—wonderfully believable—and yet if one stands back—one sees that they more or less fit a traditional pattern of a family with a homosexual son. Even in the first paragraph we get (appropriately) gender stereotyping when the narrator comments on Laird's openness: "No one [Janet] knew talked that way—no man, at least." The implication surely is this: Men talk one way, women another—and a gay man, dying of AIDS, may talk like a woman. By the way, students may have a good deal to say on the alleged differences between the ways women and men speak—especially if the students have used a freshman reader that includes essays by such popular writers as Robin Lakoff and Deborah Tannen.

Although in this story the mother is infinitely more interesting than the father, students might begin tracking the comments about the father. He makes himself scarce now (paragraphs 4, 62), as he always did (64, 66, 68-69, 73); he has often let his son know that he is disappointed in the boy (72); he knows that his son is homosexual but apparently can't bring himself to admit it or discuss it with the boy (121). Of course—and it is important that this point comes up in class—we know the father chiefly through the mother. We never enter the father's mind; if he were to tell the story, we would get a somewhat different story. But we do see him weep (183), and he does suggest that bagpipes should provide the funeral music, a choice that we must believe the mother is fully in accord with. And, most moving of all, the story ends with his plaintive words, "Please tell me—what else did my boy like?" In short, the father of this gay boy held certain ideas of manliness that prevented him from being close to the boy during his life. Now that the boy is dead he admits that he failed as a father, and he desperately wants to know what his son was really like.

CHAPTER 10

The Novel

It sometimes seems that books about the novel (or books including some discussion of the novel) are as numerous as novels. Among the commentaries of the last few decades that we have found valuable are the following:

Robert Martin Adams, *Strains of Discord*

Robert Alter, *Partial Magic: The Novel as Self-Conscious Genre*

Miriam Allott, *Novelists on the Novel*

Leo Bersani, *A Future for Astyanax: Character and Desire in Literature*

Wayne C. Booth, *The Rhetoric of Fiction*

Judith Fetterley, *The Resisting Reader: A Feminist Approach to American Fiction*

William H. Gass, *Fiction and Figures of Life*

Henry Louis Gates, Jr., *The Signifying Monkey: A Theory of Afro-American Literary Criticism*

Martin Green, *Dreams of Adventure, Deeds of Empire*

Barbara Hardy, *The Appropriate Form*

W. J. Harvey, *Character and the Novel*

Robert Liddell, *Robert Liddell on the Novel* (a combined edition of *A Treatise on the Novel* and *Some Principles of Fiction*)

David Lodge, *The Language of Fiction*

Mary McCarthy, *On the Contrary*

J. Hillis Miller, *Fiction and Repetition: Seven English Novels*

Edward W. Said, *Orientalism, Culture and Imperialism*

Robert Scholes and Robert Kellogg, *The Nature of Narrative*

Eve Kosovsky Sedgwick, *Between Men: English Literature and Male Homosocial Desire* and *Epistemology of the Closet*

Philip Stevick, ed., *The Theory of the Novel*

Eric J. Sundquist, *To Wake the Nations: Race and the Making of American Literature*

Jane Tompkins, *Sensational Designs: The Cultural Work of American Fiction*

But this is mere stalling. The question is, what novel to teach? The only time we experience any success in teaching a novel in an introductory course is when the novel is fairly short, which means that we have failed miserably with *Portrait of a Lady, Bleak House,* and *The Brothers Karamazov* and even with *Crime and Punishment.* Our moderate successes are limited to traditional favorites of freshman English, things like the following:

The Adventures of Huckleberry Finn

The Awakening

Billy Budd

Daisy Miller

Ethan Frome

The Great Gatsby

Hard Times

Miss Lonelyhearts

My Antonia

Notes from Underground

A Passage to India

A Portrait of the Artist as a Young Man

The Red Badge of Courage

Seize the Day

The Stranger

Their Eyes Were Watching God

To the Lighthouse

Among more recent titles that work well are the following:

Chinua Achebe, *Things Fall Apart*

Margaret Atwood, *The Handmaid's Tale*

Anthony Burgess, *A Clockwork Orange*

Evan S. Connell, Jr., *Mrs. Bridge*

Don De Lillo, *White Noise*

E. L. Doctorow, *Ragtime*

Umberto Eco, *The Name of the Rose*

Louise Erdrich, *Love Machine*

Graham Greene, *The Human Factor*

Kazuo Ishiguro, *Remains of the Day*

Charles Johnson, *The Middle Passage*

Milan Kundera, *The Unbearable Lightness of Being*

Bobbie Ann Mason, *In Country*

Cormac McCarthy, *All the Pretty Horses, The Crossing*

Brian Moore, *The Lonely Passion of Judith Hearne*

Toni Morrison, *Beloved*

Ben Okri, *The Famished Road*

Sylvia Plath, *The Bell Jar*

Thomas Pynchon, *The Crying of Lot 49*

Philip Roth, *The Ghost Writer*

Leslie Marmon Silko, *Almanac of the Dead*

Amy Tan, *The Joy Luck Club*

Anne Tyler, *A Slipping Down Life*

Alice Walker, *The Color Purple*

Eudora Welty, *The Optimist's Daughter*

PART THREE

Poetry

CHAPTER 11

Approaching Poetry: Responding in Writing

LANGSTON HUGHES

Harlem (p. 302)

In the eight lines enclosed within the frame (that is, between the first and next-to-last lines) we get four possibilities: The Dream may "dry up," "fester," "crust and sugar over," or "sag." Each of these is set forth with a simile, for example, "dry up / like a raisin in the sun." By the way, the third of these, "crust up and sugar over—like a syrupy sweet," probably describes a dream that has turned into smiling Uncle Tomism. Similes can be effective, and these *are* effective, but in the final line Hughes states the last possibility ("Or does it explode?") directly and briefly, without an amplification. The effect is, more or less, to suggest that the fancy (or pretty) talk stops. The explosion is too serious to be treated in a literary way. But, of course, the word "explode," applied to a dream, is itself figurative. That is, the last line is as "literary" or "poetical" as the earlier lines, but it is a slightly different sort of poetry.

A word about the rhymes: Notice that although the poem does use rhyme, it does not use a couplet until the last two lines. The effect of the couplet (load / explode) is that the poem ends with a bang. Of course, when one reads the poem in a book, one sees where the poem ends—though a reader may be surprised to find the forceful rhyme—but an audience hearing the poem recited is surely taken off-guard. The explosion is unexpected (especially in the context of the two previous lines about a sagging, heavy load), and powerful.

Note: Later in the textbook we present Hughes in depth.

See *The Collected Poems of Langston Hughes*, ed. Arnold Rampersad (1995), an excellent edition. Rampersad's two-volume biography (1986, 1988) is superb. On the poetry: Onwuchekwa Jemie, *Langston Hughes: An Introduction to the*

Poetry (1976). See also: James A Emmanuel, *Langston Hughes* (1967); *Langston Hughes, Black Genius: A Critical Evaluation,* ed. T. B. O'Daniel (1972); Richard K. Barksdale, *Langston Hughes: The Poet and His Critics* (1977); Steven C Tracy, *Langston Hughes and the Blues* (1988); and R. Baxter Miller, *The Art and Imagination of Langston Hughes* (1989).

TOPIC FOR CRITICAL THINKING AND WRITING
One might keep the first line where it is, and then rearrange the other stanzas—for instance, putting lines 2-8 after 9-11. Which version (Hughes's or the one just mentioned) do you prefer? Why?

A "Voices and Visions" videocassette of Langston Hughes is available from Longman.

CHAPTER 12

Lyric Poetry

One can engage in more profitable activities than in fretting about whether a given poem is a narrative poem or a lyric, but the topic is worth at least a little thought. Something, of course, depends on the way in which the text is rendered. Spirituals, for instance, often have considerable narrative content, and yet one feels that their affinities are with the lyric and that the story is subordinate to the state of mind. This sense of lyrical meditation is heightened by the refrains—repetitions that do not advance the story and that help to communicate and to induce a visionary state. An instructor who wants to pursue this topic may want to discuss such work as "Didn't My Lord Deliver Daniel," which is included in this text.

There is much fascinating material about the theory of nineteenth-century lyric poetry in M.H. Abrams, *The Mirror and the Lamp*. See also C. Day Lewis, *The Lyric Impulse*, and W.R. Johnson, *The Idea of the Lyric: Lyric Modes in Ancient and Modern Poetry*.

Versions of "Michael" were in print in the 1870s, and the song is still popular. Among effective recordings is one by Pete Seeger on Columbia (CS9717). "Careless Love" easily leads to a discussion of the blues. Here is a brief part of Ralph Ellison's comment on the genre in an essay on Richard Wright in Ellison's *Shadow and Act*: "Their attraction lies in this, that they at once express both the agony of life and the possibility of conquering it through sheer toughness of spirit. They fall short of tragedy only in that they provide no solution, offer no scapegoat but the self."

In the chapter on "Rhythm," we quote a remark by Ezra Pound that an instructor may wish to use in connection with "Michael," "Careless Love," or "The Colorado Trail." Pound says, "Poetry withers and dries out when it leaves music or at least imagined music, too far behind it. Poets who are not interested in music are, or become, bad poets." In "Colorado Trail," surely the repetitions of sounds help to make the poem singable and memorable. Ask students if they find "Blow winds blow" as attractive to the ear (as well as to the mind) as the poem's "Wail winds wail," or "all along the length of" as attractive as the poem's "all along, along, along." One can also try to account for the difference between, say, "Annie was a pretty girl," and "Laura was a pretty girl." Our own feeling is that the liquids in Laura (l, r) go better with the other liquids in the line ("pretty girl"), but other ears may hear something different.

ANONYMOUS

Western Wind (p. 511)

"Western Wind" has been much discussed. Probably most readers will find acceptable R. P. Warren's suggestion (*Kenyon Review*, 1943, 5) that the grieving lover seeks relief for the absence of his beloved in "the sympathetic manifestation of nature." But how do you feel about Patric M. Sweeney's view (*Explicator*, October 1955) that the speaker asserts that "he will come to life only when the dead woman returns, and her love, like rain, renews him"? In short, in this view the speaker "cries out to the one person who conquered death, who knows that the dead, returning to life, give life to those who loved them." We find this reading of the poem hard to take, but (like many readings) it is virtually impossible to *dis*prove.

One other point: Some readers have asked why other readers assume that the speaker is a male. A hard question to answer.

APHRA BEHN

Song: Love Armed (p. 512)

Although the allegory may at first seem unfamiliar to relatively inexperienced readers, if you ask students whether they have ever heard of any connections between love and war, they will quickly come up with phrases such as "the battle of the sexes" and "all is fair in love and war," and someone will mention that Cupid is armed with a bow and arrows. And although we don't want to push this delightful poem too far in the direction of realism, probably many students will find Behn's characterization of love as "tyrannic" quite intelligible.

It happens, however, that what especially interests us about the poem is the issue we raise in our first question: Why do people enjoy songs about unhappy love? Because it gives us a chance to impose form onto suffering, and thus implies a kind of mastery over suffering? In any case, many students will be familiar with the motif, and will be able to offer explanations accounting for the pleasure they take in the material.

Aphra Behn was not only a poet, but also a playwright and novelist, and when teaching her poetry, we often take note of her powerful narrative of slavery and colonization, *Oroonoko* (1688). On this work, which has received much attention recently, see Katharine M. Rogers, "Fact and Fiction in Aphra Behn's *Oroonoko*," *Studies in the Novel* 20 (Spring 1988), 1-15. See also George Woodcock, *The Incomparable Aphra* (1948; rpt. as *Aphra Behn: The English Sappho*, 1989); and Angeline Goreau, *Reconstructing Aphra* (1980).

W. H. AUDEN

Stop All the Clocks, Cut Off the Telephone (p. 513)

Even students who have little familiarity with traditional literature will enjoy the poem, but readers familiar with traditional elegies (such as "Lycidas") will especially enjoy it, since it is a modern version of the classical pastoral elegy. From the days of the Greek Sicilian poet Theocritus, the pastoral elegy called upon all nature to mourn for the deceased shepherd; the poet ordered the trees to shed their leaves, the streams to stop flowing, etc., all in order to express proper grief for the great loss that the speaker had experienced in the death of his beloved.

Auden wryly introduces into this form the paraphernalia of our world—clocks, telephones, airplanes, and so on—and yet keeps the basic motifs of the original. A phrase such as "let the mourners come" (4) might occur in almost any classical elegy (from Theocritus to Milton or Matthew Arnold), where customarily there is a procession of mourners. Next we would expect to hear something about the depth of their expression of grief—perhaps the heavens would reverberate with their cry. In Auden's poem, however, the invocation to mourners is followed by "Let aeroplanes circle moaning overhead / Scribbling on the sky the message He Is Dead."

But we do not take the poem as merely a joke, or as lacking in feeling. Yes, it uses hyperbole and it has comic elements, but it also seems to us to effectively express the emotions of a grieving lover, someone who—though of course knowing better—nevertheless feels that the beloved is the moon and sun, someone who might reasonably say that the beloved was "my North, my South, my East and West, My working week and my Sunday rest." Incidentally, the poem is recited in the film *Four Weddings and a Funeral.* It aroused much favorable comment—so much that the publisher promptly issued a little book with this poem and a few others by Auden, and announced on the cover that the book contained the poem from the film.

There are a number of books on Auden that can be brought to the attention of students. The best biography so far is Humphrey Carpenter, *W. H. Auden: A Biography* (1981). For social and historical context, see Samuel Hynes, *The Auden Generation: Literature and Politics in England in the 1930s* (1976). On the poetry: Monroe K. Spears, *The Poetry of W. H. Auden* (1963); and Edward Mendelson, *Early Auden* (1981).

THOMAS HARDY

The Self-Unseeing (p. 514)

We were much taken when we came across this poem while browsing though a volume of Hardy's poetry, and though we assumed Hardy might be recalling some youthful episode, we did not take it to have highly specific references. For us, the lines "She sat here in her chair, Smiling into the fire," referred, if to anyone specific, to a woman whom he loved. When we did some reading about Hardy, it came as something of a surprise to learn that all scholars take the poem to be about a specific visit to the house built by his grandfather for Hardy's father, and that the "he" who plays the fiddle refers to Hardy's dead father (the "dead feet" of line 4), and that the "she" who sat in the chair refers to Hardy's mother—who in fact still lived, now an octogenarian, in the house. This biographical information is customarily joined to a passage in Florence Emily Hardy's *The Early Life of Thomas Hardy:*

> He was of ecstatic temperament, extraordinarily sensitive to music; and among the endless jigs, hornpipes, reels, waltzes, and country-dances that his father played of an evening in his early married years, and to which the boy dances a *pas seul* in the middle of the room, there were three or four that always moved the child to tears, though he strenuously tried to hide them.... He was not over four years of age.
>
>   Qtd. in Peter Simpson, "Hardy's 'The Self-Unseeing' and the Romantic Problem of Consciousness," *Victorian Poetry* 17 (1979) 45.

The article just cited does not offer much else, but a better study, U. C. Knoepflmacher's in *PMLA* 105 (1990): 1055-70 goes so far as to say this:

> Thus, when the second stanza opens by recalling, "She sat here in her chair, / Smiling into the fire" (5-6), it seems plausible that the speaker still has before him the same woman who, now in her old age, joins her son in remembering how she smiled while watching the child entranced by the music of the father-fiddler.... (1064)

Knoepflmacher is always worth reading, but we think he is going pretty far here, where (if we understand him correctly) a reader is to assume that "she" is still alive (as indeed Hardy's mother was, at the time he wrote the poem), present at this scene in which the poet returns to the house with "the ancient floor." (Scholars explain the line "Here was the former door," by telling us, doubtless correctly, that over the course of the years the position of the door to the house had been changed.)

The question: Does this biographical knowledge improve the poem, or diminish it, or neither? In our view, it is better for "the dead feet" to refer both to the "she" who sat there and to the "he who played." That is, we prefer to read the poem as the utterance of an old person returning to a scene of early joy, once shared with people who now are irretrievably gone. You may (or may not) want to tell your students about the biographical information, and to ask them how useful it is.

In any case, we imagine that all readers will agree that the middle stanza, with its reference to the fiddler "bowing it higher and higher," is marvelous; it takes us upward (as music does) into a world of ecstasy, a world of total unself-consciousness, and then the final stanza (beginning with the speaker dancing as "in a dream") brings us out of this world where "everything glowed with a gleam" and down into the present, where the speaker, using his adult knowledge, ends by saying, "Yet we were looking away!"

Exactly what does the end mean? Two views seem to be chiefly offered. The first—surely wrong!—is that although "Everything glowed with a gleam," the foolish people did not perceive it: "we were looking away." Only the speaker, now older and wiser, sees the "blessings" (10) that the moment offered. A second view (also mistaken?) is that the poem celebrates the child's ecstasy, and laments the loss of unselfconsciousness. Our own view is that the poem looks back with love on a wonderful moment of the past, when all present were united in joy. Yes, they were unaware of the inevitability of decay ("We were looking away"), but that scarcely makes them foolish or pitiable, and in fact the poet now resurrects the moment, and so (despite the worn floorboards and the "dead feet") in a sense the ecstatic moment has triumphed (through the poet's art) over decay.

Having offered this interpretation, we don't want to insist too strongly on it. We grant that the final line, "Yet we were looking away!," strongly implies an almost culpable innocence.

We happened to discuss the poem with a former student, Steve Scipione, and he was prompted to offer a psychoanalytic reading of "The Self-Unseeing," which he is letting us use here. You may want to try out some of his points in class. He writes:

> Nowadays, Freudian literary analysis is considered a bit quaint and unsophisticated. Nevertheless: I see in the poem intimations of Freud's so-called primal scene. You recall the primal scene: The child witnesses his parents in the act of copulation and experiences a welter of conflicting feelings. Is daddy hurting mommy? Certainly the action is fierce enough—he seems to be wrestling with her, subjugating her in some way. And mommy is making noises that sound like pain; or are they pleasure noises? Whatever, it's very much between the two of them. The child is excluded. Ignored, relegated to the role of watcher, the powerfully jealous child is powerfully drawn by the evidence of pleasure and powerfully frightened by the implications of pain.
>
> Look at the middle stanza, which focuses on the two parents only: She, smiling into the fire (of passion?); he arching (his writhing back?) his bow (phallus?) "higher and higher" with an increasingly ecstatic motion. This stanza is bracketed by a stanza that describes an ancient room (a room now empty of former pleasures) and by a puzzling stanza that initially presents a dancing "I" that somehow turns into a "we" that emphatically (exclamation point) averts its gaze.
>
> Let's assume that the central stanza does in fact represent a screen memory of a copulating couple, now translated into an image of a fiddler bringing a smile to the face of seated woman. What screen memory is being translated in the other two stanzas?
>
> At the risk of sounding like the most literal-minded hunter of Freudian symbols, let me suggest the first stanza represents the maternal body. Freud often said that a house and its rooms—familial, hollow, waiting to be filled—symbolized the female body. The door; does it perhaps signify the "lower entrance" to that body? We infer that the "hollowed" floor had often been invaded by relentless "feet"—pacing, dancing feet that wore it "thin" by repeated visits. Feet too are sexualized appendages. I trust I don't have to belabor this symbolic interpretation any further.

Of course this is just the sort of interpretation that makes students shake their heads. "Look," says the literal minded-student. "The first stanza describes an old room. The second stanza describes a man playing music for a woman in that room. What's so mysterious about that?" But the last stanza resists a straighforward literal reading. The vague imagery, the shift from "I" to "we," the confounding last line—what's going on here?

Let's go back to Freud and recall the biographical context. The child Hardy is four years old, right in the middle of the Oedipal years when his desire for his mother is checked by the fear of being punished for this outlaw desire by his father. His memory of the primal scene is activated as he dances to his father's music, the same music that brings a pleased smile to his mother's face. The feeling of ecstatic fusion ("we")—the pleasure he shares with both of them at this moment—is dissipated—no, confused—by the sudden inchoate surge of ambivalence and shame and, yes, fear. He doesn't belong in this scene. This is between mommy and daddy. But he wants to be part of this scene! No he doesn't—he's hurting mommy and angering daddy! Oh oh!

I'm suggesting that the confusing last stanza reflects the confused feelings of the child. His dancing feet parallel the father's "dead feet" of the first stanza. The child wants to be walking in his father's shoes, or dancing on his father's floor. But that's forbidden, and even dangerous (those feet are, after all, dead). And he wants to gleam with the same lambent glow that lights his mother's smile. But that too would be sharing the warmth of a forbidden fire.

The very word "childlike" in the first line of the final stanza suggests this confusion and ambivalence, the desire to be part of the parental dyad and the need to distance the self from it. Initially the reader assumes that the first line of the final stanza puts the "I" right in the scene with the mother and father: The child is dancing to the music played by the father for the mother. But no, look closer: Isn't it instead an adult, dancing "childlike," recalling "that [long ago] day"? The truth is, it's both: at once a fusing, and a distancing.

This oscillation between distancing and fusing is played out in other ways. Formally the poem divides present from past (the present room of stanza one, the past event of stanza two) but through repetition brings the two together ("Here is the ancient floor"; "She sat here in her chair"). It posits a separation of mother, father, and child in time (the narrator is in the present room, the parents occupy the room in the past) and space (the narrator is here, the mother sat there, the father stood there); but then it metaphorically joins them (in stanza one the parental dead feet parallel the child's dancing feet of the third stanza; in stanza two the mother and father are lit by fire, while in stanza three "everything"—presumably including child and parents—glows and gleams.)

That takes me to that puzzling last line. Why "we," and why are "we" looking away? Here are three possible answers: (1) The "we" conflates the remembered child and the remembering adult; (2) it conflates the child who has wishfully imagined himself at one with his parents—fused in their erotic embrace—and the child who must "look away" from the forbidden primal scene into which he has blundered; or (3) both of the above. In this reading of the final stanza, the fusing / distancing pattern I've been tracing, rooted in the ambivalence of the primal scene, emerges in the puzzling shift from "I" to "we."

Of course I'm not suggesting that Hardy was deliberately writing a poem about the primal scene. I'm suggesting that the primal scene wrote the poem through Hardy. What is mysterious, vague and powerful in the language and arrangement of the poem is what is mysterious, vague and powerful about the incident to Hardy. He was trying to convey this experience and his emotional response through his art, without the conceptual framework of psychoanalysis that would help him "understand" it.

To repeat: The Freudian reading that has occupied the last few paragraphs is by Stephen Scipione, who has generously allowed us to use it.

Hardy is one of our favorite lyric poets, and we make a special effort to interest students in his verse. *The Complete Poetical Works of Thomas Hardy* have been edited by Samuel Hynes (3 vols., 1982-85). A good biography is Michael Millgate, *Thomas Hardy: A Biography* (1982). For help with the poetry, we recommend: Donald Davie, *Thomas Hardy and British Poetry* (1973); F.B. Pinion, *A Commentary on the Poems of Thomas Hardy* (1976); and William Buckler, *The Poetry of Thomas Hardy: A Study in Art and Ideas* (1983).

JULIA WARD HOWE

The Battle Hymn of the Republic (p. 515)

Although in the last few decades women in considerable numbers have written poetry on political and social issues, in earlier periods their chief topics were love, children, death, and God, for the most part treated personally, intimately, rather than publicly. But religion allowed, in hymns, for personal expression on a public topic, and the Abolitionist movement especially provided a subject about which women could exhort society to action.

Lines 1-4 of "The Battle Hymn of the Republic" are indebted to Revelations 19:11 ("And I saw heaven opened, and behold a white horse; and he that sat upon him was called Faithful and True, and in righteousness he doth judge and make war"), 14 ("And the armies which were in heaven followed him upon white horses"), 15 ("And out of his mouth goeth a sharp sword, that with it he should smite the nations and he shall rule them with a rod of iron: and he treadeth the winepress of the fierceness and wrath of Almighty God"). Isaiah 63:3-6 ("I have trodden the winepress...; I will tread down the people in mine anger"), describing God's punishment of His enemies, also exerted an influence. Line 15 is indebted to Genesis 3:15 (God tells the serpent that woman's seed shall bruise the serpent's head), and in line 18 "sift" is related to Isaiah 30:28 (God will "sift the nations"). The "fiery gospel" of the third stanza perhaps comes from Deuteronomy 33:2 ("from his right hand went a fiery law"). The lillies of line 21 probably come from the Song of Songs and the Sermon on the Mount. The connection between holiness and freedom (23) is common in Paul, though of course in "The Battle Hymn" (published in 1862) the allusion to freedom in line 23 is to freeing the black slaves.

In *Redeemer Nation*, Ernest Tuveson briefly discusses the poem in the context of American apocalyptic writing. He points out that although many who have sung the hymn have thought that the biblical images are merely "fitting metaphors for a war between right and wrong," the images in fact convey "a message about the precise place and point of the war in the pattern of salvation." (The idea is that the Civil War was the fruit of the accumulated evils of the reign of Satan; the day of the Antichrist is ending.)

The hymn has recently been the subject of some controversy. In July of 1986 a committee of the United Methodist Church (a denomination formed in 1968 when the Methodist Church and the Evangelical United Brethren merged) narrowly voted to eliminate "The Battle Hymn of the Republic" (along with

"Onward, Christian Soldiers") from the hymnal. The committee received thousands of letters of protest and reversed its decision in July of 1987. Students might well be invited to discuss the appropriateness (or inappropriateness) of the military metaphor and the reasons for the appeal of the hymn.

Two other issues: "Glory, Glory, Hallelujah" (a shout of triumph at the fall of Babylon) was not in the "Hymn" when it was first published. The final stanza, with its two lines about Christ, may seem incongruous or inept, but it introduces the Incarnation and Atonement, which made possible the last triumphs over evil on earth. Hermes Nye sings "The Battle Hymn" on a record titled *Ballads of the Civil War*, Vol. 1 (Folkways FA 2187 [FP 48/ 7]).

Students, we have found, are very interested in the Civil War, and eager to learn more about it. Instructors might recommend: James M. McPherson, *Ordeal by Fire*, 2 vols. (2nd ed., published in paperback, 1993). This is also a good opportunity for us to mention a valuable reference work: *Notable American Women: A Biographical Dictionary*, ed. Edward T. James (3 vols., 1971), though the scholarship in it now needs updating, its entries are detailed and thorough. On Julia Ward Howe, see 2:225-29.

SPIRITUALS

Deep River; Didn't My Lord deliver Daniel (p. 516-517)

The introductory note in the text mentions that one of the chief themes is the desire for release, and that this theme is often set forth with imagery from the Hebrew Bible, but some additional points should be mentioned. Most of what follows here is derived from Albert J. Raboteau, *Slave Religion* (1978).

Although the passages about release undoubtedly refer to the release from slavery, the songs should not be taken only as disguised statements about secular life. Many slaves—like at least some of their masters—believed that the Bible was the book of the acts of God, which is to say that they "believed that the supernatural continually impinged on the natural, that divine action constantly took place within the lives of men, in the past, present, and future" (Raboteau 250).

Raboteau makes a second very important point:

> Identification with the children of Israel was, of course, a significant theme for white Americans, too. From the beginnings of colonization, white Christians had identified the journey across the Atlantic to the New World as the exodus of a new Israel from the bondage of Europe into the promised land of milk and honey. For the black Christian, as Vincent Harding has observed [in *The Religious Situation*, ed. Donald R. Cutter], the imagery was reversed: the Middle Passage had brought his people to Egypt land, where they suffered bondage under Pharaoh. White Christians saw themselves as a new Israel; slaves identified themselves as the old. (250-51)

Instructors who have time for some additional reading may wish to consult—for a survey of scholarship on the topic—John White, "Veiled Testimony: Negro Spirituals and the Slave Experience," in *Journal of American Studies* 17

(1983): 251-63. White is especially concerned with adjudicating between those who see spirituals (of the type that we reprint) as highly revolutionary and, on the other hand, those who see the songs as in effect serving the cause of the masters, since the songs seem to suggest that suffering in this world is transient, and that God will later reward the sufferers. (As an example of this second view, White quotes E. Franklin Frazier, an African-American scholar who in *The Negro Church in America* [1964] rejected "the efforts of Negro intellectuals. . . encouraged by white radicals, to invest the spirituals with a revolutionary meaning.")

Other recommended works (in addition to Raboteau and White): John Lovell, *Black Song: The Forge and the Flame* (1972); James H. Cone, *The Spirituals and the Blues* (1972); and Lawrence Levine, *Black Culture and Black Conciousness* (1977).

Obviously these songs (like all oral literature) really ought to be heard, not simply read. Many excellent recordings are available, but if you are lucky you may find a student who will give a live performance in class.

LANGSTON HUGHES

Evenin' Air Blues (p. 518)

Though perhaps when we first think of blues we think of songs of disappointed love, blues include songs concerned with other kinds of loneliness, and some at least implicitly relate this loneliness to an oppressive society that is built on segregation and that engenders wandering and alienation. Hughes's "Evenin' Air Blues," then, is genuinely related to the blues tradition, though not surprisingly the note of social protest is a little more evident.

The last stanza, chiefly by virtue of its first line, seems to make a natural conclusion, but as in most blues, the stanzas can pretty much stand independently; perhaps less blueslike is the perfection of the rhyme (one almost feels that the single near-rhyme (by the standards of standard English) *fine:mind* in the first stanza is a conscious imitation of such blues rhymes as *ride:by* or *dime:mine*. The blues often uses a three-line stanza, in which the second line repeats the first; Hughes's six-line stanza, in which the fourth line repeats the second, is a variation on the usual form.

A "Voices and Visions" videocassette of Langston Hughes is available from Longman.

LI-YOUNG LEE

I Ask My Mother to Sing (p. 518)

Singing is infectious; the speaker asks his mother to sing, and his grandmother joins her. The reference to the deceased father—who would have joined in too if he had been there—adds a note of pathos and thus anticipates the second stanza, where we learn that the song is about the land of the speaker's ancestors, a land he has never seen.

The song apparently is joyful (picknickers—though admittedly the picnic is dispelled by rain), but since it is about a lost world it is also sorrowful (the women begin to cry). Yet, even singing about sorrow provides the singer with joy, or, we might say, the making of a work of art (here, singing a song) is pleasurable even when the content is sorrowful. One way of mastering sorrow, of course, is to turn it into art.

EDNA ST. VINCENT MILLAY

The Spring and the Fall (p. 519)

We begin with the rhyme scheme of the poem.

year	*a* (with internal *a*)
dear	*a*
wet	*b*
year	*a* (with internal *b*)
peach	*c*
reach	*c*
year	*a* (with internal *a*)
dear	*a*
trill	*d*
year	*a* (with internal *d*)
praise	*e*
ways	*e*
falling	*f* (with an internal *f*; but as an off-rhyme)
calling	*f*
hear	*a*
year	*a* (with internal *d*)
days	*e*
ways	*e*

Obviously there's lots of rhyme here; this is a highly lyrical lyric, close to song. In addition to the repetition of sound gained through rhyme, there are other repetitions—not only in the form of alliteration (e.g., 'bough. . . blossoming,' "rooks. . . raucous") and consonance (e.g., "trees. . . see") but also in the form of entire words: the first half of the first line is repeated verbatim in the second half of the line; "In the spring of the year" (1) becomes "In the fall of the year" (7), words repeat verbatim in the second half of the line, and in the third stanza the two phrases about the seasons are joined in line 10, but with a significant change: "the" year becomes "a" year.

Many highly lyrical poems employ what can be called a repetitive or perhaps an intensifying structure, each stanza going over the same ground, deepening the feeling but not advancing a narrative, even a narrative of the progress of a feeling. "The Spring and the Fall," however, is a lyric that includes a narrative, a progression, as a reader probably suspects immediately from the title. The first stanza deals with spring, the second with fall. Further, in the first stanza the lovers are physically and emotionally united (they walk together, and he obligingly—lovingly—presents her with "a bough of the blossoming peach"); in the second stanza the lovers are together only physically, not emotionally: "He laughed at all I dared to praise." Instead of giving her a gift, he laughs at (not with) her, and we hear of rooks making a "raucous" sound. The last line of the second stanza explicitly announces the break: "And broke my heart, in little ways." (The word "way," incidentally, was introduced in the first stanza—the peach-bough he gave her a sign of his love, "was out of the way and hard to reach." And in the last stanza "ways" appears again, in the last line, where we are told that when love went it "went in little ways.")

Another notable difference between the first two stanzas; ordinarily the stanzas in a lyric poem repeat a metrical pattern, but in this poem the last two lines of the second stanza are shorter than the last two lines of the first two stanzas, thus conveying a sense of something cut short. The difference is made especially evident by the fact that the change is unanticipated; the first two lines of the second stanza closely resemble (as one expects) the first two lines of the first stanza.

The narrative, then, in effect is completed at the end of the second stanza. Or nearly so: although at the end of the second stanza we learn that the speaker's heart was broken "in little ways," we don't learn until the last two lines of the third stanza that what especially hurts is that love went "in little ways." The third stanza, as has already been mentioned, brings the two seasons together; its first four lines seem joyous and loving, but its last two lines comment on the end of this love affair. The third stanza differs from the first two in several technical details. For example, as we have already mentioned, the first line of the first stanza, like the first line of the second stanza, repeats a phrase ("In the spring of the year, in the spring of the year," "In the fall of the year, in the fall of the year"). The third stanza, however, reflecting a different state of mind, begins with a different form of repetition: "Year be springing or year be falling." Another difference, admittedly small, is that the third stanza is the only stanza to use a feminine rhyme ("failing... calling").

We think that Millay is an underrated poet, and urge students to turn to *Collected Poems: Edna St. Vincent Millay,* ed. Norma Millay (1956). The critical work on her verse is somewhat disappointing, though we can recommend Norman A. Brittin, *Edna St. Vincent Millay* (1967), and James Gray, *Edna St. Vincent Millay* (1967), as useful points of departure.

WILFRED OWEN

Anthem for Doomed Youth (p. 520)

Here are our responses to the questions we put in the text:

1. An anthem is (a) a hymn of praise or loyalty or (b) a sacred composition set to words of the Bible. In Owen's poem, "orisons," "prayers," "save," "choirs," "flowers," "holy glimmers," and even "die" and "pall" might be found in an anthem, but among the unexpected words and phrases are "die as cattle," "stuttering rifles'... rattle," "mockeries," "demented," and perhaps "blinds."

(One might, or might not, want to talk about the onomatopoeia in "stuttering rifles' rapid rattle.")

2. This question anticipates the next chapter, "The Speaking Tone of Voice," but we see no reason not to anticipate it. We'd characterize the tone thus: The first line asks a pained question, but in "monstrous anger" (2) we begin to hear indignation, and in line 3 ("stuttering rifles' rapid rattle") bitterness. In this poem the word "mockeries" is not unexpected; the speaker is not, of course, mocking the dead, but his pain and indignation seem to find an outlet in mockery. For instance, in calling his poem an "anthem" he mocks traditional praises of the glory of dying in war. (Owen's "Dulce et Decorum Est" pretty decisively sums up Owen's view not only of the First World War, but of all wars. A different poet, however, might have mocked not war in general but only a specific war. That is, a satiric poet might have used the word "anthem" ironically, mocking a specific war precisely because it is ignoble in comparison with those wars for which anthems might fittingly be composed.) He finds some comfort, however, in the "holy glimmers of good-byes" which shine in the soldiers' eyes, in the "pallor of girls' eyes," which are the pall, and in the "tenderness of patient minds," which serves as "flowers" (a floral tribute more worthy than wreaths accompanied by conventional funeral oratory). What sad comfort there is, then, is provided by those who die and their loved ones, not by church and state. By the last line the indignation has quieted, though the sadness remains.

It is interesting to compare the final version with the first draft of the poem, printed in Owen's *Collected Poems* and in John Stallworthy's *Wilfred Owen*. The first version, untitled and chiefly unrhymed, goes thus:

> What minute bells for these who die so fast?
>   Only the monstrous anger of our guns.
> Let the majestic insults of their iron mouths
>   Be as the priest-words of their burials.
> Of choristers and holy music, none;
>   Nor any voice of mourning, save the wail
> The long-drawn wail of high, far-sailing shells.
>   What candles may we hold for these lost souls?
> Not in the hands of boys but in their eyes
> Shall many candles shine, and [?] light them.
> Women's wide-spreaded arms shall be their wreathes,
> Their flowers, the tenderness of all men's minds,
> And every dusk, a drawing-down of blinds.

Owen showed the draft to Siegfried Sassoon, who suggested some changes and who also suggested a title, "Anthem for Dead Youth." Owen accepted the changes and the title and wrote at least three more versions, facsimiles of which can be found in Stallworthy. When Owen showed the final version to Sassoon, Sassoon suggested changing the title to "Anthem for Doomed Youth."

There are some excellent secondary sources, to which students can be referred for background and context: Bernard Bergonzi, *Heroes' Twilight: A Study of the Literature of the Great War* (1965); Paul Fussell, *The Great War and Modern Memory* (1975); and Samuel Hynes, *A War Imagined: The First World War and British Culture* (1990). See also *The Penguin Book of First World War Poetry,* ed. Jon Silkin (2nd ed., 1981).

WALT WHITMAN

A Noiseless Patient Spider (p. 521)

Whitman's "A Noiseless Patient Spider" is in free verse, a form discussed later in the text in connection with Whitman's "When I Heard the Learn'd Astronomer," but most instructors find it appropriate to say a few words about the form at this stage. In fact, of course, the poem is not terribly "free;" each stanza has five lines, helping to establish the similitude of spider and soul, and the first line of each stanza is relatively short, the other lines being longer, helping to establish the idea of "venturing, throwing." The near-rhyme at the end helps to tie up the poem, as though finally the bridge is at least tentatively "form'd," the "anchor" holding, but the fact is that the action is not yet complete, the soul is not yet anchored. A discussion of this poem will also necessarily get into Whitman's use of figurative language. Implicitly, the speaker's soul is a noiseless, patient spider, "ceaselessly musing, ceaselessly venturing," building a "bridge" in the vastness (i.e., uniting the present with eternity Or are the filaments that the soul flings poems that unite mankind?).

In addition to the biographies by Gay Wilson Allen (1967) and Justin Kaplan (1980), we admire Paul Zweig's sensitively written study, *Walt Whitman: The Making of the Poet* (1984). A brisk, informative overview of the period can be found in David S. Reynolds, *Walt Whitman's America: A Cultural Biography* (1995). Harold Bloom's chapter, "Walt Whitman as Center of the American Canon," in his book, *The Western Canon* (1994), is also stimulating, though students unfamiliar with the culture and canon wars may lack the context to perceive Bloom's polemical aims here.

TOPICS FOR CRITICAL THINKING AND WRITING

1. In about 250 words describe some animal, plant, or object that can be taken as a symbol of some aspect of your personality or experience.
2. The text gives Whitman's final version (1871) of "A Noiseless Patient Spider." Here is Whitman's draft, written some ten years earlier. Compare the two poems and evaluate them.

The Soul, Reaching, Throwing Out for Love

The soul, reaching, throwing out for love,
As the spider, from some little promontory, throwing out filament after
    filament, tirelessly out of itself, that one at least may catch and form a
    link, a bridge, a connection
O I saw one passing along, saying hardly a word—yet full of love I detected
    him, by certain signs
O eyes wishfully turning! O silent eyes!
For then I thought of you o'er the world,

O latent oceans, fathomless oceans of love!
O waiting oceans of love! yearning and fervid! and of you sweet souls
    perhaps in the future delicious and long:
But Death, unknown on the earth—ungiven, dark here, unspoken, never
    born:
You fathomless latent souls of love—you pent and unknown oceans of love!

A "Voices and Visions" video cassette of Walt Whitman is available from Longman.

JOHN KEATS

Ode to a Grecian Urn (p. 522)

Let's begin at the end, with the issue of the punctuation of the last two lines. Does the urn speak the two lines, or does it speak only "Beauty is truth, truth beauty"? The matter has been thoroughly discussed by Jack Stillinger, in an appendix to his book called *The Hoodwinking of Madeline* (1971). The problem is this: when the poem was first published, in *Annals of the Fine Arts* (1819), the lines were printed thus:

Beauty is Truth,—Truth Beauty—That is all
    Ye know on Earth, and all ye need to know.

When Keats published the ode in his book *Lamia and Other Poems* (1820), the lines were punctuated thus:

"Beauty is truth, truth beauty,"—that is all
    Ye know on earth, and all ye need to know.

The two printed versions thus set off "Beauty is truth, truth beauty" as a unit separate from the remaining words. But Keats probably did not supervise the publication in *The Annals,* and because he was ill when *Lamia* was in production he may not have read the proofs, or may not have read them attentively. Many scholars therefore do not feel obliged to accept the punctuation of the two printed texts. They point to the four extant manuscript transcripts of the poem (none by Keats, but all by persons close to Keats). Because none of these transcriptions uses quotation marks or a period after "beauty," these scholars argue that the punctuation suggests that the urn speaks all of the last two lines:

Beauty is Truth,—Truth Beauty,—that is all
    Ye know on earth, and all ye need to know.

Stillinger points out that none of the six readings (the four transcripts and the two published versions) offers conclusive proof of Keats's intention. He goes on to summarize the interpretations, and we now summarize Stillinger:

1. **Poet to Reader.** The urn speaks the first five words of line 49 ("Beauty is truth, truth beauty"), and the poet, addressing the reader, speaks the rest of

the last two lines ("that is all / Ye know on earth, and all ye need to know"). The objection to this view is that earlier in the last stanza the poet and the reader are "us," and the poet says that later woes will belong to a generation other than "ours." Why, then, does the poet shift the address to "ye," where we would expect "we"? Second, the statement is obviously false; we need to know much more than that "Beauty is truth, truth beauty."

2. **Poet to Urn.** The poet speaks the end of line 49, and all of the last line, to the urn. The poet tells the urn that *it* need know no more—but that we need to know a great deal more. The objection, Stillinger points out, is that "ye" is normally a plural pronoun—though in fact Keats did sometimes use it as a singular. A second objection: What can Keats possibly mean by saying to the urn, "that is all / Ye know *on earth*..."?

3. **Poet to Figures on Urn.** The poet speaks the end of 49 and all of the last line to the figures on the urn. This fits with "ye" as a plural. The objection is that the figures are not "on earth," and, further, that the poet is no longer thinking of them as alive and capable of hearing. Further, *why* should the figures on the urn know this and only this?

4. **Urn to Reader.** The urn speaks all of the two last lines. The objection is that the statement seems to defy common sense, and more important, it is *not* the way the *Lamia* volume punctuated the line. Some critics have suggested that the quotation marks were meant to set off these five words as a sort of motto within a two-line statement by the urn.

It is our impression that most editors today disregard the *Lamia* punctuation, put the whole of the two lines within quotation marks, and take the lines as spoken by the urn to the reader. In any case, a reader is still left to wonder whether the passage is profound wisdom or is nonsense.

Now to begin at the beginning. In the first line "still" probably has several meanings (motionless; as yet; silent); the urn is the "foster-child of silence and slow time" because its real parent is the craftsman who made it, but it has been adopted, so to speak, by silence and the centuries. Although the poet begins by saying that the urn can tell a tale "more sweetly" than a poet can, in fact by the end of the stanza it is clear that the urn cannot tell a tale; it can only (of course) show some isolated moment, and let the viewer try to guess what actions came before and will come after. It is worth mentioning, too, that this stanza praises the urns staying-power ("slow time") but is rich in words that imply transience: "Sylvan," "flowery," "leaf-fringed," "haunts" (suggesting the insubstantial or ethereal). The stanza ends with urgent questions conveying agitation and implying that the urn cannot tell a tale satisfactorily.

The second stanza begins on a note of composure; in the space between the stanzas, so to speak, the poet has stilled his questioning spirit, and has progressed to a state where he can offer something for meditation ("Heard melodies are sweet, but those unheard / Are sweeter"). As the stanza continues, a slightly painful note is introduced: the pastoral landscape will never die—but the lover will never kiss the woman. The poet urges the lover not to grieve, which means that he in fact introduces into this Arcadian world the idea of potential grief. Although the stanza ends by asserting the youth's eternal love, and the woman's eternal beauty, there is something almost painful in the last words of the next-to-last line of the stanza, "though thou hast not thy bliss."

The third stanza begins with a renewed note of joy, again apparently gained in the blank space that precedes the stanza, though perhaps we may also detect a note of hysteria in the repetition of "Ah, happy, happy boughs." This stanza too, despite its early expressions of joy, moves toward distress. We are told that the figures on the urn are "far above" human passion, but the last lines dwell on the pains of human passions: "a heart high-sorrowful and cloyed, / A burning forehead, and a parching tongue."

We cannot quite say that the fourth stanza begins with the by-now expected note of composure, because in fact it begins with a question, but it is true to say that in fact this stanza too begins in a quieter mood. The poet is contemplating with interest a new scene on the urn, a scene showing a "mysterious priest" and a "heifer lowing at the skies, / ... her silken flanks with garlands drest." As the poet describes this highly picturesque scene, again we hear a note foreign to the beginning of the stanza. The poet begins by conveying his interest in what he sees—"the mysterious priest," the "heifer," and the "folk, this pious morn"—but then his mind turns to the "little town" that is "emptied of this folk" and whose "streets for evermore / Will silent be." The last two lines of the stanza are deeply melancholy: "not a soul to tell / Why thou art desolate, can e'er return." Jack Stillinger, in an essay on the odes (reprinted from his *Twentieth Century Views*) in *The Hoodwinking of Madeline* suggests that "'Desolate' in line 40 is the counterpart of 'forlorn' in *Ode to a Nightingale*. It brings the speaker back to his sole self" (106).

The fifth stanza begins with the expected renewed joy, but it is worth noticing that the urn, which in the first stanza was a "Sylvan historian" capable of telling a "flowery tale" now is a "shape" and a "silent form" and a "Cold Pastoral." The poet by now has clearly seen that what he at first took for a world of idealized love is "cold," and its figures are "marble men and maidens." That is, if it is perfect and permanent it is also cold, bloodless, without the passion that (however painful) is what we want from life. Stillinger puts it this way:

> Like the nightingale, [the urn] has offered a tentative idea—momentarily "teas[ing]" the speaker "out of thought"—but has also led the speaker to understand the shortcomings of the ideal. (108)

Stillinger's comment on the last two lines is also worth quoting:

> The final lines present a special problem in interpretation, but it is clear that, while the urn is not entirely rejected at the end, its value lies in its character as a work of art, not in its being a possible substitute for life in the actual world. However punctuated, the urn's "message" amounts to what the speaker has come to realize in his speculations—that the only beauty accessible to mortal man exists "on earth." The urn is "a friend to man" for helping him to arrive at this conclusion through just such ponderings as we have witnessed in the course of the poem. (108-09)

For students, we advise they read Keats in (or alongside) *The Poems of John Keats*, ed. Miriam Allott (1970), which includes detailed annotations. W. J. Bate's biography (1963) is an impressive work, but the shorter studies by Douglas Bush (1966) and Robert Gittings (1968) may be better for introductory students. Among critical studies, we have benefited from Christopher Ricks, *Keats and Embarrassment* (1974), and Helen Vendler, *The Odes of John Keats* (1983). Also useful is *Twentieth Century Interpretations of Keats's Odes,* ed. Jack Stillinger (1968). For paper assignments, students can consult Jack Walter Rhodes, *Keats's Major Odes: An Annotated Bibliography of the Criticism* (1984). Ian Jack, in *Keats and the Mirror of Art* (1967), has an interesting well-illustrated chapter on urns—and pictures of urns that Keats is likely to have seen, but, unfortunately, no one urn is the model; in fact, "that heifer lowing at the skies" probably came not from an urn but from the Elgin Marbles. Jack's concern is only with identifying motifs; he does not offer an interpretation of the poem.

E. E. CUMMINGS

anyone lived in a pretty how town (p. 524)

It can be useful to ask students to put into the usual order (so far as one can) the words of the first two stanzas, and then to ask students why Cummings's version is more effective. Here are a few rough glosses: 4: "danced his did" = lived intensely (versus the "someones" who in 18 "did their dance," that is, unenthusiastically went through motions that might have been ecstatic); 7: "they sowed their isn't they reaped their same" gives us the little-minded or small-minded who, unlike "anyone," are unloving and therefore receiving nothing; 8: "sun moon stars rain" = day after day; 10: "down they forgot as up they grew" implies a mental diminution that accompanies growing up; 17: "someones," that is, adults, people who think they are somebody; 25: "anyone died," that is, the child matured, stopped loving (and became dead as the other adults). The last two stanzas imply that although children grow into "Women and men" (33), the seasons continue the same. (This reading is heavily indebted to R. C. Walsh, *Explicator* 22 no. 9 [May 1964], Item 72. For a more complicated reading, see D. L. Clark, *Lyric Resonance,* pp. 187-94.)

Norman Friedman has written two books, *E. E. Cummings: The Art of His Poetry* (1960) and *E. E. Cummings: The Growth of a Writer* (1964), and edited a third, *E. E. Cummings: A Collection of Critical Essays* (1972). Also helpful is Cary Lane, *I Am: A Study of E. E. Cummings' Poems* (1976).

An audiocassette of E. E. Cummings reading is available from Longman.

PAUL LAURENCE DUNBAR

Sympathy (p. 526)

It is worth getting students to talk about the title. Most will say that it suggests a feeling of pity, but some may be familiar with another sense of the word, "fellow-feeling," or "feeling-along-with" (it comes from a Greek word whose elements are *like + feelings*). The speaker's "sympathy," then, is not merely that he feels sorry for the caged bird, but that he *shares the feelings* of the bird. Incidentally, after graduating from high school Dunbar worked as an elevator operator, and it has been suggested—we can't recall where we read this—that he well might have seen a literal as well as a metaphorical connection between himself, working in a cage-like elevator, and the bird.

We value Dunbar as a poet, in, for example, *Lyrics of Lowly Life* (1896), and as a writer of short stories, in such collections as *The Strength of Gideon and Other Stories* (1900). Secondary studies include: *A Singer in the Dawn: Reinterpretations of Paul Laurence Dunbar*, ed. Jay Martin (1975); and Peter Revell, *Paul Laurence Dunbar* (1979).

LINDA PASTAN

Jump Cabling (p. 527)

The physical appearance of a poem on the page is always important. As anthologists, we are unhappy that we must add line numbers, and that a poem sometimes begins near the bottom of a right-hand page so that most of the poem is invisible at the start. With Pastan's poem, the appearance is especially important. True, if "Jump Cabling" is read aloud, something of the physical appearance can be conveyed (1) by pausing, to indicate the space between the two columns—the space between the two cars or the two people—and (2) by not pausing when one reads the final line, still, this is a poem that must be seen as well as heard.

We take the poem to be about what it explicitly says it is, but obviously the journey together will include bodily contact. The words *touched, intimate workings, underneath*—and we can include *lifted the hood*—add a strong sexual element.

DOROTHY PARKER

General Review of the Sex Situation (p. 527)

The title suggests an academic treatise, so that's the first joke. The second joke perhaps is that the poem is so short, the "general review" of an immense topic is reduced to eight end-stopped lines, i.e. the topic is treated in a tiny space, in a no-nonsense manner, and with the implication that there is no more to be said. Further, this authoritative characterization of the presumably inevitable differences between the two sexes—no talk about "the construction of gender" here—concludes with the suggestion that *of course* things are a mess, but what can we expect.

On Parker: Arthur F. Kinney, *Dorothy Parker* (1978). See also *The Collected Dorothy Parker* (1973); and *The Portable Dorothy Parker*, ed. Brendan Gill (rev. ed., 1973).

CHAPTER 13

The Speaking Tone of Voice

GWENDOLYN BROOKS

The Mother (p. 533)

It's our guess that discussion in class will concentrate on the last three lines. For what it's worth, we find those lines convincing, partly because of their simplicity (no metaphors, no inversions, no unusual diction) and partly because of the repetition. Of course the repetition *might* suggest insincerity, the speaker's awareness that she does not sound convincing and so she piles it on (some readers may feel that the lady doth protest too much), but we do not hear any such suggestion.

GWENDOLYN BROOKS

We Real Cool (p. 534)

The unusual arrangement of the lines, putting what ordinarily would be the first syllable of the second line at the end of the first line, and so on, of course emphasizes the "we"—and therefore emphasizes the absence of "we" in the final line, which consists only of "Die soon," the "we" having been extinguished. The disappearance of the "we" is especially striking in a poem in which the "we" is so pleased with itself.

By emphasis we don't necessarily mean a heavy stress on the word. An emphasis can be gained by the slightest of pauses (even though the word is not followed by a comma or a shift in tone). In *Report from Part One*, Brooks comments on this poem:

> The ending WE's in "We Real Cool" are tiny, wispy, weakly argumentative "Kilroy-is-here" announcements. The boys have no accented sense of themselves, yet they are aware of a semidefined personal importance. Say the "we" softly. (185)

"We" presumably refers to a gang of seven confident pool players, but if seven is traditionally a lucky number, it brings these people no luck. The subtitle allows one to infer that at the Golden Shovel they are digging their own graves.

Students might be directed to Brooks's autobiography, *Report From Part One* (1972) See also D. H. Melhem, *Gwendolyn Brooks: Poetry and the Heroic Voice* (1987).

An audio cassette of Gwendolyn Brooks reading is available from Longman.

STEVIE SMITH

Not Waving but Drowning (p. 535)

All his life the dead man in Stevie Smith's "Not Waving but Drowning" sent messages that were misunderstood. His efforts to mask his loneliness and depression were more successful than he intended. His friends mistook him for a "chap" who "always loved larking," as they now mistake the cause of his death. But true friends would have seen through the clowning, the dead man seems to protest, in lines 3 and 4 (when of course it is too late to protest or to explain). The second stanza confirms his view of the spectators. They are imperceptive and condescending; their understanding of the cause of his death is as superficial as their attention to him was while he was alive. But they didn't know him "all [his] life" (11). The dead man thus acknowledges, by leaving them out of the last stanza, that, never having risked honest behavior, he is at least as responsible as others for his failure to be loved and to love.

Stevie Smith is another underrated modern poet, whom students enjoy when they encounter her work. Her *Collected Poems* were published in 1976. See also Jack Barbera and William McBrien, *A Biography of Stevie Smith* (1985). There are good studies of Smith's poetry in Calvin Bedient, *Eight Contemporary Poets* (1974); and Christopher Ricks, *The Force of Poetry* (1984).

ROBERT BROWNING

My Last Duchess (p. 536)

Robert Langbaum has a good analysis of "My Last Duchess" in *The Poetry of Experience.* On this poem, see also Laurence Perrine, *PMLA* 74 (March 1959): 157-59. W.J.T. Mitchell, in "Representation," in *Critical Terms for Literary Study,* ed. Frank Lentricchia and Thomas McLaughlin, discusses the poem at some length. One of his points is: "Just as the duke seems to hypnotize the envoy,

Browning seems to paralyze the reader's normal judgment by his virtuosic representation of villainy. His poem holds us in its grip, condemning in advance all our attempts to control it by interpretation.... "

It may be mentioned here that although every poem has a "voice," not every poem needs to be a Browningesque dramatic monologue giving the reader a strong sense of place and audience. No one would criticize Marvell's "To His Coy Mistress" on the grounds that the "lady" addressed in line 2 gives place (in at least some degree) to a larger audience—let us say, a general audience—when we get to "But at my back I always hear / Time's winged chariot hurrying near."

See also James A.W. Hefferman, in *Museum of Words: The Poetics of Emphasis from Homer to Ashberry.* For background and context, see *A Browning Handbook,* ed. W. C. DeVane (rev. ed., 1955); and Norman B. Crowell, *A Reader's Guide to Robert Browning* (1972). See also: Ian Jack, *Browning's Major Poetry* (1973); and Herbert Tucker, *Browning's Beginnings* (1980). For a cross-section of critical essays: *Robert Browning,* ed. Isobel Armstrong (1974). Biographies include Betty Miller, *Robert Browning: A Portrait* (1952).

ROBERT HERRICK

To the Virgins to Make Much of Time (p. 539)

On Herrick's "To the Virgins," see E. M.W. Tillyard in *The Metaphysical and Milton;* Tillyard argues effectively that in "To the Virgins," "the trend of the poem is urgency, touched with reflection."

This wonderful lyric seems ideally suited to introduce students to matters of persona and tone. We have found that when asked, "Who is speaking?" most students will answer, "A man." (Possibly some offer this opinion simply because a man wrote this poem.) A few will say that a w omen is the speaker, and we have found it interesting to ask them why. (Those who say that a woman is the speaker usually suggest that she is unmarried and is speaking regretfully.) Almost all students hear the voice of an older person, though they cannot always say why. Similarly, although a few students find the speaker aggressively offering unsolicited advice, most hear a friendly voice. True, the first and last stanzas begin with imperatives ("Gather ye rosebuds," "Then be not coy"), but most students hear in "Old Time," "a-flying," and "a-getting" an engaging old-codgerliness. They may hear, too, even a touch of elderly loquacity in the explanation of a fairly obvious figure: "The glorious lamp of heaven, the sun."

One other point about Herrick's poem: The shift to "you" in the last stanza (from the earlier "ye") gives the moral great emphasis.

The *carpe diem* motif allows the poem to be related easily to Marvell's "Coy Mistress." What is especially interesting, however, is the difference in tone, even though the poems share both a motif and a structure—the logical argument.

Is the poem offensive to women? Some of our students have found it so. Our hope is that readers will be able to read the poem not so much as advice to women to submit passively to marriage, as advice (which can apply to males as well as to females) "to make much of time." Against "dying" and "setting," we can "gather," "smile," and "run."

John Press (1961) and Roger B. Rollin (1966) have good introductions to Herrick's life and work.

TOPICS FOR CRITICAL THINKING AND WRITING

This seventeenth-century poem suggests that a woman finds fulfillment only in marriage. Can the poem, then, be of any interest to a society in which women may choose careers in preference to marriage?

THOMAS HARDY

The Man He Killed (p. 540)

The speaker's diction is that of a simple, uneducated rustic ("old ancient," "Right many a nipperkin," "list," "off-hand-like"). He tells us (15) that he enlisted because he was out of work and broke, but line 10 reveals that he also responded to customary wartime propaganda and appeals to patriotism. He is still too trusting to reject what he was told about his "foe," but in the third stanza the repetitions, abrupt pauses, and attempts to reassure himself in "of course he was," and "That's clear enough" all indicate his struggle to overcome incipient doubts. The heavy pauses in the fourth stanza show the difficulty a man unused to thinking about large matters has when what he has been taught by his "betters" conflicts with his own feelings. In the fifth stanza he resolves his doubts with a platitude—war is "quaint and curious"—but we feel that he'll be retelling his story at one pub or another and pondering his experience for the rest of his life.

One can have a field day talking about irony; here the ironic distance between poet and speaker and between speaker and reader, the "irony of fate" in which the soldier is trapped, the dramatic irony in the fact that the speaker had to kill a man before he could recognize him as a potential neighbor or friend, a man like himself. And, finally, this simple man is one of us. Like him, we are mere pawns trapped between forces whose meaning, though it continues to elude us, we continue to question.

TOPICS FOR CRITICIAL THINKING AND WRITING

What state of mind would you have to be in to think of war as "quaint and curious"? To think of a man you killed as a "foe"? *Is* the speaker convinced by the words he utters? Whether your answer is "Yes" or "No," why do you think so?

WALTER DE LA MARE

An Epitaph (p. 541)

The form of course is an epitaph (literally, "over a tomb"), and it is also an epigram, not in the relatively late sense of a witty comment but in the old sense of something intended to be engraved or inscribed: "writing [engraved] on," "inscription." (Because inscriptions were brief they customarily were highly packed, and in time the word became applied to brief witty writings, but originally an epigram simply was "an inscription.")

The words are imagined to be carved on a tombstone, and the speaker is the tombstone itself ("When I crumble...."). The form was common in the ancient world, and is especially known in the *Greek Anthology*, a collection edited and reedited many times, from the earliest version by the poet Meleager around 60 B.C. until versions as late as the tenth century A.D., by which time the *Greek Anthology* included some 4,500 poems, by more than 300 poets. Sometimes the tombstone itself speaks (as in de la Mare's poem), but sometimes the deceased person speaks, as in what is perhaps the most famous of all ancient epigrams, Simonides's sepulchral epigram spoken by one of those who died at Thermopylae. When the huge Persian army led by Xerxes sought to conquer Greece, the small Greek army established itself at a narrow pass at Thermopylae. The Greek position was betrayed, and the soldiers withdrew, except for some three hundred soldiers from the Greek city-state of Sparta (also called Lacedaemon), who remained and fought to the death. A monument was said to have been erected on the spot:

> Go, tell the Lacedaemonians, passer-by,
> That here obedient to their laws we lie.

Here's another version:

> Stranger, let Sparta learn that here we lie,
> Obedient to her call who bade us die.

(A literal translation might go thus: "Stranger, tell the Spartans that we lie here obeying their orders.")

De la Mare's "An Epitaph" has a slightly archaic flavor in the fourth line, where the accent in "West Country" falls on the final syllable (a common occurrence in ballads, for instance in "Sir Patrick Spence," where the accent on "sailor" is on the second syllable).

The poem consists of relatively short lines, and it is fulll of heavy pauses. What is the effect? To us, given the subject matter, the pauses contribute to the speaker's sense of a painful loss. The one line that is enjambed is the next-to-last, when the stone speaks of crumbling, and we take this over-running to be imitative of the stone losing its form. Notice, too, that in the first line the stone speaks of "a most beautiful lady," thus preserving at least the memory of the lady's beauty, but in the last line—when the stone imagines its own demise—the lady's beauty is utterly gone, and we hear only of "This lady," and indeed the context ("who will remember / This lady") suggests that the lady as well as her beauty is gone.

Students might turn next to de la Mare's *Selected Poems*, ed. R. N. Green-Armytage (1954); and *A Choice of de la Mare's Verse*, ed. W. H. Auden (1963).

GERARD MANLEY HOPKINS

Spring and Fall: To a Young Child (p. 542)

In our experience, students will have considerable difficulty if they simply read the poem silently to themselves, but if they read (and reread) it aloud, it becomes clear—and more important, it becomes something they value.

We begin, then, as we usually do with poems, by having a student read the poem aloud, and then we invite comments about the title and its connection with the two people in the poem. Students usually see that the poem presents youth and age, that Margaret is associated with spring and the speaker with the fall, and this leads to discussion of the Fall in Christian thought. Many students, however, do not know that in Christian thought the disobedience of Adam and Eve brought consequences that extended to nature, and that the perennial spring of Eden therefore yielded to autumn and winter; that is, "Goldengrove" inherited death. ("Goldengrove," incidentally, might seem to suggest preciousness and eternity, but here the golden leaves are a sign of transience and death.)

In the original version of "Spring and Fall" (1880), line 8 ran, "Though forests low and leafmeal lie." When he revised the poem in 1884, Hopkins changed "Though forests low and" to "Though worlds of wanwood," thus introducing the pallor of "wanwood" and also wonderfully extending the vista from "forests" to "worlds." Margaret's sorrow for the trees stripped of their golden foliage is finally sorrow for the Fall, whose consequences are everywhere. Her mouth cannot formulate any of this, but her spirit has intuited it ("ghost guessed").

On "Spring and Fall," see Paul L. Mariani, *A Commentary on the Complete Poems of Gerard Manley Hopkins*; Marylou Motto, *The Poetry of Gerard Manley Hopkins*; and Peter Milward's essay in Milward and R. V. Schoder, *Landscape and Inscape*. George Starbuck has a modern version ("Translations from the English") in his book of poems, *White Paper*.

Recent work on Hopkins includes: *Gerard Manley Hopkins (1844-1889): New Essays on His Life, Writing, and Place in English Literature*, ed. Michael E. Allsop and Michael W. Sundermeier (1989); Robert Bernard Martin, *Gerard Manley Hopkins: A Very Private Life* (1991); and Norman White, *Hopkins: A Literary Biography* (1992).

COUNTEE CULLEN

For a Lady I Know (p. 543)

Although Cullen sometimes wrote about African-American life he also wrote on other topics and in traditions other than the vernacular tradition employed by Langston Hughes.

"For a Lady I Know" is indeed about white/black relations, but it is in the tradition of the polished epigram of Martial and other Roman satirists and their successors. "Low" diction occurs in "snores," but for the most part the diction is refined, echoing the language that the "lady" might use: "lies late," "poor black cherubs," "rise at seven," "celestial chores." The satiric force of the poem comes largely from stating a repulsive idea elegantly.

LYN LIFSHIN

My Mother and the Bed (p. 543)

Students enjoy this poem, and classroom discussion may be animated, especially concerning the second question in the text, which asks if bitterness overshadows geniality.

Our first question, concerning the unexpected extra spaces in the poem, calls attention to the need to pay close attention to—to enjoy—the physical appearance of the poem. Of course readers of this book have already seen, in Pastan's "Jump Cabling" in the preceding chapter, a poem whose meaning is partly conveyed by its appearance on the page, but it is useful to remind students to consider the physical appearance of every poem. Long lines convey a feeling different from short lines, and the breaks between stanzas can say a lot. True, we should read poems aloud, if possible, but we should also look at them closely—"hear with eyes," in Shakespeare's words—and take their appearance seriously.

E. E. CUMMINGS

next to of course god america i (p. 545)

"Next to of course god america i" uses Cummings's characteristic unconventional typography, but here the effect is not so much to break with lifeless convention as it is to emphasize the mindless, unvarying, unstoppable jabbering of politicians.

An audiocassette of E. E. Cummings reading is available from Longman.

MARGE PIERCY

Barbie Doll (p. 546)

The title alerts us to the world of childhood, so we are not surprised in the first line by "This girlchild" (like "This little pig") or by "peepee" in the second line. The stanza ends with the voice of a jeering child. The second stanza drops the kid-talk, adopting in its place the language of social science. (The stanza has much of the sound of Auden's "The Unknown Citizen.") We have not, then, made much progress; the "girlchild" who in the first stanza is treated like a Barbie doll is in the second treated like a healthy specimen, a statistic. The third stanza sounds more intimate, but she is still an object, not a person, and by the end of this stanza, there is a painful explosion. The two preceding stanzas each ended with a voice different from the voice that spoke the earlier lines of the stanza (in 6, "You have a great big nose and fat legs," we hear a jeering child, and in 11, "Everyone saw a fat nose on thick legs," we hear an adolescent imagining how others see her), but the third stanza ends with something of the flatly stated violence of a fairy tale: "So she cut off her nose and her legs / and offered them up." In the fourth and final stanza she is again (or better, still) a doll, lifeless and pretty.

In recent years, in addition to white Barbies there have been African-American, Hispanic and Asian Barbies, but until the fall of 1990 the TV and print ads showed only the fair-skinned blue-eyed version. For additional information about Barbie, see Sydney Ladensohn Stern and Ted Schoenhaus, *Toyland: the High-Stakes Game of the Toy Industry*, and M.G. Lord, *Forever Barbie*. Barbie's wardrobe has changed from flight attendant to astronaut, and from garden-party outfits to workout attire. She has a dress-for-success and a briefcase—but they are pink.

Piercy has written many books of poetry and novels. We suggest that students turn to the poems in *Circles on the Water* (1982), *My Mother's Body* (1985), and *Available Light* (1988). See also: *Ways of Knowing: Essays on Marge Piercy*, ed. Sue Walker and Eugene Hamner (1991).

MARGE PIERCY

What's That Smell in the Kitchen? (p. 547)

Putting aside the title (in which, at least in retrospect, perhaps we hear the voice of the oafish husband comfortably seated in the TV room), the first words of the first line ("All over America women are") might lead us to expect some sort of feminist/Whitmanesque assertion of glorious unity, or of flourishing individuality, and in a sense we get something like this, but in a comic domestic vein. The burnt dinners are fully explained in the final line, but the reason becomes evident fairly soon in the poem—certainly by line 9, with its punning glance at kitchen utensils in "Anger sputters in her brainpan."

MITSUYE YAMADA

To the Lady (p. 548)

First, some background. In 1942 the entire Japanese and Japanese-American population on America's Pacific coast—about 112,000 people—was incarcerated and relocated. More than two-thirds of the people moved were native-born citizens of the United States. (The 158,000 Japanese residents of the Territory of Hawaii were not affected.)

Immediately after the Japanese attack on Pearl Harbor, many journalists, the general public, Secretary of the Army Henry Stimson, and congressional delegations from California, Oregon, and Washington called for the internment. Although Attorney General Francis Biddle opposed it, on February 19, 1942, President Franklin D. Roosevelt signed Executive Order 9066, allowing military authorities "to prescribe military areas. . . from which any or all persons may be excluded." In practice, no persons of German or Italian heritage were disturbed, but Japanese and Japanese-Americans on the Pacific coast were rounded up (they were allowed to take with them "only that which can be carried") and relocated in camps. Congress, without a dissenting vote, passed legislation supporting the evacuation. A few Japanese-Americans challenged the constitutionality of the proceeding, but with no immediate success.

Many students today may find it difficult to comprehend the intensity of anti-Japanese sentiment that pervaded the 1940s. Here are two samples, provided by David Mura, whose poem about the internment camps appears on page 509 of the text. Lt. General John DeWitt, the man in charge of the relocation plan, said:

> The Japanese race is an enemy race and while many second and third generation Japanese born on United States soil, possessed of United States citizenship, have become "Americanized," the racial strains are undiluted. To conclude otherwise is to expect that children born of white parents on Japanese soil sever all racial affinity and become loyal Japanese subjects. . . . Along the vital Pacific Coast over 112,000 enemies, of Japanese extraction, are at large today. There are indications that these are organized and ready for concerted action at a favorable opportunity. The very fact that no sabotage has taken place to date is a disturbing and confirming indication that such action will be taken.

One rubs one's eyes in disbelief at the crazy logic that holds that *because* "no sabotage has taken place," such action "will be taken." The second quotation Mura has called to our attention is a remark made in 1942 by Senator Tom Steward of Tennessee:

> They [the Japanese] are cowardly and immoral. They are different from Americans in every conceivable way, and no Japanese. . . . should have the right to claim American citizenship. . . . A Jap is a Jap anywhere you find him. They do not believe in God and have no respect for an oath of allegiance.

By the way, not a single Japanese-American was found guilty of subversive activity. For two good short accounts, with suggestions for further readings, see the articles entitled "Japanese Americans, wartime relocation of," in *Kodansha Encyclopedia of Japan*, 4:17-18, and "War Relocation Authority," in 8:228.

It may be interesting to read Yamada's poem aloud in class, *without* having assigned it for prior reading, and to ask students for their responses at various stages—after line 4, line 21, and line 36. Line 14 poses a question that perhaps many of us (young and old, and whether of Japanese descent or not) have asked, at least to ourselves. The question, implying a criticism of the victims, shows an insufficient awareness of Japanese or Japanese-American culture of the period. It also shows an insufficient awareness of American racism; by implying that protest by the victims *could* have been effective, it reveals ignorance of the terrific hostility of whites toward persons of Japanese descent.

The first part of the response shows one aspect of the absurdity of the lady's question. Japanese and Japanese-Americans were brought up not to stand out in any way (certainly not to make a fuss), and to place the harmony of the group (whether the family, or society as a whole) above individual expression. Further, there was nothing that these people could effectively do, even if they had shouted as loudly as Kitty Genovese did. For the most part they were poor, they had no political clout, and they were hated and despised as Asians. The absurdity of the view that they could have resisted effectively is comically stated in "should've pulled myself up from my / bra straps" (echoing the red-blooded American ideal of pulling oneself up by one's bootstraps), but of course the comedy is bitter.

Then the speaker turns to "YOU," nominally the "lady" of the title but in effect also the reader, and by ironically saying what we would have done points out what in fact we did not do. (The references to a march on Washington and letters to Congress are clear enough, but most students will not be aware of the tradition that the King of Denmark said that he would wear a Star of David [line 27] if Danish Jews were compelled by Nazis to wear the star.)

Thus far the speaker has put the blame entirely on the white community, especially since lines 5-21 strongly suggest that the Japanese-Americans *couldn't* do anything but submit. Yet the poem ends with a confession that because Japanese-Americans docilely subscribed to "law and order"—especially the outrageous Executive Order 9066—they were in fact partly responsible for the outrage committed against them. The last line of the poem, "All are punished," is exactly what Prince Escalus says at the end of *Romeo and Juliet*. Possibly the echo is accidental, though possibly the reader is meant to be reminded of a play, widely regarded as "a tragedy of fate," in which the innocent are victims of prejudice.

LOUISE ERDRICH

Dear John Wayne (p. 550)

The title suggests a fan letter (and therefore a naive, adoring writer-speaker), but the poem turns out to be a witty, vigorous satire, with a good deal of Swiftian *saeva indignatio* under the wit.

The mock heroic diction of "to *vanquish* hordes of mosquitoes" quickly yields to the simplicity of "Nothing works," but the mosquitoes as enemies reappear in "They break through the smoke-screen for blood," where the line also evokes thoughts of cowboys and Indians in battle. Other elevated passages include "There will be no parlance" and "die beautifully," but such terms are mixed with "ICBM missiles" and "this wide screen," so they are undercut; the apparent heroism is Hollywood phoniness, as phony as John Wayne's smile, "a horizon of teeth."

Satire, of course, is a way of talking seriously, of expressing indignation under a veil of comedy. If the absurdity of what is happening on the screen causes the Indians to laugh and "fall over the hood, / slipping in the hot spilled butter," these lines about Native Americans eating popcorn remind us of the cliché about people slipping in blood during battle, and the cliché reminds us of the reality of the battles in which, finally, the whites took the land from the Native Americans.

CHAPTER 14

Figurative Language: Simile, Metaphor, Personification, Apostrophe

If the idea that metaphors are like riddles is appealing, ask the class why the camel is "the ship of the desert." They will see that the figure goes beyond saying that the camel is a means of transportation, for the figure brings out both the camel's resemblance (at a great distance) to a sailboat and the desert's resemblance to an ocean.

If one wants to get into this business of metaphors as riddles (and we recommend it), one can have great fun in class by assigning Craig Raine's "A Martian Sends a Postcard Home," printed later in the text.

On figurative language, consult Monroe Beardsley, *Aesthetics;* Isabel Hungerland, *Poetic Discourse,* W. K. Wimsatt, Jr., and Cleanth Brooks, *Literary Criticism,* pp. 749-50; and Terence Hawkes, *Metaphor.* Probably as good as any statement about figurative language is Shelley's, that the language of poets "is vitally metaphoric; that is, it marks the before unapprehended relations of things and perpetuates their apprehension."

At some point during our classroom discussion of metaphor we usually manage to give students Kenneth Burke's comment on metaphor (from his essay on Marianne Moore): Metaphor is "a device for seeing something *in terms of* something else. It brings out the thisness of a that, or the thatness of a this!"

ROBERT BURNS

A Red, Red Rose (p. 553)

Probably few instructors will feel the need to discuss this poem in class, but we include it in the book because we like it and because it offers figures that are easily perceived. What do we like about it? Well, we like the figures (even though they are obvious); we like the repetition: "red, red rose" (1), "And I" (7, 11, 15), "Till a' the seas gang dry" (8, 9), "my dear" (9, 11), and especially "luve" (a noun in 1 and 3, referring to the beloved; a noun in 6, referring to the speaker's mental state; a verb in 7; a noun in 13 and 15). We like the fact that the poem scarcely advances, but keeps returning to the beloved. Of course, one can find a structure (e.g., the song moves from the local and familiar ["a red, red rose"] to the remote ["ten thousand mile"]), but chiefly one feels that the poet keeps coming back to his beloved and to his love for her.

David Daiches, in *Robert Burns*, p. 312, praises the poem for its "combination of swagger and tender protectiveness." Somehow, this characterization doesn't seem exactly right to us, and you may want to ask your students if his view corresponds to theirs:

> Nowhere in literature has that combination of swagger and tender protectiveness so characteristic of the male in love been so perfectly captured, and it is all done by simple similes and simple exaggeration.

Burns is best studied in the one-volume edition in the Oxford Standard Authors series, ed. James Kinsley (1969). An older but still valuable book on Burns is John Delancey Ferguson, *Pride and Passion* (1939). See also: *Critical Essays on Robert Burns*, ed. Donald A. Low (1975); and *The Art of Robert Burns*, ed. R. D. S. Jack and Andrew Noble (1982).

SYLVIA PLATH

Metaphors (p. 555)

Sylvia Plath's "Metaphors," in nine lines of nine syllables each, with nine metaphors, is a sort of joking reference to the nine months of pregnancy, which is what this riddling poem is about.

There are many biographies and critical studies of Plath, but the best place to start is with Janet Malcolm's fascinating account of Plath, her husband (and poet) Ted Hughes, and her biographers, *The Silent Woman: Sylvia Plath and Ted Hughes* (1994).

A "Voices and Visions" videocassette and an audiocassette of Sylvia Plath are available from Longman.

RICHARD WILBUR

A Simile for Her Smile (p. 556)

The comparison is not of her smile to the approaching riverboat (the "packet," in line 9), but of the pause in the speaker's mind (a pause that follows the "hope, the thought" of her smile) to the pause in traffic when the boat approaches the drawbridge. In the second stanza some of the words describing the life around the speaker can easily be thought to refer also to the woman: "the packet's *smooth* approach," "the *silken* river." Probably the last line, with its rather grand image ("And slow cascading of the paddle wheel"), comes as a pleasant surprise.

There is no need to get into matters of versification (though no harm, either), but you may want to point out that the poem is divided into two sestets, and that the open space between them corresponds to the space made as the drawbridge starts to rise. The space also stands for the silence that comes over the horns and motors.

For more of Wilbur's poetry, see his *New and Collected Poems* (1988). Critical studies include: Donald Hall, *Richard Wilbur* (1967); *Richard Wilbur's Creation*, ed. Wendy Salinger (1983); and Bruce Michelson, *Wilbur's Poetry: Music in a Scattering Time* (1991). See also the special issue of the journal *Parnassus*, Spring-Summer 1977; and *Conversations with Richard Wilbur*, ed. William Butts (1990).

JOHN KEATS

On First Looking into Chapman's Homer (p. 557)

In "On First Looking into Chapman's Homer," Keats uses figures to communicate to the reader the poet's state of mind. Figures of traveling (appropriate to a poem about the author of *The Iliad* and *The Odyssey*, and also, via "realms of gold" or El Dorado, to the Elizabethans) give way in the sestet to figures of more breathtaking exploration and discovery; (By the way, it is not quite right to say that at line 9 we pass from the octave's images of land to the sestet's images of discovery. An important shift occurs in line 7, with "Yet" no less important than line 9's "Then." "Breathe" in line 7 is probably transitional, linked to the octave's idea of foreign travel and also to the sestet's early reference to the skies.)

It is probably fair to say that the octave (or at least its first six lines as compared with the sestet) has a somewhat mechanical, academic quality. "Realms of gold," "goodly states," "bards in fealty to Apollo," "demesne," etc., all suggest something less than passionate utterance, a tone reinforced by the rather mechanical four pairs of lines, each pair ending with a substantial pause. But in the sestet the language is more concrete, the lines more fluid (it can be argued that only line 10 concludes with a pause), and the meter less regular, giving a sense of new excitement that of course corresponds to the meaning of the poem.

Almost all critics agree that Keats erred in giving Cortez for Balboa, but C. V. Wicker argues in *College English* 17 (April 1956): 383-87 that Keats meant Cortez, for the point is not the first discovery of something previously unknown, but an individual's discovery for himself of what others have earlier discovered for themselves. Still, it seems evident that Keats slipped, and instructors may want to spend some class time discussing the problem of whether such a factual error weakens the poem.

In line with much contemporary criticism that sees poetry as being reflective discourse concerned with itself, Lawrence Lipking, in *The Life of the Poet*, sees this poem as being about Keats's discovery of Keats. Well, yes, in a way, but surely the poem is also about the discovery of the world's literature, a world other than the self. See also P. McNally, in *JEGP* 79 (1980): 530-40.

MARGE PIERCY

A Work of Artifice (p. 558)

Bonsai is the art of dwarfing trees by pruning the branches and roots and by controlling the fertilization. The grower shapes the tree by wiring the trunk and the branches. The important point, so far as Piercy's poem goes, is that a bonsai (the word can be used of a specimen itself, as well as of the art) is *not* a special hybrid dwarf, but is a tree distorted by the grower. (The somewhat freakish shape of the poem perhaps imitates the miniaturized tree.) Lines 1-8 give students the gist of what they need to know about bonsai. Students will readily see that Piercy's bonsai is a metaphor; the real "work of artifice" that the poet is concerned with is the female shaped by a dominant male society. The metaphor extends through line 16, when it yields to the closely related image of "the bound feet" (footbinding was practiced in China until well into the twentieth century) and then by easy association to "the crippled brain," which in turn yields to "the hair in curlers." Students might be invited to comment on the connection between these last two images: In what way is "hair in curlers" a kind of crippling (not only of the hair, but also of the woman's mind, which is persuaded or bullied into distorting itself in order to be acceptable to men)? The last two lines remind us of an advertisement, perhaps for a soap or skin lotion, but we can't identify it. In any case, in "the hair you love to touch" the reader gets the modern American male's version of the gardener who soothingly "croons" (11) to his tree while he maims it.

EDMUND WALLER

Song (p. 560)

If the previous chapters have already been read, students will have encountered roses in "To the Virgins to Make Much of Time" and in Burns's "A Red, Red Rose." In the next chapter they will encounter Blake's "The Sick Rose." In line 2, "wastes" is perhaps more potent than many students at first find it, for it implies not simply squandering but destroying, as in, for instance, "to lay waste a city." Thus the idea of death, explicit in lines 16-17, is present almost from the start of the poem.

WILLIAM CARLOS WILLIAMS

The Red Wheelbarrow (p. 897)

Roy Harvey Pearce, in *The Continuity of American Poetry* (p. 339), regards

William Carlos Williams's "The Red Wheelbarrow" as sentimental (but of some value), and says that what depends is the poet: "He assures himself that he is what he is by virtue of his power to collocate such objects into sharply annotated images like these." Charles Altieri, in *PMLA* 91 (1976): 111, suggests that although the items are stripped of associations, "No poem in English is more metonymic. Three objects evoke a mode of life in the sparsest, most succinct manner possible. The poverty of detail, like that in the rural paintings of Andrew Wyeth, at once intensifies the starkness of rural life and exemplifies it." Altieri also points out that in each of the last three stanzas, the first line "depends" on the second, for the word that ends each first line is often a noun ("wheel," "rain," "White"), but in the poem turns out to be an adjective. Thus the reader's mind "is made to hover over details until its waiting is rewarded, not only within the stanza, but also as each independent stanza emerges to fill out this waiting and to move us beyond details to a complex sense of a total life contained in these objects." John Hollander (*Vision and Resonance*, 111) suggests that cutting "wheelbarrow" and "rainwater" (with no hyphens to indicate that "rain" and "wheel" are parts of the compounds) helps to convey what the poem is about: seeing the constituents of things in the freshness of light after rain.

Two older studies remain useful: Linda Wagner, *The Poems of William Carlos Williams* (1964); and James E. Breslin, *William Carlos Williams: An American Artist* (1970). Paul Mariani's biography, *William Carlos Williams: A New World Naked* (1981), is detailed and definitive, but for students, Reed Whittemore's *William Carlos Williams: Poet From Jersey* (1975), might be a better place to start.

Also recommended: *The Oxford Companion to Twentieth-Century Poetry in English, ed.* Ian Hamilton (1994).

A "Voices and Visions" videocassette and an audiocassette of William Carlos Williams are available from Longman.

ALFRED, LORD TENNYSON

The Eagle (p. 562)

Tennyson's concise account in "The Eagle" seems literal enough, but from the first the bird is personified, by being called "He" instead of "it" and by being given "hands" instead of talons. Note also that "his mountain walls" implies that the bird is lord of a fortress. "Wrinkled sea" and "crawls" are other obvious figures, giving us the sea from a human-bird's eye view. The simile "like a thunder bolt he falls" returns us from the eagle's point of view to the observer's. "Ringed with the "azure world," we should mention, has been interpreted as expressing the bird's view of the earth spread out in a circle before him, but "azure" may indicate that the description is not of the earth but of the sky around the bird, and so the line is from an observer's point of view.

Robert Graves assaults the poem in *On Poetry: Collected Talks and Essays,* pp. 402-405. Graves suggests that if the eagle's claws are hands, when we are told that the eagle "stands" he must be standing on his wings, and Graves claims that line 3 adds nothing: "Since the eagle perches on his crag close to the sun, a background of blue sky has already been presumed." Graves goes on to complain that "lands" has been chosen for the rhyme with "hands" and "stands," not for the sense, because "the eagle can stand only in one land." And "close to the sun" is objectionable; "What," Graves asks, "are a few hundred feet, compared with 92,000,000 miles!"

In teaching "The Eagle," we have occasionally found that a student too familiar with the ways of English teachers may insist that the bird is symbolic of something or other. Christ has been suggested, on the grounds that the bird descends from heaven ("Close to the sun") to earth, and the word "falls" has been said to contain an allusion to the Fall of Man. Such a symbolic rendering can be gently but firmly rejected, though perhaps it contains a germ of truth: The bird is presented as an intent watcher of the world beneath it. To this degree perhaps one can say that the bird resembles the keen-eyed poet, though this is not to claim that the bird is a symbol for the poet. The bird is a bird, in fact an eagle.

Christopher Ricks skillfully edited Tennyson's poetry in a one-volume edition in 1969, and in a revised three-volume edition in 1988. Ricks's *Tennyson* (1972) and A. Dwight Culler's *The Poetry of Tennyson* (1977) are fine critical studies.

CHRISTINA ROSSETTI

Uphill (p. 563)

How can one be sure that the poem is metaphorical? This is part of what we are getting at in our first question, in which we ask the student to respond to a reader who assumes the speaker is making inquiries preparatory to a bit of touring. The question is not meant to be frivolous. Instructors know that this is a poem about larger matters, but that's because instructors are used to reading poems and are therefore used to figurative language. Most students are unfamiliar with the way poems work—which is why they sometimes read too literally and why, on other occasions, they read too freely, ignoring some passages and imposing highly personal readings on others.

Our second question asks, Who is the questioner? The poem is not a Browningesque dramatic monologue, and we think it is enough to say that the questioner is the poet, or the poet as a universal spokesperson. By the way, we don't know exactly what to make of the suggestion of a student that the answerer in "Uphill" is a ghost, that is, someone who has made the journey and who therefore answers authoritatively.

As for our final question in the text, we do find the answers (with their dry understatement, as in "You cannot miss that inn," i.e., "Don't worry, you will certainly die") chilling as well as comforting, but we are unconvinced that a reader is supposed to imagine a dialogue between the poet and a revenant. Rather, we believe (guided by Jerome J. McGann's essay on Christina Rossetti in his *The Beauty of Inflections*) that the poet is speaking with what McGann calls "her divine interlocutor" (242). McGann points out that the ending of "Uphill" is easily misinterpreted. Rossetti is not saying that the pilgrimage of the Christian soul ends with an eternal sleep. Rather, she is alluding to the Anabaptist doctrine known as "Soul Sleep" (technically, psychopannychism), which holds that at death the soul is put into a condition of sleep until the millennium. On the Last Day the soul awakens and goes to its final reward. McGann fully discusses the point in his essay.

From time to time, we have taught students who have become very interested in Rossetti's verse. For specialized work, we can recommend *The Complete Poems of Christina Rossetti,* ed. R. W. Crump, 3 vols. (1979-90). But students might profit even more from reading Rossetti in the midst of other Victorian women poets; see *Victorian Women Poets: An Anthology,* ed. Angela Leighton and Margaret Reynolds (1995). See also Dolores Rosenblum, *Christina Rossetti: The Poetry of Endurance* (1986); Antony H. Harrison, *Christina Rossetti in Context* (1988); and Angela Leighton, *Victorian Women Poets* (1992), 118-63.

RANDALL JARRELL

The Death of the Ball Turret Gunner (p. 564)

We reprint here a good explication, by a student, of the poem:

Reading the first line aloud, one pauses slightly after "sleep," dividing the line in half. The halves make a sharp contrast. The point of transition in this line is "I fell," a helpless movement from the mother to the State, from sleep to the State. The mother and the State make an evident contrast, and so do "sleep" and "the State," which resemble each other in their first sound and in their position at the end of a half-line but which have such different associations, for sleep is comforting and "the State" is associated with totalitarianism. ("The country" or "the land" might be comforting and nourishing but "the State" has no such warm suggestions.) We will soon see in the poem that life in the "belly" of the state is mindless and cold, a death-like life which ends with sudden and terrible death. A mother, even in her "sleep," naturally protects and nourishes the child in her warm womb; the State unnaturally cramps the man in its icy belly. He "hunched in its belly" until his "wet fur froze." We gather from the title that "its" refers not only to the State but also the airplane in whose womb-like ball turret he led his confined existence and died. Given the title, the fur probably literally refers to the fur lining of the jackets that fliers wore in World War II, and it also suggests the animal-like existence he led while confined by this unfeeling foster parent, the State-airplane.

His unnatural existence is further emphasized by the fact that, in the airplane, he was "Six miles from earth." From such an existence, far from the "dream of life" that people hope for, and still hunched in the turret like a baby in the womb, he was born again, that is, he awoke to (or became aware of) not a rich fulfillment of the dream but a horrible reality that is like a nightmare. "Woke to black flak" imitates, in its rattling k's at the end of words, the sound of the gunfire that simultaneously awakened and killed him. His awakening or birth is to nightmarish reality and death. It is not surprising, but it is certainly horrifying, that in this world of an impersonal State that numbs and destroys life, his body is flushed out of the turret with a hose. That this is the third horrible release: the first was from the mother into the State; the second was from the belly of the State into the belly of the airplane; and now in shreds from the belly of the airplane into nothing. That this life-history is told flatly, with no note of protest, increases the horror. The simplicity of the last line more effectively brings out the horror of the experience than an anguished cry or an angry protest could do.

Jarrell is a splendid critic, whose likes and dislikes are illuminating. See *Poetry and the Age* (1953) and *Kipling, Auden, and Co.* (1980). *The Complete Poems* (1969) is available, but for students, *The Selected Poems* (1991), is a preferable point of entry. William Pritchard, *Randall Jarrell: A Literary Life* (1990), is helpful.

Jarrell reads and discusses the poem on Caedman cassette SWC 1363.

SAMUEL JOHNSON

On the Death of Mr. Robert Levet (p. 565)

Students may find this elegy lacking in feeling, or, more precisely, they may think that the lack of expression of personal grief suggests the author was indifferent or even insincere. But Johnson is writing a public poem, not a personal one, and though he is fairly specific, even going so far as to name Levet, he is speaking not as Levet's friend but as the objective observer of a man who lived a good life. The point, so to speak, is *not* "I have lost a dear friend"; rather, the point is, "The world has lost a good man."

Further, Levet in some ways stands for all of us, and indeed the poem begins with a generalization about life, about *our* lives, rather than about Levet's. "Condemned to Hope's delusive mine," i.e. toiling in this world of illusions, *we* see our friends ("Our social comforts") die, one by one ("drop away"). The second stanza introduces Levet, the latest to die, and announces that he embodied certain virtues: "Officious, innocent, sincere." The next four stanzas let us see him in action.

Students may not at first realize that Johnson is relying heavily on personifications. For instance, "lettered Arrogance" (9) means, in this context, "educated people—such as persons with medical degrees—who are proud, and scornful of others." Levet visited "fainting Nature" (sick human beings) who lived "In Misery's darkest caverns" (hovels, or perhaps even jails). Death is not just a word here, Death is personified, first in line 14, where he prepares a blow against "fainting Nature," and again in the last stanza where he breaks "the vital chain" that binds Levet— an image that connects with the first line of the poem, where all of us are said to be "Condemned to Hope's delusive mine," i.e. as (in effect) slaves in a mine.

Because this poem uses the Parable of the Talents (see lines 27-28), if you teach "On the Death of Robert Levet" you may want to connect it to Milton's "On His Blindness," which uses the same parable. Johnson's use of the story is unusual. In the original, the man with the one talent did not use it effectively; Johnson's Levet has indeed only one talent (i.e. he was not a man of great abilities)—but he does effectively use the little that he has.

The essential secondary work is, of course, James Boswell's *The Life of Samuel Johnson* (1791). It can be supplemented by two excellent modern biographies written by John Wain (1975) and W. J. Bate (1977). Among the many critical studies, two merit special notice: Bate's *The Achievement of Samuel Johnson* (1955); and Paul Fussell, *Samuel Johnson and the Life of Writing* (1971).

Johnson is a compelling personality and literary voice, and we find we often cite him on this or that occasion throughout the introductory courses that we teach. For example: "Curiosity is one of the permanent and certain characteristics of a vigorous mind"; "A man ought to read just as inclination leads him; for what he reads as a task will do him little good"; "Worth seeing? yes, but not worth going to see."

Anything that can be done to make Johnson come alive for students is worthwhile, both because it might lead students to his writings, and, more generally, because it might help to flash before students' eyes the pleasure and interest of older literatures that are encountered too rarely.

TOPICS FOR CRITICAL THINKING AND WRITING

1. How is the figure of the mine (line 1) continued in other stanzas?
2. Lines 27-28 allude to the Parable of the Talents (Matthew 2.1430). How does Johnson add a twist to the parable?
3. Does the lack of personal expression of grief suggest insincerity? Explain.

SEAMUS HEANEY

Digging (p. 566)

The comparison of the pen resting in the hand, "snug as a gun," may especially remind a reader that in Ireland literature has often been closely connected with politics and with war, but of course the idea of the pen as a weapon is widespread, best known in the adage that "The pen is mightier than the sword." Less well known, but in the same vein, is Napoleon's preference of newspapers to battalions.

The image of the weapon is then largely replaced by the lines about the speaker's father digging—now flowerbeds, but twenty years ago he dug nourishing potatoes—but such words as "lug," "shaft," and "cool hardness" (though said of potatoes) keep the gun in our midst, at least faintly. Similarly, the emphasis on the father's posture (careful, professional, expert) suggests the discipline of a marksman—and of a writer.

Heaney then goes further back in time, to his grandfather digging not potatoes but turf, the fuel that cooks the potatoes and that heats a home, thus a substance no less necessary to life than food. But the evocation of these pictures of father and grandfather digging serves to remind the poet that he has "no spade to follow them" (24). What, then, is his place in the family, and his role in society? What nourishment, what fuel can he contribute? And so we come back to the pen: "The squat pen rests" (30, a repetition of the first half of line 2). "I'll dig with it" (31). The "squat pen" is the poet's spade and gun, to be used with the energy and precision with which his father and grandfather used their spades, and to be used, presumably, with the same life-sustaining effect.

For further reading, see *Selected Poems, 1966-1987* (1990). Heaney's sharp, sensitive prose writings include: *Preoccupations: Selected Prose, 1968-1978* (1980); *The Government of the Tongue* (1988); and *The Place of Writing* (1989). Critical studies: Blake Morrison, *Seamus Heaney* (1982); *The Art of Seamus Heaney,* ed. T. Curtis (1982); Robert Buttel, *Seamus Heaney* (1985); and Neil Corcoran, *Seamus Heaney* (1986). The journals *Salmagundi* no. 80 (1988) and *Agenda* 27, no. 1 (1989) have devoted issues to Heaney's work.

LOUISE ERDRICH

Indian Boarding School: The Runaways (p. 567)

The runaways think of railroad tracks as "old lacerations" (4) and scars (6), and of their own "worn-down welts" as a highway—all of this, of course, a reflection of their experience of "ancient punishments" (16) at school. Even the names they inscribed in the wet cement of sidewalks and the outlines and veins of leaves they pressed into the cement are imagined as the scars of "old injuries" (24). In short, the violence done to the children is seen as reflected in violence done to the land.

CHAPTER 15

Imagery and Symbolism

For a discussion of the difference between *natural* symbols (items that are meaningful on the literal level but that mean much more too) and symbols that have no literal existence, such as a man who does not cast a shadow, see N. Friedman, "Symbol," in *The New Princeton Encyclopedia of Poetry and Poetics,* ed. Alex Preminger and T.V.F. Brogan.

The references suggested for Chapter 14 are relevant here too. In addition, see Barbara Seward, *The Symbolic Rose.*

Among the highly relevant poems in Chapter 20 are Donne's "Valediction," Keats's "To Autumn," Ginsberg's "A Supermarket in California," and especially Pound's "In a Station in the Metro." William Carlos Williams's "Spring and All" is an interesting example of a poem with almost no figurative language—until near the end.

WILLIAM BLAKE

The Sick Rose (p. 570)

"The Sick Rose" has been much interpreted. usually along the lines given in the text. (See Reuben Brower, *The Fields of Light* and Rosenthal and Smith, *Exploring Poetry.*) But E. D. Hirsch, Jr., in *Innocence and Experience,* argues that "The rose is being satirized by Blake as well as being infected by the worm. Part of the rose's sickness is her ignorance of her disease. Her ignorance is her spiritual disease because in accepting 'dark secret love' she has unknowingly repressed and perverted her instinctive life, her 'bed of crimson joy.'" Hirsch argues his point for a couple of pages.

We especially like Helen Vendler's comment on this poem in her introduction to *The Harvard Book of Contemporary American Poetry:*

> The world of the poem is analogous to the existential world, but not identical with it. In a famous created world of Blake's, for instance, there is a rose doomed to mortal illness by the love of a flying worm who is invisible. We do not experience such a poem by moving it piecemeal into our world deciding what the rose "symbolizes" and what the worm "stands for" On the contrary, we must move ourselves in to its ambience, into a world in which a dismayed man can converse with his beloved rose and thrust upon her, in his anguished jealousy, diagnosis and fatal prognosis in one sentence... After living in Blake's world for the space of eight lines, we return to our own world, haunted and accused.

Allen Ginsberg has "tuned" the poem (MGM Records FTS-3083).

WALT WHITMAN

I Saw in Louisiana a Live-Oak Growing (p. 571)

Whitman spent two months in New Orleans, in the spring of 1848.

As Whitman sees it, the tree is like him in that it is "rude, unbending, lusty" (this is the Whitman who from the first version of *Leaves of Grass* onward celebrated himself as "one of the roughs, a kosmos, / Disorderly, fleshly and sensual... eating drinking and breeding"), but the tree is *un*like him in that it grows in solitude.

In line 3 "uttering" ("uttering joyous leaves") strikes us as especially interesting, since it attributes to the tree a voice, or, rather, sees its organic growth as akin to human speech. Whitman conceived himself as one who by nature writes poetry, as a tree by nature produces leaves.

On at least one occasion Whitman suggested that the poems in "Calamus" could be thought of as something like a group of sonnets, and some readers have felt that this poem has the feel of a sonnet with an octave and a sestet, even though it is not rhymed, is not in iambic pentameter, and has thirteen rather than fourteen lines.

The first four lines can be thought of as a quatrain (or, in terms of the structure of the whole, as roughly equivalent to the octave in an Italian sonnet) in which the poet presents the image—the tree—and relates it to himself. Then, at the beginning of line 5, comes a turn (the *volta* in an Italian sonnet), strongly marked by "But," and we get a sort of comment on the first unit, rather as a sestet in an Italian sonnet may comment on the octave. (Here the second unit runs to nine lines rather than to six.) The gist is this: the poet dwells on his difference from the tree—even as he talks about the souvenir twig that he has brought back with him. One can of course divide this second unit variously, for instance one can distinguish between the first five lines (5-9)—a group about the twig—and the remaining four lines (10-13)—a group in which the poet's thought returns to the original tree that is not only like him ("joyous") but is also unlike him ("without a friend a lover near").

JOHN HAINES

The Whale in the Blue Washing Machine (p. 574)

One of us not long ago started a discussion of Haine's poem by showing the class a book of photographs of whales that dramatized their immense size, power, and uncanny grace. Some of the students had been on whale-watching trips, and offered their accounts of the awesome sights they had seen. Several students too, of course, referred to Melville's *Moby Dick.* These first few minutes helped students to register the eerie incongruity that Haines presents and explores—the whale that swims in the household, where there are indeed "depths" enough to allow him to live.

The main focus will fall on the symbolic meanings of the whale, which students enjoy debating and arguing about. But we have found it important at the same time, to ask students to consider specific word choices throughout (why "household" rather than "house," for example) and to discuss the tone of particular stanzas (do we smile or feel a breath of baffled unease at the conjuction of the pulsebeat of the whale, the spinning washer, and the clanking dryer?).

The poem also offers at least one interesting allusion—it seems unintentional—that students can be referred to. Haines's evocation of the "kitchen darkness," "steamy windows," and the "streets draining away the fog," has affinities with the movements of "yellow fog" that T.S. Eliot describes in stanza two of "The Love Song of Alfred J. Prufrock."

SAMUEL TAYLOR COLERIDGE

Kubla Khan (p. 575)

Among the interesting discussions of "Kubla Kahn" are Brooks and Warren *Understanding Poetry,* 4th ed.; Humphry House, *Coleridge* (House's material on "Kubla Khan" is reprinted in *Romanticism and Consciousness,* ed. Harold Bloom); Harold Bloom, *The Visionary Company;* Walter Jackson Bate, *Coleridge;* and Jerome J. McGann, *The Romantic Ideology.*

Most critics tend to see the fountain, river, and chasm as symbols of the poet's consciousness and "the pleasure dome" as a symbol of poetry. Charles Patterson (*PMLA* 89 [October 1974]: 1033-42) believes that the river (suggestive of poetic consciousness) is called "sacred" because it is "given over to and seemingly possessed by a god presenting through the poet's furor divinus a vision of beauty." The "deep delight" of line 44 is, Patterson suggests, "a daemonic inspiration, an unrestricted and amoral joy like that of the pre-Christian daemons." Patterson's judicious article deserves close study. Given the continuing interest in drugs, the instructor also may wish to consult Elisabeth Schneider, *Coleridge, Opium, and Kubla Khan,* or Alethea Hayter, *Opium and the Romantic Imagination.* Apparently it is unsound to attribute the poem to opium. As someone has said, Coleridge didn't write "Kubla Khan" because he took opium;

he took opium because he was the sort of person who writes poems like "Kubla Khan."

Blake's "Lamb" and "Tyger" printed later in our text, are useful when talking about symbolism, as are Keats's "La Belle Dame sans Merci" and Yeats's "Sailing to Byzantium."

We start our students with Humphrey House, *Coleridge* (1953); and Walter Jackson Bate, *Coleridge* (1968). On the Wordsworth-Coleridge relationship: Paul Magnuson, *Coleridge and Wordsworth* (1988); and G. W. Ruoff, *Wordsworth and Coleridge* (1989).

TOPIC FOR WRITING

"Kubla Khan" as a celebration of the energy of life. (It can be argued that even the references to ice and to the "sunless sea" and "lifeless ocean" in this context suggest mystery rather than lifelessness; certainly the Khan, the river, the fountain, the dome, the wailing woman, and the poet—among other things—combine to give a vision of a powerful and mysterious creativity.)

LORNA DEE CERVANTES

Refugee Ship (p. 578)

Most students will quickly grasp the significance of the title: like a refugee on a ship, the speaker is isolated from her origins and she is uncertain—indeed desperate—about her future. In the original version (see question 3 in the text) the repetition in the last two lines ("a ship that will never dock / a ship that will never dock") perhaps indicates a condition of numbed hopelessness, a sense that she is doomed to drift forever and will never be able to achieve a stable identity. (We are *not* saying that repetition always has this effect. The repetition in the last two lines of Frost's "Stopping by Woods" probably has quite a different effect.) But in the revision, printed in our text, the line is in Spanish rather than in English, which suggests to some readers of our acquaintance that she is no longer "orphaned" from her Spanish name, and that Spanish is no longer "foreign" (line 7) to her.

The change, thus interpreted, is somewhat puzzling, since the recovery of Spanish (i.e., the regaining of her Spanish heritage) would seem to contradict the idea of the boat never landing. A related point: the original poem (1974) did *not* end with a period (it had no final punctuation), so it seemed inconclusive, unfinished, unending, and thus appropriate to the idea of a speaker who can't find her identity. The period at the end of the revision (1981) of course adds a note of finality—but is the idea that the ship will never dock, or (since the final line is in Spanish) that the Spanish heritage has been regained?

Still another conspicuous difference between the original and the revision is in a figure of speech in line 9 of the revision, where the speaker refers to her "bronzed skin." In the original (see below, line 10) she spoke of her "brown skin." Students might be asked to comment on the change. Our own view is that "bronzed" is somewhat more elevated, perhaps even suggesting heroic monuments in bronze. Other changes are in the lineation, and from "I am an orphan to my spanish name," by virtue of the lowercase initial letter, somewhat diminished. Here is the 1974 version.

Refugee Ship

like wet cornstarch I slide past *mi abuelita's* eyes
bible placed by her side
she removes her glasses
the pudding thickens

mamá raised me with no language
I am an orphan to my spanish name
the words are foreign, stumbling on my tongue
I stare at my reflection in the mirror
brown skin, black hair

I feel I am a captive
aboard the refugee ship
a ship that will never dock
a ship that will never dock

By the way, in class a Chicano student brought up a point that provoked considerable discussion. He mentioned that many people with Spanish names are by no means rightly characterized as "Hispanic," since they are descended largely or entirely from Native Americans, and they were deprived of their own languages by the Spaniards. Some of these people may think of themselves as "Spanish," but in Cervantes's words they really are "orphaned," persons who have lost their original (i.e., indigenous) culture. The student was somewhat surprised to find himself saying that just as these people who have lost their original identity have came to regard themselves as Spanish or "Hispanic," so the Chicanos of today may in time forget their "Spanish" identity (really something imposed on many of them) and they may become as assimilated to the Anglo world as they now are to the "Spanish" world. That is, although the student fully sympathized with the speaker's anguish, he found it ironic that she presumably regards the grandmother as at ease in a Spanish culture that probably struck the grandmother's ancestors as foreign and undesirable.

Most students probably will feel that the second and third stanzas present few if any difficulties, but they may be puzzled by the first stanza, especially by the images of "wet cornstarch" and "pudding." We confess our own uncertainty. Perhaps part of the idea is that "wet cornstarch" has no permanent shape, no identity, just as the speaker feels she has no identity. Or, on the contrary, is the point that "wet cornstarch" is sticky, thereby suggesting that the speaker can't move easily, can't get anywhere (like a ship that can't dock)? (But the speaker does not in fact say that she feels "like wet cornstarch;" rather, she is saying something about the way in which the grandmother perceives, or doesn't perceive, her.) A more evident point is that cornstarch is white, which perhaps is the way the grandmother sees the speaker. That is, although the speaker has "bronzed skin, black hair," since she speaks English rather than Spanish (her mother's words are "foreign") she is an Anglo to the grandmother.

And what about "the pudding" in the last line of the first stanza? Again, it's our understanding that the first stanza gives the speaker's interpretation of the way in which the grandmother perceives her. "The pudding thickens," then, is a description of the way in which the grandmother, who has removed her glasses, perceives the speaker. Someone who is not wearing the glasses that she needs might well feel that the scene is "thickening." But why "pudding"? Probably there is a connection with "cornstarch," but exactly what is the connection? Is a pudding thought to be (like the wet cornstarch of the first line) shapeless? But in fact a pudding that thickens (with the aid of cornstarch) is not shapeless; it has considerable consistency or identity.

For a very different attitude toward being a Latina in the United States, see Aurora Levins Morales's poem. "Child of the Americas," later in our text.

ADRIENNE RICH

Diving into the Wreck (p. 579)

Most responses identify the wreck as either (1) the speaker's life (persons familiar with Rich's biography may identify it specifically as her unhappy marriage to a man who committed suicide in 1970, about three years before the poem was published) or (2) more broadly, our male-dominated society. Another way of putting it is to say that the poem is about sexual politics. The poem is discussed by Wendy Martin and by Erica Jong in *Adrienne Rich's Poetry,* ed. Barbara C. Gelpi and Albert Gelpi. Part of the following comment is indebted to their discussions.

Armed with a book of myths (an understanding of the lies society has created?) and a camera and a knife (an instrument of vision and an instrument of power?) she goes, alone, in contrast to Cousteau assisted by a team, to explore the wreck. (This sort of exploration can be done only by the individual. One might add, by the way, that it is a new sort of exploration, an exploration for which Rich had no maps. Before the second half of the twentieth century, there was virtually no poetry about what it was like to be a wife or a woman living in a male-dominated society. The earlier poetry written by women was chiefly about children, love, and God.) More exactly, she is there, exploring the wreck ("I came to explore the wreck" implies that she is speaking from the site itself). She has immersed herself in the primal, life-giving element and has now arrived in order "to see the damage that was done / and the treasures that prevail," that is, to see not only what is ruined but also what is salvageable. Her object is to find truth, not myth (62-63).

Lines 72-73, in which she is both mermaid and merman, and line 77, in which "I am she; I am he," suggest that she has achieved an androgynous nature and thus has become the sort of new woman who will tell the truth. According to lines 92-94, the names of such true persons, or androgynes, persons who may rescue civilization, do not appear in the book of myths.

On Rich, see Jane Cooper, *Reading Adrienne Rich: Reviews and Revisions, 1951-1981* (1984); Claire Keyes, *The Aesthetics of Power: The Poetry of Adrienne Rich* (1986).

For a selection of Rich's poetry, see *The Fact of a Doorframe: Poems Selected and New, 1950-1984* (1984). Rich is also the author of three collections of essays—*On Lies, Secrets, and Silence* (1979); *Blood, Bread and Poetry* (1986); and *What Is Found There: Notebooks on Poetry and Politics* (1993)—and a controversial study of motherhood, *Of Woman Born: Motherhood as Experience and Institution* (1976).

We'll mention here a reference work we have found useful: *The Oxford Companion to Women's Writing in the United States*, ed. Cathy N. Davidson and Linda Wagner-Martin (1995).

WALLACE STEVENS

The Emperor of Ice-Cream (p. 581)

On "The Emperor of Ice-Cream," first a comment by Stevens, in a letter (*Letters of Wallace Stevens*, Holly Stevens, ed.) of 16 May 1945. He says of "concupiscent curds" that the words "express the concupiscence of life, but, by contrast with the things in relation to them in the poem, they express or accentuate life's destitution, and it is this that gives them something more than a cheap lustre: (500).

If "emperor" suggests power and splendor, "ice cream" suggests pleasure, especially sensuous enjoyment, triviality, and transience. Put together, and in this context of a wake, the implication is that a human for a while shapes and enjoys the tawdry world, as the dead woman embroidered fantails on her sheets, which were too short. We can take pleasure in the world (there is certainly pleasure in the shifting diction and in the alliteration in line 3, "In kitchen cups concupiscent curds"), but if Stevens insists on the pleasure (cigars, ice cream, flirting girls), he also insists on looking at ("Let the lamp affix its beam") transience ("last month's newspapers," the dresser lacking knobs) and death (the corpse's horny feet). The two stanzas juxtapose a world of concupiscence and a world of death. The pleasures described, then, to return to Stevens's letter, "accentuate life's destitution."

In another letter, published in the *Southern Review* (Autumn 1979): 773-74, Stevens freely paraphrases part of the poem: "let us have a respite from the imagination (men who are not cigar makers, blondes, costumes, theology), and, in short, suppose we have ice cream. Not that I wish to exalt ice cream as an absolute good, although my little girl might. It is a symbol, obviously and ironically, of the materialism or realism proper to a refugee from the imagination." Stevens goes on, however, to insist that "ambiguity [is] essential to poetry."

We marvel at Stevens's deft, moving combinations of words, but he is a hard poet to teach well. Students wonder, "just what is he trying to say?"; and we confess that versions of the same question have occurred to us even during our most sympathetic readings of Stevens. To appreciate Stevens, we think it is best to keep the emphasis on the sounds and rhythms and clever, uncanny organizations of his language.

There are many critical studies, including those by A. Walton Litz (1972); Helen Vendler (1969); Harold Bloom (1977); and Alan Filreis (1992). See also the biography by Joan Richardson (2 vols., 1986, 1989). The problem for students, however, is the wide range of interpretive disagreement, which perplexes rather than enlightens them. The *meaning* of a Stevens poem is not an easy thing to arrive at, and, again, it might be better to suggest to students that they make this issue secondary in their reading of this poet's work. Enjoy his *art,* his craftsmanship, his patterns of sounds. Find poems that you like—a simple but, in this instance, a good approach; and look for connections and echoes among them.

Stevens, from *Opus Posthumous* (1957): "A poem is a meteor.... All poetry is experimental poetry.... Poetry is a purging of the world's poverty and change and evil and death. It is a present perfecting, a satisfaction in the irremediable poverty of life.... Poetry is a search for the inexplicable."

Edmund Wilson: "[Stevens's] gift for combining words is baffling and fantastic but sure: even when you do not know what he is saying, you know that he is saying it well."

Randall Jarrell: "At the bottom of Stevens's poetry, there is wonder and delight, the child's or animal's or savage's—man's— joy in his own existence, and thankfulness for it."

For students interested in Stevens's verse, the handiest place to start is with *The Palm at the End of the Mind,* ed. Holly Stevens (1971).

A "Voices and Visions" videocassette of Wallace Stevens is available from Longman. An audiocassette of Wallace Stevens reading is also available from Longman.

A Note on Haiku (p. 582)

The haiku in our text, along with the editorial comment, is enough to give students an idea of the form, and to allow them to write their own haiku. We have found that most students enjoy—because they can achieve at least a decent degree of success—writing haiku.

For collections of haiku, with substantial commentaries, see Harold G. Henderson, *An Introduction to Haiku,* and Kenneth Yasuda, *The Japanese Haiku.* For a shorter but still moderately detailed history of the form, see the article on haiku in *The Kodansha Encyclopedia of Japan.* We summarize the last part of the Kodansha article, "On Writing Haiku in English." As you will see in a moment, the author takes us through several versions of a haiku. You may want to write the first version on the board, discuss it, and then move on to the second, and so on.

The author begins by saying what a haiku does: "When a haiku is successful, it endows our lives with freshness and new wonder and reveals the charm and profundity of all truly simple things." Almost any subject is possible, from the stars on a stormy night to a heron in the evening breeze. He gives as an example (in the traditional 5-7 syllable pattern) a roadside encounter:

Meeting on the road,
we chat leisurely awhile
and go on our ways.

"The problem with this verse," he says, "is that it tells us something but evokes nothing. It is flat and one-dimensional." What is needed, among other things, is a sharper "cutting" (usually indicated by a colon or dash) after either the first or the second line, thus:

A roadside meeting:
we chat leisurely awhile
and go on our ways.

But there still is not enough of a cutting here; there is no imaginative distance between the two elements. Another try:

A baby's crying:
we chat leisurely awhile
and go on our ways.

Here, however, the distance between the two parts is too great. One would have to be deaf or cruel to chat while a baby cries. The two images don't somehow connect. The next version:

A peaceful country:
we chat leisurely awhile
and go on our ways.

Not bad; the peaceful country provides a grand background for this pleasant encounter between two friendly people; or, to put it the other way around, the encounter between the two people "crystallizes the abstract notion of a peaceful country."

The two parts of the poem, then, must be remote to a degree and yet must somehow connect, and each must enhance the other. Further, in the traditional Japanese haiku there must be a seasonal theme. When does a leisurely chat occur? Probably not in winter (too cold to stand chatting); nor does spring (the author says) seem right for this sort of talk, since spring is the time for "the fresh encounters of the young." Autumn? No, "Autumn is too suggestive of reflective maturity and eventual partings." Only summer is right:

Another hot day:
we chat leisurely awhile
and go on our ways

But the author of the article says, the word "leisurely" is wrong here; one wouldn't chat in a leisurely fashion on a hot day. A summer chat is characterized not by leisureliness but by "involuntary lethargy." The final version:

Another hot day:
yawning "good-bye" and "take care"
we go on our ways.

The author's final judgment of this work: "Not a haiku masterpiece, but not discreditable for a first try."

Reminder: Ezra Pound's "In a Station of the Metro" (Ch. 25) is deeply influenced by Pound's reading of haiku. We discuss the poem at some length in this manual.

    Note: In Chapter 19 we give literal translations of several haiku, and invite students to turn the translation into poems.

CHAPTER 16

Irony

SHARON OLDS

Rites of Passage (p. 587)

One of our students wrote a good paper about this poem, calling it a "poem about perspective." We liked the way he noted the difference in size between the speaker and her son and the other "short men" attending the party, and his movement from this observation to verbal details that illuminate the speaker's point of view. This student said that the speaker in fact takes two points of view—two perspectives—on the boys, seeing them as children and as small adults (i.e., the persons they will grow up to be), We think it's helpful to ask students to consider how the speaker perceives the boys, how they view themselves ("they eye each other"), and—a broader issue—how Olds means for readers to understand the lesson of poem. What exactly is its tone? What is our own perspective on its descriptions supposed to be?

Here one can focus on Olds's title. What is a "rite of passage" and in what respect is this birthday party an example of one? Turn next to specific moments in the poem's language, as when the speaker quotes the boys' warnings: "I could beat you up" and "We could easily kill a two-year-old." Students, we have found, react very differently to these phrases. Some judge them to be comic—it's funny and familiar to hear little boys making large threats—whereas others maintain that Olds wants us to hear these words as ominous, as a sign of the hard masculine world that these "short men" will inhabit (and promote) when they get older.

The discussion of "Rites of Passage" is always lively, and becomes more so as it proceeds. A student in one of our classes wondered is this a political poem? Is Olds using this scene to assail patriarchy, a system in which boys "naturally" assume manly poses and, while still small, are already looking and sounding like "bankers" and "Generals"? It is intriguing, too, to invite students to imagine other perspectives on this same subject. Would the boy's father (note that no mention is made of him) interpret the scene differently from the mother? Is there a similar kind of typical scene at a girl's birthday party against which this one could be compared?

Responses to these questions can be keyed to the poem's final phrase: "celebrating my son's life." The word "celebrate" can be connected to the word "rites"—it has a sacred and solemn meaning, as in celebrating a marriage or a mass. More commonly, "celebrate" suggests showing joy at an event; being part of a festive, happy occasion; rejoicing in an opportunity for honoring someone (i. e., celebrating a person's achievements). Does Olds want her readers to hear her final line as ironic, or, as students have sometimes told us, does she instead mean it more straightforwardly, as if she were saying, "I've made my amused, satiric points but it's really a happy day after all, and I do love my son?" Don't neglect the word "my," however. It's one of those small words that students tend to pass by, but it's an important one. It indicates the speaker's connection to the child (he is *her* child), renewed at the end of the poem. Yet while the speaker takes responsibility for him in one sense, this is balanced against the detachment, the separation, evident in the speaker's perception that her small boy is a man in miniature, not her child as much as an adult in the making. The words in this last line are finely placed, reaching a complicated, disquieting balance.

DANIEL HALPERN

How to Eat Alone (p. 588)

One way to begin discussion of this poem is to write on the board a sentence from one of Montaigne's essays: "A man should not so much respect what he eateth as with whom he eateth." Most of us like to think of mealtime as an experience when we enjoy being with family and friends. The meal tastes better because of the company we are with. Eating alone is something all of us have done, but that we are not likely to want to do often.

Halpern's poem can be approached as a set of directions, as—appropriately enough—a kind of recipe. Note the precision of the details (e.g., "the juice of *hard* lemons"—don't make the mistake of settling for a less good kind). But consider too the larger question of to whom these directions are being given. Is the "you" in line 16 meant to refer to the reader, or is it the speaker's other self, as though he were so alone he has only himself to talk to. This question becomes all the more pressing when students turn to the ending: Is the speaker's toast one that he is delivering to himself, or is he urging us to behave this way when *we* are alone? Perhaps both interpretations are possible at one and the same time.

There is an ambiguity in the final line as well. How are we to understand the word "best"? Is this a form of high compliment, or of self-contempt? Another way to formulate the question might be: Is the lesson of the poem that each of us is the best person we know (i.e., the best company we could ever want), or, instead, that for this speaker at least, the future holds little to look forward to?

JOHN HALL WHEELOCK

Earth (p. 589)

The Martian astronomer who speaks confidently while "gazing off into the air" seems to be a pompous ass. Of course, it is the business of astronomers to gaze (sometimes) into air, but here the description seems to imply the astronomer's contempt for, or at least indifference to, his audience.

But it probably is more complicated. First, "drily" suggests that the astronomer may himself be speaking ironically. (The Elizabethans called irony "the dry mock.") Our students, by the way, seem to divide evenly between those who believe the astronomer is being satirized and those who believe the astronomer is speaking ironically. In any case, what he says makes sense; earth is inhabited by "intelligent beings" (4), and if the earth blows up, as here it is imagined to do, it will be because these people have blown it up. Yet the poem, ostensibly spoken by an astronomer who praises the intelligence of earthlings, of course condemns the misapplied intelligence.

For the report of another Martian, see Craig Raine, "A Martian Sends a Postcard Home" later in the text.

PERCY BYSSHE SHELLEY

Ozymandias (p. 590)

James Reeves, in *The Critical Sense*, does a hatchet job on Shelley's "Ozymandias" (Ozymandias, incidentally, was the Greek version of the name User-ma-Ra, better known as Ramses II, the name the Greeks used for the thirteenth century B. C. pharaoh who, like other pharaohs, built monuments to celebrate his own greatness. One such monument was a colossus sixty feet tall, carved in stone by Memnon. Diodorus, a Sicilian Greek historian of the first century, saw the statue and wrote that it was inscribed, "I am Osymandyas, king of kings; if any would know how great I am, and where I lie, let him excel me in any of my works." At some later date, the statue tumbled, leaving only fragments.) Reeves's objections include: "vast" (2) means "of great extent," but the legs would be tall rather than vast; "in the sand" (3) is hardly necessary after "in the desert"; if the visage is "shattered" (which Reeves takes to mean "broken to pieces"), it would be difficult to recognize the facial expression; the speaker says that the sculptor "well ... read" the subject's passions, but we cannot know if this is true, since we have no other information about the subject; if it is argued that the inscription is evidence of cold-hearted tyranny, the sestet should begin "For," not "And"; to speak of "the decay" of a "wreck" is tautological; in lines 13-14 "boundless" makes unnecessary "stretch far away," and "bare" makes "lone" unnecessary. Some of Reeves's objections are telling, some are niggling; in any case, the power of the poem is chiefly in the essential irony and the almost surrealistic scene of legs arising in the desert, the face on the ground nearby, and no trunk anywhere.

A small point: Lines 4-8 are unclear, for it is not certain if "the hand ... and the heart" belong to the sculptor, in which case the idea is that the sculptor "mocked" ("mimicked," "imitated in stone") the passions and "fed" them by creating them in stone, or if the hand and the heart belong to Ozymandias, whose hand mocked the passions of his foes and whose heart fed his own passions.

Shelley's friend, Horace Smith, a banker with a taste for literature, wrote a sonnet on Ozymandias at the same time that Shelley did. You may want to ask students to compare the two poems:

On a Stupendous Leg of Granite, Discovered Standing by Itself in the Desert of Egypt

In Egypt's sandy silence, all alone,
Stands a gigantic Leg, which far off throws
The only shadow that the desert knows.
"I am great Ozymandias," said the stone,
"The King of kings; this mighty city shows
The wonders of my hand." The city's gone!
Naught but the leg remaining to disclose
The sight of that forgotten Babylon.

We wonder, and some hunter may express
Wonder like ours, when through the wilderness
Where London stood, holding the wolf in chase,
He meets some fragment huge, and stops to guess
What wonderful, but unrecorded, race
Once dwelt in that annihilated place.

For additional background material on Shelley's poem, see H. M. Richmond, "Ozymandias and the Travellers," *Keats-Shelley Journal* 11 (1962): 65-71. For a discussion of Shelley's poem and Smith's, see K. M. Bequette, "Shelley and Smith: Two Sonnets of Ozymandias," in *Keats-Shelley Journal* 26 (1977): 29-31.

There are excellent biographies by Richard Holmes (1974) and Kenneth Neill Cameron (2 vols., 1950, 1974), and many critical studies, including those by Carlos Baker (1948), Harold Bloom (1959), Earl Wasserman (1971), and William Keach (1984). The scholarship on Shelley, because of its engagement with the poet's dense ideas and passionate, but often obscure, social and philosophical views, can prove daunting to undergraduates, It might be preferable to recommend instead two books that combine primary texts with extensive annotations and contextual materials: *The Lyrics of Shelley*, ed. Judith Chernaik (1972); and *Shelley's Poetry and Prose*, ed. Donald H. Reiman and Sharon B. Powers (1977).

LINDA PASTAN

Ethics (p. 591)

First, a word about the teacher and the ethical question posed. One may wonder what kind of teacher keeps asking the same question, year after year. (On the other hand, perhaps good teachers do ask the same questions, year after year. They change the answers, not the questions.) Why, by the way, does the stated ethical problem—an old chestnut—always involve a woman rather than a man? (We are reminded of Faulkner's comment that "If a writer has to rob his mother, he will not hesitate; the 'Ode on a Grecian Urn' is worth any number of old ladies." One can hope that no one today would tolerate such talk.)

The poem begins by stating the ethical problem, but doesn't go on to answer it. Rather, it rejects the problem as arid, something perhaps fit for youngsters to debate (though in the poem the students don't care much about pictures or old people) but a concern that disappears when one is older and when one is "in a real museum" and is standing "before a real Rembrandt." We infer that the speaker, older and wiser, does care about both art and life, and knows that one doesn't have to choose between them. Art draws on life, and reveals life (lines 20-24), and both are "beyond saving by children" (25).

Although the speaker and her classmates were not much interested in the ethical problem that the teacher posed, other students may be. If so, you may want to set them loose on the first two lines of Yeats's "The Choice":

> The intellect of man is forced to choose
> Perfection of the life, or of the work.

ANDREW MARVELL

To His Coy Mistress (p. 592)

Marvell's "To His Coy Mistress" is well discussed by J. V. Cunningham, *Modern Philology* 51 (August 1953): 33-41; by Francis Berry, *Poets' Grammar;* by Joan Hartwig, *College English* 25 (May 1964): 572-75; by Bruce King, *Southern Review* 5 (1969): 689-703; and by Richard Crider, *College Literature* 12 (Spring 1985): 113-21. Incidentally, "dew" in line 35 is an editor's emendation for "glew" in the first edition (1681). Grierson suggests "glew" means a shining gum found on some trees. Another editor, Margoulieth, conjectures "lew"—that is, warmth.

Marvell's poem can be the subject of a paper involving a comparison with Herrick's "To the Virgins." Although both poems take as their theme the *carpe diem* motif, their tone and imagery differ greatly. For example, the sun in Herrick's poem ("the higher he's a-getting") does not race through the sky, but in Marvell's poem the lovers will force the sun to hurry. Or, again, in Herrick's poem the speaker is concerned not with satisfying his own desires but with the young women, whereas in Marvell's poem one strongly feels that the speaker is at least as concerned with himself as with the woman.

We have usually found it best to teach Herrick's poem before Marvell's partly because Herrick's is shorter, but chiefly because most students find it simpler.

Naturally none of the early discussions of the poem consider whether it is outrageously sexist—and, if it is, whether it should be taught. Such a discussion is probably inevitable in the classroom today, and no reader of this manual can be in need of our opinion on this topic. We will therefore comment only on some formal matters.

The poem consists of three parts, developing an argument along these lines: "If... But... Therefore." The first of these three parts is playful, the second wry or even scornful or bitter, and the third passionate. Or, to put it in slightly different terms, the poem is an argument, spoken (as the title indicates) by a male suitor to a reluctant woman. It begins with a hypothetical situation ("Had we but world enough and time") in which the speaker playfully caricatures Petrarchan conventions (fantastic promises, incredible patience). Then (21-32), with "But at my back," he offers a very different version of life, a wry, almost scornful speech describing a world in which beauty is fleeting. Finally (33-46) he offers a passionate conclusion ("Now therefore").

The conclusion, and especially the final couplet, perhaps require further comment. The "amorous birds of prey" of line 38 replace the doves of Venus found in more traditional love poetry. The destructiveness suggested by the birds is continued in the image of a "ball," which is chiefly a cannonball hurtling "thorough the iron gates of life" but is also the united lovers—that is, the ball is made up of their "strength" (chiefly his?) and "sweetness" (chiefly hers?). Some commentators find in "Tear" a suggestion of a hymen destroyed by "rough strife." The violence and the suggestions of warfare are somewhat diminished in the final couplet, but they are not absent, for the sun, though advancing, is partly imagined as an enemy that is being routed ("yet we will make him run").

We have some small uncertainties about the metrics of lines 21-22, "But at my back I always hear / Time's winged chariot hurrying near." Are "chariot" and "hurrying" disyllabic or trisyllabic? If they are trisyllabic the line contains two extra syllables, forcing the reader to hurry through the line. But of course different readers will read almost any line differently. For instance, in the first of these lines some readers will put relatively heavy stresses on the first four syllables ("But at my back"); others may rush through the first three words and put an especially heavy stress on "back," compensating for the lack of an earlier stress. In any case, these two lines surely are spoken differently from the earlier lines. Similarly, the third section, beginning with line 33, starts by sounding different. In this case almost everyone would agree that "Now therefore" gets two consecutive stresses.

Good selections of Marvell's poetry have been edited by Frank Kermode (1967), George de F. Lord (1968), and Elizabeth Story Donno (1972). Students might enjoy John Dixon Hunt, *Andrew Marvell: His Life and Writings* (1978), which includes well-chosen illustrations.

JOHN DONNE

Holy Sonnet XIV ("Batter my heart, three-personed God") (p. 593)

"Batter my heart" has been discussed several times in *Explicator* (March 1953, Item 31: December 1953, Item 18; April 1954, Item 36; October 1956, Item 2). In *College English* 24 (January 1963): 299-302, John Parrish summarized these discussions, rejecting the idea that in the first quatrain, especially in lines 2 and 4, God is compared to a tinker mending a damaged pewter vessel, and offering his own reading. All these are conveniently reprinted in the *Norton Critical Edition of John Donne's Poetry*, ed. A. L. Clements.

Our own winnowings from these essays follow. Although the first line introduces the "three-personed God," it is impossible to associate each quatrain with only one of the three persons. Still, the idea of the trinity is carried out in several ways: "knock, breathe, shine" becomes "break, blow, burn." And there are three chief conceits: God as a tinker repairing the speaker, damaged by sin; the speaker as a town usurped by satanic forces; God as a forceful lover who must ravish the sinful speaker; or (lest one get uneasy at the thought that Donne presents himself as a woman) God as a lover who must fully possess the speaker's soul (the soul is customarily regarded as female). "O'erthrow" in the first quatrain, in line 3, leads to the image of the besieged town in the second quatrain; "untrue" at the end of the second quatrain leads (because it can refer to marital infidelity) to the conceit of the lover in the third quatrain; and "ravish" in the final line can take us back to "heart" in the first line of the poem.

A useful, relatively long explication by M. T. Wanninger appeared in *Explicator* (December 1969), Item 37. M. H. Abrams, *Natural Supernaturalism*, 50-51, points out that in "Batter my heart" Donne draws on Revelation 21:5 ("Behold, I make all things new"), and that "the ultimate marriage with the Bridegroom, represented as the rape of the longingly reluctant soul" draws on "commonplaces of Christian devotion."

For a lively, provocative study, we recommend John Carey, *John Donne: Life, Mind, and Art* (1981). For an example of a New Historicist approach, see Arthur Marotti, *John Donne, Coterie Poet* (1986). We should note that we often consult editions of Donne's writings that include annotations and commentaries: *The Songs and Sonnets*, ed. Theodore Redpath (rev, ed., 1983); *John Donne's Poetry*, ed. A. L. Clements (rev. ed., 1992); and *John Donne: The Complete English Poems*, ed. A. J. Smith (1971). See also Robert H. Ray, *A John Donne Companion* (1990).

TOPIC FOR CRITICAL THINKING AND WRITING

How do you feel about an observation made in *Explicator* (Spring 1980), to the effect that "no end" (line 6) is an anagram for "Donne"? What is the point? According to the author of the note, "This anagram is, I think, another of the many ingenious samples of Donne's playing upon his name for poetic effect." Is this reading helpful? Why? Why not?

LANGSTON HUGHES

Dream Boogie (p. 594)

The *American Heritage Dictionary* defines boogie-woogie as "a style of jazz characterized by a repressed rhythmic and melodic pattern in the bass." "Repressed" has unconscious ironic echoes, since jazz grew in part from the white repression of blacks.

Many whites, noticing the musical accomplishments of some blacks, falsely assumed that these musicians were happy: If they weren't happy, why were they singing? But as Langston Hughes says in *The Big Sea*, blacks put their life into their music, singing "gay songs because you had to be gay or die; sad songs, because you couldn't help being sad sometimes. But gay or sad, you kept on living and you kept on going." In "Dream Boogie" Hughes says that if you "listen.. closely," you can hear the injustice that in part gave birth to jazz and forced blacks to express their sorrow rhythmically and in a masked form. The enthusiasm of the opening line soon yields to a hint of a menace ("rumble,"3), and the point becomes almost explicit in the reference (4) to "a dream deferred." (Instructors who already have assigned "Harlem," doubtless will make connections between the two poems.) In lines 8-9 ("You think/It's a happy beat?") the speaker pretty clearly says it is an unhappy beat, but by putting the words in the form of a question, he stops short of making a flat assertion, and of course he doesn't—and lines 22-26 are explicit, for instance, in "We knows everybody / ain't free." The next passage (27-34), including the quotation from the Pledge of Allegiance, is hard-hitting, but the speaker then shifts to another manner, using the jive-talk that to unthinking whites suggests the happiness of blacks, but the message is clear to the reader.

In the preface to *Montage of a Dream Deferred* (1951), Hughes wrote:

> This poem on contemporary Harlem, like be-bop, is marked by conflicting changes, sudden nuances, sharp and impudent interjections, broken rhythms, and passages sometimes in the manner of the jam session, sometimes the popular song, punctuated by the riffs, runs, breaks, and disc-torsions of the music of a community in transition.

A "Voices and Visions" videocassette of Langston Hughes is available from Longman. An audiocassette of Langston Hughes reading is also available from Longman.

MARTIN ESPADA

Tony Went to the Bodega but He Didn't Buy Anything (p. 596)

The basic irony of course is that Tony leaves the projects (i.e., his Hispanic background) for law school and Boston and (presumably) material success, but, finding that he is dissatisfied, he searches out the projects and a bodega. Why didn't he buy anything? Because it's enough for him to savor "la gente...hablan-do espanol." And now a smaller irony: Earlier (15) we are told that as an incipi-ent merchant he engaged in "practicing the grin on customers/ he'd seen Makengo grin," but now, luxuriating in the "beautiful" atmosphere of the bode-ga, he "grinned / his bodega grin"—without any thought of trying to charm cus-tomers. Success, we are told at the end, is a return to one's roots.

EDNA ST. VINCENT MILLAY

Love Is Not All: It Is not Meat nor Drink (p. 597)

Late in the poem a phrase in line 12 ("the memory of this night") identifies the speaker (a lover), the audience (the beloved), and the time (a night of love), but the poem begins drily, even rather pedantically. A somewhat professorial voice delivers a lecture on love, beginning authoritatively with four almost equally stressed monosyllables ("Love is not all"). Then, warming to the subject, the speaker becomes more expansive, with "It is not...nor...Nor...nor...And...and... and...and...can not...Nor...nor," all in the octave. Of course, in saying that love cannot do this and that we sense, paradoxically, a praise of love, if we have read a fair amount of love poetry, perhaps we expect the octave to yield to a sestet that will say what love *can* do. But this sestet too begins with apparent objectiv-ity, as if making a concession ("It well may be"). Then, like the octave, the sestet introduces a romantic note while nominally proclaiming realism, although its images are somewhat less exotic (there is nothing like the "floating spar" of line 3, for instance) than the images of the octave. On the other hand, insofar as it introduces a more personal or a more intense note ("the memory of this night"), and reveals that the poem is addressed to the beloved, it is *more* romantic. In any case the sestet comes down to earth, and at the same times reaches a romantic height, in its last line, which consists of two sentences: "It may well be. I do not think I would." The brevity of these two sentences, and the lack of imagery, pre-sumably convey a dry humor that the octave lacks, and at the same time they make an extremely romantic claim. (Surely "I do not think I would" is an under-statement; in effect, it is a passionate declaration.) Put it this way: although the octave asserts, for example, that love is not meat and drink and cannot heal the sick, and the first part of the sestet asserts that the speaker "might" give up the beloved's love in certain extreme circumstances, the understated passion of the conclusion serves to dismiss these assertions as unlikely—indeed, a reader feels, as untrue. Although to the rational mind "love is not all," to the lover it is "all," and a lover here is doing the talking.

CHAPTER 17

Rhythm and Versification

Paul Fussell, Jr.'s *Poetic Meter and Poetic Form,* rev. ed. (1979), is a readable discussion of metrics. Derek Attridge, *The Rhythms of English Poetry,* though more massive, is also readable and will be of special interest to teachers or students who themselves write poetry. John Hollander's *Rhyme's Reason: A Guide to English Verse* illustrates forms of verse with self-descriptive poems. Also of interest are Harvey Gross, *Sound and Form in Modern Poetry,* and *Mid-Century Poets,* John Ciardi, ed. (which includes useful comments by Wilbur, Roethke, Jarrell, and others). More difficult, and much more specialized, are W. K. Wimsatt, Jr.'s "One Relation of Rhyme to Reason," in his *The Verbal Icon,* and Charles O. Hartman, *Free Verse: An Essay on Prosody.*

We think it is a mistake to spend an hour discussing nothing but meter. It seems to us better to work some discussion of metrics into the daily meetings than to devote a meeting exclusively to this topic. This chapter is meant to provide a summary and a convenient dictionary, but instructors probably will already have made use of some of the material. For example, the instructor, in teaching Keats's "On First Looking into Chapman's Homer," may have already mentioned (in commenting on the last line, "Silent upon a peak in Darien") that when a line in a predominantly iambic poem begins with a trochaic adverb or adjective, "we often get [Paul Fussell notes in *Poetic Meter,* p. 65] an effect of sudden quiet." Incidentally, a similar metrical effect occurs in Shakespeare's Sonnet 29 (printed in Chapter 20), where the ninth line (in effect the first line of the sestet begins with a trochee ("Yet in"), marking the start of an energetic rejection of the depressed condition set forth in the octave.

A. E. HOUSMAN

Eight O'Clock (p. 602)

A. E. Housman's "Eight O'Clock" is discussed by Rosenthal and Smith, *Exploring Poetry*, and by Richard Wilbur, "Alfred Edward Housman," *Anniversary Lectures 1959* (Library of Congress), pp. 42-43. Wilbur points out that we learn almost nothing about the condemned man—not even what his crime was—we get only the last half-minute of his life. A clock strikes eight, the conventional hour for executions in England; to the victim, and to the reader, it is a machine that strikes down not merely hours but men. Note the ticking in "clock collected," and the effect of the enjambment in the seventh line, where the clock collects its strength and (after a heavy pause) strikes the hour and ends the man's life.

By the way, the Library of Congress owns a notebook draft of the poem, in which lines 3-4 run thus:

One, two, three, four, on jail and square and people
They dingled down.

Wilbur points out that the deletion of the reference to the jail is a great improvement. "Suspense," he says, "requires that the reason for the man's intent listening should not be divulged until we come to the second stanza. Contrast requires too that the "morning town," as it is called in the first stanza, be simply presented as a crowded market place down to which the steeple clock almost gaily tosses its chiming quarters."

For Housman, see *The Collected Poems* (1939; rev. ed., 1953), and, for essays as well as poetry, *A. E. Housman: Collected Poems and Selected Prose*, ed. Christopher Ricks (1988). Critical studies: *A. E. Housman: A Collection of Critical Essays*, ed. Christopher Ricks (1968); and John Bayley, *Housman's Poems* (1992).

THEODORE ROETHKE

My Papa's Waltz (p. 603)

Writing of Roethke's "My Papa's Waltz" in *How Does a Poem Mean*, John Ciardi says that the poem seems to lack a "fulcrum" (Ciardi's word for a "point of balance" or point at which there is a twist in the thought), but that the fulcrum "occurs after the last line." In his terminology, "The fulcrum exists outside the poem, between the enacted experience and the silence that follows it."

See *The Collected Poems of Theodore Roethke* (1966); *On the Poet and His Craft: Selected Prose of Theodore Roethke*, ed. Ralph J. Mills, Jr. (1965); and *Straw for the Fire: From the Notebooks of Theodore Roethke; 1948-63*, ed. David Wagoner (1972). Critical studies include: Karl Malkoff, *Theodore Roethke: An Introduction to the Poetry* (1966); and Rosemary Sullivan, *Theodore Roethke: The Garden Master* (1975).

An audiocassette of Theodore Roethke reading is available from Longman.

WILLIAM CARLOS WILLIAMS

The Dance (p. 604)

Williams's "The Dance" is in free verse, but the abundance of dactyls (as in "Breughel's great picture," "dancers go round," "squeal and the blare") gives it a sort of stamping effect appropriate to sturdy dancers wearing wooden shoes.

A "Voices and Visions" videocassette of William Carlos Williams is available from available Longman. An audiocassette of William Carlos Williams reading is available from Longman.

DYLAN THOMAS

Do not go gentle into that good night (p. 605)

One might at first think that a villanelle is an utterly inappropriate form in which to urge someone to "rage," but in Thomas's "Do not go gentle into that good night," addressed to a man on his deathbed, it proves appropriate because of its ritualistic, incantatory quality. In discussing the poem one can wonder why the night is "good." Probably because death is natural and inevitable (in 4 "dark is right"), but surely too there is a pun on "good night" as an equivalent to death. Further, "the last wave" (7) is probably both a final wave of water (suggesting the last flow of life) and a final gesture of the hand; "Grave men" (13) of course alludes both to serious men and to men near the grave.

Thomas's distinctions between "wise men," "good men," "wild men," and "grave men" have aroused various interpretations. W. Y. Tyndall, in *A Reader's Guide to Dylan Thomas*, suggests that wise men are philosophers, good men are moralists (perhaps Puritans), and wild men are "men of action and lovers of living." (He suggests that the grave men are poets.) M. W. Murphy, in *Explicator 27*, No. 6 (February 1970), Item 55, suggests that the wise men who preach wisdom are contrasted with the good men who live a life of wisdom. Both rage against death because they have accomplished nothing, the words of the former and the deeds of the latter having gone unheeded. The wild men are hedonists—who at death discover they have not caught time—and, in contrast to those Dionysian figures, the grave men are ascetic Apollonians who have missed the joys of life but who now, near the grave, see what they have missed. In short, for all men life is incomplete and too brief, and no one should "go gentle into that good night. "

We see the poem along these lines: Despite "good night," "at close of day," "the dying of the light"—terms that suggest death is to be welcomed—the speaker urges passionate resistance. The "wise men" (4-7) do not go gently, because they have come to realize that their wise words "had forked no lightning"—that is, had not given them, or anyone else, enough energetic illumination to accept death. The "Good men" of the third tercet, people who had presumably tried to do good deeds, see that their deeds are "frail." The "Wild men," the poets who "sang" of the vitality of nature, see that their celebrations were really elegies. The "Grave men" (there is, again, a pun here) are highly serious people who, nearing death and seeing the joy they have lost, also rage. The speaker, then, tells his father, who is "on the sad height" of old age, to "curse" and to "bless" him, to curse presumably because the speaker will go on living in the world that the old man is losing, and to bless him because the speaker has instructed the father on how to die properly. "Curse, bless," then leads to "fierce tears."

If you are lucky, a pedantic student may ask you why "gentle" rather than "gently" is used. One answer is that "gentle" is an adjective referring to the understood subject "you," not an adverb modifying "go." In this view, Thomas is describing a condition he hopes his father will not be in, rather than describing the father's method of going. This point is clear if for "gentle" one substitutes, say, "ignorant." On the other hand, one can argue that "gentle" is not necessarily an adjective. Some authorities point out that verbs of motion and sensation take adverbs that do not end in *ly:* cf. "Go slow," "Think fast," "Sleep sound," and "Feel good."

See *The Poems of Dylan Thomas* (rev. ed., 1974); *Collected Letters.* ed. Paul Ferris (1985); and *The Notebooks,* ed. Ralph N. Maud (1967). For criticism and bibliography: R.B. Kershner, *Dylan Thomas: The Poet and His Critics* (1976); and John Ackerman, *A Dylan Thomas Companion* (1991).

An audiocassette of Dylan Thomas reading is available from Longman.

ROBERT FRANCIS

The Pitcher (p. 606)

In presenting Robert Francis's "The Pitcher" to the class, ask if anyone knows the etymology of "eccentric" (cf. "eccentricity" in line 1). You may have to provide the answer yourself, but in any case you can explore with the students the ways in which a pitcher's art is "eccentricity."

Note that the first four stanzas do not rhyme, but they miss by only enough to "avoid the obvious" and to "vary the avoidance." "Aim" in line 1 comes as close as a word can to rhyming with "aim" in line 2, but the line drops off and misses by the merest fraction of a foot. And if "obvious/avoidance" and "comprehended/misunderstood" aren't strictly consonant, they are eccentrically so. No question about consonance or slant rhyme in "wild/willed." But perfect rhyme is reserved for the last couplet, which everyone (except the by-now-paralyzed batter) can see is a perfect strike. The rhyme scheme, the economical couplets, the tense but erratic repetition in sentence structure, the eccentric placement of caesuras (in 4 and 9), all of course contribute to the poem's wit in imitating the performance it describes.

We have found that students enjoy discussing the devices in the poem, one perception leading to another. But line 6 ("Throws to be misunderstood") and line 10 ("understood too late") can cause trouble. Is the poet saying that poets are willfully obscure? Or that they like to challenge readers so that readers can have the pleasure of (after a little thought) enjoying complexity?

GALWAY KINNELL

Blackberry Eating (p. 611)

Much of the fun of the poem is in the saying of it, the feeling of the sounds in the mouth, especially of the word *squinched*, in which the tongue presses against the palate and (given the context) crushes an imaginary blackberry in the mouth. But even in reading the poem silently one gets a sense of the pleasures of the sounds, for instance in "The stalks very prickly," and perhaps—though we may be going too far here—in these words one almost *sees* (because of the verticality of the *t*, and the *l*'s, and the *k*'s) the prickly stalks.

Exactly what does Kinnell mean when he speaks of (lines 4-6) "the stalks, very prickly, a penalty / they earn for knowing the black art / of blackberry-making"? Does "they" refer to the blackberries, and is he playfully saying the blackberries are punished with prickles because they traffic in forbidden arts ("the black art/of blackberry-making")? Or does "they" refer to blackberry-lovers, in which case he is playfully saying that those who gather the berries are punished for converting the berries into tasty objects? In any case, we think most readers will agree that the poem offers an almost sensuous delight.

X. J. KENNEDY

Nothing in Heaven Functions as It Ought (p. 613)

The poem is a Petrarchan sonnet, with the traditional contrast between the octave and the sestet. Kennedy's contrast of heaven and hell is not surprising, then, but in the contrasting rhymes and versification he plays an unexpected game. The off-rhymes and the hypermetric lines of the octave imitate the statement of the octave (things are askew), and the mechanical perfection of the sestet imitates the sestet's statement ("Hell hath no freewheeling part").

Kennedy has let us see an earlier version of the poem. You may want to invite students to compare the following version with the one in their text.

Nothing in Heaven Functions as It Ought (an early version)

Nothing in Heaven functions as it ought:
Peter snaps off a key stuck in the lock,
And his creaky gates keep crowing like a cock
(No hush of oily gold as Milton thought).
Gangs of the martyred innocents keep whoofing
The nimbus off the Venerable Bede
Like that of an old dandelion in seed.
The beatific choir take fits of coughing.
But Hell, sweet Hell, holds no unsteady part,
Nothing to rust nor rip nor lose its place.
Ask anyone: How did you come to be here?—
And he will slot a quarter into his face
And there will be a click and wheels will whir
And out will pop a neat brief of his case.

WALT WHITMAN

When I Heard the Learn'd Astronomer (p. 614)

In our discussion of the poem, we emphasize the division of the one-sentence poem into two units of four lines each, but we concentrate our discussion on the length of the lines, and we say little about the thematic contrasts in the two parts; e.g., the speaker indoors versus the speaker out of doors, the speaker with other human beings versus alone in the presence of nature, the speaker amidst noise (the lecture, the applause) versus the speaker surrounded by silence, the speaker sitting and passive versus the speaker moving and active (though the activity seems almost effortless: "rising and gliding," "wander'd off," "Look'd Up").

Notice too that we discuss the poem as an example of free verse—which it is—but we also mention that the final line of the poem is iambic pentameter. Moreover, though of course one does not want to read this line mechanically, stressing every second syllable, it is appropriate here (as rarely elsewhere in poetry) to stress the prepositions ("up" and "at") as well as the more obviously important words, "silence" and "stars."

A "Voices and Visions" videocassette of Walt Whitman is available from Longman.

CAROLYN FORCHÉ

The Colonel (p. 616)

"The Colonel" comes from a book of poems. You may want to talk about the rather undefined genre of the prose-poem. A prose-poem looks like prose but is marked by a strong rhythm (often gained by repetition of grammatical constructions) and sometimes by abundant imagery. (The idea is that the chief characteristics of poetry are rhythm and imagery, and so a short piece of prose with these features can be called a prose-poem.) Having said this, we must add that we don't think there is much point in worrying much about whether "The Colonel" is poetry or prose.

Much of "The Colonel" probably is literally true. During one of her stays in El Salvador, Forché may indeed have visited a colonel, and he may have said and done exactly what this colonel says and does. Until we are told that the ear "came alive" when dropped into the glass of water, there is nothing unbelievable in "The Colonel," partly, of course, because television has informed us that atrocities are committed daily.

Forché's first sentence ("What you have heard is true") suggests that the speaker is addressing someone who has just said, "I heard that you visited Colonel ———. Did you really? What was it like?" We get details about what seems to be a comfortable bourgeois existence ("Daily papers, pet dogs") and also some menacing details ("a pistol on the cushion beside him," "broken bottles were embedded in the walls"), all told in the same flat, matter-of-fact voice. The sixth sentence uses a metaphor ("The moon swung bare on its black cord over the house"), but even journalists are allowed to use an occasional metaphor, and a reader probably does not think twice about Forché's metaphor here, except perhaps to notice that it uses the same structure ("The moon swung bare. . .") as the previous, factual sentences ("I was," "His wife carried," "His daughter filed," "There were"). Again, for the most part the language is flat; when the speaker next uses a metaphor (the ears are "like dried peach halves") she (or he) flatly apologizes for this flight of fancy: "There is no other way to say this." But the next to last sentence takes us into a metaphorical (or mysterious) world: "Some of the ears on the floor caught this scrap of his voice."

Much of the power of "The Colonel" comes from the contrast between the picture of the colonel's bourgeois private life (pets, television, lamb, wine, etc.) and his brutal public life, a contrast that Forché emphasizes by not commenting on it (i.e., by allowing the reader to make the comment). The piece is masterful in what it doesn't say. The colonel asks how the visitor "enjoyed the country," but we don't hear the response. We can, however, guess it by what follows: "There was some talk then of how difficult it had become to govern." Presumably the colonel becomes annoyed with the visitor's comments, though at first we aren't told this in so many words. Instead we are told what the colonel did (he got a sack of ears, dumped them on the table, shook one in the faces of his guests, dropped it in a glass of water). Then we hear him: "I am tired of fooling around. . . . As for the rights of anyone, tell your people they can go fuck themselves." Irked but (as we see it) enormously confident, he says of the severed ears, "Something for your poetry, no?" Students might be invited to comment on the tone the colonel uses here. Is he complacent, wry, naive, or what?

Students might also be invited to comment on the last two sentences of "The Colonel." Does the next-to-last sentence indicate (let's say symbolically) that the oppressed people of the country know what is going on, and will ultimately triumph? Does the last sentence ("Some of the ears on the floor were pressed to the ground") mean that (1) some of the ears were pressed, presumably by being stood on, and (2) the dead were listening (and presumably waiting to be avenged)?

Forché is the editor of *Against Forgetting: Twentieth Century Poetry of Witness* (1993), a powerful collection of poems on politics, war, torture, repression, death, exile.

CHAPTER 18

In Brief:
Writing About Poetry

MARIA FUENTES

Aunt Jennifer's Screen and Adrienne Rich's Poem (Student Essay) (p. 621)

We think that Fuentes does a very good job of discussing the poem. True, she doesn't say *everything* possible about it (she might, for instance, have commented on the unusual word "denizens," or on the "chivalric certainty" of the tigers), but we think she makes important points, especially the connection between the screen as a work of art and the poem (another work of art). This point in fact is implicit from the outset, in Fuentes's title, where the balance (X and Y) implies an equivalence.

We happen to like, also, the slight personal touch ("what especially pleased me..."), which for the most part is combined with a relatively impersonal style. If you and your students are concerned with the question of how personal an essay should be, you may want to discuss this essay as one kind of example. Obviously essays can be more personal than this one, and less personal, but we think this essay strikes a good balance. Notice that in the final sentence, for instance, the language seems impersonal (there is no "I") but in fact strong opinions about the poem and about society are being conveyed.

CHAPTER 19

Poetry and Translation

An important purpose of this part of the chapter is to let students who are at ease in a language other than English—perhaps *more* at ease in it than they are in English—draw on their experience, make valuable contributions to the class, and increase everyone's understanding of poetry.

As long-time English teachers, we inevitably have read a fair number of discussions of translation, e.g. concerning Pope's *Homer*, the Greek dramatists, Roman poets, Old English poems, *The Rubaiyat*, etc. etc., to say nothing of arguments about the worth of Ezra Pound's translations of works in languages that he did not know. More recently we have encountered discussions of the problems of translating Native American poetry—a topic we touch on in our discussion of the two Arapaho poems in our chapter on poetry dealing with the making of our multi-cultural nation. Most specialists in Native American poetry insist that because such poems are not merely spoken, but are chanted and danced, a translation of the mere text, without indications of intonations, pauses, music, and so on is necessarily misleading. On this topic see Arnold Krupat, "Identity and Difference in the Criticism of Native American Literature," *Diacritics* 13 (Summer 1983): 2-13, Brian Swann and Arnold Krupat, *Recovering the Word* (1987); and Brian Swann, ed., *Coming to Light: Contemporary Translations of the Native Literatures of North America* (1995).

In discussing translations of poetry it is commonplace to say that they fall (very roughly) into three kinds: (1) literal, where the information or content is paramount, and literary values are largely or entirely ignored. (Such translations are often in prose.) (2) verse translations that seek to reproduce the form of the original (e.g., tercets, or ottava rime) and that of course seek to stay as close to the content as the translator can, within the confines of the form; (3) free translations, concerned less with the poem as information than with the poem as an aesthetic object. Translators of the last sort are likely to claim that they have aimed at catching the "spirit" of the original, which may mean that they have departed very far from the content. Persons who favor (3) point to the translations of Ezra Pound, which (from the scholarly point of view) are filled with gross errors, and in any case sometimes are from languages that Pound did not know. Pound's translations (his translation of the Old English "The Seafarer" is the usual example), these critics say, have the spirit of the original and are good poems in themselves, and therefore the translations are superior to versions that are more accurate in terms of whatever information the original conveyed.

But, again, we include this chapter not primarily in order to allow for discussions of the art or craft of translation but in order to allow non-native or bilingual speakers of English to draw on their experience, enlarge their own understanding of poetry, and contribute to the enlargement of the understanding of their classmates.

Students are keenly interested in learning about the differences in languages—for instance the use of the familiar form in French and Spanish, or the use of honorifics and the distinction between "man's language" and "woman's language" in Japanese, or the fact that Chinese poetry uses patterns of tone rather than of stress. If you make use of the sample essay, on García Lorca's "Despedida," you may want Spanish-speaking members of the class to comment on the translation of the title. How elevated or formal is "Despedida"? How does it compare with "Adios"? Is "Goodby" better translation that the student's choice, "Farewell"? But the discussion should not be limited to students fluent in Spanish. The non-Spanish speaker has a perfect right to express an opinion on whether the fact that no one says "Farewell" makes that word a poor choice in an English version. (We think it is an excellent choice, but our opinion is irrelevant to your classes.) Similarly, one does not have to know a word of Spanish to comment on the translator's decision to substitute "window" for "balcony."

Students interested in the art of translation might enjoy Edwin Honig, ed., *The Poet's Other Voice: Conversations on Literary Translation* (1985). There is also a detailed entry and bibliography in *The New Princeton Encyclopedia of Poetry and Poetics*, ed. Alex Preminger and T. V. F. Brogan (1993)—a massive work that students ought to know about.

CHAPTER 20

A Collection of Poems

We begin this chapter with some traditional (or popular) ballads, but later we print two literary the ballads: Keats's "La Belle Dame sans Merci" and Hardy's "Ah, Are You Digging on My Grave?"

Albert B. Friedman, in *The Viking Book of Folk Ballads*, reissued as *The Penguin Book of Folk Ballads*, gives additional versions of "Sir Patrick Spence," a comic version of "The Three Ravens," and an American version of "Edward." An American version of "Edward" is recorded on an album, *Child Ballads Traditional in the United States*, 1, issued by the Library of Congress (AAFS L57). Some of these may be useful in class discussion.

ANONYMOUS

Sir Patrick Spence (p. 641)

Discussion of the questions (below) ought to fill a good part of the hour and ought to help students to see the virtues in this great ballad. One might also call attention to the fact that the poem does not begin with Sir Patrick—whose initial appearance is effectively held off and built up to—and to the fact that the first lines, with their reference to the king drinking, suggest a life of courtly ease that contrasts with Sir Patrick's life of seamanship. But notice too the dark or tragic implication in the second line: the wine is "blude-reid." And we should also call attention to the contrast between the nobles, who are "loath," to wet their shoes, and Sir Patrick, who is not eager for the trip and is much more than "loath," for he knows that the trip is virtually a death mission. The nobles are associated with ladies with fans and combs. The courtiers will be mourned by the ladies, but we are not told of any mourners for Sir Patrick. However, we see

Sir Patrick as master of the lords in death by virtue of having done his duty with full awareness.

TOPICS FOR CRITICAL THINKING AND WRITING

1. The shipwreck occurs between lines 29 and 32, but it is not described. Does the omission stimulate the reader to imagine the details of the wreck? Or does it suggest that the poem is not so much about a shipwreck as about kinds of behavior? (Our own response is that the poem is much more about loyalty than about a storm at sea.)

2. Do you think that lines 17-18 warrant the inference that the "eldern knicht" (5) is Sir Patrick Spence's enemy? (Maybe. There's no way of being sure, but, as we suggested a moment ago, we think this poem is chiefly about Sir Patrick's loyalty. Whether the knight is malicious or not does not, finally, matter.)

3. What do you make of lines 13-16? (Students sometimes have trouble understanding the sharp transition. Apparently at first Sir Patrick thinks the order to sail is a joke, but then he sees it is serious, and he foresees the ironic consequences. The two states are sharply juxtaposed, without a transition.)

4. In place of lines 37-40, another version of this ballad has the following stanza:

> The ladies crack's their fingers white,
> The maidens tore their hair,
> A' for the sake o' their true loves,
> For them they ne'er saw mair.

Which version do you prefer? (We prefer the first, since we find the second melodramatic.)

5. In the other version, the stanza that is here the final one (41-44) precedes the stanzas about the ladies (33-40). Which stanza do you think makes a better conclusion? Why? (We much prefer the version given in the text, since it ends quietly and with dignity.)

6. Understatement in "Sir Patrick Spence" (or, a slightly different way of putting it: Things unsaid in "Sir Patrick Spence").

ANONYMOUS

The Three Ravens (p. 643)

"The Three Ravens," like many other ballads, is filled with mystery: How did the knight die? Why does the doe bury him? Is the doe his lover? But against these uncertainties the poem gives us considerable detail: There are three ravens, the field is "green" (death and life coexist), hounds and hawks loyally guard the knight, and the doe cares for his corpse, protecting it from the birds who would make it their "breakfast." Having given us five stanzas in which death and life and bodily self-satisfaction and loyalty are juxtaposed, the poem goes on in its next four stanzas to show us only gentleness and self-sacrifice. The final stanza, with its reference to a "leman," pretty clearly indicates that the pregnant doe is the knight's beloved and, equally important, suggests that even though the knight is dead, his life was a sort of triumph since it earned such loyalty. The last stanza offers explicit moralizing, but the poem as a whole has *shown*, not preached.

TOPICS FOR CRITICAL THINKING AND WRITING

1. The hounds and the hawks are loyal followers of the knight, as is the doe. How do the references to the hounds and hawks in some degree prepare us for the doe? Do you think this preparation is necessary? Why, or why not?
2. Why does the poet include the ravens? Do they confuse a poem on loyalty, or do they provide an effective contrast? Do the ravens help to give a fuller, more realistic picture of life? Explain.
3. What is your response to the final two lines? Do they strike you as an intrusive comment? Explain.

ANONYMOUS

The Twa Corbies (p. 644)

"The Twa Corbies," unlike the "The Three Ravens," is a poem about *disloyalty*—of hound, hawk, and lady—but we should not overlook the cozy, though macabre, domesticity of the fourth stanza, in which the corbies plan to dine and to patch their nest.

TOPICS FOR CRITICAL THINKING AND WRITING

1. The story in the poem is implied (in the second and third stanzas) rather than made explicit. In your opinion, what *is* the story? Is it the worse for being implicit? Explain.
2. Hair is usually "gowden" in ballads. What does this conventional detail tell us about the knight's age? Suppose instead of "gowden" (15) the poem said "graying." Would your response be different? How? Why?
3. What do you think the fourth stanza (especially 15-16) contributes to the poem?
4. Animals can't speak Do you therefore find the poem absurd? Explain.

ANONYMOUS

Edward (p. 645)

Bertrand Bronson, in *The Ballad as Song*, suggests that "Edward" may not be a pure folk ballad. Perhaps the strongest evidence of a "literary" touch is the fact that the surprise ending in the last line—which forces us to reconstruct our understanding of the mother—is unusual for a ballad. In traditional ballads,

Bronson points out, people ask questions in order to learn what they do not know (or, in the case of riddling ballads, in order to test someone), but in "Edward" the questions and answers serve a sophisticated technique of character revelation and of plot-telling. By the way, the motifs of questions and answers and last will and testament, found in "Edward," are also in "Lord Randal," which is fairly well known among undergraduates.

TOPICS FOR CRITICAL THINKING AND WRITING

1. The poem consists of two parts. How does the structure of the first part parallel that of the second?
2. What might have been the mother's motives? Do you think that the story would be improved if we knew the motives behind her "counseils"? Explain.
3. How can you explain Edward's statements about his wife and children?
4. Line 21 offers a surprise, but it is topped by the surprise in the final four lines. Can you reread the poem with pleasure once you know the surprises? Explain.

ANONYMOUS

The Demon Lover (p. 646)

Not all ballads, include supernatural elements, but a good many of them do. This is not to say, however, that these ballads are purely fanciful or escapist. Many of them, including "The Demon Lover," are deeply rooted also in the passions (which, finally, are mysterious) of this world.

"The Demon Lover" nicely illustrates several of the characteristics mentioned in the note on folk ballads in the text, at the beginning of "A Collection of Poems." That is, the process of oral transmission probably has eliminated the dross (the antecedent action may once have been given at length but now it can be gleaned only from the dialogue) and has left us chiefly with memorable speech, swiftly drawn pictures, and strong passions. There is no comment on the action, no reflection on the theme. Rather, whatever "meaning" the poem has is conveyed only through the action. It begins not with the introduction of a speaker, but with dialogue. In a similarly abrupt fashion, without telling us that after A spoke B replied, we get the words of the second speaker. As in most ballads (or at least in most of the ballads that are regarded as the best) the plot is vigorous but highly abbreviated, and the characters—perceived through what they say rather than through description—are sharply drawn, not in the sense that they are rounded but in the sense that they are embodiments of intense passions. (One thinks of Yeats's remark that comedy gives us "characters" but in tragedy we get not character but pure passion, intense versions of ourselves.)

Between lines 28 and 29 (between the seventh and eighth stanzas) the woman decides to go with the demon lover. In the final stanza the lover suddenly appears to become gigantic, striking the topmast (one thinks of him striking the top of the mast) and the foremast simultaneously. That is, his overwhelming power is given a physical dimension that corresponds to its force.

ANONYMOUS

John Henry (p. 648)

There is a wealth of information about the origin of "John Henry" in Guy B. Johnson, *John Henry*, and in Louis W. Chappell, *John Henry*. These books, and many other scholarly writings on John Henry, are summarized in Richard M. Dorson, "The Career of 'John Henry,'" *Western Folklore* 24 (1965):155-63, reprinted in *Mother Wit from the Laughing Barrel*, Alan Dundes. Albert B. Friedman, *The Penguin Book of Folk Ballads*, prints six versions, and the song has often been recorded, e.g., by Huddie Ledbetter, *Leadbelly's Last Sessions*, Vol. 1, Part Two (Folkways Records FA2941 C/D).

Although "John Henry" was composed by blacks, sung by blacks, sung to blacks, and is about a black hero, Eldridge Cleaver suggests (*Soul on Ice*, 164) that it suits the purposes of white racism: The black is all Body and no Brain. There is something to Cleaver's view, though ballads are scarcely likely to celebrate intellectual activity; when one thinks about the matter, one notices that ballads celebrating a white folk hero normally give him a touch of cunning and make him a fighter against injustice (e.g., Jesse James "had a hand and a heart and a brain," and he "stole from the rich, and he gave to the poor"). "John Henry" celebrates only physical strength (and sometimes sexual strength, in the reference to his women). But the vast majority of ballads celebrating white heroes are rather unimpressive sentimental pieces; "John Henry," however limited its view, has an aesthetic excellence that endures. And after all, no one expects any work of art to tell the *whole* truth.

TOPICS FOR CRITICAL THINKING AND WRITING

1. How does the first stanza contribute to John Henry's grandeur?
2. Some versions contain an additional stanza at the end:

> They took John Henry to the buryin' ground,
> And they buried him in the sand;
> And every locomotive come roarin' round
> Says "There lies a steel-drivin' man,"
> Says "There lies a steel-drivin' man."

Do you find the ending as given in the present text unsatisfactory? Do you have any doubt about John Henry's death?

WILLIAM SHAKESPEARE

Sonnet 29, Sonnet 73, Sonnet 116, and Sonnet 146 (p. 649-51)

Shakespeare's 154 sonnets were published in 1609, although it is thought that most of them were composed in the middle 1590s, around the time *Romeo and Juliet* and *A Midsummer Night's Dream* were written. Francis Meres spoke of Shakespeare's "sugared sonnets" in 1598, and two were published in an anthology in 1599. The order of the sonnets is probably not Shakespeare's, but there are two large divisions (with some inconsistent interruptions). Sonnets 1-126 seem to be addressed to, or concerned with, a handsome, aristocratic young man who is urged to marry and thus to propagate his beauty and become immortal. Sonnets 127-152 are chiefly concerned with a promiscuous dark woman who seduces a friend, at least for a while.

Wordsworth thought the poems were autobiographical ("With this key Shakespeare unlocked his heart"), to which Browning replied, "If so, the less Shakespeare he." Scholars have not convincingly identified the friend or the lady, and the whole thing may be as fictional as *Hamlet.* Certainly it *sounds* like autobiography, but this is only to say that Shakespeare is a writer who sounds convincing. The chief argument that the poems really may be autobiographical is that the insistence that the friend marry is so odd a theme. As C. S. Lewis says in *English Literature in the Sixteenth Century* what man (except a potential father-in-law) cares if another man gets married? One other point: Do the poems addressed to the beautiful friend suggest a homosexual interest? Certainly they suggest a *passionate* interest, but it doesn't seem to be erotic. "Sonnet 20," a bawdy and witty poem, expressly denies any interest in the friend's body. It seems reasonable to say that what the speaker of the sonnets wants from the friend is not sex but love.

Of the many studies, we are partial to Stephen Booth, *An Essay on Shakespeare's Sonnets* (1969), and to his edition of the sonnets (1977), which prints both the facsimile of the first edition and a modernized text, along with extremely detailed commentaries.

Sonnet 29 (When in disgrace with Fortune and men's eyes) (p. 649)

The rhyme scheme of "Sonnet 29" is that of the usual Shakespearean sonnet, but the thought is organized more or less into an octave and a sestet, the transition being emphasized by the trochee at the beginning of line 9. The sense of energy is also communicated by the trochee that begins line 10 and yet another that introduces line 11, this last being especially important because by consonance and alliteration it communicates its own energy to the new image of joy ("Like to the lark"). As in most of Shakespeare's sonnets, the couplet is more or less a summary of what has preceded, but not in the same order: line 13 summarizes the third quatrain: line 14 looks back to (but now rejects) the earlier quatrains.

The first line surely glances at Shakespeare's unimpressive social position, and line 8 presumably refers to his work. Possibly the idea is that he most enjoyed his work before it became the source of his present discomfort. Edward Hubler, in *The Sense of Shakespeare's Sonnets,* notes that "the release from depression is expressed through the image of the lark, a remembrance of earlier days when the cares of his London career were unknown."

To this it can be added that although the poem employs numerous figures of speech from the start (e.g., personification with "Fortune," synecdoche with "eyes" in line 1, metonymy with "heaven" in line 3), line 11, with the image of the lark, introduces the poem's first readily evident figure of speech, and it is also the most emphatic run-on line in the poem. Moreover, though heaven was "deaf" in line 3, in line 12 it presumably hears the lark singing "hymns at heaven's gate." "Sullen" in line 12 perhaps deserves some special comment too: (1) The earth is still somber in color, though the sky is bright, and (2) applied to human beings, it suggests the moody people who inhabit earth.

TOPIC FOR CRITICAL THINKING AND WRITING

Disregarding for the moment the last two lines (or couplet), where does the sharpest turn or shift occur? In a sentence, summarize the speaker's state of mind before this turn and, in another sentence, the state of mind after it.

Sonnet 73 (That time of year thou mayst in me behold) (p. 650)

Sonnet 73 is chiefly a meditation on growing old, though the couplet relates this topic to the theme of love that is the subject of many of Shakespeare's sonnets. All three quatrains, in varying degrees, glance at increasing coldness and darkness, and each successive quatrain is concerned with a briefer period. In the first, the human life is compared to a year; in the second, to a day; in the third, to a few hours. In the first quatrain, there is a further comparison; the boughs of the autumnal trees are compared (in "bare ruined choirs") to the churches that had fallen into decay after England broke with Rome. ("Sweet birds" refers primarily to the feathered creatures that recently sang in the boughs, but it also glances at choristers in the choirs.) Note, too, that it is reasonable to perceive, faintly, a resemblance between the shaking boughs and a trembling old person. The first quatrain, then, is rich in suggestions of ruined beauty and destroyed spirituality.

The second quatrain, by speaking of night as "Death's second self," explicitly introduces death into the poem. The third quatrain personifies the fire, speaking of its "youth" (i.e., the earlier minutes or hours of the blaze) and its "deathbed," and in its reference to ashes it introduces a common idea of the decayed body. (The idea, of course, is that the last embers lie on the ashes, which were the "youth" or earlier hours of the fire, and these ashes now help to extinguish the embers.) The year will renew itself, and the day will renew itself, but the firewood is utterly destroyed. In the final line the speaker is reduced to "that," not even "me."

"Sonnet 116" (Let me not to the marriage of true minds) (p. 650)

Although the poem is almost certainly addressed to a man, because it is a celebration of the permanence of love it can apply equally well to a woman or, in fact, to a parent or child.

The first words, "Let me not," are almost a vow, and "admit impediments" in the second line faintly hints at the marriage service in the Book of Common Prayer, which says, "If any of you know just cause or impediment. . . ." In line 2 "admit" can mean both "acknowledge, grant the existence of" and "allow to enter."

The first quatrain is a negative definition of love ("love is not..."), but the second quatrain is an affirmative definition ("O no, it is..."). The third begins as another negative definition, recognizing that "rosy lips and cheeks" will indeed decay, but denying that they are the essence of love; this quatrain then ends affirmatively, making a contrast to transience: "bears it out even to the edge of doom." Then, having clinched his case, the speaker adopts a genial and personal tone in the couplet, where for the first time he introduces the word "I."

Speaking of couplets, we can't resist quoting Robert Frost on the topic. Once, in conversation with Frost, the boxer Gene Tunney said something about the price of a poem. Frost replied: "One thousand dollars a line. Four thousand for a quatrain, but for a sonnet, $12,000. The last two lines of a sonnet don't mean anything anyway." Students might be invited to test the sonnets against this playful remark.

TOPICS FOR CRITICAL THINKING AND WRITING

1. Paraphrase (that is, put into your own words) "Let me not to the marriage of true minds / Admit impediments." Is there more than one appropriate meaning of "Admit"?
2. Notice that the poem celebrates "the marriage of true minds," not bodies. In a sentence or two, using only your own words, summarize Shakespeare's idea of the nature of such love, both what it is and what it is not.
3. Paraphrase lines 13-14. What is the speaker's tone here? Would you say that the tone is different from the tone in the rest of the poem?
4. Write a paragraph or a poem defining either love or hate. Or see if you can find such a definition in a popular song. Bring the lyrics to class.

Sonnet 146 (Poor soul, the center of my sinful earth) (p. 651)

Shakespeare's Sonnet 146 is well discussed in Edward Hubler, *The Sense of Shakespeare's* Sonnets, and more learnedly and elaborately discussed by Michael West in *Shakespeare Quarterly* 25 (Winter 1974): 109-122. Also useful is *A Casework on Shakespeare's Sonnets,* Gerald Willen and Victor B. Reed, eds. See also an article by Charles A. Huttar, "The Christian Basis of Shakespeare's Sonnet 146," *Shakespeare Quarterly* 19 (Autumn 1968): 355-65, which rejects a reading that the poem ironically argues that spiritual health is achieved by bodily subjugation. The rejected reading holds that the advice that the soul exploit the body must be ironic, since if it were not ironic, the soul would be guilty of simony, the sin of buying (or attempting to buy) salvation. According to this ironic reading, the poet really is pleading for the life of the body against a rigorous asceticism which glorifies the spirit at the expense of the body. But Huttar argues (by citing Biblical sources and Christian commentaries) that the poem argues in behalf of the traditional Christian doctrine that the soul should be the master of the body; the body (which must in any case die) should not he allowed to cause the soul to "pine." The poem, Huttar says, is close to Jesus's words in Matthew 6:20: "Lay up for yourself treasures in heaven, where neither moth nor rust cloth corrupt, and where thieves do not break through and steal."

TOPICS FOR CRITICAL THINKING AND WRITING

1. In line 2, "My sinful earth" is doubtless a printer's error, an unintentional repetition of the last words of the first line. Among suggested emendations are "Thrall to," "Fooled by," "Rebuke these," "Leagued with," "Feeding." Which do you prefer? Why?
2. How would you characterize the tone of the first two lines? Where in the poem does the thought take its chief turn? What do you think is the tone of the couplet?
3. What does "array" (line 2) mean?
4. Explain the paradox in lines 13-14.
5. In a poem on the relation between body and soul, do you find battle imagery surprising? Commercial imagery (lines 5-12)? What other imagery is in the poem? Do you think the sonnet is a dull sermon?

JOHN DONNE

A Valediction: Forbidding Mourning (p. 651)

Instructors may be so familiar with this poem that they may not recognize the difficulties it presents to students. The title itself leads many students to think (quite plausibly) that it is about death, an idea reinforced by the first simile. But this simile is introduced to make the point that *just as* virtuous men can die quietly because they are confident of a happy future, *so* the two lovers can part quietly—that is, the speaker can go on a journey—because they are confident of each other.

The hysterics that accompany the separation of less confident lovers are ridiculed ("sigh-tempests," "tear-floods"); such agitation would be a "profanation" of the relationship of the speaker and his beloved and would betray them to the "laity."

Thus the speaker and the beloved are implicitly priests of spiritual love.

The poem goes on to contrast the harmful movement of the earth (an earthquake) with the harmless ("innocent") movement of heavenly bodies, thereby again associating the speaker and the beloved with heavenly matters. (The cosmology, of course, is the geocentric Ptolemaic system.) The fourth stanza continues the contrast: other lovers are "sublunary," changeable, and subject to the changing moon. Such earthbound lovers depend on the physical things that "elemented" their love ("eyes, lips, and hands"), but the love of the speaker and his partner is "refined" and does not depend on such stuff. Moreover, if their love is like something physical, it is "like gold to airy thinness beat."

The three last stanzas introduce the image of a draftsman's (not an explorer's) compass, and they also introduce the circle as a symbol of perfection.

See Theodore Redpath's edition of *The Songs and Sonnets of John Donne,* and see especially Clay Hunt, *Donne's Poetry,* and Patricia Spacks, *College English* 29 (1968): 594-95. Louis Martz, *The Wit of Love,* 48, says of line 20: "'Care less,' but is it so? The very rigor and intricacy of the famous image of the compass at the end may be taken to suggest rather desperate dialectical effort to control by logic and reason a situation almost beyond control."

TOPICS FOR CRITICAL THINKING AND WRITING

1. The first stanza describes the death of "virtuous men." To what is their death compared in the second stanza?
2. Who is the speaker of this poem? To whom does he speak and what is the occasion? Explain the title.
3. What is the meaning of "laity" in line 8? What does it imply about the speaker and his beloved?
4. In the fourth stanza the speaker contrasts the love of "dull sublunary lovers" (i.e., ordinary mortals) with the love he and his beloved share. What is the difference?
5. In the figure of the carpenter's compass (lines 25-36) the speaker offers reasons—some stated clearly, some not so clearly—why he will end where he began. In 250 words explain these reasons.
6. In line 35 Donne speaks of his voyage as a "circle." Explain in a paragraph why the circle is traditionally a symbol of perfection.
7. Write a farewell note—or poem—to someone you love (or hate).

JOHN MILTON

"When I consider how my light is spent" (p. 653)

Milton's sonnets have been carefully edited by Ernst Honigmann (1966). Argument about the date Milton became blind need not concern us (Miltonists wonder how literally to take "Ere half my days"), but it should be noticed that one critic argues that the sonnet is not about blindness, (The common title "On His Blindness" has no authority; it was first used by a printer in 1752.) Lysander Kemp held *(Hopkins Review,* 6 [1952], pp. 80-83) that the sonnet deals with the loss not of vision but of poetic inspiration, but Kemp's view has not been widely accepted. The most sensible view (to draw on Honigmann) is that the octave assumes that God requires ceaseless labor, and the sestet enlarges the concept of service to include those who though inactive are eagerly prepared for action.

Additional notes: in line 2, "this dark world and wide" suggests not only the dark world of the blind man but is also a religious stock expression for the sinful world; in line 7, "day-labor" suggests not only labor for daily wages but also labor that requires daylight, i.e., the power of vision; in line 14, "wait" perhaps means not only "stay in expectation" but also "attend as a servant, to receive orders."

WILLIAM BLAKE

The Lamb (p. 653); The Tyger (p. 654)

E. D. Hirsch, Jr., in *Innocence and Experience,* Harold Bloom, in *The Visionary Company,* and Hazard Adams, in *William Blake,* discuss these poems. "The Tyger" has engendered much comment. Of special interest are Martin K. Nurmi, "Blake's Revisions of 'The Tyger,'" *PMLA* 71 (September 1956): 669-85; Harold

Bloom, *Blake's Apocalypse;* and two pieces by John Grant and Hazard Adams reprinted in *Discussions of Blake,* ed. John Grant. See also, for a collection of essays and extracts from books, *William Blake: The Tyger,* ed. Winston Weathers.

In the course of arguing on behalf of reader-response criticism, Stanley Fish, in *Is There a Text in This Class?,* has some fun calling attention to the diversity of opinions. He points out that in *Encounter* (June 1954), Kathleen Raine published an essay entitled "Who Made the Tyger?" She argued that because for Blake the tiger is "the beast that sustains its own life at the expense of its fellow-creatures," the answer to the big question ("Did he who made the Lamb make thee?") is, in Raine's words, "beyond all possible doubt, No." Fish points out that Raine, as part of her argument, insists that Blake always uses the word "forest" with reference "to the natural, 'fallen' world." Fish then calls attention to E. D. Hirsch's reading, in *Innocence and Experience* (1964), in which Hirsch argues that "forest" suggests "tall straight forms, a world that for all its terror has the orderliness of the tiger's stripes or Blake's perfectly balanced verses." In short, for Hirsch "The Tyger" is "a poem that celebrates the holiness of tigerness." Hirsch also argues that Blake satirizes the single-mindedness of the Lamb.

We find all of this very baffling. We are not specialists in Blake, but it seems to us that both poems celebrate rather than satirize or in any way condemn their subjects. In "The Lamb" (such is our critical innocence), innocence is celebrated; in "The Tyger," energy is celebrated. In "The Lamb" the speaker is a child, or is an adult impersonating a child. He asks the lamb a question and then gives the answer according to traditional Christian thinking. (In the Gospel of John [1:29, 35] John the Baptist twice greets Jesus as the Lamb of God, presumably drawing on the idea of the lamb as a sacrificial offering. And behind this idea is the Suffering Servant of Isaiah 53, who is compared to "a lamb that is led to slaughter.") The speaker uses a simple vocabulary (words of one and two syllables), and he uses end-stopped lines (one thought to a line). Lamb, God, speaker, and child are all united at the end of the poem.

In "The Tyger" the animal is "burning bright" because of its fiery eyes (6) and presumably because of its orange stripes, also flame-like. (Since the tiger is imagined as being created in a smithy, the poem also includes other images of fire in such words as "forge" and "furnace.")

Blake's question in effect is this: Was the tiger created in hell ("distant deeps") or in heaven ("skies")—and by Satan or by God? Blake hammers these questions into our minds, but it seems to us that Blake clearly implies an answer: The creator is "immortal," daring, "dread," and—most important—creative. In traditional Christian thinking, then, the answer is that God created the tiger. Lines 17-18 ("When the stars threw down their spears / And watered heaven with their tears") have engendered much commentary. Possibly the lines allude to the war in heaven in Milton's *Paradise Lost,* and Blake's gist might be paraphrased thus: "When the rebel angels cast down their spears in defeat, did the triumphant God smile at his success, i.e. What were God's feelings when he had to be tiger-like to an aspect of his own creation?" This makes sense to us, but we admit that, strictly speaking, in *Paradise Lost* the rebellious angels never do "cast down their spears," i.e. never surrender.

One last comment. Harold Bloom probably understands Blake as well as anyone else alive. In *The Oxford Anthology of English Literature* he gives this footnote, which we can't quite bring ourselves to believe. You may want to think about it, and to try it out on your students.

> However the poem is interpreted, the reader should be wary of identifying the poem's chanter with Blake, who did not react with awe or fear to any natural phenomenon whatsoever.
>
> Blake probably had considerable satirical intention in this lyric, as a juxtaposition of his verbal description of the Tyger with his illustration seems to suggest. [The illustration shows an unimpressive beast.] The poem's speaker, though a man of considerable imagination (quite possibly a poet like William Cowper), is at work terrifying himself with a monster of his own creation. Though Blake may mean us to regard the poem's questions as unanswerable, he himself would have answered by saying that the "immortal hand or eye" belonged only to Man, who makes both Tyger and Lamb. In "the forests of the night," or mental darkness, Man makes the Tyger, but in the open vision of day Man makes the Lamb.

TOPICS FOR CRITICAL THINKING AND WRITING

1. What do the lamb and the tiger symbolize?
2. In "The Tyger" Blake asks a great question, "Did he who made the lamb make thee?" What is the answer?

WILLIAM BLAKE

London (p. 655)

"London," from *Songs of Experience*, is a denunciation of the mind-forged manacles, that is, of manmade repressive situations, not a denunciation of cities and a glorification of rural life. The church assists in exploitation by promises of an eternal reward, the monarchy slaughters men for private gain, and marriage drives the unmarried (or the unsatisfactorily married) to harlots. "Chartered" (2)—not merely mapped but also licensed—is perhaps almost acceptable for streets, but that the river, an image of freedom, should also be chartered is unnatural and intolerable. As the poem develops, it is evident that children are licensed (as chimney sweeps), soldiers are licensed (to kill and to be killed), and harlots are licensed (bought and sold). E. D. Hirsch, Jr., *Innocence and Experience*, suggests that there is a further meaning: The English were proud of their "chartered liberties," rights guaranteed by Magna Carta, but "these chartered liberties are chartered slaveries." For "ban" in line 7 Hirsch offers four references: a summons to arms (king), a formal denunciation or curse (church), a proclamation of marriage, and a prohibition (king, church, marriage).

A few additional points: The church is "blackening" because (1) it is covered with the soot of an industrial (mechanistic) society; (2) it is spiritually corrupt; and (3) it corrupts people. The chimney-sweeper's cry appalls the church because the cry is a reproach, and "appalls" hints at "pall" (suggestive of the dead church) and at its literal meaning, "to make pale," that is, the hypocritical church is a whited sepulcher. In line 14, "the youthful Harlot's curse" may be a cry (thus linked with the infant's cry, the chimney sweeper's cry, and the soldier's sigh), or it may be the disease that afflicts her and is communicated to others. In *Poetry and Repression,* Harold Bloom offers the astounding suggestion that "the harlot's curse is not, as various interpreters have said, venereal disease, but is indeed what 'curse' came to mean in the vernacular after Blake and still means now: menstruation, the natural cycle in the human female.... [Blake knows that one] curse or ban or natural fact (menstruation) blasts or scatters another natural fact, the tearlessness of the newborn infant."

In an earlier version, "dirty" stood in lines 1 and 2 instead of "chartered," and "smites" instead of "blights" in line 16.

For an analysis of several reading of "London," see Susan R. Suleiman and Inge Crosman, *The Reader in the Text.* Also important is an essay by E. P. Thompson in *Interpreting Blake,* ed. Michael Phillips.

TOPICS FOR CRITICAL THINKING AND WRITING

1. What do you think Blake means by "mind-forged manacles" (8)? What might be some modern examples?
2. Paraphrase the second stanza.
3. Read the poem aloud, several times. How would you characterize the *tone*—sad, angry, or what? Of course the tone may vary from line to line, but what is the prevailing tone?
4. An earlier version of the last stanza ran thus

   But most the midnight harlot's curse
   From every dismal street I hear,
   Weaves around the marriage hearse
   And blasts the new-born infant's tear.

   Compare the two versions closely, and then consider which you think is more effective, and explain why.
5. Write a poem or a paragraph setting forth your response to a city or town that you know well.

WILLIAM WORDSWORTH

The World Is Too Much with Us (p. 655)

The meaning of "the world" in line 1 is clarified in line 2: "Getting and spending." Our powers are bestowed on worldly (presumably commercial) things, rather than on perceiving Nature properly. We have given our hearts away, but this gift ("boon") is sordid, for our hearts are set on wrong things. Against the "world" Wordsworth sets nature. He defines nature through images of natural beauty (sea, flowers) and through mythological allusions (Proteus, Triton). That is, nature is both beautiful and wonderful, for those who perceive it. The sea and winds are "upgathered now like sleeping flowers," but they will reveal themselves in all their beauty and mystery when we turn to them. (C.F.

Hopkins's "There lives the dearest freshness deep down things," in "God's Grandeur," later in the text.) Wordsworth does not say that paganism is preferable to Christianity; he says he would rather be a pagan than what "we" are, because the pagan still responded to the divinity in nature, whereas "we" have lost touch with it.

WILLIAM WORDSWORTH

I Wandered Lonely as a Cloud (p. 656)

On 15 April 1802, Wordsworth and his sister, Dorothy, took a walk, during which they saw some daffodils near a lake. Dorothy recorded the experience in her journal, and this entry affords us something close to the raw material out of which Wordsworth's poem was made. The entry is not, of course, Wordsworth's own experience; Dorothy's experience was not William's, and Dorothy's words cannot exactly reproduce even her own experience. (It should be noted, incidentally, that Dorothy's description is not entirely "factual"; her daffodils rest their heads, glance, dance, etc.) Still, the entry gives us something of the phenomena that stirred an emotion in Wordsworth, and for Wordsworth, poetry was made out of "emotion recollected in tranquility." Below is the entry from Dorothy's journal. (We sometimes photocopy the entry and ask the students to discuss the poem in light of the entry.)

> It was a threatening, misty morning, but mild. We set off after dinner, from Eusemere. Mrs. Clarkson went a short way with us, but turned back. The wind was furious, and we thought we must have returned. We first rested in the large boathouse, then under a furze bush opposite Mr. Clarkson's. Saw the plough going in the field. The wind seized our breath. The lake was rough. . . . When we were in the woods beyond Gowbarrow Park we saw a few daffodils close to the water-side. We fancied that the lake had floated the seeds ashore, and that the little colony had so sprung up. But as we went along there were more and yet more; and at last, under the boughs of the trees, we saw that there was a long belt of them along the shore, about the breadth of a country turnpike road. I never saw daffodils so beautiful. They grew among the mossy stones above and about them; some rested their heads upon these stones as on a pillow for weariness; and the rest tossed and reeled and danced, and seemed as if they verily laughed with the wind that blew upon them over the lake; they looked so gay, ever glancing, ever changing. This wind blew directly over the lake to them. There was here and there a little knot and a few stragglers a few yards higher up; but they were so few as not to disturb the simplicity, unity, and life of that one busy highway. We rested again and again. The bays were stormy, and we heard the waves at different distances, and in the middle of the water, like the sea. Rain came on—we were wet when we reached Luff's, but we called in.

Two years after the walk, William presumably recollected and contemplated the emotion, and wrote "I Wandered Lonely as a Cloud," leaving out the threatening weather, the plough, the boathouse, the miscellaneous flowers and even the first group of daffodils, and the people (including Dorothy). Notice, too, that the sense of effort which Dorothy records ("we thought we must have returned," "we first rested," etc.) is not in the poem: The speaker "wandered," and he lies on his couch in "vacant or in pensive mood"; if he acts, it is with sponta-neous joy, but chiefly it is the daffodils that act ("Fluttering and dancing in the breeze," "tossing their sprightly heads," etc.).

On Dorothy Wordsworth's *Journals* and William Wordsworth's "I Wandered Lonely as a Cloud," see Carl Woodring, *Wordsworth;* Edward Rosenheim, *What Happens in Literature;* David Perkins, *Wordsworth;* and especially Frederick Pottle's essay in *Yale Review* 40 (Autumn 1950): 27-42, reprinted in *Wordsworth,* Gilbert T. Dunklin, ed.

TOPIC FOR WRITING

Wordsworth first published the poem in 1807, but the version printed here (which is the one everyone knows) is that of 1815. The differences between the first and second versions are these: In the first version lines 7-12 are lacking; line 4 has "dancing" instead of "golden"; line 5 has "Along" instead of "Beside"; line 6 has "Ten thousand" instead of "Fluttering and"; line 16 has "laughing" instead of "jocund." Evaluate the revisions. In particular, what does the added stanza con-tribute?

PHILLIS WHEATLEY

On Being Brought from Africa to America (p. 657)

As the headnote informs students, Wheatley was educated by a pious white family, and was kept from the company of other blacks. It does not seem at all surprising to us, then, that the values she sets forth in this poem are those of her owner-educators, rather than (to put the point strongly) those of today's African-Americans. Among the basic views of the time were these two: (1) slav-ery conferred a benefit on the slaves, since it rescued them from pagan igno-rance and brought them, through faith in Jesus, from bondage to Satan to ever-lasting life, (2) the color of Africans suggested a special affinity with Satan, the Prince of Darkness. Thus, to Jeremiah's question in 13: 23, "Can the Ethiopian change his skin?"—in a context where Jeremiah is accusing the people of Judah of irredeemable sin—one can juxtapose a reply from Matthew 19: 26 and Mark 10: 27: "With God all things are possible."

Not everyone believed that the color of the African was a sign of special guilt, and that slavery was justified because it conferred the possibility of sal-vation, but these beliefs were widespread, and it is easy to see why. They offered whites a comforting justification for a wicked practice that they wished to continue.

We do not find it at all unsurprising that Wheatley, a black, should echo the thoughts of her white owners. What are these commonplace white thoughts? In the first line she says that "mercy" (rather than, say, a desire for material profit from her labor) brought her from her "pagan land"; in the sec-ond line she says that before she learned about God her soul was "benighted," hence her capture in Africa and her transportation to America was a boon. We do not find it hard to believe that she is utterly sincere in this belief, and we are puzzled by modern commentators who find it impossible to believe that in the eighteenth century a favored slave, brought up in a pious household, might genuinely believe that his or her physical and *spiritual* conditions were infinitely superior to those of pagan blacks in Africa. Wheatley expressed the idea elsewhere, in a poem addressed to Harvard students, "To the University of Cambridge in New England." She says,

> 'Twas not long since I left my native shore
> The land of errors and Egyptian gloom:
> Father of mercy, 'twas thy gracious hand
> Brought me in safety from those dark abodes.

This sort of thing was good eighteenth-century Christian thinking; given the conditions of her upbringing, it is almost inconceivable that Wheatley could have held another view.

But we should return to the poem in the text. The imagery of darkness continues in "sable race," which some say "is a diabolic dye." The poem ends with the thought that although Negroes (Wheatley's word) are "black as Cain," they "may be refined, and join th' angelic train." This is all evident enough, but some readers have been determined to find in the poem a message contrary to the surface statement, where imagery of darkness is associated with evil. That is, readers want to say that Wheatley is surreptitiously a protest poet. Thus, James A. Levernier, writing in *Explicator* 40:1 (Fall 1981), says that "Wheatley used her considerable linguistic talent to embed in the poem, at a very sophisticated level, a far different message than that which the poem superficially conveys" (25).

What message does he find? "By subtly inverting the connotations traditionally associated with light and dark imagery, she suggests that Christians do not always practice what they preach" (25). He finds puns on *die* and *Cain*, i.e. he says that the words call to mind indigo *dye* and sugar *cane*, produced in the Indies by slave labor.

> Aware that both dye and cane were obtained through the sufferings of blacks who not only constituted a commodity in the triangular trade, but who also labored in sugar *refineries* (yet another word which Wheatley puns on in the poem) and dye and cane plantations in the Indies, true Christians boycotted these products... The point of these puns [is]... that Christians should practice what they preach. (26)

Certainly we can all agree that Wheatley directly addresses whites ("Christians") in the next-to-last line, and reminds them that blacks no less than whites may "join th' angelic train," but whether by means of puns Wheatley stresses the monstrous behavior of whites is, well, something that is debatable.

See *The Collected Works of Phillis Wheatley*, ed. John Shields (1988), a volume in the Schomburg Library of Nineteenth Century Black Women Writers series, published by Oxford University Press. This volume is excellent in many ways, but the main selection of Wheatley's verse is a photo-offset of the 1773 edition—the archaic spellings of which may prove nettling to students.

ANONYMOUS

Cross-Section of a Slave Ship (drawing, p. 658)

As we indicate in our discussion of Phillis Wheatley's "On Being Brought from Africa to America," we do not subscribe to the argument, current today, that Wheatley's poem is consciously ironic, that Wheatley *can't* mean what she says, etc. Wheatley, we assume, as a pious Christian thought that her condition of servitude was a small price to pay for salvation, especially since she was much fussed over. But we should remember the other aspects of slavery, beginning with the voyage from Africa to the United States.

It is estimated that 10 million Africans survived the transatlantic journey (the "middle passage") to slavery. Most were sent to Brazil and the West Indies; only 4 to 6 percent of the total were delivered to the American colonies. But 66 percent of the slaves in the New World were in the American South by 1860, the result of a high birthrate and relatively stable (if precarious) family relationships.

Students might be reminded, too, that in the 1760s and 1770s—Wheatley was brought to Boston in 1761—slavery was legal in every one of the thirteen colonies. In 1763 there were, for example, 5,200 black slaves in Massachusetts, employed as seamen, farmhands, lumberjacks, craftsmen, and domestic servants.

For a powerful first-person account of the horrors of the slave trade, students could be referred to *The Interesting Narrative of the Life of Olaudah Equiano, or Gustavus Vassa, the African, Written by Himself* (1789; rpt. Bedford Books, 1995). Other useful sources include: Jay Coughtry, *The Notorious Triangle: Rhode Island and the African Slave Trade* (1981); Steven Mintz ed. *African-American Voices: The Life Cycle of Slavery* (1993); and David Northrup, *The Atlantic Slave Trade* (1994).

LYDIA SIGOURNEY

The Indian's Welcome to the Pilgrim Fathers (p. 658)

A good entry into Sigourney's poem is through its descriptive language—about, for example, the ominous landscape that the Pilgrims confronted, and even more, the figure of the Indian chief who appears to them. Notice that the chief at first seems fearsome and threatening, but Sigourney's point is precisely to show that however fierce he seemed, he came to speak welcome and bring words of peace. Indeed, Sigourney emphasizes that the Indians' "welcome" was the word that marked their downfall. She does not say so explicitly, but Sigourney leaves the implication that perhaps the Indians would have done better *not* to welcome these first settlers, who at the beginning were vulnerable, exposed intruders—"a weak, invading band."

The word choices in this poem are suggestive and pointed. Sigourney writes that the Indians and their children were "swept" from the land that belonged to them. On one level, this may seem untrue, for the Indians did resist; they did not give up as easily as the ease and absoluteness of "swept" indicates. But Sigourney wants to accent the point that, ultimately, the Indians had no chance once they welcomed the settlers and thus allowed the "weak, invading band" to remain. "Swept" is a word that captures much of the callousness of the white settlers and the helplessness of the Indians to defend their rights against a power that would soon overwhelm them.

Students who wish to explore the historical context might consult: Harold E. Driver, *Indians of North America* (1961); Alvin M. Josephy, Jr., *The Indian Heritage of America* (1968); Francis P. Prucha, *The Great Father: The United States Government and the American Indian*, 2 vols, (1984); and Russell Thornton, *American Indian Holocaust and Survival* (1987).

JOHN KEATS

To Autumn (p. 659)

The poem is discussed in books on Keats by Walter Jackson Bate, Douglas Bush, and Helen Vendler, and also in Reuben Brower, *The Fields of Light*, and in Geoffrey Hartman, *The Fate of Reading, and Other Essays*.

Some gleanings: One can see, in the three stanzas, the progress of autumn from the energetic first stanza (note "load," "bless," "bend," "fill," "swell," "set budding") with its "apples" and "mellow fruitfulness" before the harvest to the more languid second stanza with its "half-reaped furrow" and its cider press with "last oozings," and then the "stubble plains" in the third. We move from richness and fruition in the first stanza, to a sense of loss and also of drowsiness in the second, and finally to a full awareness of death in the third ("soft dying," "mourn," "wailful"), though death is seen in the context of fulfillment. Thus the images of death are in various ways modified. If the day is dying, it is "soft-dying," and if we get stubble rather than swaying grain, the stubble is "rosy."

One can also see the progress of a single day: The "maturing sun" of the first stanza may suggest noon, the resting figure of second suggests midafternoon, and then "the last oozings hours by hours" suggest late afternoon; and the third stanza explicitly indicates the end of the day, by "soft- dying day" and "gathering swallows." There is also a movement from the cottage garden with its fruit trees and flowers in the first stanza, to the granary, cider press, and fields of a farm in the second, and then to the hills and skies (though including the "garden-croft") of the third.

RALPH WALDO EMERSON

Concord Hymn (p. 661)

The poem presents a reader with no difficulties, but because we happen to be deeply attached to it—the writer of these pages was required to memorize it in the eighth grade, and has treasured it ever since—we will talk at some length about "Concord Hymn," even if sometimes tangentially.

During Emerson's lifetime the poem was published under the title of "Ode" as well as "Concord Hymn." Both titles point to the loftiness or solemnity of the theme, though "Hymn"—perhaps from the Greek *hymen*, referring to a song of joy at a marriage—today is almost always reserved for a song in praise of God.

In any case, Emerson's subject is lofty, though he treats in a simple, lucid manner. At the beginning of the poem we are a humble setting—by a "rude bridge." As Emerson says in lines 7-8, in his own day the bridge was gone. In 1874, in preparation for the centennial, a bridge was built, but it did not resemble the original and it was later replaced. The present bridge is said (Allen French's *Historic Concord and the Lexington Fight*) to be a replica of the original, though "higher and stronger." In this humble setting stand ordinary men, "farmers." And of course most of the men really were farmers; only in Boston would there be a substantial non-agricultural population. In the final stanza, after their action has been recorded, the farmers are called "heroes." But even in the first stanza there is a faintly heroic (larger-than-lifesize) note: The Concord River is a "flood," and the farmers seem to be assisted by nature itself ("Their flag to April's breeze unfurled"). Still, on the whole the scene is unprepossessing, but at this pastoral site the farmers "fired the shot heard round the world." And they really did. By Emerson's day, the country had doubled in territory, and it had become a player in the international scene. Less than a decade after Emerson wrote the poem, Matthew Calbraith Perry commanded a naval squadron off Africa in support of a British blockade of the slave trade, and in 1853 (less than two decades after Emerson wrote the poem) Perry anchored four ships in a Japanese harbor.

The Concord monument ("votive stone" in line 10, "shaft" in line 16) is an obelisk. A study of obelisks can take a student into some very interesting byways in the history of ideas and of iconography, particularly into the Egyptian Revival in Europe and England in the late eighteenth century and in the United States in the early nineteenth. Briefly, the obelisk—a four-sided tapering stone pillar, topped by a pyramid—came to America via Europe, and to Europe via Egypt. The obelisk, whose top was sometimes gilded in order to catch the first rays of the sun, may have originated as a phallic symbol, but it is usually thought to represent the *axis mundi* ("world pillar," "axis of the world"), an imaginary pillar in the center of the flat earth, supporting the heavens. It is thus the symbol of stability and of a well-ordered universe. After Rome's victory over Egypt at the Battle of Actium (31 B. C.), Augustus imported an Egyptian obelisk to serve as the gnomon for a giant sundial, and later other Egyptian obelisks were imported. In 64 A. D. Nero crucified Christians (including, according to tradition, St. Peter) in the Circus of Nero, where there was an obelisk that Caligula had imported. This obelisk was allowed to stand when St. Peter's basilica was erected on the site of the circus of Nero, because it had witnessed Peter's martyrdom, and because it was from the land where Moses had lived. The obelisk thus acquired additional suggestions of holiness.

What we have said thus far is preliminary to the Egyptian Revival, stimulated by Napoleon's Egyptian campaign (1798). Books illustrating Egyptian monuments and designs provided Europeans and Americans with a repertory of motifs that can still be seen in furniture and in architecture, for instance in libraries and in cemetery gates. The Concord obelisk still stands ("Time and nature," in accordance with Emerson's wish in lines 15-16, have indeed spared the monument), though tourists visiting Concord's North Bridge tend to focus on Daniel Chester French's statue, *The Minute Man of Concord*, on the other side of the bridge. In thinking of obelisks that are used as patriotic symbols in the United States, one should also recall the Washington Monument and the Bunker Hill Monument, although these are not true obelisks since they are not monoliths.

We've had good luck when we directed students to *Emerson in His Journals*, ed. Joel Porte (1982), a judicious culling of the sixteen-volume edition of the journals published by Harvard University Press. Though nearly half a century old, Ralph Rusk's *The Life of Ralph Waldo Emerson* (1949) remains excellent. Among recent books, one stands out: Robert D. Richardson, Jr., *Emerson: The Mind on Fire* (1995).

TOPICS FOR CRITICAL THINKING AND WRITING

1. Other poems commemorating battles are Francis Scott Key's "The Star-Spangled Banner," originally entitled "The Defense of Fort McHenry," and Melville's "The March into Virginia," both given in our text, along with Lanier's poem on the death of Stonewall Jackson, at the Battle of Chancellorsville. What other poems commemorating battles can you think of? Examine one poem, studying the particular aspects of the battle—for instance self-sacrifice, courage, pity—that the poem is chiefly concerned with, and compare it with the qualities celebrated in "Concord Hymn."

2. The memorial was (and still is) an obelisk—the "shaft" Emerson speaks of in line 16. Exactly what is an obelisk? And why do you suppose obelisks—rather, say, than boulders—are frequently used as memorials?

3. Line 11 is curious. Why does Emerson suggest that memory must "redeem" the deed of the Minutemen? (If you are in doubt about the exact meaning of "redeem," look it up in a good dictionary. You might also check the brief entry—a short paragraph—on *redemption* in *The Perennial Dictionary of World Religions*, or the long entry—almost six pages, double-columns—in *The Anchor Bible Dictionary*.) Think about what other words Emerson might have used instead of "redeem," and consider how a substitution would change the meaning of the line.

4. We hear about "sires" and "sons" (line 12) but nothing about mothers and daughters. And the "farmers" (line 3) who "fired the shot heard round the world" are men. Does the sexism of the poem disturb you? Explain.

ALFRED, LORD TENNYSON

Ulysses (p. 662)

Robert Langbaum, in *The Poetry of Experience*, and Christopher Ricks, in

Tennyson, offer some good remarks; Paul Baum, in *Tennyson Sixty Years After,* assaults the poem. Henry Kozicki, in *Tennyson and Clio* (a book on Tennyson's philosophy of history), argues that "Ulysses" reveals Tennyson's optimism about historical progress and his despair about the role of a hero. For a review of much that should not have been written, see L. K. Hughes in *Victorian Poetry* 17 (Autumn 1979): 192-203. By the way, it is worth mentioning to students that Homer's hero wanted to get home, Sophocles's (in *Philoctetes*) is a shifty politician (as is Shakespeare's), and Dante's Ulysses (*Inferno* XXVI) is an inspiring but deceitful talker whose ardent search is for *forbidden* things.

The first five lines emphasize, mostly with monosyllables, the dull world Ulysses is leaving. With line 6 ("I cannot rest from travel") we see a rather romantic hero, questing for experience, and indeed "experience" is mentioned in line 19, but it must be added that something is done in the poem to give "experience" a social context: Ulysses has fought for Troy (17), he wishes to be of "use" (23), and he wishes to do "some work of noble note" (52). Lines 22-23 apparently say the same thing four times over, but readers are not likely to wish that Tennyson had deleted the superbly appropriate metaphor of the rusting sword. "Gray spirit" (30) and "sinking star" (31) help (along with the heavy pauses and monosyllables in 55-56) to define the poem as a piece about dying, though students on first reading are likely to see only the affirmations. Even the strong affirmations in 57 ff. are undercut by "sunset" (60), "western" (61), etc. But the last line, with its regular accents on the meaningful words, affords a strong ending; perhaps the line is so strong and regular that it is a bit too easy. In line 45 Ulysses directly addresses the mariners, yet we hardly sense an audience as we do in Browning's dramatic monologues. If he is addressing the mariners, who are aboard, where is he when he refers to "this still hearth" (2) and when he says, "This is my son" (33)? (Some critics claim that lines 1-32 are a soliloquy: Ulysses supposedly would not speak publicly of Ithaca as stagnant and savage, or of his wife as "aged." Lines 33-43 are his farewell to the Ithacans, and the remainder is an address to his mariners.)

Probably the reader ought to see the poem not as a muddled attempt at a Browningesque dramatic monologue, but as a somewhat different type of poem—a poem in which the poet uses a fairly transparent mask in order to express his state of mind and to persuade his readers to share that state of mind. The poem thus is closer to, say, "Prufrock," than it is to "My Last Duchess."

TOPICS FOR CRITICAL THINKING AND WRITING
1. Ulysses's voice.
2. Ulysses: hero or suicidal egotist?
3. Ulysses as he sees himself, compared with Ulysses as we see him.

HERMAN MELVILLE

The March into Virginia (p. 664)

It is hard for anyone today to think of war as romantic— if nothing else, tele-

vised images of the dead and wounded have pushed romance out of the picture—though of course individual acts may be heroic, and possibly (a topic
much debated by philosophers) some wars may be "just." But on the whole the
war poems that have found their way into today's anthologies are not celebrations of military exploits. Poems such as Browning's "Incident of the French
Camp," Longfellow's "Paul Revere's Ride," and Kipling's "Gunga Din"—standard
stuff in schoolbooks of the 1930s—have all but vanished. In their place are such
deeply ironic favorites as Hardy's "The Man He Killed" and Wilfred Owen's
"Dulce et Decorum Est."

As we read it, Melville's "The March into Virginia" is somewhere in
between these two extremes. Certainly there is abundant irony—the boyish
"champions and enthusiasts" (lines 6-7), "Chatting left and laughing right" (30)
will move from their innocence to experience:

> But some who this blithe mood present,
>   As on in lightsome files they fare,
> Shall die experienced ere three days are spent
>   Perish, enlightened by the vollied glare....

The "lightsome files" are soon "enlightened by the vollied glare," i.e. their
superficial joy is turned into first-hand knowledge of what war—accompanied
by death—is really like. (The irony is heightened by the fact that gunfire literally produces light.) On the other hand, some of the men will survive, and will
become "like to adamant" (35), battle-hardened veterans who will continue the
fight. That these survivors, Melville tells us, will go on to a second defeat ("the
throe of Second Manassas share") does not minimize their achievement; ultimately the Union forces won the war and preserved the United States. Although
we hear in the poem a voice pitying the innocence of the inexperienced warriors, and we hear a judgment on war ("All wars are boyish, and are fought by
boys") we do not hear a denunciation of this war, or of war in general.

As we read the poem, Melville is saying that wars would not be fought if
the warriors knew more, for instance that war offers more than "glory" (26)—
but they don't know this, and so they go into battle and (often) die. He does *not*
say that the battle cannot be for a noble cause, and there is ample evidence that
Melville was a strong Unionist. We would go so far as to say that this poem
might stand, in a textbook, next to "The Gettysburg Address" and there would
be no argument, no ironic contrast between the two works, although the thrust
of each work differs greatly. In fact, although *Battle-Pieces* (the book from
which the poem comes) is dedicated "to the memory of the three hundred thousand who in the war for the maintenance of the Union fell devotedly under the
flag of their fathers," the book has much of the tone of Lincoln's Second
Inaugural Address, which concluded by exhorting the nation to proceed "with
malice toward none, with charity for all." *Battle-Pieces* includes two poems
praising a Southern general, Stonewall Jackson—the subject of the next poem in
our text and therefore the next in our discussion in this manual.

In a "Supplement" at the end of *Battle-Pieces* Melville talks at some length
about heroic ideals, both on the side of the North and the South. He sees the
Southern cause as seriously tainted, but he also sees noble ideals. Here is a small
sample from the "Supplement":

It was in subserviency to the slave-interest that Secession was plotted; but it was under the plea, plausibly urged, that certain inestimable rights guaranteed by the Constitution were directly menaced that the people of the South were cajoled into revolution. Through the arts of the conspirators and the perversity of fortune, the most sensitive love of liberty was entrapped into the support of a war whose implied end was the erecting in our advanced century of an Anglo-American empire based upon the systematic degradation of man.

Spite this clinging reproach, however, signal military virtues and achievements have conferred upon the Confederate arms historic fame, and upon certain commanders a renown extending beyond the sea—a renown which we of the North could not suppress, even if we would.... Dishonorable would it be in the South were she willing to abandon to shame the memory of brave men who with signal personal disinterestedness warred in her behalf....

Barbarities also there were [in the South], ... but surely other qualities—exalted ones—courage and fortitude matchless, were likewise displayed, and largely....

Melville takes a deeply tragic view of the Civil War, seeing it as something that may have conferred on the nation—at a tremendous cost—a wisdom that perhaps can be born only of tremendous suffering. The final paragraph of the "Supplement" begins thus: "Let us pray that the terrible historic of our time may not have been enacted without instructing our whole beloved country through terror and pity.... " Here the words "pity" and "terror" make it perfectly clear that Melville has in mind an Aristotelian concept of tragedy, and it is evident that he held the view (common in the nineteenth century and most famously formulated in the early twentieth century by A. C. Bradley in his book on Shakespeare's tragedies) that these emotions, properly evoked, bring forth a kind of wisdom otherwise unattainable.

Melville's language is sometimes condensed, but we think the only passage that may cause students any difficulty is this one, at the end of the first stanza:

Turbid ardors and vain joys
    Not barrenly abate—
Stimulants to the power mature,
    Preparatives of fate.

As we understand the words, the gist is this: The turbid ardors (tumultuous passions?) of the young do not end in nothing ("not barrenly abate"); rather, they are stimulants for the powerful actions of mature men, and it is these that produce the future ("Preparatives of fate").

One other point: After writing the preceding paragraphs we happened to come across Robert Penn Warren's *Selected Poems of Herman Melville* (1970). Warren suggests that in "berrying party" (line 18) there is "really a secret, and grim pun: *burying party*," i.e. a glimpse of soldiers burying the dead after the battle. We had read the poem dozens of times without this thought having occurred to us, and we are now inclined to think that the pun is accidental—but of course we cannot talk fruitfully about Melville's intention in this matter. In any case, our own feeling is that even if Melville did not intend the pun, now that Warren has pointed it out a reader cannot *not* think of it. It is here to stay. You may want to ask your class (1) whether they noticed it, (2) if they didn't, do they imagine that it was intended, and (3) does the author's intention—at least in this issue—matter?

Most of the work on Melville emphasizes his novels and stories. For an overview of all aspects of Melville scholarship, see the 900-page volume, *A Companion to Melville Studies* ed. John Bryant (1986). There are a number of biographies, but for students the best place to begin is with Hershel Parker's detailed, up-to-date entry in *The Norton Anthology of American Literature* (4th ed. 1994), 1:2191-2200.

TIMOTHY H. O'SULLIVAN

John L. Burns with Gun and Crutches (photograph, p. 664)

O'Sullivan was trained from the age of fifteen by the most famous of all Civil War photographers, Matthew B. Brady. In looking for a photo appropriate to Melville's poem we encountered many images of battlefields strewn with corpses, taken by Brady or by his associates such as O'Sullivan and Alexander Gardner. And given Melville's emphasis on death, such an image would have been appropriate. But Melville speaks not only of those who would "Perish, enlightened by the vollied glare," but also of the grim survivors, those who became "like to adamant" (line 35). Such a one, we think, is John L. Burns, posed here between what art historians call "attributes"—items that help to establish the identity of the sitter, in this case crutches and a gun. And, we might add, a grim face. The gun and the crutches echo each other, and these verticals are echoed also in the wooden chair in which Burns sits, in the boards of the house, and in the column at the left. As one dwells on the picture, one notices that the crutches form a triangle resting on its apex, and this form is echoed not only in the gunstock but also (inverted) in the lower limbs of Burns's legs. Inevitably, however, a viewer returns to the face.

Even in our introductory courses, we often find students who have a special passion for the Civil War period, and who find the visual material about the war highly absorbing. We recommend the following sources: *Gardner's Photographic Sketch Book of the Civil War* (1866; rpt. 1959); Roy Meredith, *Matthew Brady's Portrait of an Era* (1982); and Harold Holzer and Mark E. Neely Jr., *Mine Eyes Have Seen the Glory: The Civil War in Art* (1993).

WALT WHITMAN

Reconciliation (p. 665)

In this chapter we try to bring together poems that give some sense of the history of our multicultural nation. Although today *multiculturalism* almost implies *all cultures other than Anglo*, of course there are varieties of Anglo culture, and surely the Civil War involved (among other things) a clash of cultures.

In "Reconciliation" Whitman celebrates not simply the end of the war—though that in itself was a cause of celebration— but a loving union, or reunion, daringly symbolized by a kiss bestowed upon the dead enemy. The poem begins by announcing (1) that the very word *reconciliation* has an affinity with heaven ("beautiful as the sky"), and (2) that the fact of reconciliation will "in time" obliterate the terrible carnage of the clash of cultures. Whitman goes on to call Death and Night sisters; that is, he constructs a mythology—at least we are not aware of any system of mythology in which they are sisters. (In Greek mythology, Night is the mother of Death.) Whitman's two allegorical figures "incessantly softly wash again, and ever again, this soil'd world." Once he has given us this image, it seems obvious enough, but, again, it is new to us. Far from being portrayed as a cleansing force, Death customarily is portrayed as destructive (think of the classical image of the inverted torch, or the late medieval and Renaissance image of a skeleton carrying a scythe), or at best as offering an anodyne, a release from an unbearably painful world. Night, in traditional mythology, is not quite so grim, and is even beneficent to the extent that she brings her son, Sleep, but she is nevertheless destructive since, like Day, she leads to decay and death. In contrast, Whitman imagines Death and Night as washing (purifying) "this soil'd world"; in this specific context of this poem, which speaks of a corpse in a coffin, the allegorical figures surely are meant to be associated with persons washing (symbolically purifying) a corpse.

The purification effected by Death and Night is a purification of the speaker and of his enemy; now that the "carnage" has been washed away, the former enemies are (in the word of the title) reconciled, and the new relationship is symbolized (daringly) by a kiss. But we should notice that, almost as daring as the gesture of the kiss, Whitman daringly ends this poem with the dead man still dead; the last word in the poem is *coffin*. Unlike (say) Lanier's Stonewall Jackson, Whitman's dead soldier does not become enshrined in the heavens, nor does he, through noble words, live eternally in the minds of survivors. The closest a reader gets to heaven is in the first line, where (as we have seen) the word *reconciliation* is said to be "beautiful as the sky." Still, at least in our reading of the poem, the gesture of the kiss is so daring, so original, that it overcomes the horror of the carnage and the continuing death of the former enemy.

MATTHEW ARNOLD

Dover Beach (p. 666)

"Dover Beach" begins with the literal—the scene that hits the eye and ear—and then moves in the second stanza to Sophocles's figurative tragic interpretation, in the third to Arnold's figurative religious interpretation, and finally—the image of the sea now being abandoned—to the simile of the world as a "darkling plain" whose only reality is the speaker and the person addressed. The end thus completes the idea of illusion versus reality that began in the first stanza, where the scene that was said to be "calm" (1), "fair" (2), and "tranquil" (3) actually contained the discords implicit in "grating roar," "fling," and so on. In fact, even the "tonight" of the first line implies some conflict, for the word suggests that on other nights the sea is *not* calm.

For a thought-provoking reading of "Dover Beach," consult A. Dwight Culler, *Imaginative Reason: The Poetry of Matthew Arnold.* Culler argues (perhaps too ingeniously) that although some critics complain about a lack of unity in the imagery (no sea in the last section, and no darkling plain in the first), "the naked shingles *are* the darkling plain, and that we have no sea in the last section is the very point of the poem. The sea has retreated from the world...." To this point of Culler's we add that the "pebbles" flung about by the waves (10) are an anticipation of "ignorant armies" that are "swept with confused alarms of struggle and flight" (36).

Gerald Graff includes a chapter called "How to Save 'Dover Beach'" in his *Beyond the Culture Wars: How Teaching the Conflicts Can Revitalize American Education* (1992). As the title of the essay and the subtitle of the book indicate, Graff believes that works such as "Dover Beach" can best be taught by recognizing that many of today's readers find some of their assumptions unconvincing and even incomprehensible. Graff imagines an older male professor (OMP) who throws up his hands at his students' indifference to the poem, and a young female professor (YFP) who says she understands how the students feel. In fact Graff's YFP goes on not to express indifference but rather to offer a challenging reading of the poem, or at least of the last lines ("Ah, love...."). She says that this passage adds up to this:

> In other words, protect and console me, my dear—as it's the function of your naturally more spiritual sex to do—from the "struggle and flight" of politics and history that we men have been assigned the regrettable duty of dealing with. It's a good example of how women have been defined by our culture as naturally private and domestic and therefore justly disqualified from sharing male power. (38)

She goes on to say that it is precisely for this reason that we *should* teach the poem—"as the example of phallocentric discourse that it is." OMP objects that such a label "misses the whole point of poetry," and that YFP and her colleagues treat poems "as if they were statements about gender politics" rather than expressions of "universal concerns." YFP replies that literature *is*—among other things—about "gender politics." She goes on:

> What you take to be the universal human experience in Arnold and Shakespeare, Professor OMP, is male experience presented as if it were universal. You don't notice the presence of politics in literature—or in sexual relations, for that matter—because for you patriarchy is simply the normal state of affairs and therefore as invisible as the air you breathe. My reading of "Dover Beach" seems to you to reflect a "special-interest" agenda, but to me yours does, too. You can afford to "transmute" the sexual politics of literature onto a universal plane, but that's a luxury I don't enjoy. (39)

Again, Graff's chief point is that we should face the controversies—should let them enter into our teaching—and not ignore them. "For disagreements about 'Dover Beach' are not peripheral to humanistic culture; they are central to what we mean by humanistic culture" (56). And: "Controversies from which we have been trying to protect 'Dover Beach' can do a lot to save it" (63).

Students enjoy comparing and contrasting "Dover Beach" and "Ulysses." How is the sea described in each of them? What is the function of the "others" addressed or referred to in the poems (Achilles and Telemachus in "Ulysses," the person urged to "come to the window" in "Dover Beach")? What is the movement or progress of the speaker's attitude in the two works? What is or is not resolved in the poems' conclusions? In working with these questions, keep the students focused on specific moments in Tennyson's and Arnold's language. Especially when comparing poems, students can tend to become a bit too generalized, loose in their formulations of how the texts are similar and different. Try to guide them back to lines and passages, in order to sharpen their observations.

Often, after studying "Ulysses" and "Dover Beach," we have turned directly to Eliot's "The Love Song of J. Alfred Prufrock" (also in the text), whose themes, we suspect, Eliot may have developed in part from his reading of Tennyson's and Arnold's famous poems, with their accounts of doubt, faith, and the challenge of maintaining commitment and fulfilling the self's desires. Here again, it's important to keep moving back-and-forth from the general to the particular, with the stress falling throughout on the three poets' choices and organizations of language.

TOPICS FOR CRITICAL THINKING AND WRITING

1. What are the stated and implied reasons behind Arnold's implication that only love offers comfort?
2. The sea, described in the first stanza, puts the speaker in mind of two metaphors, one in the second stanza and one in the third. Explain each of these metaphors in your own words. In commenting on the first, be sure to include a remark about "turbid" in line 17.
3. Is there a connection between the imagery of the sea in the first three stanzas and the imagery of darkness in the last stanza?

THOMAS HARDY

The Convergence of the Twain (p. 667)

The biggest and perhaps the most luxurious ship ever built up to that time, the supposedly unsinkable *Titanic* (it had sixteen watertight compartments), collided with an iceberg and sank in the Atlantic on 15 April 1912, during her maiden voyage from Southampton to New York, with a loss of 1513 lives. Many of those who were drowned were rich and famous.

Hardy completed the poem on 24 April 1912. He lost two acquaintances in the wreck, but the poem is not an elegy; rather it is a sort of narrative and philosophical lyric which tells of the destruction (fashioned by "the Immanent Will") that awaits "the Pride of Life." The poem contains eleven stanzas, the first five of which describe the "vaingloriousness" that rests at the bottom of the sea, "Deep from human vanity." The sixth stanza, beginning, "Well," makes an emphatic transition, and the remaining five introduce the "Shape of Ice" and tell of "the intimate welding" of ship and iceberg. (Note that "welding—which almost sounds like "wedding"—leads in the last line to "consummation"; the ship [female] at last meets her "mate.") The first two lines—notably brief—of stanzas 2, 3, 4, and 5 call attention to pride ("mirrors meant / To glass the opulent," etc.) and the last line—notably long and sonorous—of each of these stanzas calls attention to the humbling of pride ("The sea-worm crawls," etc.).

The poem is not merely about the contrast between vain ambition and death; it is also about the government of the universe. The "mooneyed fishes" formulate a question in line 13, but they cannot answer it. Hardy can. For Hardy, "the Spinner of the Years" stands behind these ambitions, preparing their "mate."

SIDNEY LANIER

The Dying Words of Jackson (p. 667)

As we mentioned in the comments on Melville's "The March into Virginia," Melville's *Battle-Pieces* includes two poems on Jackson. In the first of these, Melville clearly states that Jackson "devoutly stood for Wrong," but he finds he must praise him nevertheless:

> Earnest in error, as we feel;
> True to the thing he deemed was due,
> True as John Brown or steel.

Melville's second poem on Jackson, subtitled "Ascribed to a Virginian," offers undiluted praise (or praise diluted only in so far as the subtitle implies a modification). Given the fact that Sidney Lanier's poem makes such considerable use of star imagery, it is interesting to notice Melville's comment that "Stonewall followed his star" (in fact he uses these words five times, with minor variations, and he also speaks of "Stonewall's star"). One can hardly escape the idea that Melville is suggesting a comparison with the Magi, who followed a star, i.e. who were divinely guided in their activity. True, Melville's invented speaker is a Virginian, but surely Melville would not have written the poem if he had not been immensely impressed by Jackson's deeds.

Lanier's poem begins with Jackson's dying words, in which Jackson showed himself to be, to the last, a soldier devoted to duty. Students may have trouble with the first stanza, which we interpret thus: The stars take up the work of the sun ("the glittering Day") and "rain his glory down with sweeter grace / Upon the dark World's grand, enchanted face / All loth to turn away," i.e. the world still seeks (needs?) Jackson's illuminating spirit. In the second stanza, the dying Day turns its commission over to the stars, "To stand for burning fare-thee-wells of light," i.e. in traditional elegiac form, nature itself mourns the death of the hero. Further, the heavenly imagery suggests that the dead hero is not really dead but has achieved immortality.

The third stanza explicitly compares Jackson to the sun (life-giving), and his words to the stars (i.e. heavenly, illuminating), and sets him above "the gloomy wars" in which he gave his life, i.e. the man is even greater than his deeds. The fourth stanza brings us into the delirious mind of the general (as the epigraph has already done) and sees in his dying words his solicitude for his soldiers. In the fifth stanza, Jackson, having done all that a man can do, is now ready to die, and to let God decide the battle. The final stanza continues the imagery of the sun and stars: The sun is gone (i.e. it is nighttime, and Jackson-the-sun has departed), but "thy stars remain" (i.e. Jackson's words remain, words "that miniature his deeds"). The poem thus ends where it began, with Jackson's words, and with the stars replacing the sun. But the final stanza also introduces a new note; whereas the earlier parts of the poem have emphasized Jackson's loving care, the final stanza tells him that he himself is "Thrice-Beloved," and therefore he can draw solace.

What Lanier is doing in most of the poem is what most writers of elegies do, i.e. Lanier is giving new life to the deceased. That is, he is apotheosizing Jackson, making him into a heavenly body. This is in accord with Greek and Roman thought (influenced by Persian and Babylonian thought), which worshipped stars and planets as deities, but the idea is not only pagan; Christ speaks of himself as the "bright star of dawn" in Revelation 22.16. In the next-to-last line, where Lanier says that Jackson's "great heart bleeds," he comes pretty close to evoking an image of the crucified Christ. We don't mean to say that Lanier is equating Jackson with Christ, but he does suggest that Jackson's deeds and words continue to sustain those who knew him.

ANONYMOUS

Women at the Grave of Stonewall Jackson, in Lexington, Virginia (photograph, p. 669)

Grief knows no gender, but in wartime traditionally men are supposed to embody the manly virtues, which means heroic action, and women are supposed to embody the womanly virtues, which means grief. At the sight of the death of a hero, for instance, men are (or were) supposed to remain stoic, and women are (or were) supposed to collapse, overcome by emotion. The women here have not collapsed, but presumably Jackson had died some time ago, and they are now paying tribute by their presence.

Students might be invited to discuss the usual demeanor of men versus women on occasions of mourning. They might also discuss the various forms that mourning takes in different cultures. And they might well relate this picture and Lanier's poem to Auden's elegy, "Stop All the Clocks," in our chapter on "Lyric Poetry."

The historian Roy R. Stephenson has pointed out, in a discussion of "death and mourning" in the Confederacy, that the extremely high casualty rate "made Southerners acutely aware of mortality." Of a "potential military population of about a million," he explains, "750,000 soldiers served in the Confederate armies, and approximately 250,000 died during the war—about one in four

Southern white men of military age in contrast to the Northern rate of one in ten." See *Encyclopedia of the Confederacy* (4 vols., 1993), 2:459-61.

As Stephenson and others have shown, Southern women during the first years of the war mourned their own dead loved ones in "public" ways, transforming their personal grief into a ritual that honored and heightened their sense of the rightness of the Confederate cause. As the war dragged on, however, as the casualties mounted, and as the eventual collapse of the Confederacy became clear, Southern women turned increasingly to the personal cost of the war: Above all they grieved over their lost husbands, sons, and brothers, not ever the death of the Confederate nation. Yet after the war, the elements of public ritual again became prominent, with memories of the dead tied repeatedly to the nobility of the "Lost Cause."

Students interested in this rich topic might consult: Anne Firor Scott, *The Southern Lady: From Pedestal to Politics* (1970); Rollin G. Osterweis, *The Myth of the Lost Cause: 1865- 1900* (1973); George Rable, *Civil Wars: Women and the Crisis of Southern Nationalism* (1989); and Drew Gilpin Faust, "Altars of Sacrifice: Confederate Women and the Narratives of War," *Journal of American History* 76 (1990): 1200-28.

GERARD MANLEY HOPKINS

God's Grandeur (p. 670)

The world (including the human world) has divinely created beauty in its charge (care), but "charged" in line 1 is also a scientific term (referring to electricity), leading to "flame out" in the next line; "foil" in line 2, Hopkins explained in a letter, refers to "foil in its sense of leaf or tinsel." Most of the first quatrain asserts the grandeur of God, whose divine energy may be manifested either suddenly ("flame out") or slowly ("ooze of oil / Crushed"). "Crushed," at the beginning of line 4, is part of this celebration (probably alluding to olives or seeds), but this word itself of course also suggests destruction, and the rest of the octave is about human corruption of the self and of nature. "Man's smudge" in line 7 probably alludes to original sin as well as to the destruction wreaked on the countryside by factories. The octave thus moves from an excited or urgent proclamation of God's grandeur to a melancholy reflection on our insensitivity to this grandeur. The sestet reintroduces a joyous affirmation of God's grandeur. Lines 13 and 14 allude to the traditional representation of the Holy Ghost as a dove, but Christ is here seen also as the dawning sun, giving warmth and light, and thus we go back to the reference to light in line 2; "bent world" probably evokes the curvature of the horizon, the world distorted by sin, and perhaps backbreaking labor.

Paul L. Mariani, in his excellent *Commentary on the Complete Poems of Gerard Manley Hopkins*, suggests that the last lines are connected with the first quatrain: "If we can picture the dawning sun before it breaks over the horizon, we may recall how the rich light seems precisely to gather to a greatness' in density and brightness. . . until the orb of the sun itself seems to spring forth, and then the sun flames out in strong rays like wings from its center." W. H. Gardner, in *Gerard Manley Hopkins,* II, 230, suggests that the obvious meaning of the poem is that the world is a reservoir of divine power, love, and beauty, and that the deeper meaning is that life must be jarred before the presence of God can be felt. On "verbal resonance" and other sound effects in the poem, see Brooks and Warren, *Understanding Poetry,* 4th ed., pp. 538-40. See also Terry Eagleton in *Essays in Criticism* 23 (1973): 68-75. Students might be invited to compare the poem with this entry (8 Dec. 1881) from one of Hopkins's notebooks, reprinted in *The Sermons... of Gerard Manley Hopkins,* ed. Christopher Devlin, p. 95: "All things therefore are charged with love; are charged with God and if we know how to touch them give off sparks and take fire, yield drops and flow, ring and tell of him."

TOPICS FOR CRITICAL THINKING AND DISCUSSION
1. Hopkins, a Roman Catholic priest, lived in England during the last decades of the nineteenth century—that is, in an industrialized society. Where in the poem do you find him commenting on his setting? Circle the words in the poem that can refer both to England's physical appearance and to the sinful condition of human beings.
2. What is the speaker's tone in the first three and a half lines (through "Crushed")? In the rest of line 4? In lines 5-8? Is the second part of the sonnet (the next six lines) more unified in *tone* or less? In an essay of 500 words, describe the shifting tones of the speaker's voice. Probably after writing a first draft you will be able to form a thesis that describes an overall pattern. As you revise your drafts, make sure (a) that the thesis is clear to the reader, and (b) that it is adequately supported by brief quotation.

A. E. HOUSMAN

"Shropshire Lad #19 (To an Athlete Dying Young)" (p. 671)

Brooks and Warren, *Understanding Poetry* 4th ed., print two manuscript versions of the poem—the first a very incomplete sketch, the second a rather full one.

WILLIAM BUTLER YEATS

Sailing to Byzantium (p. 672)

The literature on this poem is enormous. Among the readable pieces are M. L. Rosenthal and A. J. Smith, *Exploring Poetry;* and Elder Olson in *University Review,* 8 (Spring 1942): 209-219, reprinted in *The Permanence of Yeats,* James

Hall and Martin Steinmann, eds. Less readable, but highly impressive, are Curtis Bradford's study of Yeats's interest in Byzantium and of the manuscripts, in *PMLA 75* (March 1960): 110-125, reprinted in *Yeats,* John Unterecker, ed., and Jon Stallworthy's discussion of the manuscripts in *Between the Lines.* For a hostile discussion of the poem, see Yvor Winters, *Forms of Discovery.*

The capital of the Eastern Roman Empire (330 to 1453 A.D.) and the "holy city" of the Greek Orthodox Church, Byzantium is noted for mysticism, the preservation of ancient learning, and exquisitely refined symbolic art. In short, its culture (as Yeats saw it) was wise and passionless. In *A Vision,* his prose treatment of his complex mystical system, Yeats says:

> I think that in early Byzantium, maybe never before or since in recorded history, religious, aesthetic and practical life were one, that architect and artificers—though not, it may be, poets, for language has been the instrument of controversy and must have grown abstract—spoke to the multitude and the few alike. The painter, the mosaic worker, the worker in gold and silver, the illuminator of sacred books, were almost impersonal, almost perhaps without the consciousness of individual design, absorbed in their subject matter and that the vision of the whole people. They could copy out of old Gospel books those pictures that seemed as sacred as the text, and yet weave all into a vast design, the work of many that seemed the work of one, that made building, picture, pattern, metal-work or rail and lamp, seem but a single image.

An audiocassette of W. B. Yeats reading is available from Longman.

TOPICS FOR CRITICAL THINKING AND WRITING

1. The patterns of organization in "Sailing to Byzantium."
2. The poem can be said to record a debate between opposing desires. What are those desires?
3. Summarize the poem, perhaps in three or four sentences, and then explain Yeats's view of the happiness of old age, comparing it to more customary views of old age.

WILLIAM BUTLER YEATS

For Anne Gregory (p. 673)

One can imagine Yeats, at 65, writing about a woman of 19, in response to her somewhat petulant and innocent assertion that she wants to be loved "for herself alone." Presumably she means by this her intellectual and psychological characteristics, her mind and her personality. Yeats, more or less in the role of The Wise Old Man, asserts in the first stanza that it is simply a fact that youthful lovers will be taken by her physical beauty—a beauty, by the way, that seems formidable (note "ramparts")—and thrown into despair. The old Yeats presumably remembers his own youthful feelings, but note his reference to "an old religious man" who "found a text" to prove that only God could overlook her hair and love her for herself alone. If the old man "found" the text, presumably he was looking for it. The implication seems to be that beauty captivates not only "a young man, / Thrown into despair" (1 and 2), but also "an old religious man"—to say nothing of an old irreligious man, or of Yeats—and that such a man, feeling ashamed, might well search for a text that would explain or justify his apparently indecorous feelings.

Of course Yeats is speaking somewhat playfully, even teasingly, but the overall intention is to help this young female friend ("my dear," 16) accept her exceptional beauty. She may think of her hair as yellow, and she may imagine dying it "Brown, or black, or carrot," but for Yeats, and for "young men in despair," it is "great honey-colored / Ramparts," sweet, yet magnificent and beyond reach.

If one wants to move away from the poem a bit and turn to a larger issue, one might ask whether the poem is sexist. Can we imagine a poem consisting of a dialogue between an older woman and a young man, in which the woman assures the man that young women can never love him for himself alone, but only for his blond (or raven-black) hair (or profile, or body)? If one can't imagine such a poem, *why* can't one? Is it because a sexist view prevents us from imagining an old woman giving good advice to a young man? Or is it perhaps because Yeats's poem touches on a truth, that is, young men are captivated by youthful female beauty, whereas the hypothetical poem is false; that is, young women are not taken chiefly by youthful male beauty? Or is it sexist to assume that, confronted with the opposite sex. the primary interests of young men and young women differ?

An audiocassette of W. B. Yeats reading is available from Longman.

TOPICS FOR CRITICAL THINKING AND WRITING

1. What can you imagine Anne saying that provoked the poem?
2. In the first stanza Anne's hair is described both as "great honey-colored ramparts" and as "yellow." Why does the speaker use these two rather different characterizations? Judging from the second stanza, how would Anne describe her hair?
3. If you did not know that Yeats was 65 when he wrote the poem, would you be able to deduce from the poem itself that the speaker of the first and third stanzas is considerably older than Anne?
4. Anne says that she wants to be loved "for myself alone." Exactly what do you think this expression means?
5. Why would "an old religious man" search until he found a text that would prove that only God could love her for herself alone? Do you think Yeats shares this view?
6. In a sentence or two characterize Yeats as he reveals himself in this poem and then characterize Anne.

EDWIN ARLINGTON ROBINSON

Richard Cory (p. 674)

The point is not that money doesn't bring happiness; even a thoroughly civilized spirit (grace, taste, courtesy) does not bring happiness. The protagonist's name is significant. "Richard" suggests "Rich," and probably his entire name faintly suggests Richard Coeur de Lion (and *coeur* – heart and core, and also suggests *cour* = court). These suggestions, along with "crown," "favored," "imperially," "arrayed," "glittered," "king," emphasize his superiority. Other words emphasize his dignity, courtesy, and humanity: "gentleman," "clean favored," "quietly," "human," "schooled," "grace." Everything combines to depict him as a man of self-sufficiency, dignity, and restraint—yet he kills himself. Still, even his final act has some dignity: it is stated briefly, and it takes place on "one calm summer night." Students might be asked if anything is lost by substituting (what might on first thought seem more appropriate) "one dark winter night."

If this rewriting is not bad enough, listen to Paul Simon's version of the poem. He sings it, with Art Garfunkel, on *Sounds of Silence*, Columbia CS 9269.

Useful introductions include: Emory Neff, *Edwin Arlington Robinson* (1948); and Ellsworth Barnard, *Edwin Arlington Robinson: A Critical Study* (1952). We have often gotten good results simply by referring students to the *Collected Poems* (1937).

The poet James Dickey on Robinson's verse: "No poet ever understood loneliness or separateness better than Robinson or knew the self-consuming furnace that the brain can become in isolation, the suicidal hellishness of it, doomed as it is to feed on itself in answerless frustration, fated to this condition by the accident of birth, which carries with it the hunger for certainty and the intolerable load of personal recollection."

JAMES WELDON JOHNSON

To America (p. 675)

The poem consists entirely of questions, and this fact about its structure is a good place to begin discussion. Students are able to grasp readily enough that this African-American poet is speaking on behalf of his race to white Americans. But they might not see at first the meaningful choice of title. Johnson does not say "white America," but simply "America," implying the way in which the idea of America has been wedded to whiteness, and at the expense of the black Americans who did so much to build the nation. In Johnson's view, white Americans tend automatically to define the nation as *their* nation, and not as one in which black persons should be incorporated as equals.

See Eugene Levy, *James Weldon Johnson: Black Leader, Black Voice* (1973).

WILLIAM CARLOS WILLIAMS

Spring and All (p. 675)

This, the first poem in a book (1922) of the same title, is preceded by eleven pages of prose, the gist of which is the defense of a "new" American experimental writing. This introduction concludes with the words "THE WORLD IS

NEW," and then the poem bursts upon us. It begins with the reference to the hospital (stock responses—which Williams dedicated his life to opposing—conjure up ideas of sickness and death, reinforced in "cold" and "dried," but it turns out that the poem moves on to the recovery of health, which after all is what hospitals are for); it moves on to a vivid and concrete description of bushes and trees that appear "Lifeless," then to a spring that "quickens," and finally back to the bushes and trees that "begin to awaken." What is "contagious" turns out to be not sickness, death, winter (all stock responses), but spring, and probably this contagious quality of spring is what the "All" of the title implies.

Characteristically, Williams seems "unpoetic": Although in line 2 "the surge of clouds" is metaphoric (clouds as waves), and in line 7 "standing water" is a metaphor (though only a dead metaphor), one can say that in the first part of the poem figurative language is conspicuously absent. Not until line 15 ("dazed spring approaches") does figurative language emerge; the following stanza (16-20) continues the image of nature as human ("They enter the new world naked"), making it clear that the hospital is as much a place of birth as of death, and essentially a place where life is preserved, but the poem also continues to record sharp literal perceptions ("the stiff curl of wild carrot leaf"), enhancing the last, metaphoric words: "rooted they / grip down and begin to awaken." The slight increase in the number of verbs (they are sparse in the beginning) helps to suggest the life that is pushing through the deadness. Whether literal or metaphoric, the lines seek (to borrow words which Williams used of his *Kora in Hell*) "to refine, to clarify, to intensify that eternal moment in which we alone live." See also, for a long discussion, Bram Dijkstra, *Cubism, Stieglitz, and the Earlier Poetry of William Carlos Williams.*

A "Voices and Visions" videocassette of William Carlos Williams is available from Longman. An audiocassette of Williams reading is also available from Longman.

EZRA POUND

The River-Merchant's Wife: A Letter (p. 676)

One of Pound's comments to William Carlos Williams may be useful (from *Letters of Ezra Pound, 1907-41,* edited by D. D. Paige, 3-4):

> To me the short so-called dramatic lyric—at any rate the sort of thing I do—is the poetic part of a drama the rest of which (to me the prose part) is left to the reader's imagination or implied or set in a short note. I catch the character I happen to be interested in at the moment he interests me, usually a moment of song, self-analysis, or sudden understanding or revelation. And the rest of the play would bore me and presumably the reader.

Pound learned much from Browning's dramatic monologues, and this comment could, in a general way, apply to Browning's poems. But it is worth exploring with students the way in which "The River-Merchant's Wife" differs from "My Last Duchess." For one thing, Pound's speaker (like many of the speakers in his early poems) is relatively naive, and so the poem gives us an impression of a "pure" and universal sort, whereas Browning's gives us an impression of a particular case history. Moreover, Browning customarily gives us considerably more sense of a particular period than Pound does or, to put it a little differently, Browning—even in "My Last Duchess"—gives us a greater sense of a particular character interacting with particular circumstances of the age. Pound based his poem on a prose translation by Ernest Fenollosa of a poem by the Chinese poet Li Po (in Japanese, called Rihaku). A transcription of the Fenollosa manuscript is printed in Michael Reck, *Ezra Pound: A Close-up*, 168-71.

For Pound, see *Selected Poems* (1949; rev. ed. 1957); *Literary Essays* (1954). A good introduction is M. L. Rosenthal, *A Primer of Ezra Pound* (1960); for a more advanced approach, we recommend Hugh Kenner, *The Pound Era* (1972).

TOPICS FOR CRITICAL THINKING AND DISCUSSION

1. Is the writer of the letter nagging her husband to return? Or is she conveying her love and with admirable concreteness and restraint.
2. Ford Maddox Ford, reviewing the book in which the poem appeared, said in 1927:

> The quality of great poetry is that without comment as without effort it presents you with images that stir your emotions; so you are made a better man; you are softened, rendered more supple of mind, more open to the vicissitudes and necessities of your fellow man. When you have read 'The River Merchant's Wife' you are added to. You are a better man or woman than you were before.

Do you believe it? If so, are we in this case "added to" because we see a model for behavior? But how, then, would "My Last Duchess" add to us?
3. The last sentence is the longest, and immediately follows two sentences so short that they both fit in a single line. What, then, is the effect of the last sentence?

EZRA POUND

In a Station of the Metro (p. 677)

While these two lines have not generated quite as much commentary as the "two-handed engine" in "Lycidas," they have generated a good deal—beginning with Ezra Pound. In *T.P.'s Weekly* (6 June 1913) Pound talked about the poem, and then elaborated his comment, as follows, in *Fortnighly Review*, (1 September 1914):

> Three years ago in Paris I got out of a "metro" train at La Concorde, and saw suddenly a beautiful face, and then another and another, and then a beautiful child's face, and then another beautiful woman, and I tried all that day to find words for what this had meant to me, and I could not find any words that seemed to me worthy, or as lovely as that sudden emotion. And that evening, as I went home along the Rue Raynouard, I was still trying, and I found, suddenly, the expression. I do not mean that I found

words, but there came an equation... not in speech, but in little splotches of color....

The "one image poem" is a form of super-position, that is to say, it is one idea set on top of another. I found it useful in getting out of the impasse in which I had been left by my metro emotion. I wrote a thirty-line poem, and destroyed it because it was what we called work "of second intensity." Six months later I made the following hokku-like sentence ["In a Station of the Metro"]. I dare say it is meaningless unless one has drifted into a certain vein of thought. In a poem of this sort one is trying to record the precise instant when a thing outward and objective transforms itself, or darts into a thing inward and subjective.

What is left for commentators to say about the poem? A great deal, since Pound says nothing about any of the specific words in the poem. Thomas Hanzo in *Explicator*, February 1953, made the following points:

1. "In the first line the word 'apparition' suggests the supernatural or the immaterial and a sudden and unexpected appearance."
2. "Since only faces are mentioned," we have a sense of "bodiless" substances. "The faces are likened to 'petals on a wet, black bough.' We know therefore that they are the faces in the windows of a train which has drawn up at the station, for the likeness can only be between the faces framed in the windows of the long, dark train and petals which have fallen on a bough after a rain."
4. "The important point of similarity is that the train has made one of its momentary stops, just as the bough is only momentarily black because it is wet from the rain which has just broken the petals from their stem."
5. What interests Pound is *not* that beauty can be found in a subway (a point made by Brooks and Warren), "but that the vision of beauty has occurred in the one instant before it vanishes, when it has been released from the accidents and particularly of its material embodiment."

John Espey, writing in the June 1953 issue of *Explicator,* took issue with some of Hanzo's points. Espey argued that Pound's comment (unlike Hanzo's) keeps the faces "precisely where the poem places them, 'in the crowd,'" rather than in the windows of subway cars drawn up for a moment at the station. Further, Espey points out, the Parisian subway cars were not dark either inside or out, since they were illuminated and they had colorful exteriors.

What to do? Hanzo's comment that the detached petals can be taken to refer to faces in the windows strikes us as reasonable and perceptive, especially since "apparition" allows for a sort of disembodiment corresponding to faces viewed without bodies, but against this is Pound's own statement that the faces were in the crowd—presumably the crowd he saw on the platform as he got out of the car. Well, we all know that we don't have to take the author's word (Wimsatt and Beardsley taught us this truth in "The Intentional Fallacy"); still, one wants to think as carefully about an author's comments as one does about a critic's.

Let's start over. We can probably all agree that although the most memorable (because the most visual?) thing in the poem is the image of "Petals, on a wet, black bough," the word "apparition" is extremely important, since it (paradoxically) makes somewhat ghostly or unreal the vivid image of the faces as petals. Yoshiyuki Iwamoto, in *Explicator* February 1961, presses this point. He begins by arguing that the second line adds up to something like this: Life is violent (the rainstorm), and such violence is essential to the continuity of life. But, he says, the word "apparition" calls all of this into doubt, and thus the poem as a whole is linked to Buddhist thought about the unreality of the tumultuous life that we think is real. There is surely plenty here that can provoke lively debate in class.

Other points:

1. "The transition from the Metro station to the wet boughs somewhere outside liberates us from 'space limits,' and the transition from the present faces to the remembered petals breaks down 'time limits,'" (Hugh Witemeyer, *The Poetry of Ezra Pound* [1969], p. 34.)
2. Perhaps we can more humbly reword Witemeyer's point along these lines: the second line perceives beauty in the subway (underground, enclosed) and also takes us out of the subway, above ground and in the open air, and in connection with "apparition" suggests the mystery of existence. (If we seem to be making a fuss about "apparition," consider how different the poem would be if the word were "appearance.")
3. Can one go further and say that this poem, often thought of as simply a vivid image, not only suggests (a) the fragility or transience of life, and (b) the mystery of life, but it also suggests (c) the pathos of urban, mechanized life?

A "Voices and Visions" videocassette of Ezra Pound is available from Longman. An audiocassette of Ezra Pound reading is also available from Longman.

H. D.

Helen (p. 678)

Most students know something about Helen of Troy—her extraordinary beauty; her marriages to Menelaus and Paris; and the fact that the Trojan war, which Homer recounts in the *Iliad,* was waged over her. But whenever we teach this poem, we use it as an occasion to send students to the library to read about Helen in such reference works as *The Oxford Classical Dictionary,* ed. N. G. L. Hammond and H. H. Scullard (2nd ed., 1978) and *The Oxford Companion to Classical Literature,* ed. M. C. Howatson (new ed., 1989). Both have lengthy entries on Helen of Troy, and flesh out well the bare bones of the students' knowledge. Most of us consult reference books, dictionaries, specialized encyclopedias often—it's hard to imagine doing research and teaching without them. But many students are unfamiliar with scholarly tools of this kind; they know about general multivolume encyclopedias and handy desktop-size dictionaries, and that's about it. Reference works come as a revelation to many students whom we have taught, and we try to get them into the habit of making use of these books, not only for reading literature but, even more, for paper-writing assignments, so that students can comment in detail on allusions, references, names, and terms that a poem relies upon.

H.D.'s poem depends for its effect on the aura of Helen, known and expressed throughout the ages. And it is made all the more evocative through the clear, clean, precise choices of language that H. D. has made—"the still eyes in the white face," "the beauty of cool feet." The verbs are effectively placed—for example, the sharply focused "hates" in line one, and the keenly rhymed combination of "reviles/smiles" in line two.

Note: As a way of indicating Helen's mythic status, we make sure to quote Marlowe's famous lines from *Doctor Faustus:* "Was this the face that launched a thousand ships/And burnt the topless towers of Ilium?" It doesn't hurt to mention other sources (e.g., Goethe's *Faust),* including a few that might be less well known, such as the line from Shakespeare's *All's Well That Ends Well:* "Was this fair face the cause, quoth she,/Why the Grecians sacked Troy?"

Students respond well to H. D.'s poetry, and might be directed toward her longer work, *Helen in Egypt* (1961), and to her *Collected Poems, 1912-1944,* ed. Louis L. Martz (1983). Useful secondary sources include: Barbara Guest, *Herself Defined: The Poet H. D. and Her World* (1984), Susan Stanford Friedman, *Penelope's Web: Gender, Modernity, H. D.'s Fiction* (1990), and *Signets: Reading H. D.,* ed. Susan Stanford Friedman and Rachel Blau DuPlessis (1990).

T. S. ELIOT

The Love Song of J. Alfred Prufrock (p. 679)

Among the useful introductory books are Elizabeth Drew, *T. S. Eliot;* Northrop Frye, *T. S. Eliot;* and Grover Smith, *T. S. Eliot's Poetry and Plays.* On "Prufrock," see also Rosenthal and Smith, *Exploring Poetry;* Hugh Kenner, *The Invisible Poet: T. S. Eliot,* 3-12; and Lyndall Gordon, *Eliot's Early Years.* It is well to alert students to the fact that "Prufrock" is not a Browningesque dramatic monologue with a speaker and a listener, but rather an internal monologue in which "I" (the timid self) addresses his own amorous self as "you." (Not every "you" in this poem, however, refers to Prufrock's amorous self. Sometimes "you" is equivalent to "one.") Possibly, too, the "you" is the reader, or even other people who, like Prufrock, are afraid of action.

Among the chief points usually made are these: the title proves to be ironic, for we scarcely get a love song; "J. Alfred Prufrock" is a name that, like the speaker, seems to be hiding something ("J.") and also seems to be somewhat old-maidish ("Prufrock" suggests "prude" and "frock"); the initial description (especially the "patient etherised") is really less a description of the evening than of Prufrock's state of mind; mock heroic devices abound (people at a cocktail party talking of Michelangelo, Prufrock gaining strength from his collar and stickpin); the sensuous imagery of women's arms leads to the men in shirt-sleeves and to Prufrock's wish to be a pair of ragged claws.

We print the original (1915) version, from *Poetry* magazine, but in line 19 we give *soot* instead of *spot* (an obvious typo in *Poetry*). When the poem later appeared in book form it differed only in punctuation (e.g., square brackets instead of parentheses) and one verbal change—*no doubt* instead of *withal* in line 114.

In graduate school, one of us had the privilege of studying Eliot's poem with an eminent critic of modern literature, who has written well about Eliot, Joyce, and Pound. A student in this class, somewhat impatiently, asked, "So what does the poem mean?" To which the instructor replied: "It doesn't mean anything."

That reply seems at first a bad one that is likely to add to students' confusions and perplexities when they encounter "The Love Song of J. Alfred Prufrock" for the first time. It doesn't mean *anything*? But what the instructor was getting at, and what he proceeded to describe, was the ample pleasure that the reader can take—and that Eliot took himself—in the mixed playful and serious rhymes ("In the room the women come and go / Talking of Michaelangelo"); in the clever imagery (e. g., yellow fog that's like a cat); and in the management of sounds ("I grow old... I grow old / I shall wear the bottoms of my trousers rolled") that echo the verbal patterns that such nineteenth-century poets as Longfellow and Tennyson mastered.

On one level, Eliot is engaged in an act of high literary seriousness, as the allusions to Dante, Shakespeare, and the Bible attest. But these features of the poem sometimes prove more appealing to critics and scholars than to beginning students, who do not always possess the background needed to appreciate and ponder them. You'll want to talk about the allusions and give students some help with them. But remember, too, that there are many kinds of verbal effects in the poem, many different moments in the organization of its language. You can read lines and stanzas aloud and linger over them with students. This is obvious enough, but it works especially well in Eliot's case, and overcomes students' worry that this poem is "too hard" for them.

Sometimes students do indeed find "The Love Song of J. Alfred Prufrock" intimidating—which, with its epigraph in Italian, probably was one aspect of Eliot's intention. But only one: the poem is actually quite engaging to students, quite accessible, when it is read aloud, and when Eliot's phrases and lines are enjoyed in all their craftsmanship.

An audiocassette of T. S. Eliot reading "The Love Song of J. Alfred Prufrock" is available from Longman. A "Voices and Visions" videocassette of T. S. Eliot is also available from Longman.

TOPICS FOR CRITICAL THINKING AND WRITING

1. How does the speaker's name help to characterize him? What suggestions—of class, race, personality—do you find in the name? Does the poem's title strike you as ironic? If so, how or why?
2. What qualities of big-city life are suggested in the poem? How are these qualities linked to the speaker's mood? What other details of the setting—the weather, the time of day—express or reflect his mood? What images do you find especially striking?

3. The speaker's thoughts are represented in a stream-of-consciousness monologue, that is, in what appears to be an unedited flow of thought.
Nevertheless, they reveal a story. What is the story?

JOHN CROWE RANSOM

Piazza Piece (p. 682)

"Piazza Piece" is a sonnet, and sonnets often treat the theme of love, but few if
any others treat the old theme of "Death and the Maiden." It should be read
aloud, and when it is read aloud, the apparently odd placement of "listen to an
old man not at all" seems perfectly right, catching the old-fashioned tone of the
suitor.

Not all students will know that "piazza" (Italian for square) in parts of the
United States denotes a porch, verandah, or balcony; nor will they know that in
the earliest days of automobiling the roads were not paved or covered with
asphalt, so riders—in open cars, of course—wore dustcoats, coats that were
ankle-length. Ransom, a Southerner who was born in 1880, catches the polite-
ness and nostalgia that characterized (and still characterize) much of the South
when a respectable woman was still "a lady," and a man was "a gentleman," and
"Sir" was in common use.

Students can be directed to two collections, Ransom's *Selected Poems* (1945)
and *Selected Poems* (1963). But they need to know that the first excludes many
poems that Ransom had published previously, and the second, while more
capacious, includes revised (and many have argued, *inferior*) versions of his
earlier work. See Thomas Daniel Young, *Gentleman in a Dustcoat: A
Biography of John Crowe Ransom* (1976), and, on the poetry, Robert
Buffington, *The Equilibrist: A Study of John Crowe Ransom's Poems, 1916-1963*
(1976).

TOPICS FOR CRITICAL THINKING AND WRITING

1. Who speaks the first eight lines? What words especially characterize him?
He is a "gentleman in a dustcoat," but who else is he? What is a "dustcoat" or
a "duster"? Why is this garment especially appropriate here? Characterize
the speaker of the six remaining lines.
2. In lines 9-10, she is waiting for her "true love." In line 14 she is still "waiting."
For whom does she think she is waiting? For whom does the reader know
she is waiting? How do you know?

CLAUDE MCKAY

America (p. 683)

This poem bears almost the same title as the one by James Weldon Johnson, and
makes an excellent comparison with it. Johnson speaks of "us," but McKay's

focus is highly personal—how he responds to America, its ideals and values. This poem is very effective in showing students the complex response that many minority poets have expressed toward the nation. America makes McKay angry—it feeds him "bread of bitterness." (Note that McKay characterizes America as female at first, though later he uses the image of "a king in state.") Yet America also invigorates McKay, supplying him with the strength that he needs to combat America at its worst. For McKay, America is both enemy and ally, cruel foe and potent supporter and friend.

Lines 11-14 are somewhat puzzling. Does the image of "priceless treasures sinking in the sand" intimate that America's monumental glory will persist decades into the future (like the Egyptian pyramids), or that America, however mighty now, will one day be no more than a historical memory, fading into oblivion, covered up by the sands of time?

See Wayne Cooper, *Claude McKay: Rebel Sojourner in the Harlem Renaissance* (1987); and James R. Giles, *Claude McKay* (1975).

ARCHIBALD MACLEISH

Ars Poetica (p. 683)

See Donald Stauffer, *The Nature of Poetry,* 121-25, and W. P. Standt in *College English* 19 (October 1957) 28-29. Standt points out that in the first and second sections there are similes, but in the third section we move from similarity to identity; i.e., metaphors replace similes. Moreover, identity is stressed in the quasi-mathematical formula at the beginning of the third section.

This poem, like Moore's "Poetry," easily gets the class into a discussion of the nature of art. (Moore's poem is not concerned explicitly with "modern" poetry, but with new poetry of any period.) And a discussion of MacLeish's poem inevitably gets into whether MacLeish practices his precepts; the abundant detail gives us a sense of felt reality ("be"), but doesn't MacLeish also "mean"? Certainly "a poem should not mean but be" has meaning; and note, too, that MacLeish is not content to give us "An empty doorway and a maple leaf," for he prefaces this with an explanation, telling us that it stands "for all the history of grief."

It is useful to ask students to comment in detail on the figures. The figure of an empty doorway and an autumn leaf standing for grief is clear enough, but how is "a poem... motionless in time / As the moon climbs"? Perhaps the idea is that a poem, because it stirs the emotions, seems to move, yet it is itself unchanging.

MacLeish can be studied in detail in the following sources: *Letters of Archibald MacLeish, 1907 to 1982,* ed. R. H. Winnick (1983); *Archibald MacLeish: Reflections,* ed. Bernard A. Drabeck and Helen E. Ellis (1986); and Scott Donaldson, *Archibald MacLeish: An American Life* (1992).

An audiocassette of Archibald MacLeish reading is available from Longman.

WILFRED OWEN

Dulce et Decorum Est (p. 684)

There are plenty of comments about the horrors of war—for instance Tacitus's "They make a desert and call it peace," and Sherman's "War is Hell"—but even Tacitus and Sherman probably believed that war is necessary and can be heroic. It's our guess that they would even have agreed with Horace: *"Dulce et decorum est/ Pro patria mori."*

Owen is asserting that modern war is so dehumanizing that Horace's line—if it were ever true—is now certainly false. We say "dehumanizing" because even from the start Owen gives us images of ruined creatures: "Bent double," "old beggars," "hags." There is nothing here of Tennyson's Light Brigade charging manfully into the Valley of Death.

Death comes to a battered, knock-kneed, limping soldier who is seen as "flound'ring" rather than falling in some heroic pose. The speaker relives the sight of witnessing (through the eyepiece of his gas mask) his companion destroyed by what seemed to be a sea of poison gas, but equally horrible is the memory of the appearance of the dead body when it was carted away.

It's probably true to say that as long as war was (for the most part) something executed by professionals in remote places, politicians and poets and even the mass of citizens comfortable at home could find it easy to praise war. Speaking of war as it was in the eighteenth century, the Swiss philosopher Emerich de Vattell (1714-1767) said, "The troops alone carry on war, while the rest of the nation is at peace." But modern war—it is sometimes said that the Civil War was the first modern war—is quite another thing. First, an army can get its supplies from remote sources, which means from the civilians back home, who therefore become fair game for the enemy. Second, newspaper photography and television have brought the horrors of the battlefield into the home—and this, in effect, is what Owen does in the poem.

What of the structure of the poem? The first stanza (8 lines) consists of two quatrains (*ababcdcd*). Line 4 ends with a period, so why did Owen not begin a new stanza with line 5? Apparently he thought of the first two quatrains as an octave—possibly he even began by thinking he would write a sonnet. The next stanza is a sestet, rhyming *efefgh*. The fifth and sixth lines of this sestet will rhyme with the next two lines, so from the point of view of the rhyme scheme Owen has again written two quatrains, but he interrupted the second of these two, separating it from its last two lines by putting a space between lines 14 and 15. Surely this arrangement of lines has a meaning, and probably has an effect. Although the speaker uses "we" in line 2 and "our" in line 4, and thus identifies himself with the scene, until the last line of the sestet (i.e., until the second half of line 14) the impression is chiefly of a description of something out there, rather than a revelation of the self. But if for fifteen and a half lines the speaker seems chiefly to be an observer, the second half of the sixteenth line emphatically introduces the speaker's response: "I saw him drowning." In the next stanza, which consists of only two lines (15-16), considerable emphasis is given to the dead man, but an even greater emphasis is given to the speaker's response to the sight:

In all my dreams, before my helpless sight,
He plunges at me, uttering, choking, drowning.

The final stanza (twelve lines—three quatrains, the third of which grimly rhymes "glory" with *"mori")* begins by drawing the reader ("you") into the nightmare world of the narrator and the dead soldier. The speaker insistently holds onto this "you," addressing him (or her?) not only in line 17, but also in 21 and ironically (as "My friend") in line 25. The poem ends with a noble Latin sentiment, but this ending is scarcely designed to provide a quiet or upbeat ending; rather, it is designed to keep the squirming reader squirming.

E. E. CUMMINGS

in Just- (p. 685)

Of course a reader's response to any sort of print on a page is partly conditioned by the appearance of the page. Nice margins and creamy paper can make a so-so story seem pretty good, and double columns and thin paper that allows for show-through can make reading even an absorbing work difficult. And probably any poet would be distressed to find the first twelve lines of his or her sonnet printed on a right-hand page, and the final couplet—invisible to the reader of the three quatrains—on the next page.

Our point, again, is that the physical appearance of any work counts, but of course with cummings's work it counts a great deal more, in a variety of ways. For instance, "eddieandbill" catches the child's way of speaking, and also conveys a sense of an inseparable pair, just as "bettyandisabel" does. (When the youngsters grow up, they will be Eddie and Betty, and Bill and Isabel, but cummings is giving us children in the stage when boys play with boys and girls with girls.) As for the variations in which the words "far and wee" appear, we can say only that the spaces (in line 5, "far   and wee"; in line 13, "far   and   wee"; in lines 22-24, "far / and / wee") convey the variations in the balloonman's whistle, and the last of these perhaps suggests that he is moving away.

The allusion to Pan (via the goatfoot and the whistle) seems clear to us. Pan is the woodland god of Arcadia, a land usually depicted as a world of perpetual spring. Of course Pan is especially associated with the pursuit of nymphs, but cummings here gives us a rather sexless world, though we can hardly repress the thought that this world of childhood (with its inseparable boys and its inseparable girls) and of springtime play (marbles, dancing) will in time become something else.

One other point: Most students, in the course of class discussion, will see that the repeated "wee" (5, 13, 14) works several ways. The balloon man is "little" (3); his whistle makes the sound of "wee"; "wee" is a child's exclamation of delight; and "we" children go running to buy balloons.

E. E. Cummings reads on two audiocassettes that are available from Longman.

W. H. AUDEN

Musée des Beaux Arts (p. 686)

Useful pieces on "Musée" are in *College English* 24 (April 1963): 529-31; *Modern Language Notes* 76 (April 1961): 331-36; *Textual Analysis,* ed. Mary Ann Caws (a relatively difficult essay by Michael Riffaterre); and *Art Journal* 32 (Winter 1972-1973): 157-62—the last useful primarily because it includes reproductions of Brueghel's work and it reprints other poems relating to his pictures. We reproduce Brueghel's picture of Icarus (in the Brussels Museum of Fine Arts, hence Auden's title); for a larger color reproduction see Timothy Foote, *The World of Brueghel.* Auden glances at some of Brueghel's other paintings (the children skating in *The Numbering of Bethlehem* are indifferent to Joseph and Mary, who are almost lost in a crowd; the dogs and the horses in *The Massacre of the Innocents),* and his poem accurately catches Brueghel's sense of nature undisturbed by what rarely happens to the individual.

As Otto Benesch points out (*The Art of the Renaissance in Northern Europe,* 99), in *Icarus* Brueghel gives us a sense of cosmic landscape. Plowman, shepherd, and fisherman go about their business, unaware of Icarus, who is represented in the lower right-hand corner simply by his lower legs and feet, the rest of him being submerged in the sea. Daedalus is nowhere represented; the yellow sun sets in the west, and the sea, coasts, and islands are transfigured with a silvery light. It should be noted that in Ovid's account in *Metamorphoses* 8: lines 183-235, the plowman, shepherd, and fisherman beheld Icarus and Daedalus with amazement, taking the two for gods. Given Brueghel's diminution of Icarus—legs and feet, unnoticed by the other figures in the picture—it is fair to say that Brueghel is offering a comment on the pride of scientists. James Snyder, who makes this point in *Northern Renaissance Art,* 510, also calls attention to the shiny pate of a recumbent man, a dead man, at the left margin, halfway up and all but invisible even in the original painting. This image, Snyder says, "assuredly is meant to express the old Netherlandish saying, 'No plow stops over the death of any man,' or over Brueghel's Everyman, a clever footnote that reveals, after all, that peasant wisdom can be as profound as that of the ancients."

Students are first inclined to see Auden's poem as an indictment of indifference; our own view is that Auden gives the daily world its due, especially in such phrases as "doggy life" and "innocent behind"; that is, he helps us see that all of creation cannot and need not suffer along with heroes. Auden's poem evoked a pleasant reply by Randall Jarrell, "The Old and the New Masters," *Collected Poems* (1959) 332-33. It begins, "About suffering, about adoration, the old masters / Disagree...."

An audiocassette of W. H. Auden reading is available from Longman.

W. H. AUDEN

The Unknown Citizen (p. 687)

In "The Unknown Citizen" the speaker's voice is obviously not the poet's. The speaker—appropriately unidentified in a poem about a society without individuals—is apparently a bureaucrat. For such a person, a "saint" is not one who is committed to spiritual values, but one who causes no trouble.

An audiocassette of W. H. Auden reading is available from Longman.

TOPICS FOR CRITICAL THINKING AND WRITING

1. What is Auden satirizing in "The Unknown Citizen"? (Students might be cautioned to spend some time thinking about whether Auden is satirizing the speaker, the citizen, conformism, totalitarianism, technology, or what.)
2. Write a prose eulogy of 250 words satirizing contemporary conformity, or, if you prefer, contemporary individualism.
3. Was he free? Was he happy? Explain.
4. In a paragraph or two, sketch the values of the speaker of the poem, and then sum them up in a sentence or two. Finally, in as much space as you feel you need, judge these values.

ELIZABETH BISHOP

The Fish (p. 686)

Bishop's poem gives a highly detailed picture of a "venerable" heroic fish that, with its "medals" and its "beard of wisdom," becomes a symbol of courageous endurance. From the colors of the fish, seen and imagined ("brown skin," "darker brown," "rosettes of lime," "tiny white sea-lice," "white flesh," "dramatic reds and blacks," "pink swim-bladder," "tinfoil"), and from the colors of the old fish-lines, the poem moves to the rainbow in the oil in the bilge (the lowest part of the hull). The rainbow—the sign of hope and of God's promise to Noah to spare humanity—grows in the imagination until it fills "the little rented boat," illuminating (we might say) the speaker, who, perceiving the heroic history of the captive, forbears to conquer and returns the fish to the water.

For a discussion of the poem, see Bonnie Costello, *Elizabeth Bishop.*

TOPICS FOR CRITICAL THINKING AND WRITING

1. Underline the similes and metaphors, and think about their implications. Of course they help to describe the fish, but do they also help to convey the speaker's attitude toward the fish?
2. Why does the speaker release the fish at the end of the poem.

ELIZABETH BISHOP

Poem (p. 690)

First, the title. We tell students in our composition classes that a piece of writing—whether by a student or by a professional—begins with the title; this poem provides a sort of test case. Bishop's titles are usually less laconic than this one, so we assume that this title too is significant. The poem is partly about a painting, and therefore about the effects of works of art; this title, then, reminds us at the start that we are confronting a work of art, or, to put it a little differently, Bishop's poem is itself, as an artifact, analogous to Uncle George's picture, a work of art, a concrete embodiment of a perception, and an object that will stimulate the mind of the perceivers.

We find touches of wry humor in "that awful shade of brown" ("awful" is also deeply disturbing), in the reference to "the artist's specialty," and in the bird that looks like a flyspeck—or the flyspeck that looks like a bird (12, 25, 26-27); there is a sort of humor, too, in the remembered monologue of the giver of the picture, presumably the speaker's mother or father (39-44). But any wryness that occurs after this last passage lacks humor; the remaining lines are not quite bitter, but they convey a strong sense of diminution or loss, as in "Which is which? / Life and the memory of it cramped, / dim, on a piece of Bristol board. . . ," and especially in "the little of our earthly trust. Not much / About the size of our abidance / along with theirs; the munching cows. . . ."

"Earthly trust" and "abidance" in the lines just quoted have a puritanical ring—though there is probably also a pun in "earthly trust," given the earlier financial references ("dollar bill," "never earned any money in its life," and "handed along collaterally"—another pun here). At the start the diminutive is engaging (the "tiny" cows, the "wisp" of the steeple), but soon the references to the small and the transient or the brief become disquieting. The picture is "done in an hour, 'in one breath'"; Uncle George abandoned Canada; "Life and the memory of it cramped, /dim, on a piece of Bristol board"; the speaker of the remembered conversation, who will "probably never / have room to hang these things again," is quite likely moving to smaller quarters. (Such a move is usually provoked by the loss of part of one's family.) We get "little. . . for free" (58), and though what we get on earth we treasure in memory, it cannot last. Right now, at least in memory, there are "spring freshets," but autumn and winter will come: the elms will be "dismantled" (64); that is, their covering or mantle of leaves will fall, or perhaps the branches will be lopped and the trees themselves will be chopped down. Although the reference to dismantling is powerful, it is not the last word; the poem ends with "the geese," and, after all, the little picture itself continues to survive. Art—including Bishop's poem (again we emphasize the importance of the title)—is one of the things we "get for free." (One might, in class, compare this poem with Keats's "Ode on a Grecian Urn," another poem about transience and art.) Helen Vendler, in *Part of Nature, Part of Us*, at the end of her discussion of Bishop's poem, offers a somewhat different interpretation:

> As lightly as possible, the word "dismantled". . . refutes the whole illusion of entire absorption in the memorial scene; the world of the poet who was once the child now seems the scenery arranged for a drama with only too brief a tenure on the stage—the play once over, the set is dismantled, the illusion gone. The poem, having taken the reader through the process that we name domestication and by which a strange terrain becomes first recognizable, then familiar, and then beloved, releases the reader at last from the intimacy it has induced. Domestication is followed, almost inevitably, by that dismantling which is, in its acute form, disaster. . . .

Earlier in the essay Vendler points out that "the place" depicted in the painting is described three times: first, visually; then, after "Heavens, I recognize this place," as a remembered landscape (but the painting remains a painting, consisting of "titanium whited," etc.); and finally as something not merely seen by the eye or contemplated by the mind but perceived (Vendler says) "by the heart, touched into participation." See, in addition to Vendler, Bonnie Costello, *Elizabeth Bishop.*

ROBERT HAYDEN

Frederick Douglass (p. 692)

The second question, below, asks why the subject of the sentence is delayed so long. We take it that Hayden is seeking to instill in the reader a sensation corresponding (in an infinitely tiny way, of course) to the agonized sense of waiting that African-Americans for more than a century have experienced.

Another point: The words "mumbo jumbo" in line 6 perhaps deserve a comment. Among certain West African tribes, Mumbo Jumbo is or was revered as a god who protects the people from evil. In white America, where African religion was scarcely regarded with sympathy or even with tolerance, the words came to mean gibberish. Hayden neatly turns the tables, applying the term not to the language of Africans or African-Americans but to the language of white politicians.

We are always seeking opportunities to urge students to read the *Narrative of the Life of Frederick Douglass* (1845); the best edition has been prepared by David Blight, and is published by Bedford Books (1993). Biographies of this extraordinary nineteenth-century orator, writer, and reformer have been written by Benjamin Quarles (1948) and William McFeely (1991).

TOPICS FOR CRITICAL THINKING AND WRITING

1. When, according to Hayden, will Douglass "be remembered"? And *how* will he be remembered?
2. "Frederick Douglass" consists of two sentences (or one sentence and a fragment). In what line do you find the subject of the first sentence? What is the main verb (the predicate) and where do you find it? How would you describe the effect of the long delaying of the subject? And of the predicate?
3. Does Hayden assume or seem to predict that there *will* come a time when freedom "is finally ours" (line 1), and "belongs at last to all" (line 3)?
4. Hayden wrote "Frederick Douglass" in 1947. In your opinion are we closer now to Hayden's vision or farther away? (You may find that we are closer in some ways and farther in others.) In your answer—perhaps an essay of 500 words—try to be as specific as possible.
5. "Frederick Douglass" consists of fourteen lines. Is it a sonnet?

ROBERT HAYDEN

Those Winter Sundays (p. 692)

Students can learn something about writing by thinking about the length of the four sentences that constitute this poem. The first stanza consists of a fairly long sentence (four and a half lines) and a short one (half a line, completing the fifth line of the poem). The brevity of that second sentence reinforces the content—that no one thought about the father—and the brevity also, of course, adds emphasis by virtue of its contrast with the leisurely material that precedes it. Similarly, the fourth sentence, much shorter than the third, adds emphasis, an emphasis made the more emphatic by the repetition of "What did I know?"

Next a confession: We thought about glossing "offices" in the last line, for students will almost surely misinterpret the word, thinking that it refers to places where white-collar workers do their tasks. But we couldn't come up with a concise gloss that would convey the sense of ceremonious and loving performance of benefits. And it may be just as well to spend some class time on this important word, because the thing as well as the word may be unfamiliar to many students. After the word has been discussed, the poem may be read as a splendid illustration of an "office." Like the father in the poem, who drives out the cold and brings warmth (by means of love, of course, as well as coal) to an unknowing child, an "austere and lonely" writer performs an office, shaping experience for another person's use.

One may want to raise the question in class of whether the knowledge that the author was black affects the poem's meaning.

TOPICS FOR CRITICAL THINKING AND WRITING

1. In line 1, what does the word "too" tell us about the father? What does it suggest about the speaker (and the implied hearer) of the poem?
2. What do you take to be the speaker's present attitude toward his father? What circumstances, do you imagine, prompted his memory of "Those Winter Sundays"? What line or lines suggest those circumstances to you?
3. What is the meaning of "offices" in the last line? What does this word suggest that other words Hayden might have chosen do not?

DUDLEY RANDALL

The Melting Pot (p. 693)

It is often said that America is a land of immigrants—that all of us are or are descended from immigrants. But the fact remains that African "immigrants" were the only ones brought to North America forcibly, against their will, as slaves. The history of African-Americans is inextricably tied to, yet separate from, the history of other races and ethnicities. And is a bitter version of this point that Randall satirically presents through the voice of his character Sam in this poem.

Students might be asked to respond to the effectiveness of Sam's declaration, "But I'll be just what I am," which concludes the poem. One of our students noted in class that these words are a powerful affirmation of identity, but, she wondered, is it possible for any group to stand apart from the other groups it lives among? In its ironic, barbed, clever way, Randall's poem is a suggestive commentary on African-American histories.

Note: The phrase "melting pot" comes from a play about Jewish immigrant life, *The Melting Pot*, by the Jewish author and philanthropist Israel Zangwill (1864-1926). The play opened in New York in 1908 and was a great success.

Jesse Jackson (1969): "I hear that melting-pot stuff a lot, and all I can say is we haven't melted."

Jimmy Carter (1976): "We become not a melting pot but a beautiful mosaic. Different people, different beliefs, different yearnings, different hopes, different dreams."

Helpful studies include: John Bodnar, *The Transplanted: A History of Immigrants in Urban America* (1985); Nathan Glazer, ed., *Clamor at the Gates: The New American Immigration* (1985); Maldwyn Allen Jones, *American Immigration* (1960); and David M. Reimers, ed., *Still the Golden Door: The Third World Comes to America* (1985). Students might also be referred to the *Harvard Encyclopedia of American Ethnic Groups*, ed. Stephen Thernstrom (1980), and to John Higham's important book on immigration and nativism, *Strangers in the Land: Patterns of American Nativism, 1860-1925* (1963).

GWENDOLYN BROOKS

Martin Luther King Jr. (p. 694)

Four years before King's death the African-American journalist Lerone Bennett wrote: "His grace, like Gandhi's, grows out of a complicated relation not to oppression, but the ancient scourges of man to pain, to suffering, to death. Men who conquer the fear of these things in themselves acquire extraordinary power over themselves and over others." King was assassinated in Memphis, Tennessee, on April 4, 1968—a white man named James Earl Ray was later convicted for the murder. Immediately upon King's death, race riots erupted in Detroit, Washington D.C., and more than a dozen other major cities. Nearly 100,000 persons, including national and world leaders, attended King's funeral on April 9th.

Brooks's poem places special emphasis on King as a preacher of the word "Justice" and it ends with the speaker's pledge that this word will, despite King's death, continue to be spoken and will surely be achieved. Yet students disagree about the kind of Justice that Brooks envisions. Some connect it to the healing and anointing powers that the speaker attributes to him, whereas others see something destructive in the "burning" that King's word causes—a sign, perhaps, of the revolutionary dimension of his program. Interestingly, students have sometimes interpreted this poem as a call for, or prophecy of, revenge—that Justice will eventually be done, and America, forced to pay for the crime of King's murder.

Students will probably know about the controversy that arose in 1980s about making King the focus of a "national" holiday, and will be aware of the resentments that many persons still harbor toward him for the social changes he pioneered. It is worth pointing out to students that in fact there is no such thing as a *national* holiday. The president and Congress can legally designate holidays for federal employees, and the states can follow the lead, but neither congress nor the president can declare a national holiday. Aside from New Year's Day, Independence Day, Labor Day, Thanksgiving, and Christmas, are states do not celebrate holidays on the same day. Most states, for example, celebrate Veterans Day on the fourth Monday in October, but a few use the old November 11th date. In 1986, King's birthday, January 15th, was declared a *federal* holiday, not a national one.

Instructors might mention to students the following books: D. H. Melhem, *Gwendolyn Brooks: Poetry and the Heroic Voice* (1987); and Harry Shaw, *Gwendolyn Brooks* (1980).

On King, see Taylor Branch, *Parting the Waters: America in the King Years, 1954-1963;* and David J. Garrow, *Bearing the Cross: Martin Luther King, Jr., and the Southern Christian Leadership Conference* (1986).

ANONYMOUS

Mourners Follow Martin Luther King's Coffin (photograph, 694)

On the day of Martin Luther King's funeral, the Ebenezer Baptist Church, in Atlanta, Georgia, overflowed, and some ten thousand mourners gathered outside of the church. The coffin was placed on a mule-drawn farm wagon, symbolizing the Poor People's March to Washington. King had planned the March, but interrupted his plans to go to Memphis, Tennessee, to assist striking sanitation workers. It was in Memphis that he was assassinated. The thousands of people who followed the coffin were paying homage to King and were also implying that his work was still to be done. King was buried in Atlanta's South View Cemetery, under a marble monument inscribed with the words of a slave spiritual that he had often quoted: "Free At Last, Free At Last! Thank God Almighty! I'm Free At Last!"

Nearly all students have seen film of King's might, delivery of these words at the close of his "I Have a Dream" speech, given before the Lincoln Memorial on August 28, 1963, as the keynote address of the March on Washington. But they would benefit from knowing King's other writings and speeches, gathered in the collection *A Testament of Hope: The Essential Writings of Martin Luther King, Jr.,* ed. James M. Washington (1986).

HENRY REED

Naming of Parts (p. 695)

Most students will immediately hear—if the poem is read aloud in class—two voices. One voice is that of a riflery instructor, who maddeningly uses—four times in the first four lines—what has been called the "Kindergarten We"; and he uses it again in lines 6, 12, 20, 21, and 30. But from the middle of the fourth line of each stanza to the end of the stanza there is a countervoice, or, rather, we hear the thoughts of the recruit, whose mind turns from the numbing lecture to thoughts of "the neighboring gardens" (5) and of spring. Some of the instructor's phrases (e.g., in 10, where he speaks about slings, "Which in your case you have not got") are echoed but given a different context by the student ("in our case we have not got," in 12, the silence of the trees in spring).

The poem is delightfully comic, not least because of the boring talk of the instructor, because of the contrast between his talk and the recruit's thoughts, with puns on "easing the spring" (22, 24, and 25) and "point of balance" (27, 28), and with mildly dirty allusions, but we don't think we are being hypersubtle when we say that these sexual puns arise from a not-at-all-comic desperation in the recruit's mind. Forced to listen to the droning instructor, who is talking about how to kill, the recruit mentally escapes to the abundant life going on around him. There is an assault in nature, too ("The early bees are assaulting and fumbling the flowers," 22), but that assault (in contrast to the instructor's lesson) is life-producing.

ANTHONY HECHT

The Dover Bitch (p. 696)

Andrews Wanning, to whom the poem is dedicated, is a teacher of literature. Like the title, the subtitle ("A Criticism of Life") is derived from Matthew Arnold, who in "The Study of Poetry," *Essays in Criticism, Second Series,* speaks of poetry as "a criticism of life." Hecht's poem, which at first glance is a parody of Arnold, therefore is also a criticism of poetry (though Arnold's "Dover Beach"—in our text—survives it), and, as we will argue in a minute, also a criticism of life. Inevitably Hecht's poem must be discussed in connection with Arnold's, but sooner or later the discussion probably ought to get to matters of tone in "The Dover Bitch."

Much of Hecht's poem purports to give the girl's point of view, though we should remember that the speaker is not the girl but a rather coarse fellow who knows her. This speaker sympathizes with her (to "be addressed / As a sort of mournful cosmic last resort / Is really tough on a girl"), but his sensibilities are not of the finest (he tells us that although she is "Running to fat," he gives her "a good time"). If he introduces a note of sexuality that is conspicuously absent from Arnold's poem and that affords some comedy, one's final impression may be that the poem shows us the bleak, meaningless, loveless world that Arnold feared. As Christopher Ricks puts it *Victorian Studies* 6 (1968), Hecht's "brilliant and poignant poem is by no means flippant. . . . Having subjected Arnold to an unprecedented skepticism, [the poem suddenly reveals] the superiority of Arnold—and of all he epitomized—to that knowing speaker whose worldliness was at first refreshing. The poem, we realize, is in important ways a tribute to Arnold, though hardly a reverential one. . ." (539-40).

Hecht is also a stimulating critic; his books include: *Obbligati: Essays in Criticism* (1986), *The Hidden Law: The Poetry of W. H. Auden* (1993), and *On the Laws of the Poetic Art* (1995).

MITSUYE YAMADA

The Question of Loyalty (p. 697)

In our earlier discussion of a poem by Yamada ("To the Lady", in Chapter 13), we give some background information about the evacuation of Japanese and Japanese-Americans from the west coast in the early 1940s.

The mood of the times demanded a single, unquestioning loyalty. This demand, however, was not engendered simply by World War II. It came out of the idea that the United States was a melting pot, a term first used, or at least popularized, by Israel Zangwill, in a play called *The Melting Pot* (1908): "America is God's crucible, the great Melting-Pot where all the races of Europe are melting and re-forming." At about the time Zangwill wrote *The Melting Pot,* Theodore Roosevelt said,

> There is no room in this country for hyphenated Americans. . . . The one absolutely certain way of bringing this nation to ruin, of preventing all possibility of its continuing to be a nation at all, would be to permit it to become a tangle of squabbling nationalities. (1915)

Five years later Roosevelt was to say,

> There can be no fifty-fifty Americanism in this country. There is room here for only 100% Americanism, only for those who are Americans and nothing else.

It is our impression that most of the immigrants who came at the end of the nineteenth century, or in the early decades of the twentieth, turned their backs on the country of their origin and came here to be 100% Americans. Of course they retained many of their ways, and perhaps especially their foods, but they were fleeing poverty or political persecution; having made a living or even a good living here, they had little reason to look back with much affection. Further, in the days before World War II, it was difficult to maintain contact with the old country; ocean voyages took time and money, and long distance telephone calls were almost unthinkable, except to report a death in the family. Today it is different; many middle-class immigrants, such as physicians and college professors, come here not because they are terribly oppressed but because they seek greater economic opportunity. They have no dislike of their native land; they keep in contact by telephone, and they fly back for frequent visits. But even many immigrants who are relatively poor can maintain contact with their native lands.

Further, there are many people of this sort, partly because many people in the United States were born abroad. According to today's newspaper (*The New York Times*, 30 August 1995), the percentage of the country that is foreign-born is accelerating. In 1994 it was 8.7 percent, or 22.6 million people (about four million of whom are thought to have entered illegally). The figures for California and New York, the states with the highest proportions of foreign-born residents, are 25% and 16%.

You don't need to hear our ideas on why foreign-born people today can be Americans and can yet retain affectionate ties with their native lands. Yamada's poem takes us to an earlier era, when one could *not* be "doubly loyal" (line 14). It's obvious that she fully sympathizes with her mother, although she herself took a different course: "I was poor / at math. / I signed / my only ticket out." The wry joke about being poor at math—as though the mother has really posed a mathematical problem—conveys self-condemnation, and yet one wonders if she is not right when she says that signing was in fact a necessity, the "only ticket out."

ALLEN GINSBERG

A Supermarket in California (p. 698)

The poem evokes Walt Whitman by name and evokes his poetry in the long, unrhymed lines and in the catalogs of commonplace objects of American life. But Ginsberg's America is not Whitman's, for Ginsberg makes the point that Whitman too was lonely while he lived and finally encountered the loneliness of death. The allusion to the Spanish poet García Lorca is to his poem on Walt Whitman, and also calls to mind yet another homosexual poet whose love was unreciprocated. As we see it, the "self-conscious" poet, his head aching (1), draws inspiration from Whitman, who lived in an earlier and more innocent age, an age when a man could unselfconsciously celebrate male beauty and comradeliness. But that age is "the lost America of love" (11), and in any case the Whitman who celebrates it and who is the poet's "courage-teacher" (13) was himself "lonely" (again 13) and, like all mortals, at last lost all. By the way, in the first sentence, Ginsberg seems to confuse Lethe (the river of forgetfulness) with Styx (the river across which Charon poled his ferry).

Whenever we teach Ginsberg, we get lots of questions about his friend Jack Kerouac and the members of the Beat Generation of the 1950s. Students might be referred to: Jane Kramer, *Allen Ginsberg in America* (1969); John Tytell, *Naked Angels: The Lives and Literature of the Beat Generation* (1976); Barry Miles, *Ginsberg: A Biography* (1989); Carolyn Casady, *Off the Road: My Years with Casady, Kerouac, and Ginsberg* (1990); *The Portable Jack Kerouac*, ed. Ann Charters; and *Jack Kerouac: Selected Letters, 1940-1956*, ed. Ann Charters (1995).

On Ginsberg's verse: *On the Poetry of Allen Ginsberg*, ed. Lewis Hyde (1980).

JAMES WRIGHT

Lying in a Hammock at William Duffy's Farm in Pine Island, Minnesota (p. 699)

It seems to us that the title is somewhat paradoxical, in its implication of utter relaxation and apartness—lying *in* a hammock, *at* someone's farm, *in* an island—and (on the other hand) the almost pedantic or fussy specification of the locale. And we find the rest of the poem paradoxical too.

The speaker's eye ranges. He takes in the view above (a natural starting-place for someone lying in a hammock), then looks "Down the ravine," then "to my right," and then, at the end, up again ("I lean back"), when he observes the chicken hawk. In a sense he ends where he began, but meanwhile he has explored (or at least surveyed) a good deal. He has, from his sleep-like condition in the hammock, begun by seeing a bronze-colored butterfly "Asleep," then has heard the distant cowbells, and has seen "The droppings of last year's horses" (so we get some extension into time as well as into space), and then glances again at the skies. This exploration—all from the hammock—is marked by keen yet imaginative observations.

Let's go back a moment, to the first perception, the "bronze butterfly / Asleep." The poet is describing the color, but the effect is paradoxical, giving the reader a fragile insect made of an enduring material. From perceptions of colors ("bronze," "black," "green") we go to aural perceptions ("the cowbells follow one another") and then back to visual perceptions (the horse droppings, now "golden stones"). In all of this beauty there is a keen sense of isolation—the cows and horses are not present, and even the chicken hawk is looking for home. Now, "as the evening darkens," the speaker has an epiphany, uttered in the final line.

The final line probably comes to the reader as a shock, and perhaps the reader is uncertain about how to take it. Is the speaker kidding? Or is he saying, in dead seriousness, all creatures except me seem to have their place in a marvelously beautiful, peaceful nature, whereas I am not even in my own home? Our own impression is that, whatever he says, *we* feel that he has not wasted his life, since he has so interestingly recorded his perceptions.

TOPICS FOR CRITICAL THINKING AND WRITING

1. How important is it that the poet is "lying in a hammock"? That he is at some place other than his own home?
2. Do you take the last line as a severe self-criticism, or as a joking remark, or as something in between, or what?
3. Imagine yourself lying in a hammock—perhaps you can recall an actual moment in a hammock—or lying in bed, your eye taking in the surroundings. Write a desctiption, ending with some sort of judgement or conclud-

ing comment, as Wright does. You may want to parody Wright's poem, but you need not. (Keep in mind the fact that the best parodies are written by people who regard the original with affection.)

JOHN HOLLANDER

Disagreements (p. 700)

We especially like the nonstop verbal and syntactical activity in Hollander's poem. It includes a wonderful mix of colloquial phrases, Latinate words, parallelisms ("the state of the nation but our state of contention"), and sharp, funny word choices and images in which the poet clearly takes delight (e. g., "snaffle," "braying out," the line about Punch and Judy). As much as any poem we know, this one needs to be read aloud in the classroom, so that readers hear Hollander's skill at evoking the shifts and jumps in the disagreement he describes.

One of us had good luck with a writing assignment that asked students to take, as a point of departure for examining the poem, a line from Beaumarchais's *The Barber of Seville* (1775): "It is not necessary to understand things in order to argue about them." Students might also be encouraged to think about the poem as a story: Is the state of disagreement by the end different from what it was at the beginning?

Advanced students will benefit from Hollander's excellent books of literary criticism, including *Vision and Resonance: Two Senses of Poetic Form* (1975); *Rhyme's Reason: A Guide to English Verse* (1981); and *Melodious Guide: Fictive Pattern in Poetic Language* (1988).

ADRIENNE RICH

Living in Sin (p. 701)

If some of the woman's perceptions seem to indicate hyperesthesia (she hears "each separate stair... writhe"), for the most part her perceptions are fairly ordinary: "last night's cheese," bugs among the saucers, and so on. The man, however, does not perceive even these, and for the moment—since we see him through her eyes—he seems utterly oafish. Notice the description of the apartment, imagined as an attractive still-life ("A plate of pears, / a piano with a Persian shawl, a cat / stalking the picturesque amusing mouse,") in contrast to the apartment with "dust upon the furniture of love," scraps of food, a piano that is "out of tune," and a lover (temporarily absent) who needs a shave. Later she is back in love—more concerned with the man than with the things around them—but this is not a love poem, and the real interest is in the woman's diminished (more reasonable) view of love, even though she is now back in love. The "sin" of the title is not a matter of cohabiting without the blessing of the church; rather, the "sin" is that she has seen through the myth of romantic happiness in difficult circumstances. If the stairs no longer "writhe," she is nevertheless conscious of them and of the "relentless day." Presumably never again will she think the studio will "keep itself"; now she knows that love is not the whole of life.

ADRIENNE RICH

Rape (p. 701)

We can think of a number of earlier poems about rape—one of them, Yeats's "Leda and the Swan," is in our text—and it occurs to us that in virtually all of them the suffering of the woman is transformed by a mythic vision. (So far as we know, all poems on Philomela turn the violated woman not only into a bird, as Ovid did, but also into a symbol that presumably should be contemplated with sweet melancholy.)

Rich's poem is different. The violated woman is not metamorphosed and mythologized. She is, at the end of the poem as at its beginning, an ordinary woman, a "you" who lives in a violent male world, a world in which everyone else is rapist, cop, father, stallion, unsympathetic confessor. The victim of the rape is victimized a second time when she is required to tell her story: "[T]he maniac's sperm still greasing your thighs, / ... You have to confess / to him, you are guilty of the crime / of having been forced." In Ovid, the authorities (the gods) take pity on the victim and metamorphose her, but in Rich's poem the police officer takes pleasure in the victim's distress: "the hysteria in your voice pleases him best." The first rapist is a "maniac," but the second, the police officer-confessor, is empowered by society, and so at the end the victim is diminished rather than elevated into the world of myth.

DEREK WALCOTT

A Far Cry from Africa (p. 702)

Many students—partly because they think that puns are always comic and that literature is always serious—will not see the double meaning in the title: (1) the poem is a lament from Africa, violated by colonialism and also by Africans themselves, and (2) the poet—a West Indian who lives part of the year in the West Indies and part in the United States—is a very considerable distance away from Africa.

Walcott, a black, sees not only the wickedness of British colonial rule but also the wickedness that Africans visit upon other Africans. Further, Walcott's tongue is English; he utters his cry (to use a word from the title of the poem) in English, not in an African language. In short, the two meanings of the title embody the themes of the poem—the pain that Africa is experiencing (inflicted not only by colonialists but also by Africans), and the dilemma of the English-speaking poet, who is black but who lives thousands of miles from Africa and who feels a loyalty to (and a love for) "the English tongue."

The place to begin is with Walcott's *Collected Poems, 1948-1984* (1986), but your more advanced students might enjoy exploring his epic poem, *Omeros* (1990). See also: *The Art of Derek Walcott*, ed. Stewart Brown (1991); Rei Terada, *Derek Walcott's Poetry: American Mimicry* (1992); and *Critical Perspectives on Derek Walcott*, ed. Robert D. Hamner (1993).

SYLVIA PLATH

Daddy (p. 703)

C. B. Cox and A. R. Jones point out, in *Critical Quarterly* 6 (Summer 1964): 107-122, that literature has always been interested in perverse states of mind (Greek and Roman interest in the irrational; Elizabethan interest in melancholy, jealousy, madness, etc., and Browning's dramatic monologues). The "fine frenzy" of the poet himself (in the words of Shakespeare's Theseus), once associated with inspiration and even divinity, in the twentieth century links the poet with the psychotic personality. And apparently a sensitive (poetic) mind can make only a deranged response in a deranged world. Plath's "Daddy" begins with simple repetitions that evoke the world of the nursery rhyme (and yet also of the witches in *Macbeth*, who say, "I'll do, I'll do, and I'll do"). The opening line also connects with the suggestion of the marriage service ("And I said I do") in line 67. The speaker sees herself as tormented yet also as desiring the pain inflicted by her father/love ("Every woman adores a Fascist"). She recognizes that by accepting the need for love she exposes herself to violence. The speaker's identification of herself with Jews and the evocation of "Dachau, Auschwitz, Belsen" suggest some identity between the heroine's tortured mind and the age's. Death, Cox and Jones go on to say, is the only release from a world that denies love and life. The "Daddy" of the poem is father, Germany, fatherland, and life itself, which surrounds the speaker and which the speaker rejects.

In *Commentary* (July 1974 and October 1974), there is an exchange of letters on the appropriateness of Plath's use of Nazi imagery in a poem about her father. Roger Hoffman, in the July issue, argues that the imagery is valid because in a child's mind an authoritarian father is fearsome. Irving Howe, in October (9-12), replies that this argument is inadequate ground "for invoking the father as a Nazi." The speaker of the poem is not a child, Howe says, but "the grown-up writer, Sylvia Plath." He goes on: the "unwarranted fusion of child's response and grown-ups' references makes for either melodrama or self-pity." Howe also rejects Carole Stone's argument (July) that the images are acceptable because "one individual's psyche [can] approximate the suffering of a people." Howe replies that the victims of the concentration camps didn't merely "suffer"; they were methodically destroyed. He questions the appropriateness of using images of the camps to evoke personal traumas. There is, he says, a lack of "congruence" between the object and the image, "a failure in judgement." Some useful criticism can also be found in *The Art of Sylvia Plath*, ed. Charles Newman.

A "Voices and Visions" videocassette of Sylvia Plath is available from Longman. An audiocassette of Sylvia Plath reading is also available from Longman.

TOPIC FOR WRITING

The speaker expresses her hatred for her father by identifying him with the Nazis, herself with the Jews. Is it irresponsible for a poet to compare her sense of torment with that of Jews who were gassed in Dachau, Auschwitz, and Belsen?

AMIRI BARAKA

A Poem for Black Hearts (p. 706)

Most students know something about Malcolm X, and many of them will have seen the film by the African-American director Spike Lee that appeared in 1992. Still, it is useful to remind students that Malcolm X broke bitterly with the Black Muslims in 1963-64, having become pained by the corruption he perceived in the Black Muslim leadership, especially in the case of Elijah Muhammad, whom Malcolm X had revered as his spiritual father. After an inspirational journey to Mecca, the holy city of Islam, where he saw equality among different races, Malcolm X stopped preaching that all whites were evil and began work on a movement of his own, the Organization of Afro-American Unity. He was assassinated—it is widely believed—by Black Muslims in New York City on February 21, 1965.

This poem is a good one to compare and contrast with Brooks's on King. Both poems were written two years after the death of the figures they commemorate—which suggests that both were the product of reflection on the death and its aftermath. But where Brooks is mostly understated, with firm but short lines and stanzas, Baraka is angry, honoring Malcolm X and issuing an appeal for vengeance.

Baraka's poem always generates intense debate and discussion. The reference to breaking the face of "some dumb white man," for example, can prove upsetting. But we have had students remark that this very phrase may evoke sympathy, too: He is just some dumb white man, who maybe did not at all deserve the fate he suffered. Which then leads to the question whether Baraka intended such a reading of the phrase, or, instead, whether some readers want to find it there to mute the impact of his harsh words. Some students have also noted an irony in Baraka's indictment of whites and determination to rally black men for revenge, since it was a group of African-Americans who killed Malcolm X.

Ossie Davis: "Malcolm was refreshing excitement; he scared hell out of the rest of us, bred as we are to caution, to hypocrisy in the presence of white folks, to the smile that never fades" (1965).

Maya Angelou: "Malcolm was a path, a way into ourselves" (1981).

Students might be directed to *The Autobiography of Leroi Jones/Amiri Baraka* (1984), and to two scholarly works: Kimberly W. Benston, ed., *Iamamu Amiri Baraka*, and William J. Harris, *The Poetry and Poetics of Amiri Baraka: The Jazz Aesthetic* (1985).

Biographies of Malcolm X are somewhat disappointing; the best is Peter Goldman, *The Death and Life of Malcolm X* (snd. ed., 1979). The most valuable approach to him is through his own words, in George Breitman, ed., *Malcolm X Speaks* (1965), and *The Autobiography of Malcolm X* (1965).

MARY OLIVER

The Black Walnut Tree (p. 707)

The poem presents students with few or no difficulties. Further, they will all be familiar with the experience of talking about doing something practical and then not doing it, because of the tug of sentiment, or, more generally, simply because one *feels* that the rational course of action is not always the right course.

LUCILLE CLIFTON

in the inner city (p. 708)

This poem—from a book called *Good Times*—catches a distinctive voice, meditative and colloquial, the colloquialisms never slipping into merely cute dialect or local color.

PAULA GUNN ALLEN

Pocahontas to her English Husband, John Rolfe (p. 709)

According to legend, Pocahontas (c. 1596-1617), whose name means "playful one," saved the English Captain John Smith from execution at the hands of Algonquin Chief Powhatan and his men in 1607. Scholars have disagreed about the exact nature of what happened. If it was a ceremonial feast whose customs Smith misunderstood, Smith's life may not really have been in danger. It appears that after this incident, Pocahontas—twelve years old at the time—mediated between the English settlers and the Indians and helped for several years to improve relations between them before hostilities broke out again.

In 1613, Captain Samuel Argall captured Pocahontas and held her hostage, as part of his effort to compel Powhatan to cease war against the English. She converted to Chritianity, took "Rebecca" as her Christian name, and in 1614 married John Rolfe, who became wealthy from developing and cultivating a new species of tobacco. In 1616, the Virginia Company brought Rolfe, his wife, and their son to England, in order to promote the splendors of the "new world" and spur emigration to America and investments there.

Pocahontas/"Rebecca" became widely known and was even presented at court. She died March, 1617, aboard a ship bound from England to Virginia. Rolfe was killed in an Indian attack in 1622. Their son and his descendants lived in Virginia.

We have found that a good strategy in teaching this poem is to begin with "perfidious" in line two. The Latin root means faithless, dishonest; the word itself suggests deceit, treachery, and is sometimes particularly associated with Judas, the betrayer of Christ. We then ask students to circle words that express other dimensions of Pocahontas's critique of Smith and to note along the way how she characterizes *his* perceptions of *her*.

See Philip L. Barbour, *Pocahontas and Her World* (1970); Frances Mossiker, *Pocahontas: The Life and Legend* (1977); Robert S. Tilton, *Pocahontas: The Evolution of an American Narrative* (1994); and Klas Lubbers, *Born for the Shade: Stereotypes of the Native American in United States Literature and the Visual Arts* (1994).

Allen has also written or edited a number of scholarly books, including *Studies in American Indian Literature: Critical Essays and Course Designs* (1983) and *The Sacred Hoop: Recovering the Feminine in American Indian Traditions* (1986). Instructors might also turn students toward Brian Swann, ed., *Coming to Light: Contemporary Translations of the Native Literatures of North America* (1955).

VICTOR NEHLIG

Pocahontas and John Smith (painting, p. 709)

Although all schoolchildren learn how Pocahontas saved John Smith in Virginia, historians are skeptical about the story. The gist of the narrative, though with different characters and a different setting—a Spaniard named Juan Ortiz, and a Ucita woman known as Ulele, in Florida—had been recorded almost eighty years before John Smith set foot in Virginia. The Ortiz/Ulele story, which is said to have occurred in 1528, was first published in English around 1605, two years before Smith sailed from London to America. Of course history may have repeated itself; the gist of the Ortiz/Ulele drama in Florida may have been reenacted with Smith and Pocahontas in Virginia, in December, 1607, the date Smith gave, but the evidence is non-existent. The episode does not appear in Smith's earliest account of his adventures, *A True Relation. . . of Virginia* (1608)—Smith first mentioned it in 1616—nor does any other colonist of the time mention it. Some modern historians explain the absence of an earlier account as in accordance with orders given not to publish anything that might scare off potential colonists. In any case, the gist of Smith's story, whether or not it happened, is that the beautiful Pocahontas, moved by pity or love or both, intervened and persuaded her savage father to spare Smith's life. (The father is customarily called Powhatan, a name given him by the British, but in fact Powhatan was the name of the Indian nation, not of an individual.) The basic idea behind the story is that although Indians by and large are savages, some savages are capable of virtuous deeds. The further implication is that savages can be brought, perhaps by slow degrees, to recognize the superiority of white, Christian culture, and to adopt it. This idea achieved its most memorable formulation in Kipling's poem, "The White Man's Burden." Speaking of white, we want to mention that in Nehlig's picture the Indian princess's skin is notably lighter than that of the other Indians, hinting at or symbolizing her superior nature.

The male figures, in poses calculated to display their muscles, are indebted to Michelangelo. Europeans could never quite decide if Indians were ugly, deformed creatures with wicked minds or were by nature perfectly-proportioned and mentally uncorrupted Adam-like creatures. If the latter, their unspoiled minds and their simple, primitive existence made them "noble savages," a topic discussed at length in Hugh Honour's fascinating book, *The New Golden Land* (1975). On this topic see also Julie Schimmel's chapter, "Inventing 'the Indian,'" in *The West as America: Reinterpreting Images of the Frontier, 1820-1920*, ed. William Truettner (1991). This book—originally the catalog for an exhibition—is extremely well illustrated but it is often naive in its relentless political correctness. The authors are shocked, truly shocked, that painters and writers in the nineteenth century did not represent Indians accurately—which is to say in the way that these late twentieth-century academicians see them.

The composition of Nehlig's painting, with one figure standing higher than all of the others, and seeming to preside over the action, is obviously indebted to baroque paintings that show such scenes as Solomon judging the two harlots who quarreled over the baby, or God watching Abraham as he prepares to sacrifice Isaac. But there must also be a strong influence of baroque scenes of martyrdom, with Pocahontas substituting for an intervening angel; certainly the light behind her is a secular equivalent of an angel's aureole.

In *Pocahontas: The Evolution of an American Narrative* (1994), Robert S. Tilton studies representations of the Pocahontas story in painting, fiction, drama, and historical writing from the earliest days of the colonies through the Civil War. Students might enjoy reading Tilton's book, with its many helpful illustrations. The full history of the impact of European settlement on the native peoples of the Americas receives detailed, disturbing treatment in David E. Stannard, *American Holocaust: Columbus and the Conquest of the New World* (1992).

BOB DYLAN

The Times They Are A-Changin' (p. 710)

In *The Unraveling of America* (1984), the historian Allen J. Matusow notes that the song "The Times They Are A-Changin'" quickly "became a generational anthem," adding that "it was no less appropriate for Dylan to sing at the 1963 March on Washington than for Martin Luther King to deliver a sermon there."

It is sometimes hard to convey to students why Dylan was such an important figure, and why his music was so radical and evocative, so much a part of the angry rebelliousness, sense of newness, and spirit of hopefulness of the 1960s. Some students will have seen Dylan's recent appearances on MTV, but these make him seem just another aging rock star from long ago.

On the other hand, students do find that "The Times They Are A-Changin'" fits perfectly with what they know (or have heard) about the 1960s. And most students seem able to look closely at details of the language—the criticism of senators and congressmen, the complaint about unsympathetic parents—and make connections between these and the antiwar movement, civil rights campaign, and student activism that were so central to the 1960s.

Yet it is a curious fact about the song that it came early in the decade—in 1963—and in this sense it did not so much reflect what was widespread as tell and prophesy of what was its opening phases. Making this point is a good way to help students understand how lyric and song can at least in part create the conditions that they describe, serving as a source of inspiration and empowerment.

Other important Dylan songs from this era include: "Blowin' in the Wind," which became especially important to those involved in civil rights struggles; and "A Hard Rain's A-Gonna Fall," which was inspired by the Cuban missile crisis of 1962. Curiously, this social protest album, *The Freewheelin' Bob Dylan* (1963) was followed by *Another Side of Bob Dylan*, where, as the music critic Jon Wiener has noted, Dylan "dismissed social issues and sang personal songs that expressed, among other feelings, considerable bitterness toward women."

Instructors might also ask students if "The Times They Are A-Changin'" speaks directly to them. Is it a great lyric of the 1960s, but only that? Or is it a lyric that in a timeless manner dramatizes the changes and transitions that each new generation faces? In this respect, the general nature of Dylan's language is worth remarking on. There is no reference in it to a specific historical figure or event; and except for the mention of senators and congressmen, there is nothing in "The Times They Are A-Changin'" that even ties it to the United States.

See Anthony Scaduto, *Bob Dylan* (1973); and Robert Shelton, *No Direction Home: The Life and Music of Bob Dylan* (1987).

PAT MORA

Sonrisas (p. 712)

First, a reminder that another poem by Mora, "Immigrants," appears in Chapter 1.

Most students will quickly see that the two stanzas stand for the "two rooms" (worlds, we might ordinarily say) in which the Chicana speaker lives. (Interestingly, the word "stanza" comes from an Italian word meaning "room," "stopping place"; a stanza is a room in a poem.) The first room in "Sonrisas" is a room of Anglo culture, "careful," usually unsmiling, and when there are smiles the smiles are "beige" (cautious, neutral, certainly not enthusiastic). This is a world of "budgets, tenure, curriculum," that is the orderly world of the establishment. The second room is a room of Chicano culture, a world of coffee-breaks, "laughter," "noise," scolding (presumably affectionate) and "dark, Mexican eyes" that contrast with the beige smiles and eyes of unspecified color in the first stanza. If the first stanza hints at the world of power and therefore of money (in "budgets, tenure, curriculum"), this stanza hints very gently at a world of relative poverty in "faded dresses," but it seems evident that for the speaker this world is more attractive, more (we might say) human.

GLORIA ANZALDÚA

To live in the Borderlands means you (p. 713)

As we say in our headnote in the text, obviously the "borderlands" are not merely physical locales. Among other things, they are the multicultural heritage *within* a single individual, as expressed, for example, in Joseph Bruchac's poem, "Ellis Island," where he finds his cherished Slovak heritage doing violence to his Native American heritage.

The poem is macaronic, that is, the writer uses one language chiefly but includes foreign words. The origin of the term *macaronic* is uncertain, but is commonly said to be due either to the fact that *maccarone* is a mixture (a dumpling made of flour, butter, and cheese) or that macaroni is heaped on a plate and sauce is dribbled over it. Earlier macaronic poetry was chiefly comic ("Mademoiselle got the croix de guerre / For washing soldiers' underwear, / Hinky, dinky, parlez-vous"), but some was serious, and in modern times it usually is serious. Consider, for instance, Eliot's use of foreign terms in *The Waste Land*. Today it is especially common in serious poems by chicanos or by persons from Puerto Rico; obviously it indicates, among other things, that the writers value Spanish as well as English.

The entire poem is of great interest, but the second stanza especially strikes us, with its assertion that the *india* had been betrayed for 500 years, and that

> denying the Anglo inside you
> is as bad as having denied the Indian or Black....

The first point, about the *india*, strikes us as especially contemporary, because until almost yesterday all Spanish-speaking people of South America were called "Hispanic," even though many of them were evidently of Indian origin. It's our impression that only recently, perhaps along with a heightened awareness of ethnic values in the United States, are persons of Indian origin insisting on this heritage, rather than gliding over it and characterizing themselves as Hispanic—a Eurocentric term that implies a European heritage.

If in your classes you have students from Central or South America, you may want to ask them how they identify themselves—as Hispanics, Latinos/Latinas, chicanos? It is our impression that most people from central or

South America define themselves in terms of the country of their origin, rather than with any of these all-embracing terms. But in so far as one of the broader terms is used, it probably is *Latino/Latina*, rather than *Hispanic*; both are Eurocentric, but the former is not English and therefore seems to be preferred by people who wish to distinguish themselves from Anglo culture.

DON L. LEE

But He Was Cool or: he even stopped for green lights" (p. 714)

Lee's poetry, like some of the poetry of Imamu Amiri Baraka (LeRoi Jones), owes something to William Carlos Williams and to Williams's descendants, the Beat poets, though the Beats were indebted to the rhythms of jazz, and so ultimately the chief sources are black speech and black music. The influence of black speech is apparent in a quality that Stephen Henderson (*Understanding the New Black Poetry*, pp. 33-34) calls "virtuoso naming and enumerating," a "technique [that] overwhelms the listener," which may be derived from "the folk practice of fiddling and similar kinds of wordplay." There is also a fondness for hyperbole, combined with witty, elegant coolness.

JOSEPH BRUCHAC III

Ellis Island (p. 715)

Ellis Island, in Upper New York Bay, southwest of Manhattan Island, from 1892 until 1943 was the chief immigration station of the United States. In its first year, it saw 450,000 immigrants arrive, and in its peak years in the first decade of the twentieth century the annual number exceeded a million; the total number of Ellis Island graduates was over seventeen million. When the island closed, immigration was at a low point, and for some years the buildings fell into ruin. They have now been renovated and form a museum of immigration. In 1965 Ellis Island became part of the Statue of Liberty National Monument (the statue—on its own island, separated from Ellis Island by a few hundred yards of water—had been declared a national monument in 1924).

In our discussion of Emma Lazarus's "The New Colossus" we mention that in the first decade of the twentieth century about 8.7 million immigrants entered the country, most of them via Ellis Island. This means, of course, that the great-grandparents or even the grandparents or parents of an enormous number of today's Americans are alumni of the island, and it has a hold on their affections.

Bruchac begins by calling up an image of two of his grandparents who had endured the long journey and "the long days of quarantine." He implicitly contrasts their journey and their anxiety—about 10% of the visitors were denied admission for reasons of health—with "a Circle Line ship," a ship that makes a daily pleasure cruise of a few hours around the islands, chiefly patronized by tourists. He goes on to evoke "the tall woman, green / as dreams of forests and meadows," i.e. the green patina of the *Statue of Liberty* connects it with nature.

In the second stanza he says that like millions of others he has come to the island, but of course there is a distinction between the millions who, pursuing a dream (lines 10 and 17) came as immigrants and the millions who now come as tourists, perhaps in homage to their ancestors and to the nation that accepted them.

There is, then, a contrast between the first and second stanzas, but the two harmonize. The third stanza, however, introduces a serious complication: If the immigrants were pursuing a dream, they nevertheless also were invading the "native lands" (20-22) of others. (Bruchac himself, as we mention in the head-note, is part Native American and part Slovak.) The Native Americans are characterized as people "who followed / the changing Moon," people who have or who had "knowledge of the seasons / in their veins," so they too, like the green statue, are associated with nature. Is the reader to think that these people are gone-or, on the contrary, that their heritage lives on, for example in the "veins" of the poet? To our mind, the fact that Bruchac *ends* the poem with a reference to a knowledge that is in the "veins," suggests that he sees the heritage as still living—and the violence wrought by later immigrants as also still living.

ANONYMOUS

Slavic Women Arrive at Ellis Island, Winter 1910 (photograph p. 716)

We chose this image partly because it relates closely to Joseph Bruchac's poem (he mentions his Slavic heritage), but also because it gives a somewhat unusual image of Ellis Island, which is rarely associated with snow, or, for that matter, with an all-female group. Probably the husbands of these women had come earlier, found work, and then had sent for their wives. And probably, too, what the women carry on their backs and over their arms is all that they have brought with them.

We have sometimes used this photograph and others in this section as an occasion for recommending novels and stories about immigrant life. See, for example, Abraham Cahan, *Yekl, a Tale of the New York Ghetto* (1896) and *The Rise of David Levinsky* (1917); and Anzia Yezierska, *Bread Givers* (1925). For an evocative account of the East European Jews, see Irving Howe, *The World of Our Fathers* (1976).

LOUISE GLÜCK

The School Children (p. 717)

On the surface, the poem seems loaded with pictures of cute children on their way to school, bringing the traditional apples for the teachers: "with their little satchels," "apples, red and gold," "their overcoats of blue or yellow wool." Even "how orderly they are" (said of the nails on which the children hang their coats) can be taken as a benign comment on this happy scene.

But by the time we finish the second stanza we realize that this is not a Norman Rockwell scene. The children must cross to "the other shore" where they are confronted by people "who wait behind great desks." Further, these people are not presented warmly. Rather, they are presented (we never see them) as godlike figures who wait "to receive these offerings."

The third stanza is perhaps even more menacing, with that orderly row of nails, waiting to accept the pretty coats. The text speaks—horribly—of "the nails / on which the children hang...." As we continue to read the sentence the meaning changes radically, of course, and we see that it is not the children but "their overcoats" that hang on the nails, but the thought lingers; the mind retains a vision of the children hanging from nails.

The last stanza reintroduces us to the teachers, who "shall instruct them in silence," a menacing expression that we take to mean (1) shall teach them silently (a terrifying way of teaching), and (2) shall teach them to be silent (a terrifying condition). The stanza does not end, however, with the teachers or with the children. Rather, it ends with the mothers, who "scour the orchards for a way out," i.e. who seek to equip their children with the "offerings" (line 7) that the gods require. That is, the mothers seek (by propitiating the gods) to protect their children from the severe socialization that awaits them, but it is already too late, because "the gray limbs of the fruit trees" (it is now autumn) bear "so little ammunition."

In the last stanza, why "The teachers *shall* instruct them," and "the mothers *shall* scour the orchards," rather than "will instruct" and "will scour"? Although older handbooks say that *shall* expresses simple futurity in the first person (and *will* expresses determination in the first person), it is our impression that *shall* has almost disappeared. Indeed, part of what made Douglas MacArthur's "I shall return" so memorable was that he used an unusual construction. To our ear, the use of shall in the last stanza of Glück's poem has a voice-of-doom quality; the teachers must act as they will, and the mothers must act as they will— and the children will be the victims.

TOPICS FOR CRITICAL THINKING AND WRITING

1. Which words in the poem present a cute picture-postcard view of small children going to school?
2. Which words undercut this happy scene?
3. In the last-stanza we read that "the teachers shall instruct" and "the mothers shall scour." What, if anything. is changed if we substitute *will* for *shall*?

TESS GALLAGHER

The Hug (p. 717)

We have sometimes begun discussion of this poem by asking students to imagine it for a moment ending at line ten, with the word "you." This shortened poem would place the emphasis on the sudden pleasure of an embrace exchanged between two lovers. But the actual poem continues, of course, into "the hug" between the speaker and a homeless man. Much of the middle of the poem describes how this hug happens and what it feels like. Yet it seems that Gallagher wants also for the reader to bear in mind the speaker's relation to her lover. She's surprised that her lover offers her to someone else. Maybe this is better than if he (as maybe lovers typically do) claimed the right of sole possession, but it's a little unnerving to be let loose in this way.

What is the meaning of the final two lines? These appear to intimate that perhaps this momentous hug has done something to the speaker's feeling for her lover: will there be no place "to go back to" now that she has exchanged this grandly peculiar embrace with a person she doesn't know? How well does she know her lover if she was so surprised at his willingness to let another man hold her? The detail about the button on the homeless man's coat is comically exaggerated ("a planet in my cheek"), but has a pointedness to it as well: this unexpected incident leaves a mark. The poem could have ended with another embrace between the lovers, like the one at the outset. But it doesn't.

NIKKI GIOVANNI

Master Charge Blues (p. 718)

For some comments on blues, see the note on Langston Hughes's "Evenin' Air Blues," in this manual, p. 153.

CRAIG RAINE

A Martian Sends a Postcard Home (p. 719)

We like to begin most discussions by talking about the title—about what expectations are set up by the title—and we especially recommend the procedure for this poem. Most students will find the combination of "Martian" and "postcard" at least a bit incongruous (Martians have spaceguns and "thoughtgrams"); some students (even without having read the poem) will guess that the poem will be the report of a traveler impressed by the strange things he sees on earth. And, of course, an outsider's report of something strange (here, a Martian's report of things on earth) may itself seem to be strange when read by those who are familiar with the thing described (here, by us earthlings). A large part of the point of such writing is to help us to see freshly things we have taken for granted.

The Martian, in his report, gets a few things slightly wrong. He thinks that all books are called "Caxtons" and that all cars are called "Model T." Probably the hardest part of the poem is the opening, the first four lines, describing books (" mechanical birds with many wings") which can make one cry ("cause the eyes to melt") and can make one laugh ("cause. . . the body to shriek without pain"). The car (13), the rear-view mirror (15-16), and the watch and clock (17-18) cause little difficulty; the telephone (19-24) is fairly easily guessed, even though American phones, unlike English phones (at the time when the poem was written) do not make a snoring noise when lifted from the cradle. The bathroom (25-30) is only a little more riddling. Raine (at a poetry reading) mentioned that the Martian, who during his short visit presumably saw only children cry, assumes that when adults suffer and cry, they do so privately, in the "punishment room" (26) where there is water but no food. (Martians apparently do not excrete.) In the final two lines, the Martian, speaking of couples dreaming, thinks they are reading "with their eyelids shut." The poem thus ends, as it begins, with reading.

But what does one make of what the Martian makes of us? He (or she?) seems to be very decent, sensitive to earthly phenomena, and endowed with the gift of metaphor, the sign of the poet. (In fact, when Raine reads the poem to audiences, he usually says that the Martian is not only a Martian, but also a metaphor for the poet.) The passage on mist is a good example: "the world is dim and bookish / like engravings under tissue paper" (9-10). (In our discussion of metaphor in the text we make the point that metaphors are closely related to riddles. In Richard Wilbur's "Love Calls Us to the Things of This World," the description of laundry drying in the breeze is a fresh, metaphoric view of what used to be a familiar sight. Many passages in Raine's poem are similarly close to riddles.)

The Martian reports phenomena, but (luckily for us?) does not judge our actions. Earthlings thus come off pretty well, especially if we contrast this poem with another Martian report, John Hall Wheelock's "Earth" (text, 197).

One other point: We have been able to explain a few puzzling details (especially the mistaken account of why adults go to the bathroom) because the poet has told us what's going on. But is the poet's intention binding? Suppose a reader says that the last two lines describe not people dreaming, but people falling asleep while watching television. Are they wrong?

YUSEF KOMUNYAKAA

Facing It (p. 721)

The title is both literal (he is facing the wall) and figurative (he is confronting the terrible memories of past experiences).

Soldiers in other wars, too, underwent traumatic experiences, and the experience of a combatant is almost bound to include episodes that seem unreal or surreal. But the fact that the Vietnam War had so little popular support—was not convincingly bolstered by the idea that it was being fought for a good cause—was particularly disconcerting and demoralizing. Much of Komunyakaa's poem catches a sense of unreality, and a sense of the loss of self. Thus, a black man looking at his reflection in the black wall finds his reflection literally disappearing; at the same time, if the wall has caused his reflection to disappear, it has nevertheless caught the man himself, drawn him back into the horrible experiences that the wall in effect memorializes. (Strictly speaking, the wall memorializes those who died, not the war itself. That is, the Memorial does not say that the war was either good or bad, only that certain people died in the war.)

From the title on, the speaker is "facing it"—facing the painful memories aroused by standing in front of the wall and confronting or reliving the war experiences. He sees a vision of the booby trap that killed a comrade, Andrew Johnson, and, as reflected in the wall, the loss of the arm of a veteran, who therefore is standing near the poet. At the end of the poem the violence is transformed by the return to the world outside of the wall. In the wall the poet sees a woman "trying to erase names," that is, apparently engaged in a futile action, though one hopes that the memories of the war can be diminished if not erased. But then he corrects himself, and realizes that the wall is in fact mirroring an act of affection: "No, she's brushing a boy's hair".

Some of your students may have visited the wall. If so, you may want to ask them to report their experience.

TOPICS FOR CRITICAL THINKING AND WRITING

1. The poem's title is "Facing It." What is the speaker facing? How would you describe his attitude?
2. Three people, whose names we don't know, briefly appear on the wall. How might we describe their actions? Try to paraphrase: "I'm a window. / He's lost his right arm / inside the stone.
3. At the poem's end, has the speaker "faced it"? What is your evidence?
4. If you have seen the Vietnam Veteran's Memorial, describe it and your reaction to it in a paragraph or two. If you haven't seen it, try to describe it from "Facing It" and any written or photographic accounts you have seen.

J. SCOTT APPLEWHITE

Vietnam Veterans Memorial (p. 721)

The monument was commissioned by the Vietnam Veterans Memorial Fund, which held a design competition. Any U.S. citizen over the age of eighteen could enter design. The criteria were as follows: The monument had to (1) be reflective and contemplative in character; (2) be harmonious with its surroundings; (3) include the names of the nearly 58,000 persons who died or who remain missing in action; (4) make no political or military statement about the war; (5) occupy no more than two acres of land. The competition was won by Maya Ying Lin, an undergraduate at Yale University. Her design consists of two 250-foot walls of polished black granite, meeting at a 136-degree angle. The walls are ten-feet tall where they meet, but taper off into the sloping ground. The names of the dead are inscribed, chronologically in order of death. The names begin not at the left end of the monument, but at the intersection of the two walls, at the top of the right-hand wall. The names continue along the wall, and when space on the right-hand wall is exhausted (where the tip of the wall points to the Washington Monument) they continue at the western end of the left-hand wall (whose tip points to the Lincoln Memorial). Thus, the names of the first who died in the war (on the left-hand side of the right-hand wall) are adjacent to the names of the last to die (on the right-hand side of the left-hand wall).

When the winning design was announced—there were 1,421 entries—it met with much opposition. It did not convey heroism, it was not made of white marble (the traditional material of memorials) and it was not representational. Despite the controversy the memorial was built—though as a compromise, a flagpole and a realistic sculpture of three soldiers (two white, one black) were erected nearby. Today the monument is universally recognized as a masterpiece, though it is very difficult to explain why visitors find it so deeply moving. Something has to do with the site (pointing, as we have said, to the Washington Monument and the Lincoln Memorial), something has to do with the sequence in which the names are inscribed, but much has to do with the reflective black granite sinking into the sloping grass. The criteria, you will recall, included the monument be reflective—and it *is* reflective, in a literal way that the committee doubtless had not envisioned. Visitors looking for the names of friends and loved ones see themselves in the monument. It is not too much to say that the living and the dead meet here, set in an area rich in historical associations. Perhaps we can also say that although the Vietnam Veterans Memorial is indeed a memorial, it is not gloomy, chiefly because it is animated by images of the living, but also because of the site, a grassy slope in an area flanked by memorials to Washington and Lincoln.

One wonders, too, to what extent viewers are moved by the knowledge that the memorial was created by a young woman—an undergraduate!—of Asian ancestry. It is appropriate at this point to quote Maya Lin's own comment on her work. We find it interesting but far from definitive:

> I thought about what death is, what a loss is. . . a sharp pain that lessens with time, but can never quite heal over. A scar. The idea occurred to me there on the site. Take a knife and cut open the earth, and with time the grass would heal it. As if you cut open the rock and polished it.
>
> —*American Institute of Architects Journal* 72 (May 1983): 151.

Useful discussions of the memorial can be found in Jan C. Scruggs and Joel L. Swerdlow, *To Heal a Nation*, and in an article by Charles L. Griswold in *Critical Inquiry* 12 (1986): 688-719. (Griswold's article is reprinted in *Critical Issues in Public Art*, ed. Harriet F. Senie and Sally Webster.) Somehow, no discussion does much to account for the experience of visiting the memorial.

WENDY ROSE

Three Thousand Dollar Death Song (p. 722)

Surely the gist of the poem is clear—that whites buy and sell Indian bones is a sign of the white violation of Indian culture—but we find that we differ in one respect from most other readers of the poem. Our students and colleagues assume that the "museum invoice" of the epigraph indicates that the museum bought the nineteen skeletons for $3,000. But an invoice is a list of goods shipped or services rendered, so if the word is used in the strict sense, the museum *sold* the bones. (Another possibility, of course, is that the "museum invoice" is an invoice not prepared by the museum but something in the files of the museum, in which case it could indeed indicate that the museum purchased the bones.) The point is not crucial—in either case the whites are dealing in sacred Indian material—but we do think that the skeletons probably were sold rather than bought by the museum. Line 24, "we explode under white students' hands," would thus mean that the bones were sold to a medical school or to some other educational institution that would use the bones for anatomical study. (If the museum bought the bones, then perhaps the line alludes to student anthropologists who study the bones in the museum.)

The poem begins by pretending to be businesslike (" in cold hard cash?...Or in bills?. . . Or / checks"), but the businesslike tone is obviously a transparent satiric mask for the speaker's indignation. The indignation becomes explicit with the reference in line 6 to "paper promises."

The second half of the poem moves from the assault on the bones to the larger issue of how the white world not only turned the Indian "dead into specimens" (34) but also stole everything from the Indians—"turquoise / and copper, blood and oil, coal / and uranium," of course, and even (and this is a surprising note in such a list) "children" (50). But the speaker warns (possibly drawing on Ezekiel 37:1), "watch our bones rise" (43).

The central point is the white despoilment of Indian culture, and we don't want to trivialize this issue by turning to what may seem to be a minor matter, but we do want to say that one way of approaching the poem is to ask students if they have ever seen any Native American artifacts in a museum. If so, how were the objects treated? Were they treated as the Other, something odd, primitive, crude, uncivilized or even barbaric, less than (for example) the beautiful art objects of white culture? Museum administrators face a real problem here; if they treat the material in a more or less ethnographic way, the museum is open to the charge of condescending to the culture ("See how curious the customs of these people were!"). If, on the other hand, they treat the material as important works of art, objects of rare beauty, the museum is open to the charge of taking objects out of their indispensable cultural context and seeing them as "mere" esthetic objects rather than as, say, part of the religious life of a people.

JOY HARJO

Vision (p. 723)

The view that the earth is sacred is found in many societies, but it is apparently especially strong in the thought of Native Americans.

Some students—not necessarily only those who are Native Americans—may know something about Native American beliefs, and they may provide a way of entry to the poem. It may also happen that some students may know that according to Genesis 9:12-17, God established the rainbow as a token of a covenant with Noah and his descendants. If this concept comes up, you may want to contrast it with Harjo's poem and to compare Harjo's poem with Wordsworth's "My Heart Leaps Up":

> My heart leaps up when I behold
> A rainbow in the sky:
> So was it when my life began;
> So is it now I am a man;
> So be it when I shall grow old,
>   Or let me die!
> The Child is father to the Man;
> And I could wish my days to be
> Bound each to each by natural piety.

For Wordsworth, "piety" is "natural piety," something rooted in the human being's perception of (responsiveness to) nature, rather than something based on Scripture. We take it that Harjo's vision is close to Wordsworth's.

We are not saying, of course, that the visions are the same, but we do find a close resemblance in the emphasis on the perception of nature as animating the human. For Harjo, the rainbow animates the earth, giving "horses / of color" to humans, "horses that were within us all of this time / but we didn't see them...."

NILA NORTHSUN

Moving Camp Too Far (p. 724)

The first stanza evokes the world of the Indian, though the very first words ("I can't") make it clear that this world is lost, at least to the speaker. We are in the world not of the Vanishing Red (cf. Frost's poem with this title) but of the Vanished Red.

The second stanza begins by evoking a contrast (that's what second stanzas often do)—but a moment later the contrast proves to be illusory, since the affirmative words ("i can see an eagle") become negative ("almost extinct"). The second stanza, then, does not really contrast with the first; rather, it intensifies the first (again, that's what second stanzas often do). Further, the second stanza builds to a climax of degradation; the affirmative "i can dance to indian music" descends into "rock-n-roll hey-a-hey-o," and then to the further, and final—and surprising, but in retrospect almost inevitable collapse of "& unfortunately / i do." The degradation is evident, and what perhaps is most painful is that the speaker implicitly accepts at least some of the responsibility.

For background information, consult Klaus Lubber, *Born for the Shade: Stereotypes of the Native American in United States Literature and the Visual Arts, 1776-1894* (1994).

EDWARD S. CURTIS

Plains Indians (photograph, p. 725)

We chose this photograph chiefly because we think it is beautiful, but also because it includes a travois, (a sledge or a platform resting on two trailing poles), a device mentioned in Nila northSun's poem.

Seeing the Indians as "the vanishing race," Curtis (1868-1952) was determined to record their life before it disappeared. To accomplish his goal, for thirty years, beginning in 1898, he traveled tens of thousands of miles on foot, by mule, by horseback, by boat, and by automobile, taking 40,000 pictures and making 10,000 recordings of songs. In the process he impoverished himself and ruined his health. The published result of his work was *The North American Indian*, twenty illustrated volumes of text and twenty portfolios of photographs. About 300 copies were printed, most of which were unsold at his death.

Curtis's pictures, so obviously beautiful, have been much criticized by today's anthropologists. He cropped and retouched his photographs, and, worse, he often posed his subjects, sometimes even equipping them with costumes that today's sharp-eyed scholars have identified as not rightly belonging to the tribes he was depicting. The charges against him are true, but at least two things should be remembered: The standards of anthropology have changed since Curtis's day, and, second, *all* photographers *make* rather than *take* pictures. That is, even if they do not pose their subjects, photographers make a selection from what is before them. Why, a critic might indignantly ask, did you choose to record *this* person or this activity rather than *that* one? Moreover, photographers step backward or forward, choose an angle, and, for that matter, choose a lens and a kind of film and later a kind of paper that will produce a certain kind of image, thereby turning nature into art. In the present example, quite possibly Curtis chased some child in trousers out of the way, told the two adults to look into the distance, and possibly even placed the rifle in the man's hands. We don't know, but we do think he produced a memorable picture of one aspect of life on the plains.

For an interesting criticism of Curtis, see Christopher M. Lyman, *The Vanishing Race and Other Illusions: Photographs of Indians by Edward S. Curtis* (1982). Lyman's comments make sense—and yet the beauty of the pictures that Lyman reproduces somehow leaves us with the feeling that the criticisms are trivial.

JIMMY SANTIAGO BACA

So Mexicans Are Taking Jobs From Americans (p. 726)

The title, the first line, and indeed the whole poem, have the flavor of ordinary but forceful speech, and we think this closeness to pugnacious speech, on both sides of the fence, accounts for much of the work's power. That is, it is not enough for a poem to set forth admirable sentiments, let's say sympathy for the disenfranchised. We want it to be *a poem*, not just the expression of ideas we approve of.

Here we find art in the contrast between the title, which evokes the ordinary world, and the first line and a half, which give us a preposterous world of mounted bandits, and then the third line, which gives us, even more preposterously, a bandit asking us to hand over not money but our job: "Ese gringo, gimmee your job."

To our ear, the most successful lines in the poem are of this sort—lines that show an ear for common speech and a sense of the absurd—and the least successful are the straight, earnest lines of the advocate, such as "I see the poor marching for a little work, / I see small white farmers selling out / to clean-suited farmers living in New York." But we realize that what we have been saying, which in some measure separates literature from political activity, may be unconvincing to others.

In fact, *are* Mexicans taking jobs from Americans? Well, first of all, many of these "Mexicans" are themselves Americans of Mexican origin. Second, although the subject is much disputed, some reputable authorities insist that much of the work that chicanos do—as migrant laborers, domestic workers, gardeners, and so forth—is in fact so low-paying that Anglos and African Americans will not do it. That is, the jobs wouldn't exist except for the fact that "Mexicans" are willing to do them.

RITA DOVE

Daystar (p. 727)

The poem comes from Dove's Pulitzer-prize book *Thomas and Beulah* (1986), which contains sequences of poems about African-Americans who migrated from the South to the North.

In thinking about a poem, one can hardly go wrong in paying attention to the title. Here, why "Daystar"? "Daystar" can refer either to a planet—especially Venus—visible in the eastern sky before sunrise, or to the sun. Both meanings are probably relevant here. The speaker's brief period of escape from (at one extreme) the children's diapers and dolls and (at the other) Thomas's sexual demands are perhaps like the brief (and marvelous) appearance of a planet at a time when one scarcely expects to see a heavenly body; and this moment of escape—a moment of wonderful independence—is perhaps also like the sun, which stands in splendid isolation, self-illuminating. Sometimes, as she sits "behind the garage," she is closely connected to the visible world around her (the cricket, the maple leaf), but sometimes, with her eyes closed, she perceives only her self. (The mention, in the last line of the poem, of "the middle of the day" perhaps indicates that the chief meaning of "daystar" here is the sun, but we see no reason to rule out the suggestion of the other meaning.)

JUDITH ORTIZ COFER

My Father in the Navy: A Childhood Memory (p. 728)

Most students will quickly see the imagery of death ("stiff and immaculate / in the white cloth, / an apparition") and the Christian imagery ("halo," "When he rose," "kept vigil," "like an angel / heralding a new day"). The sailor-father comes back to the living world from "below," and thus would seem to resemble the risen Jesus. But, at least as we understand the poem, it is the living (the speaker and her siblings) who, so to speak, bring life to the "apparition," whereas in Christian thinking it is Jesus who animates human beings, that is gives them the possibility of eternal heavenly life.

DAVID MURA

An Argument: On 1942 (p. 728)

Mura is a *sansei,* a third-generation Japanese-American. Born in 1952, he did not experience internment in the relocation camps of 1942. The poem is rooted in the fairly widespread difference today between the attitude of, on the one hand, most of those who experienced the camps (chiefly *issei* [first-generation] and their American-born children, *nisei* [second-generation]), and on the other hand, many *sansei,* who were born after World War II, and who cannot understand how their parents and grandparents allowed themselves to be so subjugated.

Mura's poem—in effect an argument between the poet and his mother—begins in the son's voice. Between the fourth and the fifth lines, however, the mother interrupts (or at least she does so in the son's imagination), and the poet reports her words: "—No, no, she tells me. Why bring it back? The camps are over." The mother wishes to forget the experience, or at least not to dwell on it, but her son, she says, is "like a terrier... gnawing a bone." For her, the experience was chiefly boring (line 9). (Of course one can say that she has repressed her memories of humiliation—but one can also entertain the possibility that for a child the experience was indeed chiefly boring.) For the son, who did not experience it but who now looks at it through the eyes of a mature Japanese-American writing in the late 1980s, the thought of the indignity is galling.

What does a reader make of the conflict? Presumably the reader can hold both views, sharing the youth's sense of outrage but also understanding the mother's view—which, incidentally, is given the climactic final position: "David, it was so long ago... how useless it seems..." In fact, it seems entirely possible that the poet himself holds both views. At least to our ear he voices them with equal effectiveness.

After we had written the preceding remarks we received the following comment from David Mura:

> The poem starts with an imaginary poem in my voice, a lament for the world that was destroyed by the internment order. I'm both attracted to and wary of the romantic

cast to such a voice, and in the poem, my mother gives another version of the past, one which downplays the effect of the camps and argues against over-romanticizing both the past and past sufferings. In the end, I think there's a great deal of denial in my mother's version of the past, and yet, her version is a reality with which I must contend; after all, she was there, and I wasn't (of course, her presence at these events doesn't necessarily mean her interpretation of them can't be wrong). Both her version and my version exist in the poem as realities which the reader must confront. As with much of my work, I think of this poem as a political poem.

For another poem about the internment of Japanese-Americans in 1942, see Mitsuye Yamada, "To the Lady," also in our book.

LAUREEN MAR

My Mother, Who Came From China, Where She Never Saw Snow" (p. 729)

This poem is a good one for encouraging students to consider tone of voice—how Mars's description of her mother both provides a portrait of the mother and intimates the daughter's feelings about her. "A pounding needle" is a nice detail to notice in this regard. It evokes the sound of the labor that the mother performs, and the weight of the work under which she bends. "It is easy," the narrator/daughter says twice, perhaps using the phrase that the mother might have employed herself to keep her daughter from being upset by what she saw her mother subjected to day after day. But the daughter knows that it is always the same task that the mother must undertake, and that at least once the needle stabbed through her hand.

The bare phrase "Twenty-four years" is also very effective, capturing in a breath the great span of time that the mother has done this monotonous work. And it connects sharply with the line that follows: "It is frightening how fast she works." The mother works each moment at extraordinary speed, and the daily job, though tiring and tedious on one level, makes the years whizz by.

The daughter realizes that this work has consumed twenty-four years. Students might be asked to comment on the tone of this phrase, and the larger question of whether we learn from the poem how the mother perceives herself. At no point do mother and daughter exchange a word or a glance—which is possibly why our students have on occasion described Mars's poem as vivid and keen in its details, yet cold, disquietingly distant.

See Michael H. Hunt, *The Making of a Special Relationship: The United States and China to 1914* (1983); and Akira Iriye, *Across the Pacific: An Inner History of American-East Asian Relations*

AURORA LEVINS MORALES

Child of the Americas (p. 730)

The author, born in Puerto Rico of a Puerto Rican mother and of a father whose origins went back to the ghetto in New York and beyond that to Europe, came to the United States when she was thirteen, and has lived in Chicago, New Hampshire, and now in the San Francisco Bay Area. Her heritage and her experience thus are considerably different from those of most Puerto Ricans who are now in the United States.

Wheras other Latinas in this book emphasize the difficulties of their divided heritage (see Pat Mora's "Immigrants" and Lorna Dee Cervantes's "Refugee Ship"), Morales celebrates her diversity and apparently is at ease as a Latina in the United States: She is "a light-skinned mestiza of the Caribbean, / a child of many diaspora," she was born "at a crossroads," she is "a U.S. Puerto Rican Jew, / a product of the ghettos of New York," "Spanish is in [her] flesh," but in the next-to-last stanza she insists that she is "not african," "not taína," "not european." Most significantly, she insists that she is not fragmented but is, on the contrary, "whole."

In short, Morales holds to the old idea of the United States as a melting pot, an idea not heard so often today. The conception of the melting pot has largely given way to the conception of America as a "gorgeous mosaic," a "salad bowl," a kaleidoscope, i.e., a place where there is great variety but where each ingredient maintains its identity.

MARTIN ESPADA

Bully (p. 731)

The editors of *Literature* belong to a generation that was taught, in grade school and in high school, that Teddy Roosevelt was a hero. Some of his words entered the classroom, just as half a century later some of the words of John Kennedy—notably the Inaugural Address—entered the classroom. In school we heard such Rooseveltisms as "I wish to preach, not the doctrine of ignoble ease, but the doctrine of the strenuous life" (1899), "In life, as in a football game, the principle to follow is: Hit the line hard" (1901), and "There is no room in this country for hyphenated Americanism. . . . The one absolutely certain way of bringing this nation to ruin, of preventing all possibility of its continuing to be a nation at all, would be to permit it to become a tangle of squabbling nationalities" (1915). In the fifth question below, we quote yet another (in)famous remark, expressing the opinion that all immigrants should be required to learn English within five years. Persons who doubt that Roosevelt was regarded as one of America's greatest heroes need only call to mind Mount Rushmore National Memorial, in South Dakota, where an enormous bust of Roosevelt, along with busts of Washington, Jefferson, and Lincoln, is carved. Although the sculptures (visible for some sixty miles) were not finished until the 1950s, the monument was dedicated in 1927, and in effect it represents the values of the 1920s.

In our third question below we ask about the word "bully," as an adjective and as a noun. Roosevelt used the adjective, meaning "excellent," in a famous comment, to the effect that the presidency is a "bully pulpit." But given

Roosevelt's enthusiasm for military action, in particular for the Spanish-American War (a war whose name somehow omits the efforts of the Cuban patriots who fought for independence), it is hard not to think of the other and more common meaning of the word. Certainly in this poem entitled "Bully," where it is said of Roosevelt that "each fist [is] lonely for a sabre," the image that comes across is of someone who pushes other people around. A century ago Roosevelt stormed San Juan with his Rough Riders, but today Puerto Rican children invade Roosevelt High (line 11). The end of the poem, with its reference to Roosevelt's "Victorian mustache / and monocle," present a hopelessly outdated and somewhat comic figure who contrasts with the vitality of the "Spanish-singing children."

TOPICS FOR CRITICAL THINKING AND WRITING

1. If you're not sure what Theodore Roosevelt was famous for, consult an encyclopedia. What *was* he famous for? In the first stanza, what words best express Espada's attitude toward him?
2. In the second stanza, what does Espada mean when he says "Puerto Rico has invaded Roosevelt"? What does he mean by an "*army* of Spanish-singing children"? Who are the *Taino*?
3. What does "bully" mean as a noun? As an adjective?
4. Roosevelt was a great believer in what is called The Melting Pot Theory of America. What is this theory? Do you think there is a great deal to it, something to it, or nothing to it? Why?
5. Here is a quotation from one of Roosevelt's speeches:

   Every immigrant who comes here should be required within five years to learn English or leave the country.

   What do you think of this idea? Why? Suppose that for some reason (perhaps political, perhaps economic) you decided to spend the rest of your life in, say, Argentina, or Germany, or Israel, or Nigeria. Do you think the government might reasonably require you to learn the language? Why?

SHERMAN ALEXIE

On the Amtrak from Boston to New York City (p. 732)

This piece takes the Anglo reader deep into the heart of the "Other." On the surface, the speaker is an affable guy—in a conversation with a stranger he nods his head acquiescently, he does not embarrass the woman by telling her she is talking foolishly, and he even brings her an orange juice from the food car. But we feel his rage at her superficiality, and at Don Henley's show of concern for Walden. We also intensely feel his impotence as he makes plans (34-37), which of course he will not act on, for the next occurrence of the same situation. The last line makes it explicit that whites are his enemy, but the reader knows that the whites who meet him on the train will never know it.

The woman's idea that "history" has been made only by whites is presented here in such a way that it is obviously absurd. But it is an idea that almost all whites have held until very recently. For instance, Robert Frost in "The Gift Outright" (in this chapter) speaks, without any irony, of the pre-white world as "unstoried, artless, unenhanced."

CHAPTER 21

Three Poets in Depth

EMILY DICKINSON

There are two useful guides to Dickinson Criticism, both of which are edited by Joseph Duchac: *The Poems of Emily Dickinson: An Annotated Guide to Commentary Published in English, 1890-1977* (1979), and *The Poems of Emily Dickinson: An Annotated Guide to Commentary Published in English, 1978-1989* (1993).

A "Voices and Visions" videocassette of Emily Dickinson is available from Longman.

EMILY DICKINSON

These are the days when birds come back (p. 737)

The time is Indian summer, that is, a day that seems summery but is late, hence it is a sort of sophistry of mistake or fraud. (By the way, it is not true that birds, deceived by Indian summer, return.) Lines 10-11 introduce religious imagery ("ranks of seed their witness bear," and the pun on alter-altar, which suggests a communion scene), anticipating the more overt religious images in the next two stanzas.

Some readers take the poem to suggest that just as the season can be deceptive, communion too can be deceptive or illusory. Other readers see the poem moving the other way: from the illusory season, which evokes nostalgic thoughts, to the real or firm joys of Christian immortality. Charles Anderson, in *Emily Dickinson's Poetry*, gives a substantive analysis. He suggests that the season's ambiguity provokes the question, "Does it symbolize death or immortality," and he answers that Dickinson does not give an answer but gives us "warring images poised in ironic tension."

TOPICS FOR CRITICAL THINKING AND WRITING

1. What season or weather is being talked about? Why does Dickinson use the words "mistake" (line 6) and "fraud" and "cheat" (line 7)?
2. Explain the pun on "altered" in line 11.
3. Take the first three stanzas as a group and summarize them in a sentence or two. Do the same for the last three. Then, in a sentence or two, state the relationship between these two halves of the poem.
4. Why "a child" in line 15?

EMILY DICKINSON

Papa above (p. 737)

At one extreme, we have encountered readers who find the poem a bitter protest masquerading as a prayer, a scathing attack on the anthropomorphic God of Judaism and Christianity; at the other extreme we have encountered readers who find nothing but piety in the poem, albeit piety in a very Dickinsonian idiom, a piety rooted in affection for God's creatures, even the mouse or rat. Our own hear genial—even affectionate—satire of anthropomorphism, and we also hear acceptance of the strange government of the world. Chiefly, we think, the poem expresses—again, in a characteristically Dickinsonian way—the "primal sense of awe" that Charles R. Anderson commented on.

"Papa above" begins with a domesticated version of the beginning of the Lord's Prayer (Matt. 6.9-13, "Our Father who art in heaven"; Luke 11:2-4, "Father"). In "Regard a Mouse O'erpowered by the Cat" we hear a solemn (and perhaps a wondering) voice, although we grant that one might hear some comedy in the let-down. That is, a reader who expects, after the invocation of the deity, something like "Regard the sufferings of mortals," or some such thing, is surprised to find that the speaker calls attention to a mouse. Or if the reader expects something that continues the idea of the Lord's Prayer, the shift from the expected "Give us this day our daily bread" to a picture of a mouse overpowered by the claws or jaws of a cat is indeed shocking, first because of the implied violence, and second because of the ironic contrasts between the meal Jesus spoke of and the meal Dickinson shows.

In the next two lines ("Reserve within thy kingdom / Mansion for the Rat!") we hear primarily a serious if not a solemn voice, though others hear mockery in the juxtaposition of "Mansion" and "Rat." In any case, there is surely a reference to the comforting words Jesus offered to his disciples (John 14.2) when he assured them of reunion in heaven: "In my Father's house are many mansions." But a heavenly mansion (dwelling place) for a rat? We are by no means convinced that Dickinson must have abhorred mice and rats, and that therefore "A 'Mansion for the Rat" must be ironic. As we see it, the poem thus suggests that the mouse (or rat), destroyed at the moment, has its place in the enduring heavenly scheme. Again, some readers take this to be so evidently absurd, or so disgusting that they believe Dickinson is satirizing the idea of a divinely governed universe; others find a tolerant pantheism.

The first two lines of the second stanza get us almost into a Walt Disney world of cute animals—here the mouse is "Snug" and it is able to "nibble all the day"—but in the final two lines the camera draws sharply back from the domestic scene and gives us a world of immense space and time, a world indifferent to ("unsuspecting" of) the mouse (and by implication indifferent to all of us). If there is any satire here, we think it is of persons who believe the "Cycles" are concerned with their existence, but we do not take these lines to be the fierce condemnation of the Judeo-Christian God that some readers take them to be.

The poem raises enough difficulties in itself, but you may want to ask students to compare it with Frost's "Design" (also in the text). Is Frost's "Design" a sort of restatement of Dickinson's "Papa above"? Or is Frost's poem something of a reply? On the Argument from Design, see also (in "A Collection of Poems") Addison's "Ode."

EMILY DICKINSON

Wild Nights—Wild Nights! (p. 737)

A reader tends to think of Emily Dickinson as the speaker of "Wild Nights" and therefore is perhaps shocked by the last stanza, in which a woman apparently takes on the phallic role of a ship mooring in a harbor. But perhaps the poem is spoken by a man. (In one of her poems the speaker says, "I am a rural man," in another the speaker refers to "my brown cigar," and in "A narrow fellow in the Grass"—included in our text—the speaker identifies himself as male in lines 11-12.)

Possibly we are superficial readers, but we don't attach to "Might I but moor—Tonight—/ In Thee!" the strong sexual associations that several critics have commented on. Some but not all assume that the image suggests male penetration. Albert Gelpi, in *The Tenth Muse* (1975), pp. 242 -43 says that "the sexual roles are blurred." He adds, "Something more subtle than an inversion of sexual roles is at work here, and the point is not that Emily Dickinson was homosexual, as Rebecca Patterson and John Cody have argued," but he doesn't clarify the point. (Patterson's discussion is in *The Riddle of Emily Dickinson* [1951]; Cody's is in *After Great Pain* [1971].) Paula Bennett, in *My Life a Loaded Gun* (1986), drawing on a discussion by L. Faderman, seems to reject the idea of a male speaker. She says that "the imagery of the poem, with its emphasis on entering rather than being entered, is... far more appropriate for one woman's experience of another than for a woman's experience with a man" (61). Christine Miller too insists that the speaker is a woman. In *Feminist Critics Read Emily Dickinson*, ed. Suzanne Juhasz (1983), Miller says that the speaker is a woman but she adds that "The woman is the ship that seeks to 'moor—Tonight—/ In Thee!'—an activity more representative of male than of female social behavior" (137). Our own simple view: a reader need not find an image of penetration in "moor;" rather, we think that in this poem the word suggests a longed-for security.

Is the poem sentimental? We don't think so, chiefly because it is brief, controlled, and (in "Tonight") it does not claim too much.

In *Explicator* 25 (January 1967), Item 44, James T. Connelly pointed out that in letter No. 332 (T. H. Johnson's edition, *Letters*, II, 463), Dickinson writes, "Dying is a wild Night and a new road." Looking at the poem in the light of this letter, Connelly concludes that "to die is to experience a wild night on a turbulent, surging sea. Only by plunging into this uncharted sea of Death can one at last reach the port of rest and calm. The poem, thus considered, is an apparent death wish: a personification and apostrophe to Death whose presence and company are paradoxically exhilarating luxury." We are unconvinced, partly because the poem speaks not of "a wild night" but of "Wild Nights," and we cannot see how the plural form lends itself to this reading.

TOPICS FOR CRITICAL THINKING AND WRITING

1. Probably "wild nights" refers chiefly to a storm outside of the lovers' room, but it can of course also describe their love. "Luxury" (from the Latin *luxuria,* which meant "excess" or "extravagance") in line 4 probably retains some of the meaning that it first had when it entered into English, "lust" or sensual enjoyment. What does the second stanza say about the nature of their love? How does the third stanza modify the idea?
2. What makes this lyric lyrical?
3. Do you think that the poem is sentimental? Explain.

EMILY DICKINSON

There's a certain Slant of light (p. 738)

The poem seems difficult to us, and any questions about it therefore lead to difficulties, but perhaps our fifth question, below, on the rhyme scheme, is fairly straightforward. Some students may recognize that metrically the poem is close to the "common meter" or "common measure" (abbreviated C. M. in hymnals) of a hymn. (C. M. can be defined thus: stanzas of four lines, the first and third in iambic tetrameter, the second and fourth in iambic trimeter, rhyming *abcb* or *abab.)* In fact no two stanzas in the poem are metrically identical (if we count the syllables of the first line of each stanza, we find seven, six or seven, six, and eight), but despite such variations, the meter and especially the rhyme scheme (*abab*) seem regular. The second and fourth lines of each stanza have five syllables, and these lines end with exact rhymes, though the first and third lines of each stanza rely less on rhyme than on consonance. The regularity of the rhyme scheme, especially in such short lines, is something of a tour de force, and (because it suggests a highly ordered world) it might seem more suited to a neat little poem with a comforting theme than to the poem Dickinson has given us. Further, since the meter and some of the rhymes might occur in a hymn ("Despair," "Air"; "breath," "Death"), there is an ironic contrast between the form (a hymn, that is, a poem celebrating God's goodness) and the content of the poem.

But what, in fact, is the content? And what is the "certain Slant of light" that, perceived on "Winter Afternoons," makes "Shadows—hold their breath"? No two readers seem to agree on the details, but perhaps we can offer a few inoffensive comments. Like Hopkins (cf. "God's Grandeur" [670]), Dickinson sees a divinity behind phenomena, but her nature-suffused-with-divinity differed greatly from his. "There's a certain Slant of light" begins with "light," which might suggest life and eternal happiness (think of Newman's "Lead, kindly light"), but soon becomes darker, and ends with "the look of Death." The ending is not really a surprise, however, since the "certain Slant of light" is seen on "Winter Afternoons," that is, a season when the year may be said to be dying and when light is relatively scarce, and a time of day when light will soon disappear.

This "Slant of light," we are told, "Oppresses, like the Heft / Of Cathedral Tunes." Surely "Oppresses" comes as a surprise. Probably most of us think that cathedral tunes (even funeral music) exalt the spirit rather than oppress it, and so most of us might have written something like, "That elevates, like the Lift / Of Cathedral Tunes." But of course most of us couldn't have written even this, since we would not have had the imagination to think of light in aural terms ("Tunes") and in terms of weight ("Heft").

In any case, a certain appearance in nature induces in the poet a sensation that requires such words as "Oppresses," "Hurt," "Despair," "affliction," "Shadows," and "Death." These words might appear in a traditional hymn, but, if so, the hymn would move toward the idea that God helps us to triumph over these adversities. Dickinson, however, apparently is saying that on these wintry afternoons the slant of light shining in the air gives us a "Heavenly Hurt," that is, it moves us to a painful consciousness of God and nature, and to a sense of isolation. In the final stanza presumably we are back to the "Winter Afternoons" of the first. Projecting herself into the surrounding world, the speaker personifies nature: "the Landscape listens"—but hears nothing further. (By the way, "listens" to or for what? A "Slant of light"? Again, as in the earlier comparison of light to "Cathedral Tunes," Dickinson uses synesthesia.) If during the moment when one perceives the light or "listens" there is no further insight, and certainly no amelioration of the "Heavenly Hurt," when "it goes" there is an intensification of despair, since one is left with "the look of Death." Is Dickinson evoking an image of the remote stare of a corpse? And is she suggesting that this stare corresponds to the paralyzed mental condition of those who have perceived the "Slant of light"?

Earlier in this brief discussion we contrasted Hopkins with Dickinson. But, as Charles R. Anderson points out in *Emily Dickinson's Poetry*, there is a connection between the two. The perception in this poem resembles Margaret's perception in "Spring and Fall" (542), where the child senses "the blight man was born for."

TOPICS FOR CRITICAL THINKING AND WRITING

1. In the first stanza, what kind or kinds of music does "Cathedral Tunes" suggest? In what ways might they (and the light to which they are compared) be oppressive?

2. In the second stanza, the effect on us of the light is further described. Try

to paraphrase Dickinson's lines, or interpret them. Compare your paraphrase or interpretation with that of a classmate or someone else who has read the poem. Are your interpretations similar? If not, can you account for some of the differences?

3. In the third stanza, how would you interpret "None may teach it"? Is the idea "No one can instruct (or tame) the light to be different"? Or "No one can teach us what we learn from the light"? Or do you have a different reading of this line?

4. "Death" is the last word of the poem. Rereading the poem, how early (and in what words or images) is a "death" suggested or foreshadowed?

5. Describe the rhyme scheme. Then, a more difficult business, try to describe the effect of the rhyme scheme. Does it work with or against the theme, or meaning, of the poem?

6. What is the relationship in the poem between the light as one might experience it in New England on a winter afternoon and the experience of despair? To put it crudely, does the light itself cause despair, or does Dickinson see the light as an image or metaphor for human despair? And how is despair related to death?

7. Overall, how would you describe the tone of the poem? Anguished? Serene? Resigned?

EMILY DICKINSON

I got so I could hear his name (p. 738)

This poem is not as well-known as others, but we think it is one of Dickinson's best, and it is one that students find very powerful. They respond to it, and are especially eager to probe its complexities, because they feel the immediacy of its subject. It is something that has happened to them, or that they fear might happen. One of our students in an American literature class said, "This is exactly what it feels like to have your heart broken."

The poem does express *that,* but it is also about somehow trying to recover from the pain. What measures might be taken to overcome a devastating loss? Dickinson is stunningly effective, we believe, in noting the physical closeness that the persons in her poem shared, and the wrenching experience of their separation—"all our Sinews tore." The detail about the letters is very powerful as well, for it describes precisely the terrible way we return to memories, to signs of the beloved's presence, when what we want is to get beyond them.

This is, then, a poem about feeling and confronting pain and seeking a means of self-control. In the final three stanzas, the speaker turns to God—though notice the distancing effect of "I think, they call it 'God'." Perhaps this higher force, outside the wounded self, might be able to heal it. Students find the last stanza somewhat obscure, and we agree. But the main thrust is clear enough: the speaker is uncertain whether any power exists that might aid her, and, if there is, whether this power would ever care about the pain felt by just one person. A good question to ask is how much or how little closure takes place in the final line. Does the speaker reconstitute, at least partially, her shattered self, through the process of articulating and working through, cathartically, her pain? Or is the poem the record of a pain that persists, that the speaker cannot find a remedy for?

Dickinson has legions of admirers, but in our experience, many students have trouble with her intense, gnomic, highly condensed verse. This, again, is a poem to which students do feel connected, and it is valuable as a point of entry into the study of Dickinson's life and work. See Richard B. Sewall, *The Life of Emily Dickinson* (2 vols., 1974), and Cynthia Griffin Wolff, *Emily Dickinson* (1986).

Two charged, self-dramatizing comments by Dickinson on herself, both from undated letters to the critic, editor, and journalist, Thomas Wentworth Higginson: "I had no portrait, now, but am small, like the Wren, and my Hair is bold, like the chestnut Bur, and my eyes, like the Sherry in the Glass, that the guest leaves"; and "I had no monarch in my life, and cannot rule myself; and when I try to organize, my little force explodes and leaves me bare and charred."

EMILY DICKINSON

The Soul Selects her own Society (p. 739)

Richard Sewall, in *Voices and Visions*, ed. Helen Vendler, calls this poem Dickinson's "most famous 'choice' poem" (72), and indeed he leaves the choice of its subject to the reader; it may be read as concerned with the choice of a lover, or a friend, or a kind of spiritual life. Even without being certain of the subject of this poem, one can sense how the form contributes to meaning. The even-numbered lines are shorter than the odd-numbered lines that precede them, and each even-numbered line ends emphatically with a monosyllable, thus contrasting with the previous lines with their feminine endings. And in the final stanza the short lines are even shorter (a mere two syllables each); the tight-lipped speaker leaves no doubt about the determination of the soul which has made a choice and now rejects all other suppliants, however noble. But details remain uncertain, and critics have not been so tight-lipped.

W. C. Jumper, in *Explicator* 29 (September 1970), Item 5, suggests that the soul (feminine because Latin *anima* is feminine) has a "divine Majority" because Thoreau had said in *The Duty of Civil Disobedience* that "any man more right than his neighbors, constitutes a majority of one." Jumper points out that the second stanza makes ironic use of two folktales, "The Querulous Princess" and "The King and the Beggar Maid." In the first of these tales, the wooers arrive in chariots, but the winner of her hand is he who will bow his head to enter through a low gate; in the second tale, the king kneels before a beggar maid and wins her. In "The Soul selects" the soul rejects two such humble wooers, having already made her choice.

The word "Valves" in the penultimate lines has especially disconcerted critics. *Explicator* 25 (April 1967), Item 8, suggests that it is connected with "Door" in line 2 via two old meanings: (1) the leaves of a double or folding door and (2) the halves of the shell of a bivalve such as an oyster, which closes its valve when disturbed and thus remains "like Stone." Sewall takes "Valves" to refer to a double door and says that "the line simply dramatizes further the action of line two" (73).

EMILY DICKINSON

This was a Poet—It is That (p. 739)

To say "This was a Poet" is perhaps to cause a reader to think that the speaker is contemplating the ashes or the grave of a poet, or perhaps a picture of a poet, but this idea is not developed. George E. Fortenberry in *Explicator* 35:3 (1977) reads the poem as a remark Dickinson is making "about a flower she has just plucked from beside her door, and as she smells it, thinks of it as a poet resurrected as a flower" (27). (We will return to Fortenberry's view in a moment.) In our experience, most readers take "This" to refer to a poem or a book of poems; the speaker has just read something, and now contemplates on the nature of the writer.

The first two stanzas form a single sentence, even though the second does not end with a period. At the end of the first line presumably we must supply the word "which," i.e. the poem that stands for the poet is that which distilled (extracted the essence of, stops from perishing) or "Arrested" (line 8, i.e. caught and holds for us to see) the amazing content of what seemed to be ordinary experience but what in fact is an experience that—we now see, via the poet's presentation—causes us to "wonder" (7), i.e. brings wonder into our lives. (Students might be invited to say what they think is the value of art. Our own view is pretty much what we take Dickinson to be saying here. One might also recall Conrad's words, quoted in the text in the casebook on *Heart of Darkness,* to the effect that the writer makes us "see," i.e. somehow makes us fully experience things we would otherwise be unaware of. Also relevant of course are Marianne Moore's "Poetry" and Archibald MacLeish's "Ars Poetica," both of which are in the text.)

The awe-struck wonder of the first two stanzas gives way, in the remainder of the poem, to a more agitated tone. (There are five dashes in the first two stanzas—two in the first stanza, and three in the second—but there are six dashes in the third stanza, and nine in the fourth stanza.) The idea of the third stanza seems to be this: We see our poverty when we see the poet's wealth as a revealer, a "Discloser." In the final stanza, "Portion" probably refers to the poet's wealth, and the idea is that the poet is so unaware of his or her wealth (priceless ability)—because so inherently richly endowed—that thievery would cause no loss to the poet; the poet stands outside of the world of the rest of us ("Exterior—to Time—")—immortal. In George E. Fortenberry's view, Dickinson "compares her own poverty of portion to that of the poet, who is so unconscious of his portion that the taking (robbing) of the flower 'could not harm.' The poet's fortune is exterior to time; thus he may be resurrected as a flower" (27).

For a very different (and, for us, difficult to follow interpretation), see E. Miller Burdick, *Emily Dickinson and the Life of Language.*

EMILY DICKINSON

I heard a Fly buzz—when I died (p. 740)

Dickinson's poem juxtaposes some conventional religious images ("that last Onset," "the King," "What portion of me be / Assignable") with the buzz of a fly, rather than with, say, choirs of angels, and so, as Charles R. Anderson suggests in *Emily Dickinson's Poetry,* "The King witnessed in his power is physical death, not God." Should one go further, and suggest that Death-as-fly equals putrefaction?

The last line of the poem ("I could not see to see") especially has attracted attention. Gerhard Friedrich *(Explicator* 13 [April 1955], Item 35) paraphrases it thus: "Waylaid by irrelevant, tangible, finite objects of little importance, I was no longer capable of that deeper perception which would clearly reveal to me the infinite spiritual reality." The fall into skepticism, Friedrich says, demonstrates the inadequacy of the earlier pseudostoicism. John Ciardi took issue with this interpretation and suggested *(Explicator* 14 [January 1956], Item 22) that the fly is "the last kiss of the world, the last buzz from life," reflecting "Emily's tremendous attachment to the physical world"; the final line, in his view, simply means, "And then there was no more of me, and nothing to see with."

The Todd-Higginson editions gave "round my form" for "in the Room" (2), "The eyes beside" for "The Eyes around" (5), "sure" for "firm" (6), "witnessed in his power" for "witnessed"—in the Room" (8), and "What portion of me / Could make assignable—and then" for "What portion of me be / Assignable—and then it was" (10-11). It is worth discussing with students the differences these changes make.

EMILY DICKINSON

This World is not Conclusion (p. 740)

First, a brief comment about Dickinson and religion. She clearly was not fond of the patriarchal deity of the Hebrew Bible. "Burglar! Banker—Father," she wrote of this deity, and in a note to Thomas Wentworth Higginson she says that the members of her family, except for herself, "address an Eclipse every morning—whom they call their Father." She seems to have been amused by preachers. She said, of one, that "the subject of perdition seemed to please him somehow." Still, in the words of Charles R. Anderson, in *Emily Dickinson's Poetry* (1960), no reader can doubt that she "faced creation with a primal sense of awe" (17). And, as Anderson and everyone else points out, the Bible was "one of her chief sources of imagery" (18).

Now for "This World is not Conclusion." The first two lines sound like the beginning of a hymn ("Conclusion" presumably means "ending," not "inference drawn"). The poem is not divided into stanzas by white spaces, but clearly it moves in units of four lines. The first four lines assert that although a world beyond our own is (like music) invisible, we strongly sense it. "Positive" in line 4 perhaps refers both to our conviction that it exists and also to its goodness.

Line 5 introduces a complication: "It beckons, and it baffles." Although the rest of the stanza (i.e., lines 6-8) seems to affirm the initial confident (positive) assertion, it also raises doubts in the reader, since it dismisses "Philosophy" and "Sagacity," and it characterizes life (or is it death?) as a "Riddle."

Lines 9-12 seem more positive. They remind us that although human experience "puzzles Scholars," martyrs have given their lives to affirm religious faith, to affirm (in the words of the first line) that "This World is not Conclusion."

Lines 13-16, however, present "Faith" in a somewhat less heroic light: "Faith slips—and laughs, and rallies—Blushes, if any see." Surely this is in a much lower key than "Men have borne / Contempt of Generations," a couple of lines earlier. The enduring power of faith is still affirmed (Faith "rallies"), but in "slips" and "Blushes, if any see" we seem to be presented with a rather adolescent world. Further, the last two lines of the stanza (15-16) similarly diminish Faith, showing it clutching after "a twig of Evidence," and inquiring of a "Vane" (a weather-vane, a most unstable thing). Perhaps, too, "Vane" hints at emptiness, insubstan-tiality (Latin, *vanitas*).

The final four lines at first seem more affirmative. They begin with a strong assertion that calls up a picture of a vigorously gesticulating preacher, and they reintroduce imagery of music (now "Strong Hallelujahs roll"), but these lines at the same time are unconvincing, or, rather, almost comic. A reader may find in the preacher's abundant gestures a lack of genuine conviction. (One thinks of the marginal note in the politician's speech: "Argument weak; shout here.") The "Strong Hallelujahs" may strike a reader as less potent than the "Music" that was "positive" in lines 3-4. Are the gestures and the hallelujahs "Narcotics" that don't quite work, that is that don't quite convince us of the pious forthright assertion that "This World is not Conclusion"? Yet the poem ends with the word "soul"; if "Much Gesture, from the Pulpit" reveals a preach-er who is not wholly convincing, we nevertheless cannot therefore lapse into the belief that this world is conclusion. Something "nibbles at the soul."

TOPICS FOR CRITICAL THINKING AND WRITING

1. Given the context of the first two lines, what do you think "Conclusion" means in the first line?

2. Although white spaces here are not used to divide the poem into stanzas, the poem seems to be constructed in units of four lines each. Summarize each four-line unit in a sentence or two.

3. Compare your summaries with those of a classmate. If you substantially disagree, reread the poem to see if, on reflection, one or the other of you seems in closer touch with the poem. Or does the poem (or some part of it) allow for two very different interpretations?

4. In the first four lines the speaker seems (to use a word from line 4) quite "positive." Do some or all of the following stanzas seem less positive? If so, which—and what makes you say so?

5. How do you understand "Much Gesture, from the Pulpit" (line 17)? Would you agree with a reader who said that the line suggests a *lack* of deep conviction? Explain.

EMILY DICKINSON

I like to see it lap the Miles (p. 741)

Whoever first called a train an "iron horse" had the gift of the poet, but Dickinson goes much further in "I like to see it lap the Miles," catching the beast's energy and (in the last three lines) its docility. She is interested in the sound and sight of the train (these are playfully set forth with lots of alliteration, beginning with "like... lap... lick"), but she displays no interest in the train as a symbol of progress, no interest in people or goods getting anywhere. Indeed, her train ends up—for all its rushing and roaring—"At its own stable door."

Charles Dickens, in *American Notes* (1842), describes a train ride. You may want to ask your students to compare Dickens's account with Dickinson's.

On it whirls headlong, dives through the woods again, emerges in the light, clatters over frail arches, rumbles upon the heavy ground, shoots beneath a wooden bridge, which intercepts the light for a second like a wink, suddenly awakens all the slumbering echoes in the main street of a large town, and dashes on haphazard, pellmell, neck-or-nothing, down the middle of the road. There—with mechanics working at their trades, and people leaning from their doors and windows, and boys flying kites and playing marbles, and men smoking, and women talking, and children crawling, and pigs burrowing, and unaccustomed horses plunging and rearing, close to the very rails—there—on, on, on—tears the mad dragon of an engine with its train of cars; scattering in all directions a shower of burning sparks from its wood fire; screeching, hissing, yelling, panting; until at last the thirsty monster stops beneath a covered way to drink, the people cluster around, and you have time to breathe again.

EMILY DICKINSON

Because I could not stop for Death (p. 741)

In Dickinson's "Because I could not stop for Death," the fact that a grave is suggested in lines 17-20 eludes many students; the reference to the grave contributes to toughening the poem. This stanza, by the way, is a good example of the closeness of some metaphors to riddles, a point worth discussing in class. Allen Tate, in a famous essay, praised the poem because "we are not told what to think." J. J. McGann, rightly taking issue with Tate points out that "the message about the benevolence of Death is plain enough." McGann also takes issue with the widespread idea that in this poem death is a "gentlemanly suitor." He argues, on the contrary, that since the penultimate line speaks of "horses," Dickinson is talking not about a suitor—who would drive only one horse—but about an undertaker, who is driving a hearse. (McGann's essay originally appeared in *New Literary History*, 12 [1981], and is reprinted in *Literary Theories in Praxis* [1987], ed. Shirley F. Staton.) Selections from a number of commentaries (including, among others, Allen Tate, *Reactionary Essays;* Yvor Winters, *In Defense of Reason,* and Richard Chase, *Emily Dickinson*) are collected in *Fourteen by Emily Dickinson,* ed. Thomas M. Davis. See also Clark Griffith, *The Long Shadow,* pp. 128-34, and Charles R. Anderson, *Emily Dickinson's Poetry,* pp. 241-466.

TOPICS FOR CRITICAL THINKING AND WRITING

1. Characterize death as it appears in lines 1-8.
2. What is the significance of the details and their arrangement in the third stanza? Why "strove" rather than "played" (line 9)? What meaning does "Ring" (line 10) have? Is "Gazing Grain" better than "Golden Grain"?
3. The "House" in the fifth stanza is a sort of riddle. What is the answer? Does this stanza introduce an aspect of death not present—or present only very faintly—in the rest of the poem? Explain.
4. Evaluate this statement about the poem (from Yvor Winters's *In Defense of Reason*): "In so far as it concentrates on the life that is being left behind, it is wholly successful; in so far as it attempts to experience the death to come, it is fraudulent, however exquisitely."

EMILY DICKINSON

A narrow Fellow in the Grass (p. 742)

"Fellow" (and the pronouns "Him" and "His," rather than "it" and "its") and "rides" in the first stanza help to assimilate the snake to the human world, as does "comb" in the second stanza. In these two stanzas there is some emphasis on the unexpectedness of the snake. He is "sudden" but not menacing. And in the beginning of the third stanza he seems almost an eccentric neighbor: "He likes a Boggy Acre." In the fourth stanza the reference to a whiplash introduces a more threatening note; "Nature's People" in the next stanza seems to bring us back to the comfortable world of the first stanza, but with the last line of the poem ("Zero at the Bone") there is communicated a terror that indicates a response to the snake as supremely hostile. (The snake is, after all, a traditional image of our satanic enemy.) The contrast between "a transport / Of cordiality" (which carries a sense of warmth, that is, warm-heartedness, via *cor,* heart) and the coldness of "Zero at the Bone" could hardly be greater.

Karl Keller, in a provocative book about Emily Dickinson, *The Only Kangaroo among the Beauty,* says (268) that the poem "manages to make Freud trite." Keller says that Dickinson's "tighter breathing / And Zero at the Bone" indicate that "she finds her genitals alarmed," and that "she is shocked and attracted by the male erection ('His notice sudden is')." Keller patently misreads the poem when he says, "Her own sexual desires are she says very strongly aroused: she feels a transport / Of cordiality.'" Not so; the poem says that for "Several of Nature's People" she feels that transport "but" for this fellow she feels "Zero at the Bone."

Dickinson complained when the third line was printed with a question mark at its end. Apparently "did you not" is less a question than a tagged-on conversational filler like "don't you know" and a question mark causes too long and too strong a pause. Yet another point about the punctuation: Lines 11-16 describing the boy (the speaker is a boy not Emily Dickinson) stooping to pick up what he thinks is a whiplash but what is in fact a snake that disappears are unpunctuated (until the end of 16) and thus suggestive of the speed of the event.

TOPICS FOR CRITICAL THINKING AND WRITING

1. Many of Dickinson's poems are rather like riddles. In this poem who or what is the "narrow Fellow in the Grass"?
2. How would you describe the speaker of this poem? What relationship does the speaker seem to establish with the reader?
3. In lines 17-20 Dickinson refers to "Several of Nature's People." Who or what might these be in Amherst in the later nineteenth century? Check "transport" and "cordiality" in a dictionary to see which meanings you think are especially relevant.
4. Why does Dickinson speak of the snake as "him" rather than "it" and of the animal world as "Nature's creatures"?
5. If you have read Lawrence's "Snake," write an essay of 500 words indicating the *purposes* of Dickinson and Lawrence. Include a discussion of how effectively each poet fulfills these purposes.

EMILY DICKINSON

Further in Summer than the Birds (p. 742)

We take the opening words "Further in Summer" to mean that the crickets chirping in the grass are more advanced in their span of life (nearer to autumn and winter and death) than are birds. Moreover their song is heard later in summer and thus they remind us of the imminent end of the season. The song is pathetic partly because the creatures are so small but probably chiefly because it reminds us of the passing of time and losses and of our consequent increasing loneliness. The final stanza provides another look. The first two lines of this stanza may mean that no disturbance as yet diminishes the beauty (no grace has been remitted there is no "Furrow on the Glow" of summer) but we are somewhat inclined to take them as meaning: "Do not give back (reject) grace; the moment is undisturbed—that is continue, to experience the blessedness of the moment. If this reading is right, "Yet" in the next line does not quite mean "but"; rather it means (we think) "still," "even so."

Charles Anderson discusses the poem at some length in *Emily Dickinson's Poetry.*

TOPICS FOR CRITICAL THINKING AND WRITING

1. Paraphrase—put into your own words—the first line.
2. What is the "minor Nation," whose pathetic sounds (here said to be a celebration of the Mass) are heard in the grass?
3. In this context, what does "Grace" (line 6) mean?
4. Does "Enlarging Loneliness" (line 8) mean "making loneliness greater," or does it mean "setting loneliness free," that is, releasing us from loneliness?
5. Is Dickinson saying that nature teaches us that all of creation shares in God's grace? Or is she saying—especially in the last stanza—that we must give up our imagined idea that Christian grace is found in nature? Or is she perhaps saying something else?

EMILY DICKINSON

Tell All the Truth but tell it slant (p. 743)

A student once brought up, by way of comparison, Polonius's

> And thus do we of wisdom and of reach,
> With windlasses and with assays of bias,
> By indirections find directions out. (*Hamlet* 2.1.64-66)

The last line especially seems to have affinities with Dickinson's first line, but the thrust of the two passages is fundamentally different. Polonius, worried about the behavior of his son Laertes, is sending Reynaldo to find out if Laertes has been misbehaving. He tells Reynaldo to slander Laertes, to see if Reynaldo's hearers deny the charges. Polonius thus is advocating deceit, whereas Dickinson is saying that because truth is too bright for our "infirm Delight," if we want to communicate, we must use indirection.

For Dickinson, the truth *is* splendid—it does "dazzle"—but we can perceive this splendor only after we have become accustomed to it, and we arrive at this condition "gradually."

The word "slant" nicely plays against "Circuit," and on rereading it may be taken to anticipate the word "lightning," which is often represented by a diagonal line. In any case, one of the charms of the poem is the homely comparison in lines 5-6, where the need to tell the truth "slant" is compared to offering "explanation kind" to children who presumably have been frightened by lightning. Telling the truth "slant" or "in Circuit" is not an attempt to deceive, but to be "kind."

An extant draft of the poem shows that Dickinson contemplated two possible changes, *bold* for bright in line 3, and *moderately* for gradually in line 7.

EMILY DICKINSON

A Route of Evanescence (p. 743)

An old discussion, Grover Smith's in *Explicator* 8 (1949-50), Item 54, seems to us to remain the most interesting. Smith points out that the phrase "A route of Evanescence" is "a metonymy equating the bird with its own path across the field of vision." Smith goes on:

> The visual effect is the converse of that obtained photographically by multiple rapid-exposures of a moving object on a single plate; here the poet describes not the simultaneous presence but the simultaneous vanishing of the bird at every point....

Speaking of the "revolving Wheel"—the wheel-like optical illusion produced by the rapid up and down motion of the wings—Smith points out that Dickinson's reference to the iridescent color on the bird's head and hack uses synesthesia ("A Resonance of Emerald"). He also says that Dickinson uses onomatopoeia in this line and the next line ("A Rush of Cochineal"), though not every reader will agree that onomatopoeia occurs in "A Resonance of Emerald."

Equally challenging is his assertion that in the final two lines beside the image of the bird "is implicit that of a speeding railway train, the mail and express, and also that of the more common kind of mail—a letter.... A train travels upon a 'route,' it is borne along by many a 'revolving wheel,' its sound is a 'resonance' and a 'rush,' and on it people 'ride.'" We confess that we don't see this image in the lines, and Smith himself is apparently a bit uneasy with the idea, since he himself points out that of course no train crosses the sea from Tunis, and no "easy Morning's Ride" will get us there.

Other points: the words emerald, cochineal (associated chiefly with North Africa), and Tunis bring the precious and the remote into the familiar garden. (By the way, we have been told that when hummingbirds leave New England they go to Mexico, not to North Africa.)

One of Dickinson's copies of the poem, according to Millicent Todd Bingham's *Ancestor's Brocades* (1945), p. 37, included several alternatives for "revolving" in line 4: *delusive, dissembling, dissolving,* and *renewing.* (The present location of this manuscript is not known.)

TOPICS FOR CRITICAL THINKING AND WRITING

1. Dickinson in her letters refers to this poem as "A Humming Bird." What is she getting at in line 2?
2. Dickinson uses synesthesia (the description of a sensory impression in terms of another sense) in "A Resonance of Emerald." What is the point of describing a color ("Emerald") in terms of sound ("Resonance")?
3. In line 7, why is "Tunis" preferable to, say, "New York"?

EMILY DICKINSON

Those—dying, then (p. 744)

The faith of her ancestors is, Dickinson apparently feels, no longer possible, but it serves to enrich behavior. An *ignis fatuus* (a phosphorescent light—caused by gases emitted by rotting organic matter—that hovers over a swamp) presumably resembles, however weakly, the beautiful flames of heaven and the demonic flames of hell. It is only a will-o'-the-wisp, but at least it is *some*thing. The image of amputation is shocking, but it can be paralleled in the Bible, for example by "And if thy right eye offend thee, pluck it out, and cast it from thee. . . . and if thy right hand offend thee, cut it off, and cast it from thee" (Matthew 5:29-30).

TOPICS FOR CRITICAL THINKING AND WRITING
1. In a sentence or two, state the point of the poem.
2. Is the image in line 4 in poor taste? Explain.
3. What is an *ignis fatuus?* In what ways does it connect visually with traditional images of hell and heaven?

EMILY DICKINSON

Apparently with no surprise (p. 744)

As in most nature poems, nature is humanized—but with a difference. If a flower is Wordsworthian in being at "play," the frost is not: It is a "blonde Assassin"; blonde because it is white, and the fact that this color is usually associated with innocence makes the personification the more shocking. (See Frost's white spider in "Design," in our text). Note, too, that "at its play" can go with the frost as well as with the flower, in which case the frost is only playing, but happens to play too vigorously with a destructive (but unlamented) result. And still more shocking, at least on first reading, is the fact that God (like the sun) approves. God stands behind the world, approving of the accidental destruction of beauty and joy. One could, by agile philosophizing, justify the necessary destruction of beauty and joy—but the "accidental" destruction? The sun, as usual, measured off the days, but mysteriously withheld its warmth and allowed the frost to do its work. The flower, the sun, God, all seem indifferent; only human beings are shocked.

"Apparently," of course, has two almost opposed meanings: (1) evidently, clearly; (2) seemingly (but not really), as in "The magician apparently vanished into thin air." So the lack of surprise, and the impassivity of the sun and the approval of God *may* be unreal; maybe this is just the way things look or seem, not the way things really are. After all, it is only apparent (seemingly), not real, that flowers are "happy" and that they "play."

TOPICS FOR CRITICAL THINKING AND WRITING
1. What is the implication of the action described in lines 1-3?
2. Why is the frost's power called "accidental"?
3. Why is the assassin called "blonde"? What does this word contribute to the poem?
4. Is the last line shocking? Explain.

ROBERT FROST

Although in the text we give some of Frost's own comments on his poetry, here we want to quote two additional short comments. The first, from Frost's preface to his collection entitled *Aforesaid* (1954), is about the best way to read a poem:

> A poem is best read in the light of all the other poems ever written. We read A the better to read B (we have to start somewhere; we may get very little out of A). We read B the better to read C, C the better to read D, D the better to go back and get something more out of A. Progress is not the aim, but circulation. The thing is to get among the poems where they hold each other apart in their places as the stars do.

The second passage we want to quote, from a letter to Louis Untermeyer, 1 January 1917, is a bit more cryptic. We read it to students when we begin studying Frost's work, and we reread it occasionally during the course of the study:

> You get more credit for thinking if you restate formulae or cite the cases that fall in easily under formulae, but all the fun is outside saying things that suggest formulae that won't formulate—that almost but don't quite formulate. I should like to be so subtle at this game as to seem to the casual person altogether obvious. The casual person would assume that I meant nothing or else I came near enough meaning something he was familiar with to mean it for all practical purposes. Well well well.

A "Voices and Visions" videocassette of Robert Frost is available from Longman. An audiocasseste of Robert Frost reading is also available from Longman.

ROBERT FROST

The Pasture (p. 747)

"The Pasture" is a rare example of a poem that uses no figures of speech—no metaphors, no similes. Every word can be taken literally. But the entire poem is a sort of figure. By placing "The Pasture" at the opening of his *Collected Poems* Frost allows us to read it as a figure; the invitation to accompany the speaker on a trip to the pasture can be read as an invitation to accompany the poet on a trip to the poet's work—his poems.

Reuben Brower, in *The Poetry of Robert Frost,* rightly observes that in this poem "there is not a word or an order of words we might not use in talking," and that

> by using the commonest of leave-takings and a familiar phrase of artless begging, Frost balances perfectly the claims of both song and speech. Through the concealing art of this and other lines he aptly doubles his meanings, extending an invitation to seeing and doing country things while inviting his companion and the reader to a kind of poetry and to love. (11)

In Daniel Smythe's *Robert Frost Speaks,* Frost offers a comment on this poem:

I have always had an interest in that word, "confusion." I don't think I really thought of it in this poem, but it could be thought of in connection with it. I wrote it a long time ago. I never had a greater pleasure than on coming on a neglected spring in a pasture in the woods. We clean out the leaves, then wait by to watch the uncloudiness displace the cloudiness. That is always a pleasure to me; it might be taken as a figure of speech. It is my place to see clarity come out of talk and confusion. You didn't need to know that was in the poem. But now you see that was the way it was used. (56-57)

ROBERT FROST

Mending Wall (p. 748)

Some critics applaud the neighbor in Frost's "Mending Wall," valuing his respect for barriers. For an extreme version, see Robert Hunting, "Who Needs Mending?" *Western Humanities Review* 17 (Winter 1963): 88-89. The gist of this faction is that the neighbor wisely realizes—as the speaker does not—that individual identity depends on respect for boundaries. Such a view sees the poem as a Browningesque dramatic monologue like "My Last Duchess," in which the self-satisfied speaker unknowingly gives himself away.

Richard Poirier, in *Robert Frost*, makes the interesting point that it is not the neighbor (who believes that "good fences make good neighbors") who initiates the ritual of mending the wall; rather, it is the speaker: "I let my neighbor know beyond the hill." Poirier suggests that "if fences do not 'make good neighbors,' the *making* of fences can," for it makes for talk—even though the neighbor is hopelessly taciturn. For a long, judicious discussion of the poem, see John C. Kemp, *Robert Frost: The Poet as Regionalist* (1979).

TOPICS FOR CRITICAL THINKING AND WRITING
1. Compare and contrast the speaker and the neighbor.
2. Notice that the speaker, not the neighbor, initiates the business of repairing the wall (12). Why do you think he does this?
3. Write an essay of 500 words telling of an experience in which you came to conclude that "good fences make good neighbors." Or tell of an experience that led you to conclude that fences (they can be figurative fences, of course) are detrimental.

ROBERT FROST

The Wood Pile (p. 749)

The poem contrasts a human being who "can forget his handiwork" because he lives for "turning to fresh tasks," with nature, a "frozen swamp" that is "Too much alike to mark or name a place by;" the swamp is not even a "here," but only something that tells the speaker he is "far from home." Nature is nothing in itself—or rather, nothing meaningful to humans—until a human gives it meaning; in this poem, meaning is imposed on it by the person who built the woodpile. And even though the wood is not burning in the fireplace, it nevertheless has been made into something coherent, and it shows the mark of a human as it rots and "warm[s] the frozen swamp as best it could." Nature, then, needs a human's collaboration, and, conversely, a human needs nature's collaboration, for nature completes what a human has abandoned. On this last point, notice that "Clematis / Had wound strings round and round it like a bundle"—though the line also suggests that nature is reclaiming from humans what is hers. For an excellent discussion of the poem, see Richard Poirier, *Robert Frost.*

TOPICS FOR CRITICAL THINKING AND WRITING

1. What is the contrast that Frost makes between human beings and nature?
2. What does he say about the relationship between human beings and nature?

ROBERT FROST

The Road Not Taken (p. 750)

The diverging roads are pretty similar; the speaker chose the one less worn, as "having perhaps the better claim," but three times we are told that the difference was negligible: "just as fair"; "Though as for that, the passing there / Had worn them really about the same"; "equally." It is important to notice that although a reason is given for the choice ("it was grassy and wanted wear"), we are led to doubt that there really was a clear basis for choosing. Certainly there is no moral basis. Moreover, we may feel that had the speaker chosen the other path, the ending of the poem would have been the same; that is, he would remember the alternative path and would fantasize that he might someday return to take it, and would at the same time know that he would not relearn. And so he would find that it too "has made all the difference." The sigh imagined in the last stanza is not to be taken as an expression of regret for a life wasted, but as a semicomic picture of the speaker envisioning himself as an old man, wondering how things would have turned out if he had made a different choice—which is not at all to imply a rejection of the choice he did make.

Students are likely to take the poem too seriously, and to press it too hard for a moral, for example, that Frost says we should choose the "less traveled," the unconventional, path. We have tried to suggest that the first two lines of the last stanza are playful, a reading that is supported by a letter in which Frost spoke of the poem as "my rather private jest." (See *American Literature* 50 [November 1978]: 478-79.) As Lawrance Thompson says in his introduction to *Selected Letters of Robert Frost* (1964), p. xiv, Frost wrote the poem after returning to the United States from England. In England, his friend and fellow poet Edward Thomas liked to take Frost on woodland walks, and then fretted that perhaps he should have chosen a different path, which would have revealed different flora. This bit of biography does not prove that the poem cannot refer to moral choice, but it may help students to ease up on the highly moral interpretations that many are prone to make.

TOPICS FOR CRITICAL THINKING AND WRITING

1. Frost called the poem "The Road Not Taken." Why didn't he call it "The Road Taken"? Which is the better title, and why?
2. Consider a choice that you made, perhaps almost unthinkingly, and offer your reflections on how your life might have been different if you had chosen otherwise. Are you now regretful, pleased, puzzled, indifferent, or what? (For instance, what seemed to be a big choice may, in retrospect, have been a decision of no consequence.)
3. Suppose that someone said to you that the poem is simply about walking in the woods and choosing one road rather than another. In an essay of 250 words, set forth your response. (You may, of course, agree with the view, in which case you will offer supporting evidence.)
4. In a paragraph discuss whether it would make any difference if instead of "yellow" in the first line the poet had written "bright green" (or "dark green").
5. Why do you think that Frost says he (or, more strictly, the speaker of the poem) will later be telling this story "with a sigh"? Set forth your response in a paragraph.

ROBERT FROST

The Telephone (p. 750)

A student of ours, Jane Takayanagi, wrote an entry in a journal that we think is worth reprinting. In our opinion she is right in seeing that a quarrel has precipitated the speaker's walk ("When I was just as far as I could walk / From here today"), but it is hard to convince someone who doesn't sense it. In any case, here is the entry from her journal:

As the poem goes on, we learn that the man wants to be with the woman, but it starts by telling us that he walked as far away from her as he could. He doesn't say why, but I think from the way the woman speaks later in the poem, they had a fight and he walked out. Then, when he stopped to rest, he thought he heard her voice. He really means that he was thinking of her and he was hoping she was thinking of him. So he returns, and he tells her he heard her calling him, but he pretends he heard her call him through a flower on their window sill. He can't admit that _he_ was thinking about her.

This seems very realistic to me; when someone feels a bit ashamed, it's sometimes hard to admit that you were wrong, and you want the other person to tell you that things are OK anyhow. And judging from line 7, when he says "Don't say I didn't," it seems that she is going to interrupt him by denying it. She is still angry, or maybe she doesn't want to make up too quickly But he wants to pretend that _she_ called him back so when he says, "Do you remember what it was you said?" she won't admit that she _was_ thinking of him, and she says, "First tell me what it was you thought you heard." She's testing him a little. So he goes on, with the business about flowers as telephones, and he says "someone" called him. He understands that she doesn't want to be pushed into forgiving him, so he backs off. Then she is willing to admit that she did think about him, but still she doesn't quite admit it. She is too proud to say openly that she wants him back but does say, "I _may_ have thought as much." And then, since they both have preserved their dignity and also have admitted that they care about the other, he can say, "Well, so I came. "

Two other (small) points: (1) Why in line 11 does Frost speak of having "driven a bee away"? We think that maybe in a tiny way it shows the speaker's willingness to exert himself and to face danger. It's a miniature ordeal, a test of his mettle. (2) In line 17 the speaker says, "I heard it as I bowed." Of course "bowed" rhymes with "aloud," but putting aside the need for a rhyme, surely the phrase is better than, say, "I heard it as I stood," since it conveys a gesture of humility.

ROBERT FROST

The Vanishing Red (p. 751)

This must be one of Frost's most terrifying poems, because, in our reading of it, Frost implies that in the human heart there is a sort of maniacal hatred of what now is called The Other. He is not saying we all would kill those who are different from us, but he is saying that if we were the Miller's contemporaries, we might not judge him as we now do:

> It's too long a story to go into now.
> You'd have to have been there and lived it.
> Then you wouldn't have looked on it as just a matter
> Of who began it between the two races.

That is, for the modern reader, it seems to be a matter of who first did what to whom. Did the white people injure the Indians, so that any counterattacks by Indians are more or less excusable, or did the Indians savagely (!) attack the new immigrants. (We might remember that although we now speak of "Native Americans," these people in fact were not native to the continent; they migrated to this hemisphere, but a good deal earlier than the whites did. And while we are remembering things, we might also remember that until recently it was regularly said that when Indians killed whites it was a "massacre," but when whites killed Indians it was it was a "battle.")

Well, why isn't it a matter "Of who began it"? Or, to put the question a bit differently, why did the Miller kill the Red Man? In lines 14-18 Frost gives us as much of an answer as he will give:

> Some guttural exclamation of surprise
> The Red Man gave in poking about the mill
> Over the great big thumping shuffling mill-stone
> Disgusted the Miller physically as coming
> From one who had no right to be heard from.

"Some guttural exclamation of surprise." About what? About the Miller's prices? About the Miller's behavior? About the way the mill worked? Frost doesn't tell us—because it doesn't matter. What matters is that the Red Man expressed something and he was a person "who had no right to be heard from," in the Miller's opinion. The Red Man was, like a person, acting we might say, a non-person, and here he was, acting uppity. By the way, when the poem was originally published in *The Craftsman* (October, 1916), what is now line 18 ("From one who had no right to be heard from") was not one line but two:

> From a person who the less he attracted
> Attention to himself you would have thought the better.

The early version is interesting, but it does not convey the intensity and the craziness of the revised version, where Frost does what he can to tell us of the Miller's reason for his act: The Indian had "no right" to open his mouth.

And so the Miller decides to show John the wheel pit. (By the way, the Indian is named, but not the Miller, almost as though the Miller is not meant to be a single person.) The Miller shows John "The water in desperate straits"—in a moment John himself will be in desperate straits—then closes the trap door, whose jangling ring serves as a sort of funeral knell. Obviously self-satisfied, the Miller "said something to a man with a meal-sack / That the man with the meal-sack didn't catch—then." Frost doesn't tell us what the Miller said, but we can go back to lines 6-8, where Frost does tell us what the Miller's face seemed to say. And we can easily imagine that the last line of the poem ("Oh, yes, he showed John the wheel pit all right") is what he may have said to the man with the meal-sack. Frost tells us that whatever it was he said, it was something that the man "didn't catch—then." The "then," preceded by a dash, implies that later the man *did* get the words. Presumably at some point the Red Man was missed, perhaps the man with the meal-sack said he had seen him at the mill—and then, suddenly, the significance of the words became clear.

But we are offering mere conjectures about the narrative, about what the Miller's motive was, about what he said, about what made the man with the meal-sack later "catch" the meaning of the words. What is *not* conjecture, however, is the irony of the title. "The Vanishing Red" sounds as though the Red Man did some sort of magic trick and made himself disappear into thin air. The term (or a variant such as "The Vanishing Indian" or "The Vanishing Race") was of course a euphemism; white society liked to believe that the Indians simply faded away, not that they were killed, or that they died of diseases brought by whites. Why, according to the old mythology, did Indians "vanish"? They "vanished" because whether they were imagined as noble savages (persons living close to nature, filled with natural goodness) or imagined as diabolical figures (persons lacking the virtues of civilization), they lived in an unchanging world, a world that did not participate in progress (technology). When technology came to dominate the land—when their world was superseded—they simply vanished. Such was the comforting view held by many whites. Frost gives us quite another view of the vanishing act. (We will return to this issue in a moment.)

The poem is unusual among Frost's work not only in its subject matter but also in its form. We are not thinking so much of the fact that the lines do not rhyme—Frost wrote a fair amount of blank verse—but of the fact that the pentameter is only loosely iambic. One other point: In a conversation, Frost once mentioned that he never read this poem publicly. He put it in a class with "Out,

Out" (the poem about the boy who loses his hand while operating a buzz-saw) something too terrifying to inflict on a captive audience.

A few more words about the title, and about the representation of American Indians. First, a word about the word "Indian." It is Eurocentric, of course, and in recent years it has been somewhat displaced by "Native American," but many American Indians still prefer to call themselves Indians; in fact, it is our impression that whites are more likely than Indians to use "Native American." Second, whatever term is used, it probably erodes important ethnic and individual differences. One hears generalizations about Native Americans (or Indians) that would be inconceivable in speaking of "Europeans." For instance, in *The West as America* (1991), ed. William H. Truettner—a book that accompanied a highly controversial exhibition of art— the authors are very careful to indicate their views that the Indians were far superior to the whites who maltreated them, but we get such sweeping, unsupported comments as this: "Individuality, material status, and vanity. . . [are] all notions less highly regarded in Indian culture [than in white culture]" (149). It might come as a surprise to, say, the Sioux, the Navaho, the Pawnee, and the Seneca, that they have much in common. Still, *The West as America* is an invaluable resource for images of Indians.

Another resource is Edward S. Curtis's massive collection of photographs, *The North American Indian.* The first picture in the first volume (1907—only nine years before Frost's poem) is called *The Vanishing Race.* It shows a line of Indians riding from the foreground into a dark background—vanishing. It is conveniently reproduced as #56 in Christopher M. Lyman, *The Vanishing Race and Other Illusions* (1982).

ROBERT FROST

The Oven Bird (p. 751)

Whether or not one has ever heard an ovenbird, the idea that its song is exceptionally unmelodious is clearly suggested in lines 4, 6, and 10, where we get "he says" rather than "he sings." In case a reader missed the point while reading the first ten lines, Frost makes it explicit in line 12: "he knows in singing not to sing." Notice, too, other ways in which Frost deemphasizes the bird as a singer: The ovenbird "*makes* the solid tree trunks sound again," "he *knows*," and "he *frames*" a question.

Although Frost says in the opening line that everyone has heard the ovenbird, he carefully educates the reader who has not heard it, explaining that it is heard in the interval between "the early petal-fall / When pear and cherry bloom went down in showers" and "that other fall we name the fall." It is midsummer when leaves are abundant, but they are "old," and "the highway dust is over all." This time of stasis is no time for the usual sort of birdsong.

Ask your students how many of them have ever heard an ovenbird. (In some parts of the country few, if any, students will have heard it. By the way, the North American ovenbird is not a true ovenbird; i.e., it does not belong to the family Furnariidae, which contains birds who build elaborate domed nests of clay or who dig tunnels in the ground. The North American ovenbird is a wood warbler [Parulidae] which looks like a miniature thrush.) You might ask your students, too, after some discussion of "The Oven Bird," if they believe that in order to enjoy the poem one must have heard an ovenbird. It's our guess that Frost adequately conveys the bird's song, partly in that stressed, unexpected "Loud" at the beginning of line 2 (it gains an even greater weight by being followed by a comma), and partly in the repetition of "mid" in this line ("mid-summer," "mid-wood") there is a suggestion of the repetition in a bird's song. Notice, too, that this line almost defies scansion; certainly it can't be called predominantly iambic. The poet, like the ovenbird, "knows in singing not to sing." Line 9 ("And comes that other fall we name the fall") sounds flat, and one isn't certain about how much stress to put on "we," "name," and "fall."

ROBERT FROST

Stopping by Woods on a Snowy Evening (p. 752)

On "Stopping by Woods," see John Lynen, *The Pastoral Art of Robert Frost,* and *Frost: Centennial Essays,* ed. Jac L. Tharpe. We number ourselves among the readers who see in the poem a longing for death ("frozen lake," "darkest evening of the year," "The woods are lovely, dark and deep" seem to support this view), but that is not what the poem is exclusively about. If there is a momentary longing for death in the poem, there is also the reassertion of the will to face the tasks of living. As Frost put it, at the Bread Loaf Writers' Conference in 1960, "People are always trying to find a death wish in that poem. But there's a life wish there—he goes on, doesn't he?"

Frost reads the poem in *Robert Frost Reading His Own Poems* (Record No. 1, EL LCB, 1941), distributed by the National Council of Teachers of English.

TOPICS FOR CRITICAL THINKING AND WRITING

1. As the manuscript indicates, line 5 originally read: "The steaming horses think it queer." Line 7 read: "Between a forest and a lake." Which version do you prefer? Why?
2. The rhyming words in the first stanza can be indicated by aaba; the second stanza picks up the *b* rhyme: *bbcb.* Indicate the rhymes for the third stanza. For the fourth. Why is it appropriate that the rhyme scheme differs in the fourth stanza?
3. Hearing that the poem had been interpreted as a "death poem," Frost said, "I never intended that, but I did have the feeling it was loaded with ulteriority." What "ulteriority" is implicit? How is the time of day and year significant? How does the horse's attitude make a contrast with the speaker's?

ROBERT FROST

The Aim Was Song (p. 752)

The poem offers a playful, witty fable, in effect telling how human beings improved upon nature by inventing art. Frost talks about only one art, "song," the art dearest to him, but (as we will see in a moment) the fable implies the other arts too.

Nature is the rough wind, blowing loudly. Art is (to use Alexander Pope's words in *An Essay on Criticism*) "nature methodized." In Frost's playful terms in this poem, nature has to be "converted" (line 11, literally *turned around, transformed*) and changed into something governed "by measure." Poetry of course uses *measure*, i.e. meter (from the Greek *metron*, "measure"), but so do the other arts, such as music (where the metronome has its place), architecture (where symmetry is common), and even prose fiction (where one can chart recurring motifs, paired or contrasting characters, foreshadowing, and so forth).

Having said this, we must admit that Frost is talking chiefly about poetry, and in fact about lyric poetry (*song*) where, one might almost say, the sound is more important than the sense. After all, we *do* value some lyrics that barely go beyond *hey nonny nonny.* There is a staying-power in nonsense rhymes, counting-out rhymes, and so forth, and while no one would say that these are the highest kind of poetry, they do serve as reminders that music (measure) is at the heart of poetry.

ROBERT FROST

Two Look at Two (p. 753)

The poem begins and ends with the word "love," and all between is "love." In many of his other poems there is a failure of love—consider, as a gentle example, the brief rupture that we find in "the Telephone"—but in this poem the love is sustained, and is confirmed by nature (the "unscared" deer).

The encounter of the two lovers and the two deer is a message sent by nature, or, rather, since Frost is cautious and says "as if," it at least seems to be sent by nature:

> Still they stood,
> A great wave from it going over them,
> As if the earth in one unlooked-for favor
> Had made them certain earth returned their love.

In a later poem that we include in the book, "The Most of It," nature sends, again through a day, only a highly ambiguous sign, but in "Two Look at Two" the sign is as clear as Frost was ever willing to make it. Notice too the image of "A great wave" (line 40), which implies again that a force of nature itself is sending the message. And this natural force continues a motif introduced at the start of the poem, where Frost suggests that love carries the lovers up the mountain, and that even when they are stopped by the "tumbled wall / With barbed-wire binding" an "onward impulse" still manifests itself in their last look upward.

As for the impeding wall with its barbed wire, why does Frost include this harsh element in his poem? Among the thoughts that come to mind are (1) Life includes harsh elements as well as love, and (2) Love can go only so far without getting hurt.

One other point: Why does Frost spend so much of his space entering into the minds of the two deer, and so little entering into the minds of the two humans? Our guess is that it is because readers already know, from their own experience, something of the thoughts of the human beings who are in love. Such a line as

> "This is all," they sighed,
> "Good night to woods,"

is enough for us to know the thoughts and feelings of the lovers. For that matter, the very first words of the poem,

> Love and forgetting, might have carried them
> A little further up the mountain side,

tell us how deeply in love the two human beings are. And so Frost uses much of his space playfully imagining the thoughts of the deer. The important point is that the deer are unafraid, or in Frost's more folksy word, "unscared." The doe" sighed and passed unscared along the wall" (24), and a moment later the buck did the same: "Then he too passed unscared along the wall" (37). The idea is that the two humans are at one with each other and with nature itself, and so nature (through the deer) can send them this comforting message that "earth returned their love." Or at least it is "as if" nature sends this message. In "The Figure a Poem Makes" (reprinted in our text) Frost says that a poem is "a momentary stay against confusion." In "Two Look at Two" the deer offer a comparable "stay against confusion."

ROBERT FROST

The Need of Being Versed in Country Things (p. 757)

TOPICS FOR CRITICAL THINKING AND WRITING

1. By the end of the second stanza the reader understands that the farmhouse has been destroyed by a fire. Why do you suppose (putting aside the matter of rhyme) in line 2 Frost wrote "a sunset glow" instead of (say) "a burst of flame"? And what is the effect of the simile in line 4? That is, what do these comparisons contribute to the poem? (If you are unsure of the meaning of "pistil," check a dictionary.)

2. In the fifth stanza Frost uses personifications: "the lilac renewed its leaf," and the "pump flung up an awkward arm," and "the fence post carried a

strand of wire." What other personifications do you find in the poem? What effect do these personifications have on you? And why do you suppose there are no personifications in the last two lines of the poem?

3. In a sentence or two or three, characterize the speaker. (You can probably characterize him or her by means of an adjective or two or three; use the rest of the allotment to provide evidence, such as brief quotations.)

4. Much of the poem describes a scene, but the speaker also interprets the scene. How would you summarize the interpretation? How might you paraphrase the title? Does the speaker convince you of the "need" to be "versed in country things"?

5. Do you think the poem is sentimental? Or, on the other hand, cynical? Explain.

6. Suppose you were to write a parody of "The Need of Being Versed in Country Things." What scene might you use, or what objects might you personify? (A parody is an amusing imitation of the style of another work, often with an inappropriate subject. Thus, one might parody a sports writer by imitating his or her style, but the subject would not be an athletic event but, say, students engaged in peer review.) Suggestion: Consider the possibility of using your neighborhood or your workplace as a subject.

Our thoughts about the above questions may be of some interest.

1. Why "a sunset glow" in line 2, instead of say, "a burst of flame"? Frost's metaphor introduces, early in the poem, the motif that things are not what they seem. (Later his point will be that the birds seem to weep, but are not weeping.) The same might be said for the simile of the chimney as a pistil, in line 4, with the additional implication that the house is absorbed into nature.

2. The personifications in the fifth stanza suggest that the human perceiver of nature insists on finding human qualities in nature—a tendency that will be debunked (though that's too strong a word) by the end of the poem, where the speaker without figurative language states the facts. Other personifications in the poem are: "the will of the wind" (7) and the "murmur" (15) of the birds.

3,4. Although at the end of the poem the speaker claims to be telling it as it is—that is insisting that nature is not lamenting the catastrophe—a reader probably feels that the speaker regrets that this is so. After all, much of the poem is devoted to evoking a highly sympathetic image of a busy farm that has been destroyed and turned almost into a part of nature itself. In our reading we hear some confidence in the assertion that the phoebes are not weeping, but this confidence is undercut by or at least suffused with deep regret. Put it this way: observers should understand that nature does not weep for humans losses, but (and this is not explicitly said but we think it is evident in the tone) this is a pity.

5. Our own feeling is that the poem is neither sentimental (maudlin, and influenced more by emotion than by reason) nor cynical (sneering). As we indicated in the preceding paragraph, we hear objectivity tinged with

regret. Obviously other responses are possible.

6. This suggestion for writing calls for a parody. If you assign this topic, and receive some work of special interest, we hope that (after getting the student's permission) you will send it to us, with the student's name and address. If we think we can use it in the next edition of the book, we will get in touch with the student.

ROBERT FROST

Acquainted with the Night (p. 754)

Some years ago a student of ours, Joseph Kang, wrote an explication of this poem. It seems excellent to us, and we reproduce it here with his permission.

The words in Robert Frost's "Acquainted with the Night," except "luminary" in line 12, are all common ones, but if we look closely at these words we see some *unusual* implications. Take the title: "Acquainted with the Night." We are usually acquainted with a person or with a fact, not with the night. And so "night" must have some special suggestion that is not yet clear. And to be "acquainted" with someone or something usually implies familiarity (as in "I am acquainted with John Jones") but not thorough knowledge. "I have been one acquainted with the night," then, is an unusual and cautious statement.

The first stanza is matter-of-fact. It consists of three sentences, each beginning "I have," and each sentence fills exactly one line. It almost sounds flat, but is not flat because as I have said, "acquainted with the night" is an unusual expression. Also, the repetition of words and grammatical structure makes for special emphasis. Furthermore, when "I have walked out" turns into "I have outwalked the furthest city light," we realize that we are being told about a special journey, not just a literal walk. We don't yet know what this journey was, but even if this walk beyond "the furthest city light" was a literal walk, Frost also means for us to take it as a walk beyond man-made illumination, civilization, order. It must have been meant as an experience with something dark in the way that grief, ignorance, loss of faith, or loneliness are dark.

The second stanza resembles the previous stanza but it is more expansive. It continues the use of "I have," but now only in the first two of its three lines, and only the first line is a complete sentence. And it introduces people other than the speaker, first in "the saddest city lane" (line 4), and next in the watchman (line 5). The lane cannot literally be sad; "saddest" implies that sad people live in the lane, or that the speaker feels sad when he thinks of the people who live in the lane. The watchman perhaps is one of these, and the speaker avoids his glance, explaining only that he is "unwilling to explain" (line 6). The speaker, then, not only is walking alone but also isolates himself from his fellows. That is, he feels isolated and therefore shuns contact.

The third stanza begins with "I have," as five of the previous six lines have begun, but it is even less closely patterned on the first stanza than the second was; that is, the poem becomes looser. In fact, the thought overflows the stanza;

the first stanza of three lines was three sentences, and their tone was assertive, almost confident: "I have been one acquainted...I have walked out...and back" (there is a survivor's note of understated triumph in that "and back"), and I have "outwalked" again a note of triumph. But the quiet yet firm self-assertion then begins to dissolve. The second stanza was two sentences, and now the third stanza cannot contain even one complete sentence—the sentence flows into the next two stanzas, running almost to the end of the poem. To put it slightly differently, all but the last line of the octave (final eight lines) of this sonnet is a single sentence.

In the second stanza the speaker ignores human society, suggested by the watchman; in the third and fourth stanzas human society ignores the speaker, for the "cry" (line 8) is not directed to the speaker: it is "not to call me back or say good-bye" (line 10). In addition to this suggestion of mankind's indifference to the speaker, there is a suggestion that the speaker almost doesn't exist—even in his own perceptions: "I have stood still and stopped the sound of feet" (line 7). A paraphrase of the last six words might be, "and stopped producing the noise of footsteps." Thus, by standing still the speaker became inaudible not only to the city-dwellers but also to himself.

The "interrupted cry" on line 8 is sorrowful, for it is a "cry" and not a "call" or "shout" or "laugh." And the cry is mysterious because we do not know its cause, its source, its message, or why it is "interrupted." The fourth stanza continues to deepen the sense of mystery by referring to a clock "at an unearthly height." Maybe this is a real clock, perhaps with an illuminated face, high on a church or town hall, but it seems more likely that this "luminary" clock is something beyond "the furthest city light"; probably it is a metaphor describing the full moon, which is literally "unearthly." Its unearthliness is emphasized by the unusual use of the unusual word "luminary," for "luminary" is usually a noun meaning " a source of illumination," but here it is used as an adjective. In any case, a real clock can be right or wrong, and it can tell us that the time is right or wrong for eating, sleeping, attending class, or whatever. But this "luminary clock," at an "unearthly height," offers no heavenly guidance and it cannot be either corrected or obeyed. The speaker can only look at the clock (whether a real clock or the moon) and increasingly sense that he has nothing to communicate with.

The last line of the poem, a complete sentence in itself, repeats the first line exactly, and it restores the tone of assurance. Now we have a sharper idea of what the speaker means when he says he has been "one acquainted with the night," but we still cannot say that the "night" equals or symbolizes this or that. "Loneliness," for example, is too simple a translation, because loneliness implies isolation from people, and in the poem we sense that the speaker's isolation may be not only from other people but also from himself (from a sense of any individual purpose) and also from a meaningless universe. Moreover, we must also say—and the poem is as much about this as it is about "the night"—that the speaker is not crushed by the experience. The poem is not a lament, and not a descent into self-pity. The speaker does not sadly say "I *am* one acquainted with the night"; rather, the experience is put at a distance by being set in the past: "I *have been* one acquainted with the night." And though the memory of the experience is still sharp, the speaker keeps his response under control. The closest he comes to telling us explicitly of his feelings is in the terse first and last lines. For the most part he shows us the situation rather than tells us his feelings, and thus he conveys a sense of control—a sense, we might say, of being able to deal with the experience, to survive it (since the last line repeats the first line we can say that he literally comes out where he went in), and even to get it down on paper.

ROBERT FROST

Desert Places (p.755)

Presumably the abundant alliteration and repetition of words, especially in the first stanza but, also in the third, help to suggest the thick snow falling fast, almost uniformly covering the land. The first three stanzas emphasize blankness, but of course a reader is as interested in the speaker's tone (elegiac and sonorous, but fused with some witty word-play); the fourth stanza emphasizes the speaker's response to heavenly emptiness (i.e., to the vast spaces and to lifelessness) by diminishing them with a reference to his inner "desert places." Reuben Brower, in *The Poetry of Robert Frost*, points out that in the fourth stanza "the scary place is thrust off 'there' by the emerging man of wit, by the mind that won't give way to 'absent-spiritedness.' But the gesture is a bit flamboyant and opens up a worse form of terror by bringing fear where the poet most lives alone. The taunting threat… is now replaced by a finer and more discreet irony" in the final lines.

The expression "desert places" appears in Chapter XVIII of *The Scarlet Letter*: Hester Prynne, outlawed from society, found that "Her intellect and heart had their home, as it were, in desert places, where she roamed as freely as the wild Indian in his woods." For two articles that seek to make much of the relation to Hawthorne, see A. J. von Frank and E. Stone in *Frost: Centennial Essays*, ed. Committee on the Frost Centennial of the University of Southern Mississippi. The poem (though not the alleged relation to Hawthorne) is also discussed by Brooks and Warren, *Understanding Poetry*.

ROBERT FROST

Design (p. 755)

On Frost's "Design," see Randall Jarrell, *Poetry and the Age*; Richard Poirier, *Robert Frost*; Reuben A. Brower, *The Poetry of Robert Frost*; Richard Ohmann, *College English* 28 (February 1967): 359-67; *Frost: Centennial Essays*; and Reginald Cook, *Robert Frost: A Living Voice*, especially 263-67. Brower is especially good on the shifting tones of voice, for example from what he calls "the cheerfully observant walker on back country roads" who reports "I found a dimpled…"—but then comes the surprising "spider, fat and white"—to the "self-questioning and increasingly serious" sestet. Here, for Brower, "the first question ('What had the flower to do. . . ') sounds like ordinary annoyance at a fact that doesn't fit in." The next question brings in a new note, and irony in "kindred." For Brower, with the last question ironic puzzlement turns into vision: "What but design of darkness to appall?" And then Brower says that in the final line "The natural theologian pauses—he is only asking, not asserting—and takes a backward step."

The title echoes the "Argument from Design," the argument that the universe is designed (each creature fits perfectly into its environment: The whale is equipped for the sea; the camel for the desert), so there must be a designer, God. Notice that the word—"design"—has two meanings: (1) pattern and (2) intention, plan. Frost certainly means us to have both meanings in mind: there seems to be a pattern and also an intention behind it, but this intention is quite different from the intention discerned by those who in the eighteenth and nineteenth centuries argued for the existence of a benevolent God from the "Argument from Design."

"Design" was published in 1922; below is an early 1912 version of the poem, entitled "In White":

> A dented spider like a snow drop white
> On a white Heal-all, holding up a moth
> Like a white piece of lifeless satin cloth—
> Saw ever curious eye so strange a sight?—
> Portent in little, assorted death and blight
> Like the ingredients of a witches' broth?—
> The beady spider, the flower like a froth,
> And the moth carried like a paper kite.
> What had that flower to do with being white?
> The blue prunella every child's delight.
> What brought the kindred spider to that height?
> (Make we no thesis of the miller's plight.)
> What but design of darkness and of night?
> Design, design! Do I use the word aright?

The changes, obvious enough, are discussed by George Monteiro, in *Frost: Centennial Essays,* published by the Committee on the Frost Centennial of the University of Southern Mississippi, 35-38.

By the way, an ingenious student mentioned that the first stanza has eight lines, corresponding to the eight legs of a spider. And the second stanza has six, corresponding to the six legs of a moth. What to do? We tried to talk about the traditional structure of the sonnet, and about relevant and irrelevant conjectures, and about the broad overlapping area. About as good a criterion as any is, does the conjecture make the poem better?

TOPICS FOR CRITICAL THINKING AND WRITING

1. Do you find the spider, as described in line 1, cute or disgusting? Why?
2. What is the effect of "If" in the last line?
3. The word "design" can mean "pattern" (as in "a pretty design"), or it can mean "intention," especially an evil intention (as in "He had designs on her"). Does Frost use the word in one sense or in both? Explain.

ROBERT FROST

The Silken Tent (p. 756)

The idea of comparing a woman to a silken tent in the summer breeze seems fresh enough to us (probably swaying silken tents have been compared to young women, but did anyone before Frost see it the other way around?), and given this idea, one would expect passages about gentle swaying. If one knew the piece were going to be an allegory worked out in some detail, one might expect the tent pole to be the soul. But who could have expected the brilliant connection between the cords and "ties of love and thought," and the brilliant suggestion that only rarely are we made aware—by "capriciousness"—of our "bondage"? The paradoxical idea that we are (so to speak) kept upright—are what we are—by things that would seem to pull us down is new to most students, who think that one "must be oneself." With a little discussion they come to see that what a person is depends largely on relationships. We are parents, or students, or teachers, or—something; our complex relationships give us our identity. Sometimes, in trying to make clear this idea that our relationships contribute to (rather than diminish) our identities, we mention the scene in Ibsen's *Peer Gynt* where, in an effort to get at his essential self, Peer peels an onion, each removed layer being a relationship that he has stripped himself of. He ends with nothing, of course.

In short, we think this poem embodies a profound idea, and we spend a fair amount of our class time talking about that idea. But we also try to look at the poem closely. Students might be invited to discuss what sort of woman "she" is. What, for instance, do "midday" and "summer" in line 2 contribute? Frost could, after all, have written "In morning when a sunny April breeze" but he probably wanted to suggest—we don't say a mature woman—someone who is no longer girlish, someone who is of sufficient age to have established responsibilities, and to have experienced, on occasion, a sense of slight bondage. Among the traits that we think can be reasonably inferred from the comparison are these: beauty, poise, delicacy (in lines 1-4), and sweetness and firmness of soul (5-7).

TOPICS FOR CRITICAL THINKING AND WRITING

1. The second line places the scene at "midday" in "summer." In addition to giving us the concreteness of a setting, do these words help to characterize the woman whom the speaker describes? If so, how?
2. The tent is supported by "guys" (not men, but the cords or "ties" of line 10) and by its "central cedar pole." What does Frost tell us about these ties? What does he tell us about the pole?
3. What do you make of lines 12-14?
4. In a sentence, a paragraph, or a poem, construct a simile that explains a relationship.

ROBERT FROST

Come In (p. 756)

This poem has fairly close associations with "The Need of Being Versed in Country Things" (the speaker at the end indicates his awareness that nature is *not* to be interpreted in the way that a less knowledgeable person might interpret it) and also with "Stopping by Woods on a Snowy Evening" (the temptation to enter into the darkness—to yield to some sort of impulse of self-surrender—is rejected, in favor of the assertion of the self in business as usual). The thrush's song is understood not as a "call to come in," but as "almost" (15) such a call (*cf.* the realism of the speaker of "The Need of Being Versed"), and the speaker is "out for stars," and therefore will "not come in" (*cf.* the end of "Stopping by Woods," where the speaker asserts the need to go for miles before he sleeps).

Reuben Brower in *The Poetry of Robert Frost,* speaks of "the doubling of tones in the poem" (32). Among the examples that he gives are the title, which suggests a friendly welcome at the kitchen door, and also a more mysterious invitation, and (in line 2) the word "hark," which has an old-fashioned grandmotherly tone and also a poetic tone of religious wonder. Notice also the two sets of images, darkness (in most of the poem) and light ("But no, I was out for stars"). "Pillared dark," incidently, wonderfully connects the trees with columns, presumably those of a temple.

ROBERT FROST

The Most of It (p. 756)

The "he" of the poem is not the speaker, of course; we are totally dependent on the speaker for our impression of this person and we don't get even a single phrase of reported speech. Judging from what the speaker tells us, the "he" is a rather unimaginative person, someone who (at least in the first half of the poem) finds nothing of significance outside of himself. The world around him offers "but the mocking echo" of his own voice. As Richard Poirier suggests, in his shrewd analysis in *Robert Frost* (1977), 165, this is someone who cannot "*make* the most of it," someone, we might say, who is not a poet. But the reader, as distinct from the "he," perceives the grandeur of the surroundings—and this grandeur is so presented that as we read it we more or less project ourselves into the mind of the spectator, who stands in this landscape "bathed in a mythological heroism" (Poirier 165), and we feel we are experiencing his experience. What we and the spectator get is not what the spectator wanted at the start, but is (again in Poirier's words) "a vision of some fabulousness beyond domestication" (165).

ROBERT FROST

The Gift Outright (p. 757)

We have not exhaustively searched the literature on Frost, but if there is an important commentary on this poem we are unaware of it. Evaluative criticism, such as it is, varies widely. On the one hand, Randall Jarrell in *Poetry and the Age* (1953) called it "perhaps the best 'patriotic' poem ever written about our own country" (54-51), but on the other hand William Logan, writing in the June 1995 issue of *New Criterion*, asked if "any major poet [has] written a worse poem about America than 'the Gift Outright'" (22). Logan goes on to say that this poem and "After Apple-Picking" are "poems I can't imagine anyone liking." Neither he nor Jarrell offers anything in the way of an argument to support his evaluation (or *de*valuation, in Logan's case).

We can imagine one ground for serious complaint about the poem, and that is this: Frost asserts (line 15) that before the land became ours, by "many deeds of war," it was "unstoried, artless, unenhanced." The implication—false, of course—is that the Native Americans had not endowed it with *their* stories, i.e. myths and histories, and that they were "artless" people. But one understands what Frost means—*So far as whites were concerned*, the land was empty, unstoried, and so forth because it did not yet tell *their* stories. It is not a very attractive view, but we should remember that virtually all whites held this view until only a couple of decades ago. Further, if we think that Frost was oblivious to the treatment afforded Indians by white, we have only to read the poem, "The Vanishing Red," which we print later in this chapter.

Since the somewhat paradoxical language may cause students difficulty, we find it useful to get the class to produce a paraphrase. There is usually some stumbling, but by the time the class gets to lines 12-13, with "Such as we were we gave ourselves outright / The deed of gift was many deeds of war!"—one can pause, go back to the title, and in the light of what is now seen to be the gift (ourselves), effectively revise the paraphrase. Thus in the context of the entire poem the first line can be paraphrased, "We physically possessed the land before we had a national identity as Americans [lines 3-7 make it clear that we possessed—owned—the land], but because we ourselves were possessed by England (and presumably offered our allegiance to England, rather than being possessed by—obsessed by—the land of America), the land did not yet possess (enchant, serve as the object of our obsession) us."

The paradox in 8-11 also requires comment: By not giving ourselves fully to our new land, we weakened rather than strengthened ourselves. Only when we surrendered to it—fully gave ourselves to it—did we find "salvation." The word "salvation," of course, connects this action with a paradox central to Christianity; by dying in the old world, one gains life in the new world.

The paradoxes make for a kind of punning speech notably in "possessed," and there are also multiple meanings in "deed" (deed of gift; deeds of war), "realizing" (becoming real; dawning on our consciousness) "artless" (without fine arts; without sophistication), and "unstoried" (without a history, and perhaps without legends or narratives).

TOPICS FOR CRITICAL THINKING AND WRITING

1. Paraphrase the poem. (If you find lines 6-7 especially difficult, consider the possibility that "possess" may have multiple meanings: (1) to own; (2) to enchant. Thus, for instance, "possessed by" can mean "owned by" or "enchanted by, obsessed with.")

2. What is the gift referred to in the title? (In reading the poem, pay special attention to lines 12-13.)

3. Consult the entry on *paradox* in the glossary. Then read the pages referred to in the entry, and write an essay of 500 words on paradox in this poem.

ROBERT FROST

The Draft Horse (p. 757)

Most readers believe that the poem is an allegory—but exactly what are the constituents? That is, can we find equivalents for, say, the buggy, the horse, the "lantern that wouldn't burn," the "man [who] came out of the trees," "the night," and so forth?

Laurence Perrine, who usually was cautious, in *Explicator* 24 (1966), item 79, rather surprisingly called the poem "patently allegorical," and offered the following system of equivalents. The ride = the journey of life; the darkness = old age; the inadequate lantern = failing intellectual powers; the "too heavy" horse=the burdensome body; the man with the knife = Time (the knife or dagger being a modern version of Time's scythe); getting down and walking "the rest of the way" = living one's last years in a weakened condition.

Obviously one cannot refute any of this, but somehow it seems too narrow, too reductive. But what, then, are we to make of the somewhat different allegorical reading offered by Margaret M. Blum, in the same issue of *Explicator*? For Blum, the table of equivalents goes thus: The poem as a whole is about the liberation from belief in a benevolent God; the lantern that wouldn't burn = the traditional soul (which the speaker now finds doesn't function as it should, according to orthodox belief); the frail buggy = the decaying human body; the too-heavy horse = organized religion; the "pitch-dark limitless grove" = time merging into eternity; the man with the knife = humanistic philosophy, annihilating false beliefs; the "crack of a broken shaft" and the "invidious draft" = sudden despair; the "unquestioning pair" = people making the best of a mysterious experience. Need we say that we find this interpretation hard to take?

Also writing in *Explicator*, this time in 25 (1967), item 60, Paul Burrell finds the following: the inadequate lantern, the buggy, and the horse = "images of the makeshifts to which man learns to resign himself as he goes through this world of compromises and disappointments"; the death of the horse = "the loss of anything in life to which one has become accustomed and in which one has placed a hope." Burrell goes on to say that hope is not destroyed, however, but only modified, since the couple continues on its journey, but now of foot. "The couple, symbolizing man's interdependence and love, rejects the negative reaction of 'hate' and decides to continue. Life and man, no matter how disappointing and limited, are the values which the poet sees and can keep."

We want to summarize two other readings before offering a very brief comment of our own. Frederick L. Gwynne in *The Case for Poetry* gives an archetypal reading. For Gwynne, the horse is a scapegoat for the human beings; the man who stabs the horse is a priest, such as Frazer describes in *The Golden Bough* (Gwynne says that the words "took our horse by the head" indicate that the horse-killer acts ceremoniously) the couple, who continue on foot, decline to worship the revealed power as a purposeful providence, but they do grudgingly accept it.

Somehow, none of these readings satisfies us, chiefly, we guess, because they all press too hard, i.e. they want to work out a coherent system of one-to-one equivalents. We are more comfortable with Sandra A. Tomlinson's reading (*Explicator* 42 [1984]:28-29) that Frost is describing our mysterious journey—with inadequate equipment—through life. What of the response of the pair to the assault? Tomlinson says,

> The victimized pair respond without self-pity to the maliciousness that has left them powerless. They do not cry out to the universe for answers; for they seem to know from instinct or experience that the answers will not come. They choose instead to "accept Fate," to put the best construction they can on an apparently unmotivated act of hostility....In the conclusion, the couple absolve the murderer of his responsibility. He too may be powerless.... Their simple explanation is comic and does not, of course, explain anything at all, but their decision to continue is noble.

If someone in class raises something like this last point—the idea that the couple's response to the killing is "noble"—be prepared to hear other students say that the couple must be nuts, the sort of people who watch a flood destroys a town, or a killer mows down a classroom of children, and then say, "It must be God's will."

Our own view is that the poem is symbolic, not allegorical (i.e. that the details do not have precise equivalents). Instead of trying to find specific equivalents for such things as the horse, the lantern, the buggy, etc, we want simply to say that the poem deals with the blows (disappointments, collapses of ideals?) that most or all of us experience in a world we didn't choose and that does not conform to our desires. The couple respond as best they can; a reader can imagine that other responses are also possible, but it is hard to imagine that other responses would make for a happier life.

LANGSTON HUGHES

Students should approach poems by Langston Hughes with at least two goals in mind. It is important, first, to read each one carefully in its own right, paying close attention to the special way that Hughes handles vocabulary and imagery. Second, it is also important, and one of the pleasures of reading Hughes, to notice the connections between one poem and others, the verbal and thematic links that organize Hughes's poetic enterprise as a whole.

Readers of Walt Whitman—following Whitman's lead—often refer to the many separate poems in *Leaves of Grass* as components of a single poem, a single massive act of expression in which Whitman seeks to convey and honor the multiple meanings of America. A similar description, we think, could be offered of Hughes's collected poems, and in this context it is worth mentioning that Whitman was in fact Hughes's great model, the precursor in the American literary tradition whom Hughes wished to emulate. He wanted to achieve for his people what he believed Whitman had achieved for white America, and, as David Perkins has observed in *A History of Modern Poetry* (1976), Hughes's "oeuvre makes a remarkably broad, rich, forceful, appealing impression," like Whitman's.

Notice, then, how the poem "The Negro Speaks of Rivers," with its evocative testimony of the poet's desire to speak what he has known and deeply acquired in his soul, is connected to the lines in "The Weary Blues": "Sweet Blues!/Coming from a black man's soul./O Blues!"; and then, in turn, hear how the mood of "The Weary Blues" gets turned toward a dispirited, yet still somewhat wry, self-disdain in "Too Blue." Ponder the painful image of "the dead fire's ashes" in "The South," in contrast to the "clean flame of joy" in "Ruby Brown." Consider also the themes of injustice and betrayal—specifically, the betrayal of the American dream and the promises of equal opportunity—that ties "The South" to "Let America Be America Again."

When a poet is studied in depth, students can be encouraged to see affinities among poems, linkages in ideas and illuminations, shared patterns, and variations performed on the same or related subjects, as when, for instance, Hughes traces the plight of African-American women in "Mother to Son" and "Ruby Brown." Students will observe, too, that a number of these poems are *about* poetry, about writing, about finding a subject, a voice: "The Negro Speaks of Rivers"; "Poet to Patron"; "Theme for English B"; "Poet to Bigot."

For a discussion of Hughes's relationship to other African-American writers of the period, see Arnold Rampersad, "The Poetry of the Harlem Renaissance," in *The Columbia History of American Poetry*, ed. Jay Parini (1993). For background, see *Voices From the Harlem Renaissance*, ed. Nathan Irvin Huggins (1976), and David Levering Lewis, *When Harlem Was in Vogue* (1981).

Biographies too often make a writer's work seem less interesting and urgent than it is, but Rampersad's *The Life of Langston Hughes* (2 vols, 1986, 1988) is an exception to the rule and is highly recommended.

LANGSTON HUGHES

The Negro Speaks of Rivers (p. 761)

W. E. B. Du Bois noted in 1940 that "the longing of Black men must have respect; the rich and the strange readings of nations they have seen may give the world new points of view and make their loving, living, and doing precious to all human hearts." It is a version of this longing, this desire for expression, that is at the center of "The Negro Speaks of Rivers." It is important that students realize Hughes was still in his teens when he wrote it, and that the poem is a bold as well as beautiful one. This young man was claiming to speak as a Negro on behalf of generations of his people. There is a granduer to the aspirations he voices, and maybe behind the poem is Mark Twain's formidable rendering of the Mississippi River in *Adventures of Huckleberry Finn* and other writings. But "the Negro" whom Hughes describes knows of many rivers, in an arc of experience that spans the globe.

LANGSTON HUGHES

Mother to Son (p. 761)

The main movement of this poem is clear enough: a mother urges her son to keep moving forward, working hard, whatever the hard obstacles he faces. But what makes the poem affecting is the manner in which Hughes evokes the mother's voice. Notice, for instance, the starkness of "bare" in line seven, which dramatizes both a literal fact about the stair ("places with no carpet on the floor") and the desolating emptiness that the mother feels but still strives to overcome.

On one level, the poem is affirmative and uplifting, but the reiteration of the phrase "life for me ain't been no crystal stair" complicates the mood, perhaps darkening it. Here it can be interesting to ask students what the effect would have been if Hughes had ended the poem at line nineteen: "I'se still climbin." That would have given the poem, as it concluded, the surge of an upward movement. But Hughes had a different emotional aim; he wanted the mother to return to the hardness of her life, to her slightly comic but still wounded sense of the richer, more comfortable life that she lacks. The poem ends with the mother's voicing of what she does not have, the burden that she carries. She keeps on striving and struggling, not giving up, and she counsels her son to do likewise. But she does not deny to herself or to him that there is resistance, a weight of pain and disappointment, that she will always know is there.

Note: Be sure to make vivid for students what "crystal" is. They benefit from being reminded of its glimmering qualities (how it reflects light), and of its use in fine glassware and ornaments.

LANGSTON HUGHES

The Weary Blues (p. 762)

This poem ("weary" may pun on "wary") has been identified as one of the first by an African-American to make use of the blues form. This is a key piece of information to pass along, but it does not take us very far. The phrase "the blues" is familiar, and is widely used, yet it is hard to define. In fact, part of the point seems to be the mysterious depth and mystery of the blues: you know what it is and when you are feeling it, but cannot *say* in so many words what it is. You simply got the blues, or, if you are a musician, you are playing the blues.

As *The Oxford Companion to Popular Music* (1991) indicates, "the blues remains a hazily poetical concept that still cannot ultimately be expressed more accurately than in the words of an old slave woman, quoted in the mid-19th century, who described it as music that could only be created with 'a full heart and a troubled spirit.'"

On the other hand, the literature, both popular and scholarly, on the subject of the blues is vast. We have found it to be a good one for reports by students, particularly those with an interest in contemporary music, jazz, gospel, and rhythm and blues. Teachers might recommend Le Roi Jones, *Blues People* (1963); *The Blues Line: A Collection of Blues Lyrics*, ed. E. Sackheim (1973); Robert Palmer, *Deep Blues* (1981); and P. Oliver, M. Harrison, and W. Bolcom, *The New Grove Gospel, Blues, and Jazz* (1986). See also M. L. Hart, *The Blues: A Bibliographical Guide* (1988).

For more immediate purposes in the classroom when teaching Hughes, we have cited Ralph Ellison, "Richard Wright's Blues" (1964): "The blues is an impulse to keep the painful details and episodes of a brutal experience alive in one's aching consciousness, to finger its jagged grain, and to transcend it, not by the consolation of philosophy but by squeezing from it a near-tragic, near-comic lyricism. As a form, the blues is an autobiographical chronicle of personal catastrophe expressed lyrically."

The jazz trumpet player Wynton Marsalis, in an interview published in *American Heritage* (October 1995), speaks suggestively as well: "Blues gives the jazz musician an unsentimental view of the world. Blues is adult secular music, the first adult secular music America produced. It has an optimism that's not naive. You accept tragedy and move forward. . . . Blues is such a fundamental form that it's loaded with complex information. It has a sexual meaning, the ebb and the flow of sexual passion: disappointment, happiness, joy, and sorrow. It has a whole religious connotation too, that joy and lift."

When we teach Hughes's poem, we tend to read it aloud and then, either through a mini-lecture or student reports, to provide a cultural context for it. Next, we read the poem again, lingering over the rhymes, the alliteration ("moan with melody"), and the other expert, subtle handlings of sound. One of us, indeed, always sings the lines that Hughes identifies as coming from the song of the musician. It may not be the best singing that the lines could receive, but it does alert the class to the closeness of Hughes's poem to song, to the way in which this blues poem derives from (and is) blues music.

LANGSTON HUGHES

The South (p. 762)

Hughes builds this poem on sharp contrasts of description and feeling, beginning with the first two lines: "The lazy, laughing South/With blood on its mouth." The first line could have led to a different kind of poem—sentimental, dreamy, wistful; Hughes, we think, counts on this possibility only to strike against it in the next line, with its graphic image of savagery. This is an angry, punishing poem, possibly one that is self-punishing too, as Hughes brings forth cruel images that, one feels, are etched in his consciousness, that he cannot break free from.

As the poem moves toward its conclusion, Hughes declares he will seek liberation from the South, and in our classes we have discovered that sometimes students too quickly regard the poem as proposing a straight exchange or polarity: the South is bad, impossible for the black man or woman to love, while the North is the land of bright prospects. Here, it's helpful to show how a phrase like "kinder mistress" is balanced against the reference to "cold-faced" and the distancing "they say" (the speaker is relying on others' reports—maybe these are wrong) in the preceding lines. In addition, if there is hope, it *may* exist (which differs from saying that it *will* exist) only for the next generation, not for the speaker.

We like to take the opportunity that this poem offers to recommend C. Vann Woodward's classic study, *The Strange Career of Jim Crow* (3rd. ed., 1974), and I. A. Newby, *The South: A History* (1978). Advanced students will also find useful a good collection of essays, *Myth and Southern History,* ed. Patrick Gerster and Nicholas Cords (2nd ed., 2 vols., 1989). This is also a moment in the semester when one can refer students to Jean Toomer's collection of poems, prose sketches, and stories, *Cane* (1923), and to Richard Wright's collection of stories *Uncle Tom's Children* (1938; enl. ed., 1940), and his wrenching autobiography about growing up in the South, *Black Boy* (1945).

LANGSTON HUGHES

Ruby Brown (p. 763)

This poem works well alongside "Mother to Son," as another example of Hughes's commentary on the predicaments of African-American women. The poem itself does not record a judgment on Ruby Brown's decline into prostitution, though the details are certainly disturbing ("the sinister shuttered houses"), and the church members, it is noted, no longer mention her name. But the speaker basically tells her story; he does not criticize or condemn her. Possibly there is even a hint of an ambiguity in the phrase "good church folk." Yes, they are good, but maybe just a bit complacent as well, unsympathetic to Ruby's situation, unable to fathom why she found her life of low-pay, joyless labor so deadening.

LANGSTON HUGHES

Let America Be America Again (p. 764)

This poem is located within a tradition in prose and verse of appeals for America finally to be faithful to its professed ideals. For many African-Americans, the tenets of the Declaration of Independence have seemed hollow, true for white Americans only, and there are many examples of protest, complaint, and appeal that carry this theme. Two of the best of them were presented by African-American abolitionists during the campaign against slavery:

Frederick Douglass: You degrade us and then ask why we are degraded. You shut our mouths and ask why we don't speak. You close your colleges and seminaries against us and then ask why we don't know. (1847)

William Wells Brown: This is called "the land of the free and the home of the brave"; it is called the "asylum of the oppressed"; and some have been foolish enough to call it the "Cradle of Liberty." If it is the "Cradle of Liberty," they have rocked the child to death. (1847)

Other examples can be found in the speeches and writings of the nineteenth-century orator David Walker, the post-World War II novelist, critic, and cultural commentator James Baldwin, and the civil rights leader Martin Luther King, to name only a few. But perhaps the central point here is the distinctive cast that Hughes gives to his poem in this tradition. He insists that America "be America again," but then interjects in line five that it never was "America" to him in the first place.

So often in American political rhetoric, speakers have declared that America must restore its lost ideals, return to the better place it once was, get back to values that have been distorted or defiled. But Hughes emphasizes, instead, that for him, as an African-American, "America" has *never* been a land of liberty. For African-Americans, it's a question of reaching a place at last from which they have always been excluded.

To pitch the point in this direction, however, is both correct and somewhat misleading, for as the turn in line nineteen testifies, Hughes in this poem is linking black Americans to poor whites, Native Americans, immigrants, and others who have suffered abuse, neglect, exploitation. This poem is, Whitman-like, an act of incorporation, of bringing many groups together, as the speaker announces himself to be their spokesman and representative.

Hughes wrote this poem in the mid-1930s, when he leaned decidedly to the Left politically and was often extremely radical, even revolutionary, in the ideas and sentiments that he expressed in his verse. "Let America Be America Again" is a powerful, gripping poem, more than a poem of the 1930s alone, and students frequently have told us that they find its style and structure (e. g., the placement of parenthetical lines, the intrusion of other voices) very effective. Yet while we admire this poem, we think that like much 1930s literary polemic, it becomes over-insistent and unsatisfying as it drives toward its conclusion. Students might be asked, where does this poem lead us? Hughes says "we must take back our land again." But what does this mean? Take it back in what ways? Through violence?

Such a question might seem to press the poem unfairly, as it were (or should be) a political tract. But it's hard not to raise the question when the poem is being read closely, and "Let America Be America Again" might in fact offer a good occasion for students to think about how a political *poem* and a political speech or essay resemble or differ from one another.

LANGSTON HUGHES

Poet to Patron (p. 766)

A short poem, with a ringingly clear point expressed in its angered, impatient tone. But there are some verbal effects here that students should be helped to see and appreciate. "Throw out pieces of my heart" is a wonderfully apt phrase. It suggests what the speaker is giving up to the patron, but even more precisely, it sounds a note of self-disgust: the precious pieces of his heart are thrown away like something that has no or little value. The patron is exacting something from the speaker, and the speaker is exacting something from himself. How could he allow himself to do this?

The implication here prepares the way for the harsher line, "I must sell myself," in the next stanza. The "perfumed note" in the next-to-last line, we think, says something mocking and derisive about the patron who sends the note, yet, once more, it conveys self-contempt in the speaker who is obliged to receive it. Notice that the speaker does not conclude by renouncing the patron. He dislikes the patron's demands; and he states that working in a factory might be better. But the final lines imply that he is still connected to the patron; he hasn't broken away yet. After all, if he worked in a factory, he would not be writing poetry. If he gave up his patron, he would be sacrificing even more than he does now. In this respect, the patron is still in control, whatever the speaker's resistance to him.

LANGSTON HUGHES

Ballad of the Landlord (p. 766)

This is another of Hughes's political poems, and it is a very effective one. It is a good poem to teach with "Let America Be America Again," because in it Hughes shows what happens to a person who stands up for his rights and demands justice. As soon as he does, he is branded a dangerous radical who is bent on toppling the government and turning America upside down. The final lines are clipped and fast-paced, as Hughes bears witness to how quickly America contains (and eliminates) its internal foes. Part of the point is that versions of this same incident have occurred countless times before.

LANGSTON HUGHES

Too Blue (p. 767)

This poem can be taught effectively next to "The Weary Blues"; it has a sad, wry weariness that is evident, for example, in the speaker's amused but glum observation that it would probably take two bullets to crack through his "hard head" if he tried to shoot himself.

LANGSTON HUGHES

Harlem [1] (p. 767)

The poet-critic Claude McKay, in *Harlem: Negro Metropolis* (1940), observes: "Harlem was my first positive reaction to American life—it was like entering a paradise of my own people; the rhythm of Harlem still remains one of the most pleasurable sensations of my blood."

Hughes sometimes celebrates Harlem in the way that McKay does, but in this poem the vision is more severe and terrible: Harlem is painted as the place on the edge of hell where African-Americans face mistreatment and from where they glimpse all that is denied to them. Harlem is *here,* and "the world" is over there, gazed at from a distance.

When we teach this poem, we return for a moment to "The South," so that the students can measure what is said about Harlem in "Harlem [I]" against the freedom that the speaker (or at least his children) hopes to locate in the North. Students enjoy hearing poems in dialogue with one another, glossing and even challenging one another. Try to communicate to students how the poems of a writer like Hughes establish a structure of relationships, which, in turn, are part of the larger structure of the history of poetry within which the writer works.

See the critic Arthur P. Davis, in an essay included in *Images of the Negro in American Literature,* ed. Seymour L. Cross and John Edward Hardy (1966): "One must bear in mind that with Langston Hughes, Harlem is both place and symbol. When he depicts the hopes, the aspirations, the frustrations, and the deep-seated discontent of the New York ghetto, he is expressing the feelings of Negroes in black ghettos throughout America."

LANGSTON HUGHES

Theme for English B (p. 768)

We have found this poem to be very provocative for getting students to think about what constitutes the *identity* of a poet. The question has always been an important one, but perhaps in the highly multi-cultural 1990s it has become especially vexed and contentious. "Will my page be colored that I write," Hughes's speaker asks. Does a poem inevitably reflect the race, ethnicity, gender, and/or class of its author? Can members of a different group *really* read and understand such a poem, or is a poem a circuit of communication that passes only from the author to the members of the group whose identity he or she shares?

For Hughes, persons cannot be separated off into groups, however much they might wish they could be. "That's American," he says. If there is an essential America, it lies in the fact that in America no one is truly separate from anyone else. Everyone is "part" of one another and has much to learn: no one can claim to be beyond the need of knowing about what others have to teach them. We like at this point both to commend Hughes's faith and query students whether they can accept it for themselves.

LANGSTON HUGHES

Poet to Bigot (p. 769)

Like "Theme for English B" and "Poet to Patron," "Poet to Bigot" is a poem about writing, reading, and interpretation. Invite students to draw out the implications of the opposing images of "stone" and "flower" in the final two stanzas. But then, by way of review and summary, ask the class to describe the range of feeling, the range of voice, that Hughes exhibits in the poems included in this section of the book. "My moment is/A Flower." Call attention to the precise, concrete immediacy of this line, with its rich but fragile delicacy, and then prompt students to discuss moments in other poems where Hughes's voice displays a different tone and timbre.

PART FOUR

Drama

CHAPTER 22

Some Elements of Drama

Among useful basic studies are S. Barnet et al., eds. *Types of Drama* (an anthology with introductions and critical essays); Cleanth Brooks and Robert Heilman, eds., *Understanding Drama* (an anthology with a good deal of critical commentary); J. L. Styan, *The Elements of Drama*; and Eric Bentley, *The Life of the Drama*.

SUSAN GLASPELL

Trifles (p. 783)

Some students may know Glaspell's other version of this work, a short story entitled "A Jury of Her Peers." Some good class discussion can focus on the interchangeability of the titles. "Trifles" could have been called "A Jury of Her Peers," and vice versa. A peer is an equal, and the suggestion of the story's title is that Mrs. Wright is judged by a jury of her equals—Mrs. Hale and Mrs. Peters. A male jury would not constitute her equals because—at least in the context of the story and the play—males simply don't have the experiences of women and therefore can't judge them fairly.

Murder is the stuff of TV dramas, and this play concerns a murder, but it's worth asking students how the play differs from a whodunit. Discussion will soon establish that we learn, early in "Trifles," who performed the murder, and we even know, fairly early, *why* Minnie killed her husband. (The women know what is what because they correctly interpret "trifles," but the men are baffled, since they are looking for obvious signs of anger.) Once we know who performed the murder, the interest shifts to the question of whether the women will cover up for Minnie.

The distinction between what the men and the women look for is paralleled in the distinction between the morality of the men and the women. The men stand for law and order, for dominance (they condescend to the women, and the murdered Wright can almost be taken as a symbol of male dominance), whereas the women stand for mutual support or nurturing. Students might be invited to discuss *why* the women protect Minnie. Is it because women are nurturing? Or because they feel guilt for their earlier neglect of Minnie? Or because, being women, they know what her sufferings must have been like, and feel that she acted justly? All of the above?

The symbols will cause very little difficulty. (1) The "gloomy" kitchen suggests Minnie's life with her husband; (2) the bird suggests Minnie (she sang "like a bird," was lively, then became caged and was broken in spirit).

The title is a sort of symbol too, an ironic one, for the men think (in Mr. Hale's words) that "Women are used to worrying over trifles." The men in the play never come to know better, but the reader-viewer comes to understand that the trifles are significant and that the seemingly trivial women have outwitted the self-important men. The irony of the title is established by the ironic action of the play.

Does the play have a *theme?* In our experience, the first theme that students may propose is that "it's a man's world." There is something to this view, but (1) a woman kills her husband, and (2) other women help her to escape from the (male) legal establishment. Do we want to reverse the first suggestion, then, and say that (in this play) it is really a woman's world, that women run things? No, given the abuse that all of the women in the play take. Still, perhaps it is fair to suggest that one of the things the play implies is that overbearing male behavior gets what it deserves—at least sometimes. Of course, when put this way, the theme is ancient; it is at the root of the idea of *hubris*, which is said to govern much Greek tragedy. Glaspell gives it a very special twist by emphasizing the women's role in restoring justice to society.

On Glaspell, see: Jean Gould, *Modern American Playwrights* (1966); Arthur E. Waterman, *Susan Glaspell* (1966); and C. W. E. Bigsby, "Introduction," *Plays by Susan Glaspell* (1987). Also useful is *Modern American Drama: The Female Canon,* ed. Jane Schlueter (1990).

CHAPTER 23

Tragedy

SOPHOCLES

Oedipus Rex (p. 800)

Though interpretations are innumerable, most fall into the following categories:

1. The gods are just; Oedipus is at fault. The gods are innocent because fore-knowledge is not foreordaining. (Jesus predicted that Peter would thrice deny him, but this prediction does not mean that Jesus destined Peter to deny him.) The prophecy told what Oedipus would do, but Oedipus did it because of what he was, not because the gods ordained him to do it. As we watch the play, we see a man acting freely—pursuing a course that leads to the revelation of who he is. (See especially Bernard Knox, *Oedipus at Thebes* 33-41.) Though Oedipus is often praised for relentlessly pursuing a truth that ultimately destroys him, the fact is that—until very late in the play—he believes he is searching for someone other than himself, and moreover, in this search he too easily assumes that other people are subversive. Oedipus is rash and even cruel in his dealings with Teiresias, Creon, and the shepherd. His rashness is his *hamartia,* and the gods punish him for it. Given the prophecy that was given to Oedipus, a man less rash would have made it his business never to have killed anyone, and never to have married. (But he thought Polybos and Merope were his parents, and he knew that the old man [Laios] was not Polybos and that the queen in Thebes [Iocaste] was not Merope.)
2. The gods are at fault; Oedipus is innocent. When Oedipus asked the oracle who his parents were, the god answered in such a way as to cause Oedipus

to leave a place of safety and to go to a tragic destination. Oedipus is a puppet of the gods; his *hamartia* is not rashness (a moral fault) but simply a mistake: He *un*intentionally killed his father and married his mother. The oracle was not conditional (it did not say, "If you do such and such, then such and such will happen"). The play is a tragedy of destiny; notice that at the end of the play no one justifies the gods; that is, no one exonerates them from forcing evil on Oedipus.

3. Oedipus is on the whole admirable (he pities his suffering kingdom; he has a keen desire to know the truth), but he is not perfect. The matter of his *intention* is irrelevant because the deeds of patricide and incest (irrespective of motive) contain pollution. The gods are mysterious, and though they sometimes shape men's lives terribly, they are not evil because they cannot be judged by human standards of justice or morality.

4. Sophocles is not concerned with justice; the play is an exciting story about a man finding out something about the greatness of humanity and about human limitations.

Walter Kaufmann, *Tragedy and Philosophy*, has a long discussion of *Oedipus Rex*, in the course of which he finds five themes:

1. The play is about man's radical insecurity (epitomized in Oedipus's fall); Oedipus was the first of men, but he fell.
2. The play is about human blindness. Oedipus did not know who he was (i.e., he was ignorant of his parentage); moreover, he was blind to the honesty of Creon and Teiresias.
3. The play is about the curse of honesty. Oedipus's relentless desire to know the truth brings him to suffering. (If one wants to hunt for a tragic "flaw," one can see this trait as a flaw or vice, but a more reasonable way of looking at it is to see it as a virtue. Would we regard a less solicitous ruler as more virtuous?)
4. The play is about a tragic situation. If Oedipus abandons his quest, he fails his people; if he pursues his quest, he ruins himself.
5. The play is about justice or, more precisely, about *in*justice, that is, undeserved suffering. (Here we come back to Kaufmann's third point: The reward of Oedipus's quest for truth is suffering. It is not even clear that he is being justly punished for killing Laios, for Oedipus belongs to the old heroic world, where killing an enemy is celebrated.) Another point about the play as a play about justice: Sophocles talks of *human* justice too. When Oedipus curses the unknown killer of Laios, he does not think that the killer may have acted in self-defense. And Oedipus's desire to punish Creon and Teiresias similarly shows how wide of the mark efforts at human justice may be.

The Norton critical edition of *Oedipus Tyrannus*, ed. L. Berkowitz and T. F. Brunner, includes a translation, some relevant passages from Homer, Thucydides, and Euripides, and numerous religious, psychological and critical studies, including Freud's, whose key suggestion, in *The Interpretation of*

Dreams, is that the play "moves a modern audience no less than it did the contemporary Greek one" because there is a "voice within us ready to recognize the compelling force of destiny [in the play] . . . . His destiny moves us only because it might have been ours—because the oracle laid the same curse upon us before our birth as upon him. It is the fate of all of us, perhaps, to direct our first sexual impulse towards our mother and our first hatred and our first murderous wish against our father."

An instructor who uses this quotation in class may wish to call attention to the male chauvinism: Freud's "all of us" really means "all males," although he did make various efforts to account for the Oedipus complex in women. It may also be relevant to mention that if the Oedipus of the play did have an Oedipus complex, he would have wanted to go to bed with Merope (the "mother" who brought him up) rather than Iocaste. Note, too, that when he kills Laios, Laios is to him a stranger, not his father. Indeed, his flight from Corinth is a sign that he does *not* wish to sleep with his mother or to kill his father. But perhaps such a view is too literal. Perhaps this is a convenient place to mention that Oedipus's solution of the riddle of the Sphinx (a human being is the creature who walks on four feet in the morning, two at noon, and three in the evening) is especially applicable to Oedipus himself (the weakest of infants, the strongest of men in his maturity, and desperately in need of a staff in his blind old age), but of course it applies to all the spectators as well.

In addition to the Norton edition, the following discussions are especially interesting: Stanley Edgar Hyman, *Poetry and Criticism;* H. D. F. Kitto, *Greek Tragedy* and his *Poeisis;* Richmond Lattimore, *The Poetry of Greek Tragedy;* Cedric Whitman, *Sophocles;* Bernard Knox, *Oedipus at Thebes;* Charles Rowan Beye, *Ancient Greek Literature and Society,* especially 306-12; Brian Vickers, *Toward Greek Tragedy,* Vol. I; R. P. Winnington-Ingram, *Sophocles.*

A videocassette of Sophocles's *Oedipus Rex* is available from Longman.

TOPIC FOR WRITING
By today's standards, is Oedipus in any sense guilty, and if so, of what?

SOPHOCLES

Antigone (p. 836)

On *Antigone*, consult two books by H. D. F. Kitto, *Greek Tragedy*, and especially *Form and Meaning in Drama*. See also D. W. Lucas, *The Greek Tragic Poets;* Cedric H. Whitman, *Sophocles;* and R. P. Winnington-Ingram, *Sophocles.* Hegel's view, most often known through Bradley's essay on Hegel in Bradley's *Oxford Lectures* (and reprinted in *Hegel on Tragedy,* ed. Anne and Henry Paolucci), claims that both sides are right and that both are also wrong because they assert they are exclusively right. (For a long anti-Hegelian reading, see Brian Vickers, *Toward Greek Tragedy,* which insists that Creon is brutal and Antigone is thoroughly admirable.) Bradley says, "In this catastrophe neither the right of the family nor that of the state is denied; what is denied is the absoluteness of the claim of each."

Most subsequent commentators take sides and either see Creon as a tragic hero (a headstrong girl forces him to act, and action proves ruinous, not only to her but to him), or see Antigone as a tragic heroine (a young woman does what she must and is destroyed for doing it). The critical conflict shows no sign of terminating. Mostly we get assertions, such as D. W. Lucas's "There is no doubt that in the eyes of Sophocles Creon is wrong and Antigone right," and Cedric Whitman's "Antigone's famous stubbornness, ... the fault for which she has been so roundly reproved, is really moral fortitude." One of the most perceptive remarks on *Antigone* is by William Arrowsmith, in *Tulane Drama Review* 3 (March 1959): 135, where he says that Antigone, "trying to uphold a principle beyond her own, or human, power to uphold, gradually empties that principle in action, and then, cut off from her humanity by her dreadful heroism, rediscovers herself and love in the loneliness of her death." He suggests, too, that the play insists on "not the opposition between Antigone and Creon, but [on] the family resemblance which joins them in a common doom."

John Ferguson, in *A Companion to Greek Tragedy*, offers a fairly brief, commonsensical, scene-by-scene commentary on the play. Toward the end he argues that Hegel was utterly wrong in his view that both Creon and Antigone are right. Ferguson points out that Creon "behaves as a tyrant" and that Creon's law "is disastrous for the state." And Antigone is "wrong," Ferguson says, because although her "view of the situation is the true one," as a woman it was her duty to obey Creon. The play is about Antigone's *hubris*, and therefore it is properly titled.

We'd also recommend Charles Segal, *An Interpretation of Sophocles* (1981), which includes detailed studies of both *Antigone* and *Oedipus Rex.*

TOPICS FOR CRITICAL THINKING AND WRITING

1. What stage business would you invent for Creon or Antigone at three points in the play?
2. In an essay of 500 words, compare and contrast Antigone and Ismene. In your discussion consider whether Ismene is overly cautious and whether Antigone is overly cold in her rejection of Ismene.
3. Characterize Haimon, considering not only his polite and even loving plea when he urged Creon to change his mind, but also his later despair and suicide. In what way is he like his father and also (in other ways) like Antigone?

WILLIAM SHAKESPEARE

"The Tragedy of Hamlet" (p. 864)

Probably the best short study of *Hamlet* is Maynard Mack's "The World of Hamlet," *Yale Review* 41 (1952): 502-523, reprinted in the Signet paperback edition of *Hamlet*, in *Tragic Themes*, ed. Cleanth Brooks, and elsewhere. Maurice Charney's *Style in Hamlet* is excellent, and so too is Harley Granville-Barker's book-length essay in *Prefaces to Shakespeare*. For an essay that draws on the tenets of reader-response criticism, see Stephen Booth, "On the Value of *Hamlet*," in *Reinterpretations of Elizabethan Drama* (1969), pp. 137-176. For a sampling of recent criticism, see *William Shakespeare's Hamlet*, ed. Harold Bloom (1986).

The nature of the Ghost has produced a good deal of commentary, most of it summarized in Eleanor Prosser's *Hamlet and Revenge*. She says that for the Elizabethans a ghost can be only one of three things: the soul of a pagan (impossible in this play, for the context is Christian); a soul from Roman Catholic purgatory (impossible in this play, because it seeks revenge); or a devil (which is what Prosser says this Ghost is). Prosser argues that the Ghost is evil because it counsels revenge, it disappears at the invocation of heaven, and it disappears when the cock crows. But perhaps it can be replied that although the Ghost indeed acts suspiciously, its role is to build suspense and to contribute to the play's meaning, which involves uncertainty and the difficulty of sure action. Prosser sees Hamlet as a rebellious youth who deliberately mistreats Ophelia and descends deep into evil (e.g., he spares Claudius at his prayers only in order to damn him), but when he returns from England he is no longer the "barbaric young revenger... but a mature man of poise and serenity" (217). He is generous to the gravediggers and Laertes, "delightful" with Osric. In short, the young rebel has been chastened by experience and by the vision of death, and so he is saved. He "has fought his way out of Hell" (237). Prosser offers a useful corrective to the romantic idea of the delicate prince, as well as a great deal of information about the attitude toward ghosts, but one need not accept her conclusion that the Ghost is a devil; her evidence about ghosts is incontrovertible on its own grounds, but one may feel that, finally, the play simply doesn't square with Elizabethan popular thought about ghosts.

We comment on the Oedipus complex in our discussion of *Oedipus*. The view that *Hamlet* can be explained by reference to the Oedipus complex is most fully set forth in Ernest Jones, *Hamlet and Oedipus*. Briefly, Jones's points are that Hamlet delays because of "some unconscious source of repugnance to his task": this repugnance is rooted in the fact that Claudius had done what Hamlet unconsciously desired to do (kill Hamlet Senior and sleep with Gertrude). Thus far Jones follows Freud. But Jones adds another reason: The desire to kill the father is *repressed* in infancy, and this repression continues to operate in maturity, which means that Hamlet can scarcely act on his desire to kill Claudius, for Claudius is now in effect his father.

Hamlet is a challenging, difficult play, of course, yet it is a play that in our experience works very well for students, more so than *King Lear* and *Coriolanus*, for example, which we admire greatly but which are less familiar as cultural monuments to students. Sometimes, as the moment for reading *Hamlet* approaches, we have asked members of the class to prepare a study sheet of important issues in it. Even students who haven't read *Hamlet* before are able to make reference to the Ghost, the Oedipus complex, delay, the play within the play, revenge, Hamlet's soliloquies. Working as a group, the class can assemble an impressive list of questions, problems, and themes, which they can then bring to (and test against) their actual experience of the play.

We always use one or more film versions of *Hamlet* as a resource for teaching, such as those that star Laurence Olivier (1948), Nicol Williamson (1969), Derek Jacobi (1979), and Mel Gibson (1990). It can be very helpful if you bring to class one or more of these films—all are available in VHS format—and discuss how an actor has delivered an important speech and how the dramatic context for it has been designed. This prompts the students to focus on *Hamlet* as a *play*, as a work meant for the theater, and enables them to become sensitive to the pace, rhythm, and tone of Shakespeare's dramatic verse. The *choices* that directors and actors make, as they construct an interpretation of the play, can come alive for students when two versions of a speech or scene are compared.

CHAPTER 24

Comedy

Among useful books on comedy are Louis Kronenberger, *The Thread of Laughter;* L. J. Potts, *Comedy;* Morton Gurewitch, *Comedy;* and D. H. Munro, *Argument of Laughter* (on theories of the comic). Two interesting anthologies of essays on comedy are *Comedy,* ed. Robert W. Corrigan, and *Theories of Comedy,* ed. Paul Lauter.

WENDY WASSERSTEIN

The Man in a Case (p. 980)

In our introductory comments about comedy we mention that comedy often shows the absurdity of ideals. The miser, the puritan, the health-faddist, and so on, are people of ideals, but their ideals are suffocating.

In his famous essay on comedy (1884), Henri Bergson suggested that an organism is comic when it behaves like a mechanism, that is, when instead of responding freely, flexibly, resourcefully—one might almost say intuitively and also intelligently—to the vicissitudes of life, it responds in a predictable, mechanical (and, given life's infinite variety, often inappropriate) way. It is not surprising that the first line in Wasserstein's comedy, spoken by a pedant to his betrothed, is "You are ten minutes late." This is not the way that Demetrius and Lysander speak in *A Midsummer Night's Dream.* True, a Shakespearean lover may fret about time when he is not in the presence of his mistress, but when he sees her, all thoughts of the clock disappear and he is nothing but lover. The Shakespearean lover is, in his way, mechanical too, but the audience feels a degree of sympathy for him that it does not feel for the pendantic clock-watcher.

The very title, *The Man in a Case,* alerts us to a man who is imprisoned—

and, it turns out, a man who lives in a prison of his own making. Byelinkov says, "I don't like change very much." His words could be said by many other butts of satire—for example, jealous husbands, or misers. And of course the comic writer takes such figures and puts them in a place where they will be subjected to maximum change. The dramatist puts the jealous husband or the miser, for instance, into a plot in which a stream of men visit the house, and every new visitor is (in the eyes of the comic figure) a potential seducer or a potential thief. In *The Man in a Case,* we meet a man of highly disciplined habits, who is confronted by an uninhibited woman. If you invite students to read the first two speeches—Byelinkov's one line ("You are ten minutes late") and Varinka's rambling account of "the woman who runs the grocery store," they will immediately see the comic juxtaposition.

In this play, then, we have a pedant who unaccountably has fallen in love with a vivacious young woman. (In Chekhov's story, Byelinkov's acquaintances decided that it was time for him to get married, so they conspired to persuade him that he was in love.) The pedant is a stock comic character going back to the doctor (*il dottore,* not a medical doctor but a pedant) of Renaissance Italian comedy. Such a figure values Latin more than life. True, Byelinkov is in love, but (as his first line shows, about Varinka being ten minutes late) he remains the precise schoolmaster. Later, when Varinka says "It is time for tea," he replies "It is too early for tea. Tea is at half past the hour." Perhaps tea regularly is served at half past the hour, but, again, a lover does not talk this way; a true lover will take every opportunity to have tea with his mistress. Two other examples of Byelinkov's regimented life: his belief that "heavy cream is too rich for teatime," and his need to translate two stanzas every day because, he explains, "That is my regular schedule."

In any case, we are not surprised to hear that Byelinkov describes his career as the teaching of "the discipline and contained beauty of the classics." "Discipline" and containment are exactly what we expect from this sort of comic figure, a man who tells us that he smiles three times every day, and that in 20 years of teaching he has never been late to school. The speech that began "I don't like change very much," went on thus. "If one works out the arithmetic the final fraction of improvement is at best less than an eighth of value over the total damage caused by disruption."

Why, then, is this man talking to Varinka? Because he has fallen in love. Love conquers all, even mathematicians and classicists. For the most part, when such monomaniacs fall in love they are, as we have said, comic objects of satire, but since audiences approve of love, these figures—if young and genuinely in love—also can generate some sympathy from the audience. (Toward the end of this discussion we will talk more about two kinds of comedy, laughing *with* and laughing *at.*) Thus, when Byelinkov says he will put a lilac in Varinka's hair, he almost becomes sympathetic—but when he makes an entry in his notebook, reminding him to do this again next year, he reverts to the pedant whom we find ridiculous.

The end of the play is fairly complex: when Varinka departs, Byelinkov takes out his pad, tears up the note about the lilac, and strews the pieces over the garden. Apparently he has had enough of her; we might almost say that he has come to his senses and has realized that a man of his temperament can not possibly live with a woman of her temperament. But then we are told that he "Carefully picks up each piece of paper and places them all in a small envelope as lights fade to black." What are we to make of this? That he retrieves the paper seems to indicate that he still loves her—or does it just mean that he is fussy enough not to litter the garden and not to leave any evidence of his folly? That is, when he retrieves the paper, is he revealing that he is still the lover, or is he revealing that he is still the pedant, the man who puts everything in its place (tea at a certain hour and at no other hour)? If the former, the audience will respond with a sympathetic chuckle; if the latter, the audience will respond with a mildly scornful laugh. Much will depend on the exact gestures that accompany tearing and strewing the note, retrieving it, and putting the pieces in an envelope. If, for instance, the pieces are fussily retrieved and prissily inserted into the envelope, we will sense the pedant, the figure we laugh *at.* If however, they are tenderly retrieved and lovingly placed into the envelope, we will sense the lover, the figure we laugh *with* as well as *at.* If there were a blackout while Byelinkov picked up the papers, we are inclined to think that the total effect (because sudden and surprising) would be comic, but Wasserstein's final direction ("lights fade to black") seems to us to allow for sympathy and even pathos.

We suggest that if you assign the play you ask two students to perform it, after rehearsing with a third student who serves as a director at a rehearsal or two. Our own practice—as with scenes from Shakespeare—is to photocopy the work, and to annotate it with some suggestions for stage business. For instance, we would suggest that when Byelinkov delivers his first line ("You are ten minutes late") he says it after carefully consulting a pocket watch. For that matter, you may want to gloss the initial stage direction, "Byelinkov is pacing. Enter Varinka, out of breath." The obvious (farcical?) thing to do is to have Byelinkov pace back and forth, ceremoniously take out and consult his pocket watch, replace the watch, pace back and forth again, and then to have Varinka enter at a moment when Byelinkov is pacing *away* from her. The first two speeches make evident the contrast between the uptight Byelinkov and the effusive Varinka.

Interestingly, soon after this dialogue of opposites, the two are dancing together. Byelinkov has said he is "no dancing bear," and Varinka immediately urges him to dance with her. He complies—probably she grabs him and leaves him no choice. Strangely, when they dance he apparently enjoys the activity; at least we interpret his words "And turn. And turn" to indicate that he is caught up in the dance. A moment later he stops, to place a lilac in her hair, a charming romantic touch that surely makes him sympathetic to the audience—but equally surely he loses this sympathy and becomes merely ridiculous when he takes out his notebook and pedantically writes a memorandum.

A note on Question 1 in the text (about Byelinkov on the motionless bicycle). In Bergsonian thinking, comedy mocks those whose behavior has become fixed and obsessive. What could be more fixed and obsessive than a man furiously pedaling on a bicycle that doesn't go anywhere? Of course the theory has to be modified; the behavior of a tragic hero is also obsessive. The difference, however, is that the tragic hero is obsessed about something that the audience thinks is important (e.g., Desdemona's chastity), whereas the comic hero is obsessed with trivia.

There is, naturally, a good deal more to say about the theory of comedy, but it's probably fair to say that almost all theories of comedy fit into one of two schools: (1) comedy affords the viewer a feeling of superiority (Hobbes's "sudden glory arising from some sudden conception of some eminency in ourselves, by comparison with the infirmity of others"), or (2) comedy helps the viewer to perceive universal absurdity by causing the viewer sympathetically to identify himself or herself with some absurd action. In blunt terms, (1) laughing at (derisive laughter) versus or (2) laughing with (genial, affectionate laughter).

WILLIAM SHAKESPEARE

A Midsummer Night's Dream (p. 986)

We have taught this play many times, have seen a number of productions, and have read a fair amount of criticism, so we can't resist discussing the play here at some length. No claim is made for the originality of any of the following comments; they draw on numerous published writings and productions, but we can no longer cite their source. We want to mention, however, that some of our best class hours have been when neither we nor the students talked about the play, but when the students acted out a scene or a portion of a scene. We usually choose a passage that will take about 10 or 15 minutes to perform, photocopy the pages, write some notes suggesting bits of business, and then put a student in charge as the director. The performers are told to study the parts individually, and then to meet at least twice to rehearse under the supervision of the director. (The students are not expected to memorize the part; they perform while reading from the text. On the day that you choose the students for the performance, it's best to set a time for rehearsals; if the times are not set at once, it will be hard to get a time when they can agree.) On the first occasion that we set up a performance, we ask for volunteers, and we usually get some people who have had some experience performing, but for later scenes we sometimes draft students, though we give students the opportunity to decline if they strongly feel that they don't want to perform. We have almost never had a student refuse; and, perhaps oddly, the draftees are just about as good as the volunteers.

We have had particularly good luck with performances of 1.2 (the mechanicals meet to get parts for *Pyramus and Thisbe*) and with 4.1.49 to the end of the scene (Titania awakens, the lovers are awakened, and Bottom awakens). In the following scene-by-scene discussion, when we get to these two scenes we will talk a little about some stage business that we suggest to the students.

The title: The reference is to the summer solstice (the longest day of the year), around 23 June, but in fact the play is set in May. Still, the holiday of Midsummer Night is appropriate since this day was associated with magic (herbs gathered on this night could charm), with lover's dreams, and with madness.

11 In class we go over this entire scene, line by line, or, rather, speech by speech. It's our impression that our students do not find the process dull. Truth to tell, they seem to enjoy it immensely. If asked questions about some of the ways in which the lines work, they usually come up with very perceptive answers.

The play begins (and ends) in what passes for the real world, that is, Athens, a city that supposedly stands for reason and law. Theseus (accent on the first syllable)—the highest ranking character—speaks first, in blank verse (the form that he and Hippolyta always use, except in the fifth act, where they sometimes speak in prose). (Shakespeare does a good deal to give different kinds of speech to the different kinds of characters. The young lovers in the wood will use rhyme, the fairies will use songs, and the mechanicals will use prose.)

In his first speech Theseus introduces the motif of marriage—and also of the moon—and though he is a mature rather than an impetuous lover, he conveys impatience at having to wait for the "nuptial hour." His comparison of himself—presumably a man of some years—to a "young man" is amusing and probably true to nature. (What older man in love thinks of himself as other than youthful? Probably also true to nature is the impatience and self-centeredness glanced at in the man's conception that the stepmother or widow is "withering out" what belongs to the young man.) We read this speech aloud, discuss it, and then ask a student to read it again, so that students can hear the tones—the affection in "fair Hippolyta," the enthusiasm in "four happy days," and the pained longing in "but, O, methinks." (Speaking of longing, notice the long vowels in "O", "methinks," "slow," "old," and "moon.") In short, this is the time when we begin to talk about the marvelous flexibility of Shakespeare's blank verse.

Hippolyta in her reply introduces the motif of dreaming, with its suggestion of unreality, reinforces the motif of the moon, and in the figure of the "silver bow" manages to suggest Diana and also to suggest her own Amazon nature. Her speech ends with a reference to "solemnities," a word which, combined with Theseus's reference (a line and a half later) to "merriments," pretty much gives us the tone of the play: marriage is both a solemn and a merry affair.

In 15-18 we learn that Theseus and Hippolyta, now representatives of maturity, law, and order, were once combatants. Theseus's "I won thy love, doing thee injuries" introduces the motif of strange transformations. The chief of these are the transformations that the lovers undergo, that Titania's mind undergoes, and that Bottom undergoes, but there are other transformations: for instance, Hermia's defiance of her father turns his love to hate or at least to anger. Another word about the earlier histories of Theseus and Hippolyta: we hear, in 2.1.65 that Hippolyta has had some sort of affair with Oberon, and that Theseus was once a seducer and a rapist. By the time we have finished with the play, we can reasonably feel that Shakespeare is saying something about youthful lawless passion turning into something more decorous. In any case, Theseus's war with Hippolyta has turned into love, and so too the quarreling young lovers will ultimately be reconciled.

Into this picture of loving harmony wrought out of strife, with its promise of solemn joy ("With pomp, with triumph, and with reveling"), comes Egeus (accent on the second syllable), "Full of vexation." He is almost inarticulate—comically so—with rage: "Thou, thou, Lysander, thou hast given her rhymes..." (28), and he too speaks of "love" (29), "moonlight" (30), and "fantasy" (32). As in much comedy descended from Greek New Comedy, he insists that a harsh law be enforced. The play ultimately will brush this law aside, and Athens will thus be transformed from a constricting place to a newly enlarged and newly happy society.

His words are harsh—"As she is mine, I may dispose of her"—but they are in accord with the law (44), and Theseus at this stage can only try to persuade Hermia to obey her father. Theseus is paternalistic but very different from the irascible and tyrannical Egeus. He speaks more gently than Egeus, and he ends by saying (one hears kindness in his tone) "Demetrius is a worthy gentleman." To Hermia's pert response ("So is Lysander") Theseus continues to try to speak in kindly fashion: "In himself he is; / But in this kind, wanting your father's voice, / The other must be held the worthier." Hermia persists ("I would my father looked but with my eyes"), and Theseus patiently tries again, picking up Hermia's words: "Rather your eyes must with his judgement look." Why is Hermia so bold? She herself does not know ("I know not by what power I am made bold"), but we do—the power of love.

Theseus at some length, and with some gentleness, sets forth the grim possibilities that await Hermia, and we feel that although he represents order and maturity, and although he is well-meaning and his speech is beautiful, the choice he now offers is monstrous. He himself is aware that it is harsh, and he urges her to "Take time to pause," and he manages to introduce a reference to his own forthcoming marriage.

Lysander makes the point that Demetrius "Made love to Nedar's daughter, Helena," and so it is appropriate that the play ends with Demetrius paired with Helena, and Lysander with Hermia. As Puck will say, "Jack shall have Jill." Theseus, that embodiment of reason and authority, confesses that he has heard of Demetrius's behavior and has been negligent in speaking to him, but notice that in line 115 he invites Egeus also to a conference, for some "private schooling." One can assume that Theseus will do what he can to persuade Egeus to relent—though we never get such a scene.

Left alone, Lysander and Hermia engage in a charming duet to the effect that "The course of true love never did run smooth"—a motif that we will see exemplified in the play. As these youthful lovers exchange their patterned lines ("O cross," "Or else," "O spite," "Or else") it is hard not to smile at them, not to think of them as charming puppets, but they are scarcely objects of severe satire. If we smile at them, we also sympathize with them, even as they talk prettily about tragic love stories. One of the things that is especially interesting here is that Shakespeare introduces tragic motifs into this comedy. Lines 140-49 would not be out of place in *Romeo and Juliet*. Our point: *MSND* is a comedy of love, but Shakespeare gives us a glimpse of the tragedy of love—and later, in the story of *Pyramus and Thisbe*, he will give us a glimpse of the comedy of the tragedy of love.

And so these two eager lovers, who in line 152 talk of exhibiting "patience," immediately decide to run away from "the sharp Athenian law" (162) to the "wood" (165), the realm which Northrop Frye has called "the green world," that enchanted place that occupies the middle of so many comedies—before the lovers troop back to the ordinary world. One notices that this wood is associated (1.1.167) with an "observance to a morn of May," that is, with May Day, a holiday of love. Hermia's longish speech (168-78), in which she vows true love, interestingly is filled with references to the fragility of love, notably Aeneas's betrayal of Dido.

One should notice, too, the pairs of rhyming lines in 171-78. Although for the most part the young lovers speak blank verse, we can say that couplets are one of their characteristic idioms. Notice that the couplets continue with Helena's entrance, and they go on to the end of the scene.

In Helena's long, final speech in this scene, it's worth pointing out that when she says, "Things base and vile, holding no quantity, / Love can transpose to form and dignity," Helena might almost be describing Titania's infatuation with Bottom. It's also worth pointing out that although in *A Midsummer Night's Dream* love's obsessiveness is comic, it can be tragic elsewhere. (Some students will know *Romeo and Juliet*, or *Othello*.)

1.2 If the talk of tragic love in the first scene conceivably caused a viewer to think that perhaps the play would be a tragedy, this comic scene makes it clear that the play is a comedy. Although the play of *Pyramus and Thisbe* is a tragic tale demonstrating that "the course of true love never did run smooth," we can be assured that with these performers the play (and the larger play in which it is embedded) will afford laughter. Notice too, near the end of the scene, that Quince tells his fellows that they will meet "in the palace wood... by moonlight," thus assuring us that the story of these rustics will somehow be connected to that of the lovers.

1.2 is one of the scenes (the other is 4.1) that we usually ask students to perform in class. It calls for six performers, and although the roles are all male, there is no reason not to use women. On the photocopies that we give the actors and the director, we suggest that at the beginning of the scene the performers huddle close together (they are insecure), until Bottom confidently and grandly says "Masters, spread yourselves." We also suggest that Bottom is a know-it-all, and that in his second speech ("First, good Peter Quince") his manner is somewhat that of a teacher lecturing to children. In "A very good piece of work" he sounds rather pompous. When he comes to discussing the part of the lover ("If I do it, let the audience look to their eyes") he is perhaps not so much pompous as childishly enthusiastic and self-satisfied. (Again, our practice is to scribble suggestions of this sort on the photocopies, in order to give inexperienced readers some help, but other instructors may want to leave everything up to the students.) Presumably he recites the grotesque verse ("The raging rocks") in what he considers a lofty vein, and then, pleased with his performance, he congratulates himself ("This was lofty!") but then briskly turns back to the business at hand: "Now name the rest of the players." Still, he can't quite forget his noble performance, so he immediately adds, "This is Ercles' vein, tyrant's vein."

Other points about this scene: Flute's "I have a beard coming" should probably be said in a whimpering tone, perhaps while he feels his face. Bottom's "Well, proceed," may be uttered in a hurt tone, though Bottom regains his enthusiasm when he expresses the desire to play the lion too. When Quince insists that Bottom play only Pyramus, he is flattering Bottom as he describes the role ("for Pyramus is a sweet-faced man," etc.), and Bottom accepts, but a bit unhappily ("Well, I will undertake it"). Near the very end of the scene, Bottom's "adieu" is perhaps said rather dramatically. Quince then adds a remark, but Bottom must have the last line: "Enough; hold or cut bow strings" (perhaps the "Enough" is accompanied by the gesture of raising his hand authoritatively). Bottom is an ass, but a likeable ass despite his bullying. One thing that makes him likeable is his utter confidence, whether among mortals or fairies.

21 "Puck" is not really the character's name; rather, he is "the Puck," that is, "the spook" or "the pixy" (the words probably are all related). Since he is reputed to be mischievous, he is propitiated by being called "Goodfellow," just as the Furies in Greek mythology are called the Eumenides ("the well-meaning ones"). In this play, Puck is turned into something like Cupid, that is a blind force (he errs in applying the juice of the flower) that overrides reason. One should note, however, that although Theseus describes the power of the herb in 2. 1. 170-173, we have already seen this power at work in Hermia, who defied her father, and we have heard how it turned Demetrius from Helena to Hermia. The herb, then, is merely a sort of concrete embodiment of what we already know exists.

This scene set in the wood—traditionally a place of unreason—makes a contrast with the Athens of the first scene, though, truth to tell, despite Theseus's attempts to reason with Hermia, Athens did not seem very reasonable. In any case, the fairies' song marks the place as something very different from the blank verse world of Theseus or the prose world of the rustics.

The fuss about the changeling (20-31) is a bit of a puzzle. Why is Oberon so eager to get the boy? Perhaps the idea is that since the child is male, he belongs ultimately in the male world, and so when Titania yields the boy we see something comparable to the proper pairing of the lovers, to Jack having Jill. That is, order is restored, things are at last in their proper places. Perhaps one can go further, and say that Oberon's triumph over Titania is the proper (in the Elizabethan view) triumph of male will over female will, something comparable to Theseus's triumph over the Amazon Hippolyta. The trouble with this reading, however, is that surely readers and viewers side with Titania, who is loyal to her dead companion, and we probably see Oberon as a sort of spoiled child who petulantly wants the toy of another child.

Titania's accusations (65-73) that Oberon has courted Phillida and has some sort of attachment to Hippolyta give rise to Oberon's charge that Titania has favored Theseus. What is especially important here is the picture of Theseus as rapist and betrayer (78-80). The Theseus that we see in the play is well-meaning, fair-minded, and a self-restrained lover, but we are reminded that even this courtly figure has a badly tarnished history.

22 Again the fairies speak in a characteristic form (song). Titania is put to sleep with song, and she will be awakened by song—Bottom's raucous singing. (Later the young lovers will be put to sleep by fairy song, and will be awakened by mortal music.) If you read passages aloud in class, don't neglect the opportu-

nity to read 34-61, in which Hermia fends off Lysander. Lysander speaks romantically ("One turf shall serve as pillow for us both, / One heart, one bed, two bosoms, and one troth") but Hermia is not taken in: "Lie further off." One further point about this scene: although in 2.1 Puck says he is mischievous (43-57), he is not being mischievous when he anoints the eyes of the wrong lover. Oberon has told him he will recognize the youth by his Athenian clothes, so the mistake is an honest one.

3.1 Bottom's faith that a prologue will diminish the power of the illusion that *Pyramus and Thisbe* will create allows instructors to talk about dramatic illusion, the power of art, realism versus convention, and soon we inevitably get into some of this, but we usually make a point of reading some of the scene's lines for laughs. And we always read Bottom's song, Titania's line when she awakens, and on through Bottom's "Reason and love keep little company together."

3.2 Puck's lines in 110-21 can hardly be neglected. It's worth discussing the most famous line, "Lord, what fools these mortals be." Is this Shakespeare's judgement on humanity? (No, it's the comment of one character in the play—but one feels that there certainly is *something* to it.) One can easily get into a discussion of engagement and detachment in drama, and of Horace Walpole's famous comment that life is a comedy to those who think, a tragedy to those who feel. That is, if one *feels* for the lovers (sympathizes with them), one suffers; if one *thinks* about them (i.e., if one is detached from them), they seem absurd. Also relevant is a remark (Hazlitt, if we recall) on Pope's *The Rape of the Lock*, to the effect that it is like looking through the wrong end of the telescope.

We enjoy the misunderstandings of the lovers; we can laugh at them because we scarcely *feel* their pain, and we scarcely feel their pain because Shakespeare takes care not to make their statements too powerful. The jingling couplets, for instance, help to make the lovers somewhat puppet-like.

As we mentioned a moment ago, Puck's error is innocent, not malicious. Oberon takes care to point out, when Puck talks of "damned spirits" and of those who "themselves exile from light," that "we are spirits of another sort," and he associates himself with "the Morning's love." Appropriately, then, Puck undoes his error by bringing the lovers together and by applying the juice yet again so that (in the last words of the scene) "Jack shall have Jill... and all shall be well."

4.1 We usually ask students to perform this scene. On the photocopies that we give the students (11 roles, plus a horn player or trumpeter) we make suggestions along the following lines.

Bottom and Titania sleep (it's OK to sit) to one side; at the other side the four lovers sleep or sit. *Then* Puck enters from one side, Oberon from the other, and they stand by Titania and Bottom. Oberon's first line is spoken enthusiastically, the second is spoken in a more thoughtful, meditative tone. The five lines at the end of the speech are recited as a spell. Titania's waking words: the first line is spoken in a voice of awe, the second perhaps in a more puzzled way. When Oberon points to Bottom, Titania says, in a tone of revulsion, "O, how mine eyes do loathe his visage now!" "Now, when thou wak'st" is spoken to

Bottom. In the next line, be sure (following the text) to take hands. No need to dance, but if the spirit moves you. . . . Titania and Bottom go off to one side, where the sleeping lovers are *not*.

Theseus's words should be spoken authoritatively but genially. (He is confident of his authority and need not be pompous.) Egeus is still the crabby old man. His first three lines here perhaps are spoken (as the fourth line indicates) in "wonder," but also in a somewhat fussy and explosive way. Certainly we hear his anger in his lines about "power" and about sleeping and dreaming, "Enough, enough, my lord; you have enough... They would... they would... you and me, / You... me." The same sputtering that we heard in the first scene of the play. Demetrius speaks with puzzlement, awe. When Bottom awakens, his "Heigh-ho" is rather like an ass's braying. And when he says "me thought I had," he puts his hand on top of his head, and feels to see if he has ass's ears. (Lots of opportunity for engaging in business here; with a good deal of trepidation he feels for the ears but of course doesn't find them, then checks once more, and then expresses great relief.) His last lines here are, of course, spoken with great self-satisfaction.

4.2 This scene brings an end to the complications of the play: The lovers are properly paired, and Bottom is restored to the theatrical company. Why, then, a fifth act? Because we in the audience know that there is to be a wedding, and because we want to see a performance of *Pyramus and Thisbe*. In short, what follows gives us not the pleasure of surprise but the pleasure of the fulfillment of expectation. Further, *Pyramus and Thisbe*—intended to be tragic—shows us how the lovers' story might have turned out but, fortunately, did not.

5.1 If one doesn't read every line of this scene aloud—and there probably isn't time to do so—one must at least read the first 26 lines, about "imagination" and its effects on "the lunatic, the lover, and the poet." As Northrop Frye somewhere says, what ability in literary criticism there is in Athens is possessed by Hippolyta (23-27). The passage is so rich that pages can be (and have been) written on it, but here we will point out only that the confident Theseus, who dismisses "antique fables," is himself an antique fable, that is a character of legend. And if he is dismissive of "fairy toys," we have nevertheless seen fairies in this play, and we know that they attend upon his wedding. And we have seen that in dreams there is truth (e.g., Hermia's dream in 2.2 that Lysander laughed as her heart was being eaten away). Another word about Theseus: In 89-105 he sounds pretty complacent, and we probably should not try to whitewash him, but despite his self-satisfaction he makes some thoughtful points about taking a good intention for the deed.

The play-within-the-play. We have not been particularly lucky when we have had this scene performed in class. It looks easy, but it takes skillful actors to make it funny.

We can never refrain from reading Theseus's last speech, where he (presumably jocosely) acknowledges the existence of fairies ("'tis almost fairy time"), nor can we refrain from reading aloud the remainder of the play. In our general comment on the final act we mentioned that chiefly it fulfills our expectations—but now comes a surprise, for we probably did not expect to see the fairies again, although, come to think of it, we were told that they have come to Athens for the royal wedding. Further, their presence now reminds us that the mortal world—sometimes rational and sometimes irrational—is surrounded by a mysterious world that mortals can never comprehend. Puck speaks of the workaday world ("the heavy ploughman," "weary task," "a shroud," etc.), but these lines lead to an exorcism of evil spirits, and to a benediction by Oberon and Titania. The "glimmering light" perhaps put Elizabethan viewers in mind of midsummer eve revels when torches were ignited at a "blessing fire" and were brought from the woods to the hearth to promote good luck and fertility. Finally, in Puck's last lines he suggests that the audience may regard this whole performance as a mere dream—but we have seen in this play that dreams (e.g., Bottom's) are real.

Bibliographic Note: There are many valuable studies of the play, but among short introductions we especially recommend three: the chapter on the play in C. L. Barber, *Shakespeare's Festive Comedy* (1959); Frank Kermode's essay in *Stratford-upon Avon-Studies 3: The Early Shakespeare* (1961), ed. John Russell Brown and Bernard Harris, reprinted in the Signet Classic Edition of *A Midsummer Night's Dream*; Alvin Kernan's discussion in *The Revels History of Drama in English*, Vol 3, ed. J. Leeds Barroll et al. (1975). For a short readable book, see David P. Young, *Something of Great Constancy: The Art of "A Midsummer Night's Dream"* (1966). Also useful is a small book by Roger Warren, *A Midsummer Night's Dream: Text and Performance* (1983). Warren devotes his first 30-odd pages to a general study of the play, and the rest of the book (again about 30 pages) to an examination of several performances, from Peter Hall's 1959 production to Elijah Moshinsky's 1981 BBC Television production. If you have more time, you may want to read the essays collected by Harold Bloom in *William Shakespeare's A Midsummer Night's Dream* (1987), and study the Arden Edition of the play, edited by Harold F. Brooks (1979). This volume has a book-length introduction, detailed footnotes, and appendices on textual cruces and so forth.

A video cassette of Shakespeare's *A Midsummer Night's Dream* is available from Longman.

CHAPTER 25

In Brief:
Writing about Drama

RUTH KATZ

The Women in "Death of a Salesman" (Student Essay) (p. 1048)

We think that Katz's preliminary notes are extremely edifying—especially her renumbering (i.e. reorganization) of the items under the heading "other women." The jottings nicely illustrate the point that outlines almost always need to be revised—and of course the draft written from what one thinks is the final outline will also need revision.

Katz's paper strikes us as thoroughly admirable, especially in its use of sources. She does not simply present an anthology of comments; rather, she steadily advances her own ideas, and she quotes in order to make points, not in order to pad.

Two points about her paper: (1) Although the title reveals only the topic (we usually suggest that students reveal their thesis in their title), the first paragraph clearly reveals the thesis, so readers have a good idea of where they will be going; (2) one colleague who saw this paper expressed uneasiness about some of the diction. For instance, he was disturbed by the aggressiveness of the following passage:

> It might be nice if Linda spent her time taking courses at an Adult Education Center and thinking high thoughts, but it's obvious that *someone* in the Loman family (as in all families) has to keep track of the bills.

We understand our colleague's uneasiness, and we ourselves urge students to think twice before they adopt a wiseguy manner, but we think that on the whole the paper has an engaging human voice in it, and for that we are grateful. Whether you agree or disagree with our colleague's view, you may want to call the class's attention to this passage, and to discuss matters of tone in student writing.

Reminder: The next chapter includes *Death of a Salesman*. Ruth Katz's essay might effectively be assigned in conjunction with the play.

CHAPTER 26

Plays and Context

HENRIK IBSEN

A Doll's House (p. 1060)

First, it should be mentioned that the title of the play does *not* mean that Nora is the only doll, for the toy house is not merely Nora's; Torvald, as well as Nora, inhabits this unreal world, for Torvald—so concerned with appearing proper in the eyes of the world—can hardly be said to have achieved a mature personality.

   A Doll's House (1879) today seems more "relevant" than it has seemed in decades, and yet one can put too much emphasis on its importance as a critique of male chauvinism. Although the old view that Ibsen's best-known plays are "problem plays" about remediable social problems rather than about more universal matters is still occasionally heard, Ibsen himself spoke against it. In 1898, for example, he said, "I must disclaim the honor of having consciously worked for women's rights. I am not even quite sure what women's rights really are. To me it has been a question of human rights" (quoted in Michael Meyer, *Ibsen,* 2:297). By now it seems pretty clear that *A Doll's House,* in Robert Martin Adams's words (in *Modern Drama,* ed. A. Caputi), "represents a woman imbued with the idea of becoming a person, but it proposes nothing categorical about women becoming people; in fact, its real theme has nothing to do with the sexes. It is the irrepressible conflict of two different personalities which have founded themselves on two radically different estimates of realty." Or, as Eric Bentley puts it in *In Search of Theater* (350 in the Vintage edition), "Ibsen pushes his investigation toward a further and even deeper subject [than that of a woman's place in a man's world], the tyranny of one human being over another, in this respect the play would be just as valid were Torvald the wife and Nora the husband."

Michael Meyer's biography, *Ibsen,* is good on the background (Ibsen knew a woman who forged a note to get money to aid her husband, who denounced and abandoned her when he learned of the deed), but surprisingly little has been written on the dramaturgy of the play. Notable exceptions are John Northam, "Ibsen's Dramatic Method," an essay by Northam printed in *Ibsen,* ed. Rolf Fjelde (in the Twentieth Century Views series), and Elizabeth Hardwick's chapter on the play in her *Seduction and Betrayal.* Northam calls attention to the symbolic use of properties (e.g., the Christmas tree in Act I, a symbol of a secure, happy family, is in the center of the room, but in Act II, when Nora's world has begun to crumble, it is in a corner, bedraggled, and with burnt-out candles), costume (e.g., Nora's Italian costume is suggestive of pretense and is removed near the end of the play; the black shawl, symbolic of death, becomes—when worn at the end with ordinary clothes—an indication of her melancholy, lonely life), and gestures (e.g., blowing out the candles, suggesting defeat; the wild dance; the final slamming of the door).

For a collection of recent essays on the play, see *Approaches to Teaching Ibsen's "A Doll's House,"* ed. Yvonne Shafer. Also of interest is Austin E. Quigley's discussion in *Modern Drama* 27 (1984): 584-605, reprinted with small changes in his *The Modern Stage and Other Worlds.* Dorothea Krook, in *Elements of Tragedy,* treats the play as a tragedy. She sets forth what she takes to be the four universal elements of the genre (the act of shame or horror, consequent intense suffering, then an increase in knowledge, and finally a reaffirmation of the value of life) and suggests that these appear in *A Doll's House*—the shameful condition being "the marriage relationship which creates Nora's doll's house's situation." Krook calls attention, too, to the "tragic irony" of Torvald's comments on Krogstad's immorality (he claims it poisons a household) and to Nora's terror, which, Krook says, "evokes the authentic Aristotelian pity."

One can even go a little further than Krook goes and make some connection between *A Doll's House* and *Oedipus the King.* Nora, during her years as a housewife, like Oedipus during his kingship, *thought* that she was happy, but finds out that she really wasn't, and at the end of the play she goes out (self-banished), leaving her children, to face an uncertain but surely difficult future. Still, although the play can be discussed as a tragedy, and cannot be reduced to a "problem play," like many of Ibsen's other plays it stimulates a discussion of the questions, What ought to be done? and What happened next? Hermann J. Weigand, in *The Modern Ibsen* (1925), offered conjectures about Nora's future actions, saying,

> But personally I am convinced that after putting Torvald through a sufficiently protracted ordeal of suspense, Nora will yield to his entreaties and return home—on her own terms. She will not bear the separation from her children very long, and her love for Torvald, which is not as dead as she thinks, will reassert itself. For a time the tables will be reversed: a meek and chastened husband will eat out of the hand of his squirrel; and Nora, hoping to make up by a sudden spurt of zeal for twenty-eight years of lost time, will be trying desperately hard to grow up. I doubt, however, whether her volatile enthusiasm will even carry her beyond the stage of resolutions. The charm of novelty worn off, she will tire of the new game very rapidly and revert, imperceptibly, to her role of songbird and charmer, as affording an unlimited range to the exercise of her inborn talents of coquetry and playacting.

Students may be invited to offer their own conjectures on the unwritten fourth act.

Another topic for class discussion or for an essay, especially relevant to question 4 in the text: Elizabeth Hardwick suggests (*Seduction and Betrayal*, 46) that Ibsen failed to place enough emphasis on Nora's abandonment of the children. In putting "the leaving of her children on the same moral and emotional level as the leaving of her husband Ibsen has been too much a man in the end. He has taken the man's practice, if not his stated belief, that where self-realization is concerned children shall not be an impediment." But in a feminist reading of the play, Elaine Hoffman Baruch, in *Yale Review* 69 (Spring 1980), takes issue with Hardwick, arguing that "it is less a desire for freedom than a great sense of inferiority and the desire to find out more about the male world outside the home that drives Nora away from her children" (37).

Finally, one can discuss with students the comic aspects of the play—the ending (which, in a way, is happy, though Nora's future is left in doubt), and especially Torvald's fatuousness. The fatuousness perhaps reaches its comic height early in Act III, when, after lecturing Mrs. Linde on the importance of an impressive exit (he is telling her how, for effect, he made his "capricious little Capri girl" leave the room after her dance), he demonstrates the elegance of the motion of the hands while embroidering and the ugliness of the motions when knitting. Also comic are his ensuing fantasies, when he tells the exhausted Nora that he fantasizes that she is his "secret" love, though the comedy turns ugly when after she rejects his amorous advances ("I have desired you all evening"), he turns into a bully: "I'm your husband, aren't I?" The knock on the front door (Rank) reintroduces comedy, for it reduces the importunate husband to conventional affability ("Well! How good of you not to pass by the door"), but it also saves Nora from what might have been an ugly assault.

TOPICS FOR CRITICAL THINKING AND WRITING

1. To what extent is Nora a victim, and to what extent is she herself at fault for her way of life?
2. Is the play valuable only as an image of an aspect of life in the later nineteenth century, or is it still an image of an aspect of life?
3. In the earlier part of the play Nora tells Helmer, Mrs. Linde, and herself that she is happy. Is she? Explain. Why might she be happy? Why not? Can a case be made that Mrs. Linde, who must work to support herself, is happier than Nora?
4. Write a dialogue—approximately two double-spaced pages—setting forth a chance encounter when Torvald and Nora meet five years after the end of Ibsen's play.
5. Write a persuasive essay, arguing that Nora was right—or wrong—to leave her husband and children. In your essay recognize the strengths of the opposing view and try to respond to them.

TENNESSEE WILLIAMS

The Glass Menagerie (p. 1115)

The books on Williams that have appeared so far are disappointing. The best general survey is Henry Popkin's article in *Tulane Drama Review* 4 (Spring 1960): 45-64; also useful is Gordon Rogoff, in *Tulane Drama Review* 10 (Summer 1966): 78-92. For a comparison between the play and earlier versions, see Lester A. Beaurline, *Modern Drama* 8 (1965): 142-49. For a discussion of Christian references and motifs (e.g., Amanda's candelabrum, which was damaged when lightning struck the church), see Roger B. Stein, in *Western Humanities Review* 18 (Spring 1964): 141-53, reprinted in *Tennessee Williams,* ed. Stephen S. Stanton. Stein suggests that the play shows us a world in which Christianity has been replaced by materialism.

Perhaps the two points that students find most difficult to understand are that Amanda is both tragic *and* comic (see the comments below, on the first suggested topic for writing), and that Tom's quest for reality has about it something of adolescent romanticism. Tom comes under the influence of his father (who ran away from his responsibilities), and he depends heavily on Hollywood movies. This brings up another point: It is obvious that Amanda, Laura, and Tom cherish illusions, but students sometimes do not see that Williams suggests that all members of society depended in some measure on the illusions afforded by movies, magazine fiction, liquor, dance halls, sex, and other things that "flooded the world with brief, deceptive rainbows," while the real world of Berchtesgaden, moving toward World War II, was for a while scarcely seen. If Amanda, Laura, and Tom are outsiders living partly on illusions, so is everyone else, including Jim, whose identification with the myth of science may strike most viewers as hopelessly out of touch with reality.

The Glass Menagerie has twice been filmed, most recently in 1987, directed by Paul Newman. Newman followed Williams's sequence of scenes, and he kept almost all the dialogue, yet the film strikes us as unsuccessful. Why? Probably this "memory play" needs to be somewhat distanced, framed by a proscenium. Further, the film's abundant close-ups seem wrong; they make the play too energetic, too aggressive. Such are our impressions; instructors who rent the film (Cineplex Odeon) can ask students to set forth their own impressions—in writing.

Though the critical writing on Williams is less than stellar, we can recommend Lyle Leverich, *Tom: The Unknown Tennessee Williams* (1995), the first of a two-volume biography.

An audiocassette of Tennessee Williams reading is available from Longman.

TOPICS FOR CRITICAL THINKING AND WRITING

1. Comedy in *The Glass Menagerie.* (Students should be cautioned that comedy need not be "relief." It can help to modify the tragic aspects, or rather, to define a special kind of tragedy. A few moments spent on the Porter scene in *Macbeth*—with which almost all students are familiar—will probably

help to make clear the fact that comedy may be integral.)

2. Compare the function of Tom with the function of the Chorus in *Antigone*. (Williams calls his play a "memory play." What we see is supposed to be the narrator's memory—not the dramatist's representation—of what happened. Strictly speaking, the narrator is necessarily unreliable in the scene between Laura and Jim, for he was not present, but as Williams explains in the "Production Notes," what counts is not what happened but what the narrator remembers as having happened or, more exactly, the narrator's response to happenings.)

3. Cinematic techniques in *The Glass Menagerie*. (Among these are fade-ins and fade-outs; projected titles, reminiscent of titles in silent films; the final "interior pantomime" of Laura and Amanda, enacted while Tom addresses the audience, resembles by its silence a scene from silent films, or a scene in a talking film in which the sound track gives a narrator's voice instead of dramatic dialogue. By the way, it should be noted that Williams, when young, like Tom, often attended movies, and that this play was adapted from Williams's rejected screen play, *The Gentleman Caller*, itself derived from one of Williams's short stories.) Topic 3 and 4 are ways of getting at the importance of unrealistic settings and techniques in this "memory play."

4. Compare the play with the earlier Williams short story, "Portrait of a Girl in Class," in *One Arm and Other Stories*.

ARTHUR MILLER

Death of a Salesman (p. 1163)

(This discussion is an abbreviation of our introduction in *Types of Drama*.) The large question, of course, is whether Willy is a tragic or a pathetic figure. For the ancient Greeks, at least for Aristotle, *pathos* was the destructive or painful act common in tragedy; but in English, "pathos" refers to an element in art or life that evokes tenderness or sympathetic pity. Modern English critical usage distinguishes between tragic figures and pathetic figures by recognizing some element either of strength or of regeneration in the former that is not in the latter. Tragic protagonists perhaps act so that they bring their destruction upon themselves, or if their destruction comes from outside, they resist it, and in either case they come to at least a partial understanding of the causes of their suffering. The pathetic figure, however, is largely passive, an unknowing and unresisting innocent. In such a view Macbeth is tragic, Duncan pathetic; Lear is tragic, Cordelia pathetic; Othello is tragic, Desdemona pathetic; Hamlet is tragic (the situation is not of his making, but he does what he can to alter it), Ophelia pathetic. (Note, by the way, that of the four pathetic figures named, the first is old and the remaining three are women. Pathos is more likely to be evoked by persons assumed to be relatively defenseless than by the able-bodied.)

The guardians of critical terminology, then, have tended to insist that "tragedy" be reserved for a play showing action that leads to suffering which in turn leads to knowledge. They get very annoyed when a newspaper describes as a tragedy the death of a promising high school football player in an automobile accident, and they insist that such a death is pathetic, not tragic; it is unexpected, premature, and deeply regrettable, but it does not give us a sense of human greatness achieved through understanding the sufferings that a sufferer has at least in some degree chosen. Probably critics hoard the term "tragedy" because it is also a word of praise: To call a play a comedy or a problem play is not to imply anything about its merits, but to call a play a tragedy is tantamount to calling it an important or even a great play. In most of the best-known Greek tragedies, the protagonist either does some terrible deed or resists mightily. But Greek drama has its pathetic figures too, figures who do not so much act as suffer. Euripides's *The Trojan Women* is perhaps the greatest example of a play which does not allow its heroes to choose and to act but only to undergo, to be in agony. When we think of pathetic figures in Greek drama, however, we probably think chiefly of the choruses, groups of rather commonplace persons who do not perform a tragic deed but who suffer in sympathy with the tragic hero, who lament the hardness of the times, and who draw spectators into the range of the hero's suffering.

Arthur Miller has argued that because Oedipus has given his name to a complex that the common man may have, the common man is therefore "as apt a subject for tragedy." It is not Oedipus's complex, however, but his unique importance that is the issue in the play. Moreover, even if one argues that people of no public importance may suffer as much as people of public importance (and surely no one doubts this), one may be faced with the fact that the unimportant people by their ordinances are not particularly good material for drama, and we are here concerned with drama rather than with life. In *Death of a Salesman,* Willy Loman's wife says, rightly, "A small man can be just as exhausted as a great man." Yes, but is his exhaustion itself interesting and do his activities (and this includes the words he utters) before his exhaustion have interesting dramatic possibilities? Isn't there a colorlessness that may weaken the play, an impoverishment of what John Milton called "gorgeous tragedy"?

Miller accurately noted (*Theatre Arts,* October 1953) that American drama "has been a steady year by year documentation of the frustration of man," and it is evident that Miller has set out to restore a sense of importance, if not greatness, to the individual. In "Tragedy and the Common Man" (reprinted in our text), published in *The New York Times* in the same year that *Death of a Salesman* was produced and evidently in defense of the play, Miller argues on behalf of the common man as a tragic figure and he insists that tragedy and pathos are very different: "Pathos truly is the mode of the pessimist. . . . The plays we revere, century after century are the tragedies. In them, and in them alone, lies the belief—optimistic, if you will—in the perfectibility of man." Elsewhere (*Harper's* August 1958) he has said that pathos is an oversimplification and therefore is the "counterfeit of meaning." Curiously, however, many spectators and readers find that by Miller's own terms Willy Loman fails to be a tragic figure; he seems to them pathetic rather than tragic, a victim rather than a man who acts and who wins esteem. True, he is partly the victim of his own actions (although he could have chosen to be a carpenter, he chose to live by the bourgeois code that values a white collar), but he seems in larger part to be a victim of the system itself, a system of ruthless competition that has no place for the man who can no longer produce. (Here is an echo of the social-realist drama of the thirties.) Willy had believed in this system; and although his son Biff comes to the realization that Willy "had the wrong dreams," Willy himself seems not to achieve this insight. He knows that he is out of a job, that the system does not value him any longer, but he still seems not to question the values he had subscribed to. Even in the last minutes of the play, when he is planning his suicide in order to provide money for his family—really for Biff—he says such things as "Can you imagine his magnificence with twenty thousand dollars in his pocket?" and "When the mail comes he'll be ahead of Bernard again." In the preface to his *Collected Plays*, Miller comments on the "exultation" with which Willy faces the end, but it is questionable whether an audience shares it. Many people find that despite the gulf in rank, they can share King Lear's feelings more easily than Willy's.

Miller gathered his early plays, including *Death of a Salesman,* in *Collected Plays* (1957); this volume also contains his illuminating introduction. For critical commentary, see *Death of a Salesman: Text and Criticism*, ed. Gerald Weales (1967); and also the collections of essays edited by Robert W. Corrigan (1969); Helen Wickham Koon (1983); and Harold Bloom (1986).

Two audiocassettes of Arthur Miller reading *Death of a Salesman* are available from Longman.

TOPICS FOR CRITICAL THINKING AND WRITING

1. Miller said in *The New York Times* (February 27, 1949, Sec. II, p. 1) that tragedy shows man's struggle to secure "his sense of personal dignity," and that "his destruction in the attempt posits a wrong or an evil in his environment." Does this make sense when applied to some earlier tragedy (for example, *Oedipus Rex* or *Hamlet,* and does it apply convincingly to *Death of a Salesman?* Is this the tragedy of an individual's own making? Or is society at fault for corrupting and exploiting Willy? Or both?

2. Do you find Willy pathetic rather than tragic? If pathetic, does this imply that the play is less worthy than if he is tragic?

3. Do you feel that Miller is straining too hard to turn a play about a little man into a big, impressive play? For example, do the musical themes, the unrealistic setting, the appearances of Ben, and the speech at the grave seem out of keeping in a play about the death of a salesman?

4. We don't know what Willy sells, and we don't know whether or not the insurance will be paid after his death. Do you consider these uncertainties to be faults in the play?

5. Is Howard a villain?

6. Characterize Linda.

7. Willy says Biff can't fail because "he's got spirit, personality. . . personal attractiveness. . . . Personality always wins the day." In an essay of 500 to 1000 words, distinguish between "personality" and "character," and then describe each of these in Willy.

8. The critic Kenneth Tynan has written, in *Tynan Right and Left: "Death of*

a Salesman... is not a tragedy. Its catastrophe depends entirely on the fact that the company Willy Loman works for has no pension scheme for its employees. What ultimately destroys Willy is economic injustice, which is curable, as the ills that plague Oedipus are not." What do you think of Tynan's view?

LUIS VALDEZ

Los Vendidos (p. 1236)

Students who have been told that stereotyping people is wicked, and that characters (whether in fiction or in drama) should be well-motivated, believable, and so on may find it difficult to see anything of value in a work that uses one-dimensional stock characters. Perhaps one way to help them enjoy such a work is to talk briefly about stereotypes in films that they have enjoyed and admired. The roles performed by Chaplin, the Marx Brothers, Bogart—or even some roles in soap operas—may help them to see that stereotyped characters can be powerful.

Los Vendidos is comic in the sense of having some laughs in it, and also (at least to a degree) in the more literary sense of being a play with a happy ending. If one stands at a distance, so to speak. and looks at the overall plot, one sees the good guys outwitting the bad guys (Ms. Jimenez). In the talk about going to a party, there is even a hint of the traditional *komos* or revel.

It is of course entirely appropriate that the play include amusing passages. Valdez has said that he wanted to lift the morale of his audience (chiefly striking workers), and he wrote and staged comedies—in the sense of plays with happy endings—because he wanted to help change society. He did not want, obviously, to show the tragic nature of the human condition. He makes his aims clear in his short essay, "The Actos" (see question 6). One might ask students to think especially about whether in this play he does anything to "show or hint at a solution" to the "social problem." In some *actos* the message is clear, for instance "Join the union."

It's our view that *Los Vendidos* does not at all suffer by failing to give a "solution." (Of course it's implied that Anglos should not think of Mexican-Americans as stupid and lazy, should not expect them to be subservient, and should value them as people, but Valdez does not offer a solution for Anglo prejudice.) Much of the strength of the play seems to us to lie in the wit with which the stereotypes are presented, and also in the ingenuity of the plot, when the robots come alive and thus reverse the stereotype: the Mexican-Americans are shown to be shrewd and enterprising, and Honest Sancho is shown to be lifeless.

TOPICS FOR CRITICAL THINKING AND WRITING

At the end of the play the Mexican-Americans are shown as shrewd and enterprising. Has Valdez fallen into the trap of suggesting that Mexican-American culture is not distinctive but is just about the same as the Anglo imperialistic (capitalistic) culture that he has satirized earlier in the play?

HARVEY FIERSTEIN

On Tidy Endings (p. 1247)

The exposition continues well into the play; readers, or viewers, learn the past through explosive bits of dialogue. For instance (Question 1), we are not explicitly told that Collin died of AIDS until we are about one-quarter into the play, though the reference to death and to "Uncle Arthur" may incline us to guess that a gay man (Arthur's lover) has died, and that AIDS may have been the cause of his death. On the surface the play is *all* exposition; it seems to be almost entirely about the past. We do not see (again, at least so far as the surface plot goes) characters engaging in actions that then produce consequences that in turn cause further actions. Rather, two characters talk about a dead man.

We say "on the surface" because although nothing much seems to happen— this is not a tragedy in which we see a hero or heroine take a decisive step that will lead to death, or a comedy in which a pair of young lovers will at last be united—the real action in the play is the violent and painful education of Marion and Arthur. Both characters loved Collin, both are deeply hurt by his death and by the behavior of the other, both have some understanding of the other, but both have a great deal to learn. What do they learn (Question 7)?

Marion has already at some point come to realize that she should have included Arthur more openly in the funeral and the obituary, but during the play she learns that she is Arthur's "husband's *ex-wife*," that is, that her relationship to Collin does not equal Arthur's. As Arthur puts it, "After three years you still have no idea of who I am." She learns that although her grief is deep, it cannot equal Arthur's, not only because he is losing his home (not just a profitable piece of real estate) but also because Collin was all that Arthur had, whereas she has a home, a husband, and a son. She learns, too, or perhaps she is violently reminded, that Arthur's love prolonged Collin's life for two years beyond what the doctor thought possible, and she learns some details about Collin's last moments.

Arthur, for his part, learns that Marion knows she could not have equaled Arthur's care for and devotion to Collin. (She admits this when she says she "could never have done what you did. I would never have survived. I really don't know how you did it.") Arthur learns that Collin had not told Marion what his illness was. Further, he learns that although Marion was "jealous" she was "always lovingly" jealous. "I was happy for Collin," she explains, "because there was no way to deny that he was happy." Arthur also learns that she is a carrier, and that (since she and her husband practice safe sex) she may not be able to have the second child that she longs for. He learns, too, that he was wrong when he told Marion that she is not his friend and that he wants her out of his life. (The stage direction tells us that he is "desperate" when he says this. She *is* his friend, and he does not really want her out of his life; at the end of the play he expresses his hope that she will continue to think of him. And, finally, Arthur learns from the lips of the grudging and deeply hurt Jimmy that Collin spoke lovingly about Arthur to Jimmy.

What does Jimmy learn? It's not clear, we think, that he learns anything yet.

At the beginning of the play he makes "fey mannerisms," and he quotes a mocking phrase that his friend made about gays. (Later Arthur will say that he has noticed "the snide remarks, the little smirks" that presumably have characterized—at least recently—Jimmy's relations to Arthur.) Jimmy delivers Collin's message only when pressured by his mother, but perhaps a reader can feel that Arthur's understanding of the boy is sound. Notice that Arthur doesn't pressure him—for instance, when near the end of the play Jimmy is reluctant, as at the start, to enter the apartment, and when Marion forces the boy to give the message. Students might be invited to offer their guesses about whether Jimmy will become reconciled to Arthur.

What do readers or viewers learn? Much depends on one's point of view about whether art teaches, and, if so, how and what? At one extreme are those who hold that works of art can't teach anything because all they do is give details about one imaginary happening. At the other extreme are those who hold that works of art give us insight into reality, give us (in Picasso's famous words) "lies like truth." There is no sign that this quarrel will ever be settled.

A few words about some of the other questions posed at the end of the text. *Question 2:* First, the eagerness with which Marion waits for June shows us that Marion is in fact less composed than her initial appearance might suggest. More important, June provides something of a contrast to Marion. She is not hardhearted, but her businesslike manner helps to make us value Marion. If this assessment is right, viewers are distressed by Arthur's assaults on Marion—though probably most viewers come to understand (and forgive?) these assaults.

Question 6: Should Marion have told Jimmy why Collin left her? Answers doubtless will vary, but probably most readers will agree that the way Marion frames the explanation is grossly wrong. Collin didn't leave her in order to "go sleep with other men." "Love" might be at least part of the explanation.

A good video of the play (same title, 1988, Sandollar Productions) is available. The video is very close to the printed text, except that it begins with shots of traffic, and then of a funeral at which Arthur is in effect snubbed by the other mourners.

MARSHA NORMAN

'night, Mother (p. 1265)

First, a few words about women as playwrights. Although in England in the late seventeenth century a woman, Aphra Behn, was one of the most popular playwrights, and although in America in the mid-nineteenth century another woman, Anna Cora Mowatt, wrote *Fashion,* the best-known social comedy of the period, it is nevertheless true that very few women wrote for the theater until about 1915. And even when women did achieve some prominence as playwrights in the earlier twentieth century (for instance, Anne Nichols, author of the immensely popular *Abie's Irish Rose* [1922], and Lillian Hellman and Clare Boothe Luce in the 1930s), their plays usually did not reveal a distinctly feminist point of view. Nor were they (especially Hellman) noticeably sympathetic in their characterizations of women. In short, despite some important exceptions, women have not played a large role as writers for the theater, even though, of course, many women have made great contributions to the theater as actresses.

Honor Moore, in *The New Women's Theatre,* suggests an explanation: Theater (unlike writing fiction or poetry) is a communal activity, and men have not welcomed women into this community. "Male exclusion of women," she says, "perhaps more than any other single factor, has been responsible for the lack of a female tradition in playwriting similar to that which exists in both fiction and poetry." Then, too, writing for the theater requires larger chunks of time—for instance, whole days at early rehearsals—than most women in the past, tied to households, were able to spare.

In any case, not until the late 1960s, as part of the women's movement, did a substantial number of women begin to set forth on the stage a drama of feminine sensibility—writing, for example, about the difficult business of surviving as a woman in a man's world. As Eve Merriam said in 1976, surveying playwrighting since 1960, "First you had to write an Arthur Miller play, then you had to write an absurd play. Now there is a new freedom—you can write empathetic women characters."

Now we'll look very briefly at Marsha Norman's play. Norman gives us a figure whom she sees as very strong. In the interview that we print in the text, Norman says that Jessie achieves a "nearly total triumph. Jessie is able to get what she feels she needs. It may look despairing from the outside, but it has cost her everything she has. If Jessie says it is worth it, it is."

In this quotation Norman is pretty much saying that Jessie is a traditional tragic hero, someone who ventures boldly and, in a way, turns apparent material defeat into some sort of spiritual triumph. Interestingly, the very success of Norman's play brought fairly widespread criticism from persons interested in the development of women's theater. The two chief objections are somewhat contradictory: (1) *'night, Mother* suggests that women are self-destructive neurotics; (2) *'night, Mother* is just another drama in the male tradition—that is, it emphasizes the heroism of the isolated individual and it ignores the strength, born out of communal action, a kind of action that many women today regard as necessary if they are to escape from the assigned roles of housewife and sexual object. (Many feminist theater groups reject the usual hierarchical structure—a director dominating actors, designers, and technicians—in favor of a leaderless group.)

AUGUST WILSON

Fences (p. 1301)

Some background (taken from our *Types of Drama*) on the history of blacks in the American theatre may be of use. In the 1940s and 1950s black playwrights faced the difficult problem of deciding what audience they were writing for—an audience of blacks or of whites? The difficulty was compounded by the fact that although there were a number of black theatre groups—for example, the American Negro Theatre (founded by blacks in 1940)—there was not a large enough black theatre-going public to make such groups commercially success-ful. In fact, although the original ideal of the American Negro Theatre was "to portray Negro life. . . honestly," within a few years it was doing plays by white writers, such as Thornton Wilder's *Our Town* (not only by a white but about whites) and Philip Yordan's *Anna Lucasta* (by a white, and originally about a Polish working-class family, but transformed into a play about a black family). Further, the aim of such groups usually was in large measure to employ black actors and theater technicians; some of the most talented of these, including Harry Belafonte, Sidney Poitier, and Ruby Dee, then went on to enter the main-stream of white theatre, on Broadway, or—a short step—in Hollywood. Meanwhile, such writers as James Baldwin and Lorraine Hansberry, though writing about black life, wrote plays that were directed at least as much at whites as at blacks. That is, their plays were in large measure attempts to force whites to look at what they had done to blacks.

In the mid-1960s, however, the most talented black dramatists, including LeRoi Jones (Imamu Amiri Baraka) and Ed Bullins, largely turned their backs on white audiences and in effect wrote plays aimed at showing blacks that *they*—not their white oppressors—must change, must cease to accept the myths that whites had created. Today, however, strongly revolutionary plays by and about blacks have difficulty getting a hearing. Instead, the newest black writers seem to be concerned less with raising the consciousness of blacks than with depict-ing black life and with letting both blacks and whites respond aesthetically rather than politically. Baraka has attributed the change to a desire by many blacks to become assimilated in today's society, and surely there is much to his view. One might also say, however, that black dramatists may for other reasons have come to assume that the business of drama is not to preach but to show, and that a profound, honest depiction—in a traditional, realistic dramatic form—of things as they are, or in Wilson's play, things as they were in the 1950s—will touch audiences whatever their color. "Part of the reason I wrote *Fences*," Wilson has said, "was to illuminate that generation, which shielded its children from all of the indignities they went through."

This is not to say, of course, that *Fences* is a play about people who just hap-pen to be black. The Polish family of *Anna Lucasta* could easily be converted to a black family (though perhaps blacks may feel that there is something unconvincing about this family), but Troy Maxson's family cannot be white-washed. The play is very much about persons who are what they are because they are blacks living in an unjust society run by whites. We are not allowed to forget this. Troy is a baseball player who was too old to join a white team when the major leagues began to hire blacks. (The first black player to play in the major leagues was Jackie Robinson, whom the Brooklyn Dodgers hired in 1947. Robinson retired in 1956, a year before the time in which *Fences* is chiefly set.) For Troy's friend, Bono, "Troy just came along too early;" but Troy pungently replies, "There ought not never have been no time called too early." Blacks of Troy's day were expected to subscribe to American ideals—for instance, to serve in the army in time of war—but they were also expected to sit in the back of the bus and to accept the fact that they were barred from decent jobs. Wilson shows us the scars that such treatment left. Troy is no paragon. Although he has a deep sense of responsibility to his family, his behavior toward them is deeply flawed; he oppresses his son Cory, he is unfaithful to his wife, Rose, and he exploits his brother Gabriel.

Wilson, as we have seen, calls attention to racism in baseball, and he indicates that Troy turned to crime because he could not earn money. But Wilson does not allow *Fences* to become a prolonged protest against white oppression—though one can never quite forget that Troy insists on a high personal ideal in a world that has cheated him. The interest in the play is in Troy as a human being, or, rather, in all of the characters as human beings rather than as representatives of white victimization. As Troy sees it, by preventing Cory from engaging in athletics—the career that frustrated Troy—he is helping rather than oppressing Cory: "I don't want him to be like me. I want him to move as far from me as he can." But Wilson also makes it clear that Troy has other (very human) motives, of which Troy perhaps is unaware.

A Note on the Word *Black:* The play is set in 1957 and (the last scene) 1965, before *black* and *African-American* were the words commonly applied to persons of African descent. The blacks in the play speak of "coloreds" and of "niggers." *Black* did not become the preferred word until the late 1960s. For instance the question was still open in November 1967, when *Ebony* magazine asked its readers whether the *Negro* should be replaced by *black* or *Afro-American.* The results of polls at that time chiefly suggested that *Afro-American* was the preferred choice, but *black* nevertheless became the established term until about 1988, when *African-American* began to displace *black.*

Polls in November, 1995, revealed, however, that a majority of blacks still prefer *black* to *African-American* or to *Afro-American.* But it is our impression that in the limited world of colleges and universities, a majority prefers *African-American.*

A 30-minute videocassette of Bill Moyers' interview with August Wilson is available from Longman.

DAVID HENRY HWANG

The Sound of a Voice (p. 1354)

The play has an obvious archetypal quality, gained partly by calling the characters "Man" and "Woman" (though in one stage direction Hwang names the woman), by keeping the locale unspecified, and by including some mysterious passages in the dialogue. And it is not surprising that in the interview that we reprint, Hwang calls the play a "tragic love story." Still, we think it includes a good deal of comedy. As comic dramatists show (let's say Shakespeare, in *A Midsummer Night's Dream*), from an outsider's point of view love is an absurd business—all that fantasizing, pining, posturing, and whatnot, and perhaps lovers are the most absurd when they are the most sincere, passionately writing sonnets to their mistress's eyebrow.

We find a comic touch early in the second scene, in the banter about the Man deceiving the woman: He had said he would not deceive her, now he lies, she accuses him of deception, and he cleverly says he has seen through the lie so he has kept his promise about not deceiving her. But you don't want to hear us labor the obvious. Rather, our point is that we think the somewhat farcical business of the swordsman's attack on a mosquito has its place in the play. Incidentally, although Hwang has said he was influenced by the No drama of Japan, this business of the fly is close to a famous piece of comic business from the *commedia dell 'arte*. But there is indeed a Japanese connection too, though not in No. Legend claimed that the famous swordsman Miyamoto Musashi (known as Niten) could slice an insect. Indeed, it was said that when he was dining, he could catch a troublesome mosquito between his chopsticks.

We are inclined to think that the comic passages (e.g. the Man's comment to his belly, "You'll never leave me for another man") in the play are inseparable from the tragic story. And we take the story to be the comic-tragic battle of the sexes. Notice that the Man at first assumes the woman will be inept in the armed combat, but it turns out that she is more skillful than he is (Scene 7), and he is forced to withdraw from the game, lamely "Just practice there—by yourself." In the end, he is defeated by having fallen in love. He is, however, unwilling or unable to give himself to the woman, and she hangs herself. We don't want to seem crass—we find the ending moving—but we do want to suggest that the pathos of the woman's suicide is played against the comic obtuseness of the man who, at the end, seems not to have understood what has happened, and who "continues to attempt to play" the flute, i.e. who is still fumbling through existence.

DAVID MAMET

Oleanna (p. 1370)

Classroom discussion will probably concentrate on the degree to which we sympathize with either character. Is John a decent professor doing his best with a not-very-bright student—early in the play she seems so slow that a reader or viewer wonders how she ever got in to college—or is he a slick mouther of platitudes, skilled (at first) in dealing with students, i.e. in putting them down? Later in the play, is Carol advancing profound ideas, or is she just mouthing platitudes that come from the Group? How significant is her feminism. Is she on to something when she says that, since the tenure committee includes a woman, John's characterization of it as consisting of "good men and true" is offensive, or is she making a mountain out of a molehill? And what about her injunction to John, "Don't call your wife baby. You heard what I said."

The epigraph from Samuel Butler's *The Way of All Flesh* might suggest that Mamet's sympathies are with Carol, i.e. against a society that prevents young people from finding out the truth about themselves and about society, but the verse from the folk song suggests that anyone who thinks he or she can live in a sublimely happy world is pretty naive. It's our impression, then, that even at the outset Mamet is sympathizing with both sides and is undercutting both sides.

One other point. Mamet is notorious for using obscene language, but in this play he uses the f-word only near the end of the play, and the c-word only once, even later in the play. We take it that John's use of these words indicates—well, what *does* it indicate? A moral collapse? A putting aside of his pretentious veneer, and even a regaining of primal strength? Reasonable people may differ on the point.

TOPICS FOR CRITICAL THINKING AND WRITING

1. For the sake of argument, let's put the matter in an extreme form: John is either a decent, competent, well-meaning professor or he is a condescending, pretentious, elitist sexist pig; Carol is either an eager but confused student and perhaps the victim of a patriarchal society, or she is a radical tyrant, a feminist fascist. How would you modify these assertions?

2. One student argued that Carol is an utterly unconvincing character. In the first scene she seems too stupid to be in college, and in the third scene she is too smart, too skilled with words and too familiar with clever ideas. Do you agree or disagree? Explain your position. (One possible response would be to agree that the character is inconsistent but to argue that consistency is not an issue. The characters, one might say, are types, almost allegorical figures, not to be judged by any concept of realism.)

3. Would you agree that most of Carol's accusations are, on the surface, absurd, but that under their apparent absurdity there is a great deal of truth? Explain your position.

PART FIVE:

Critical Perspectives

CHAPTER 27

Critical Approaches

Instructors, we have found, differ widely in their discussion and use of literary theory and criticism in their introductory courses. Some have told us that they stay far away from theory; in their view, the main task is teaching students how to read and write carefully about primary texts: For these instructors, theory is likely to puzzle and confuse students rather than enlighten them. Others, however, pay a good deal of attention to theory, even featuring it in the first few weeks of the semester, They tell us that such an emphasis on theory makes students feel involved in contemporary debates and controversies about literary studies, humanities education, and the canon and culture wars, and that this thereby stimulates members of the class all the more to read, interpret and argue about the meanings of the literature itself.

We haven't resolved this issue in our own teaching and are these days pretty much content to leave it unsettled. Mostly we shift toward or away from theory depending on the mix of students enrolled in the course during a particular semester. If the group is a good one, sometimes a lot or a little attention to theory can be productive. We tend to improvise, too; if the class is radically at odds in their interpretations of a text, we might risk sketching for them the outlines of deconstruction, with its heady interest in the "undecidability" of literary works.

If you do introduce contemporary theory, remember that first-and second-year students will possess very little context for it. You will be obliged to set the stage for them, and in detail. This was brought home for one of us not too long ago, when some passages about reader-response criticism from Stanley Fish's provocative book, *Is There a Text in This Class?* (1980), cited in the midst of a discussion of Shakespeare's and Milton's sonnets, fell terribly flat. The instructor himself knew the past and present theories of interpretation that Fish was disputing and seeking to correct; the students didn't and hence were simply mystified.

Teaching theory in an introductory or even an upper-level course takes time—and maybe also the good fortune of having in the class at least a few students who quickly become enthusiastic about theory as an idea and about differences among critical approaches. "Gender" is the topic that has succeeded most often for us. Most students do have a notion of what a feminist approach might involve, and can clue in readily to gay and lesbian approaches as well; frequently, the students have picked up some background from courses in history, philosophy, and women studies that we can capitalize upon. If you stick with the topic for several or more class meetings and keep focusing the theoretical issues (e. g., what would a feminist reading of this story look like? and how would it be different from a formalist reading?) on *this* specific text, and *that* one, and so on, you may find the results rewarding for your students. It may enrich the examination of the literary works and enliven the classroom's sense of how literature affects them.

Perhaps this last point suggests our basic position: theory matters only in relation to literary works themselves, and, even more, theory should never displace literature as the primary object of attention, For students, the goal should be learning to take pleasure in various types of literature and developing skill in analyzing it well—thoughtfully, sensitively, astutely. This is hardly a modest goal. Nor is it one that proves thin or limited to students, even if theory as such is never mentioned Time and again, we have had wonderful experiences when the business of the course, from one week to the next, is reading the literary works carefully and writing short papers about them: The emphasis throughout is on close study of the organization of the writer's language, how he or she is using the verbal medium. That's something that students *enjoy* and maybe we should acknowledge this fact more than we do. Students might benefit from theory, but they are not helpless or lost without it. Show them what can be discovered through close reading of the writer's language, and that may be all the theory they will need.

Resources include: Wilfred L. Guerin, et al., *A Handbook of Critical Approaches to Literature* (3rd ed., 1992): Donald Marshall, *Contemporary Critical Theory: A Selective Bibliography* (1993), Steven Lynn, *Texts and Contexts: Writing About Literature with Critical Theory* (1994); *Teaching Contemporary Theory to Undergraduates,* ed. Dianne Sadoff and William E. Cain (1994); and *Critical Terms for Literary Study,* ed. Frank Lentricchia and Thomas McLaughlin (1990: 2nd ed., 1995).

For books that illustrate literary theory in practice, see the various titles (e. g., *The Awakening, The House of Mirth, Heart of Darkness*) in the Bedford Case Studies in Contemporary Criticism series. Recent titles (e. g., *Emma,* 2nd ed.; *Uncle Tom's Cabin*) in the Norton Critical Editions series highlight the new literary theories of the 1980s and 1990s in their selections of critical essays. A number of anthologies have also been built on this principle, combining primary texts with examples of critical approaches to them. See *Literary Theories in Praxis,* ed. Shirley F. Staton (1987); and *Contexts for Criticism,* ed. Donald Keesey (2nd ed., 1994).

For anthologies of modern theory and criticism: *Critical Theory Since 1965,* ed. Hazard Adams and Leroy Searle (1986); *Modern Criticism and Theory*, ed. David Lodge (1988); *Contemporary Critical Theory*, ed. Dan Latimer (1989); and *Contemporary Literary Criticism: Literary and Cultural Studies*, 2nd ed., ed. Robert Con Davis and Ronald Schliefer (1989).

For feminist theory and criticism: *The New Feminist Criticism: Essays on Women, Literature, and Theory*, ed. Elaine Showalter (1985); and *Feminisms: An Anthology of Literary Theory and Criticism*, ed. Robyn R. Warhol and Diane Price Herndl (1991).

CHAPTER 28

Critical Perspectives on Joseph Conrad
Heart of Darkness: A Casebook

JOSEPH CONRAD

Heart of Darkness (p. 1427)

Two casebooks—both published in 1960—let the reader easily examine a sampling of some of the most interesting earlier criticism of this work: *Joseph Conrad's Heart of Darkness: Backgrounds and Criticism*, edited by Leonard F. Dean, and *Conrad's Heart of Darkness and the Critics*, edited by Bruce Harkness. Also useful is the 3rd edition of the Norton Critical Edition (1988) of the story, edited by Robert Kimbrough.

Perhaps the most useful companion to Conrad's novel is a recent book, *Heart of Darkness: A Case Study in Contemporary Criticism*, edited by Ross C. Murfin (1989; rev. ed. 1995). Murfin's book includes the text of the novel and five new essays, each essay illustrating a contemporary critical approach: Psychoanalytic Criticism (Frederick R. Karl), Reader-Response Criticism (Adena Rosmarin), Feminist Criticism (Johanna M. Smith), Deconstruction (J. Hillis Miller), and New Historicism (Brook Thomas). Also of value is Murfin's introduction, "The Critical Background," which, after surveying some of Conrad's own statements about the novel and early reviews, moves on to Leavis, Guerard, Moser (thus far it deals with material also included in the casebooks edited by Dean and by Harkness), and then on to the present, i.e. to pieces written since 1960, by such authors as Leo Gurko, Avrom Fleishman, Bruce Johnson, David Thorburn, Claire Rosenfield, Daniel R. Schwarz, Frederick Karl, Ian Watt, and Hunt Hawkins.

From the earliest sources—the first reviews, and Conrad's own remarks—one can easily gather material for classroom discussion. To begin with the biggest question, what is the book about?

Conrad, in a letter written in 1899, a month before the first installment of the work was published, said that *Heart of Darkness* is about

> the criminality of inefficiency and pure selfishness when tackling the civilizing work in Africa.

Edward Garnett, in an unsigned review of 1902 (the year that *Heart of Darkness* was first published in book form), wrote that the book presented an

> analysis of the deterioration of the white man's morale, when he is let loose from European restraint, and planted down in the tropics as an emissary of light armed to the teeth, to make trade profits out of the subject races.

Both of these remarks severely condemn the whites who exploit Africa, and probably many instructors—particularly white instructors—have felt that the condemnation of whites is sufficient proof that the book is not racist. But a strong objection to this view has recently been offered. The gist of the objection is this: A novelist hardly has a proper view of Africans if (in effect) he says that imperialism reduces the imperialists to the barbaric condition of the savages whom they exploit. Further, it has recently been argued that Conrad's apparently favorable description of the black woman—"savage and superb, wild-eyed and magnificent"—is exactly the sort of praise that racists use; it is akin to praising African-Americans because they make good football players, or because they have rhythm. (Conrad's description of the fireman—"He ought to have been clapping his hands and stamping his feet on the bank, instead of which he was hard at work, a thrall to strange witchcraft, full of improving knowledge"—has, like the passage about Kurtz's African mistress, been criticized.)

Whether the book does in fact reveal a racist attitude toward black civilization is open to discussion, but Conrad's statement that the Europeans were "tackling the civilizing work in Africa" seems to imply that before the Europeans arrived, Africa was uncivilized—a very Eurocentric view. Of course one can reply that his comment is intended to be ironic, or that we should listen to the novel itself and not to what he says about the novel, but these replies are not thoroughly convincing.

The most forceful statement of the view that Conrad is a racist is to be found in Chinua Achebe's "An Image of Africa: Racism in Conrad's *Heart of Dnrkness.*" The essay was originally published in *Massachusetts Review* [18 (1977)]; it has been reprinted in revised form in Achebe's *Hopes and Impediments* (1988). According to Achebe, "Conrad was a thorough-going racist." The gist is that Conrad saw Africa (correctly) as un-European and therefore (incorrectly) as uncivilized. We include part of Achebe's essay in the text.

On the other hand, some writers have argued that Conrad suggests that if the Africans in *Heart of Darkness* sometimes behave barbarously, it is because the whites have destroyed traditional African societies. [See Avrom Fleishman, *Conrad's Politics* (1967).]

A second way of looking at what the book is about is to consider whether it is the story of Kutz's collapse or of Marlow's discovery. As Murfin points out,

Albert Guerard's *Conrad the Novelist* (1958) marked something of a turning point in the criticism of the book. In Guerard's view, Marlow is "recounting a spiritual voyage of self-discovery." Marlow himself says that the voyage "was the farthest point of navigation and the culminating point of my experience." Instructors interested in emphasizing this aspect of the novel might urge students to consider Marlow's response to certain early passages, for instance the anecdote of Fresleven, the women who knit, the doctor, the chain gang, and the accountant.

Though scarcely of the same magnitude as the question of racism or the question of the chief subject of the novel, the business about Marlow's lie to the Intended has also provoked very different responses. Among the most common are as follows:

1. Marlow is being loyal to Kurtz because Kurtz had finally won "a moral victory."
2. "The scene can also be read as Marlow's affirmation of fellowship with Kurtz. To accept Kurtz's pronouncement, 'The horror,' means accepting damnation; Marlow's sin, the lie, serves to confirm this" [Thomas Moser, *Joseph Conrad* (1957)].
3. Marlow (Conrad?) is weaseling on his earlier commitment to the truth.
4. The Intended, ignorant and complacent, is unworthy of knowing the truth.
5 This "pure brow" deserves to be exempted from needless suffering.
6. Marlow, like Kurtz, is contaminated; Marlow lies.

Midway in *Heart of Darkness* Marlow uses an astounding image to describe his arduous quest: "The approach to this Kurtz grubbing for ivory in the wretched bush was beset by as many dangers as though he had been an enchanted princess sleeping in a fabulous castle." What is immediately astounding is the comparison of Kurtz—at this stage a grubber and later described as one who engaged in "devilish" practices—to an enchanted princess, with implications of innocence and tranquility. Perhaps we are astounded, too, for a moment, by the introduction of the idea of a fairy-tale world, for we have been reading an account of a search in a place that, although geographically remote and sometimes associated with romance, is described here in realistic and sordid detail. Much of the book is devoted to what Conrad later called "the vilest scramble for loot that ever disfigured the history of human conscience and geographical exploration." The passage describing the "buccanneers" who constitute the Eldorado Exploring Expedition is a good example.

Yet, while reading *Heart of Darkness*, one is continually aware that one is also reading about matters other than the rapacious colonization of Africa. If we were reading the story in its first appearance in book form, *Youth. . . and Two Other Stories* (1902), the epigraph from Grimm's Fairy Tales that Conrad prefixed to this book might have alerted us that the story is not merely history with some names changed, but art, with symbolic and moral implications: "But the dwarf answered: No; something human is dearer to me than the wealth of all the world." Throughout *Heart of Darkness* Conrad gives us both the realist's detail (the smell of rotting hippo, etc.) and the fabulist's halo of implications.

Thus, the arduous journey takes Marlow past rusted useless vehicles, dying men, stupid men, all described in convincing detail, and it is at the same time a kind of mysterious descent to the underworld in a quest for knowledge, a "traveling back to the earliest beginnings of the world." Marlow himself, as has been mentioned, suggests the literal and symbolic implications in the journey. Occasionally the symbolism is highly explicit: Kurtz's "mother was half-English, his father was half-French. All Europe contributed to the making of Kurtz."

Heart of Darkness is not only the detailed story of a man's adventure in the Congo, and an indictment of Europe's assault on Africa, but it is also a revelation of certain facts (as Conrad saw them) of human nature. Briefly, Conrad's central character, Marlow, learns to understand himself through Kurtz (and we learn to understand ourselves through Marlow's story); in the voyage into Africa and the simultaneous voyage into the deepest recesses of the self he learns of man's enormous capacity for wickedness. Kurtz also learned about himself, for the last words of this degraded man were a moral judgement: "The horror! The horror!"

Shortly after the Congo voyage, when Conrad was recuperating from the diseases he had contracted there, he received an earnest letter from a relative adjuring him "to avoid all meditations which lead to pessimistic conclusions." Conrad could scarcely stop meditating, but *Heart of Darkness* shows us that his vision is not one of unmitigated pessimism. In many passages in *Heart of Darkness* Marlow emphasizes duty, an unselfish belief in service, and—another way of putting it—"restraint," no matter how severe the pressures. Putting aside fools who are too dull to know that they are being "assaulted by the powers of darkness," and "exalted creatures" who are

> deaf and blind to anything but heavenly sight. . . the earth for us is a place to live in, where we must put up with sights, with sounds, with smells, too, by Jove!—breathe dead hippo, so to speak, and not be contaminated. And there, don't you see? Your strength comes in, the faith in your ability for the digging of unostentatious holes to bury the stuff in—your power of devotion, not to yourself, to an obscure, backbreaking business.

Some of Conrad's pictures of people devoted to "obscure, back-breaking business" include ironic elements. For example, the accountant's books commendably "were in apple-pie order," but it is hard to admire the accountant unequivocally when he complains that "the groans of this sick person distract my attention." Yet it is clear that Conrad has genuine reverence for Towson's *Inquiry into Some Points of Seamanship,* whose pages, concerned with "the breaking strain of ships' chains and tackle, and other such matters," displayed "a singleness of intention, an honest concern for the right way of going to work, which made these humble pages. . . luminous with another than a professional light."

One can connect "the right way of going to work" with the writer's own work. There is something very Victorian about Conrad's—and Marlow's—emphasis on salvation through work. By the latter part of the nineteenth century the Puritan emphasis on the divinely ordained necessity of unselfish work had (for many people) lost its theological force, but dedication to unselfish work remained a code of behavior, often the only code for those who could no longer believe in God. Early in *Heart of Darkness* it is work—the sheer business of salvaging the ship and of protecting it from attack—that keeps Marlow sane and alive. This attention to surface reality does not lead to the deepest wisdom, but it keeps him going decently in a world where most of the white people have yielded to slovenliness—not only of behavior but of morals, as we see most easily in the Eldorado Exploring Expedition. Against this omnipresent flaccid evil, and later against the vigorous evil of Kurtz, Conrad juxtaposes fidelity to an ideal. He is fully aware that most colonizing is "merely a squeeze," "robbery with violence, aggravated murder on a great scale," but at moments "what redeems it is the idea only. An idea at the back of it, not a sentimental presence but an idea; and an unselfish belief in the idea—something you can set up, and bow down before, and offer a sacrifice to. . . ."

That Conrad himself held in reverence the "idea" of service through writing cannot be doubted. He gave to the task of creating fictions the same sort of patient dedication that Towson gave to his *Inquiry into Some Points of Seamanship,* and the same sort of patient dedication that earlier earned him his master's certificate in the British merchant service. The writer, he said, "descends within himself," into a "lonely region of stress and strife" which, apparently, is not very remote from a voyage into the heart of darkness. Although thoughtless people may believe that a writer is a trifler, Conrad spoke from experience when he said that writing was "hard labor for life," labor made meaningful by an idea.

Bibliographical note:

For introductory students, we have found that they do best with Conrad's stories and novellas. Such novels as *Lord Jim* (1900) and *Nostromo* (1904), however much we admire them, have proven a bit too formidable for our students, whereas we have received good responses to "The Secret Sharer," "Typhoon," and *The Nigger of the "Narcissus"* (1897). There are a number of editions of Conrad's writings that focus on his shorter works, including *The Portable Conrad,* ed. Morton Zabel (1947), which includes a helpful introduction.

Of the many critical studies, Ian Watt, *Conrad in the Nineteenth Century* (1981), is the best, though it covers only up to the year 1900. See also Thomas Moser, *Joseph Conrad: Achievement and Decline* (1957); Albert J. Guerard, *Conrad the Novelist* (1958); Frederick Karl, *A Reader's Guide to Joseph Conrad* (1960); Cedric Watts, *A Preface to Conrad* (1981); and Norman Page, *A Conrad Companion* (1985).

There are also a number of biographies; the standard work is Zdzislaw Najder, *Joseph Conrad: A Chronicle* (1983).